SACRIFICE™

SACR

WRITTEN BY **SAM HUMPHRIES**   ART BY **DALTON ROSE**

IFICE

COLORS BY PETE TOMS   LETTERS BY TROY PETERI

DARK HORSE BOOKS

To my dad, the original Sam Humphries.   —SH

To Mom and Dad, for the constant stream of pencils,
markers, and books when I was growing up. All that
I am today you two put in motion twenty years ago
at a kitchen table set with paper and pens.   —DR

COLLECTION EDITOR *DANIEL CHABON*
CONSULTING EDITOR *SCOTT ALLIE*
GRAPHIC DESIGNER *ADAM GRANO*
ORIGINAL SERIES EDITOR *ALEJANDRO ARBONA*
ORIGINAL SERIES PRODUCTION *PHIL SMITH*
ORIGINAL SERIES ART DIRECTION *DYLAN TODD*
PUBLISHER *MIKE RICHARDSON*

Special thanks to Stephen Christy, Brendan McFeely, Chip Mosher, and Chris Rosa.

Mike Richardson, President and Publisher | Neil Hankerson, Executive Vice President | Tom Weddle, Chief Financial
Officer | Randy Stradley, Vice President of Publishing | Michael Martens, Vice President of Book Trade Sales | Anita
Nelson, Vice President of Business Affairs | Scott Allie, Editor in Chief | Matt Parkinson, Vice President of Marketing |
David Scroggy, Vice President of Product Development | Dale LaFountain, Vice President of Information Technology |
Darlene Vogel, Senior Director of Print, Design, and Production | Ken Lizzi, General Counsel | Davey Estrada, Editorial
Director | Chris Warner, Senior Books Editor | Diana Schutz, Executive Editor | Cary Grazzini, Director of Print and
Development | Lia Ribacchi, Art Director | Cara Niece, Director of Scheduling | Tim Wiesch, Director of International
Licensing | Mark Bernardi , Director of Digital Publishing

Published by
Dark Horse Books
A division of Dark Horse Comics, Inc.
10956 SE Main Street
Milwaukie, OR 97222

First edition: August 2013
ISBN 978-1-59582-985-6

10 9 8 7 6 5 4 3 2 1
Printed in China

This book collects Sacrifice #1–#6, previously self-published by Sam Humphries and Dalton Rose.

SACRIFICE™

CHAPTER ONE

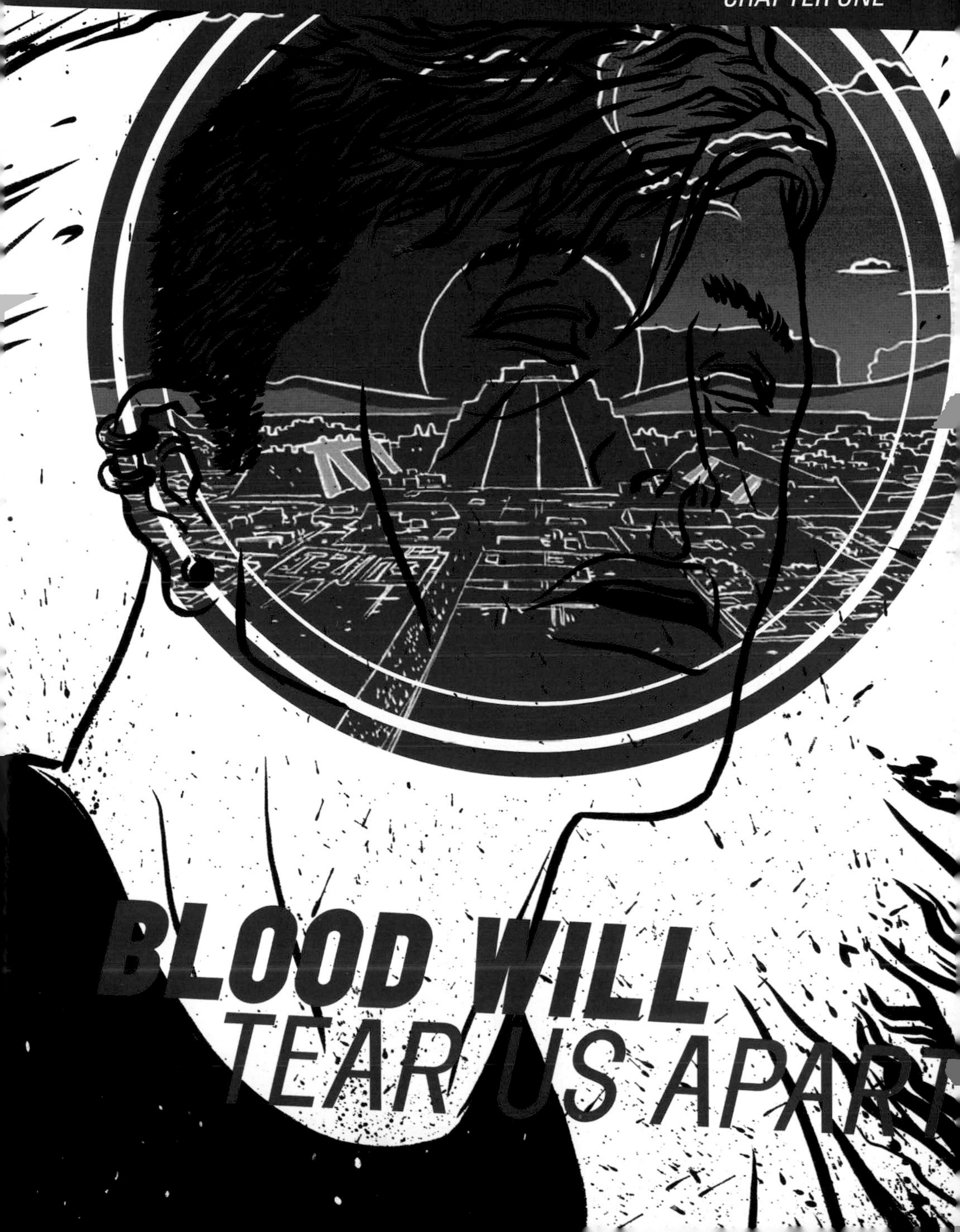

BLOOD WILL TEAR US APART

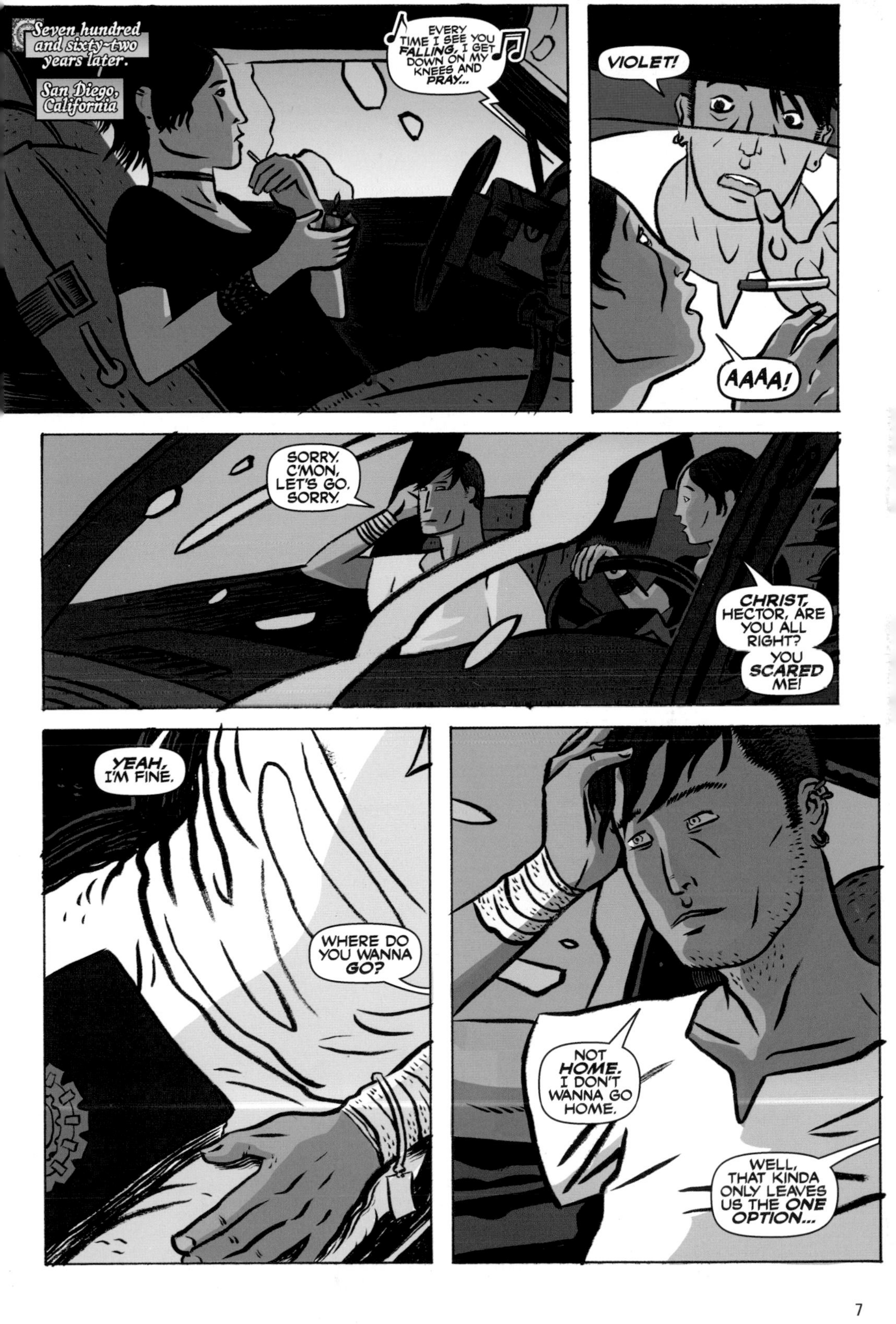
Seven hundred and sixty-two years later.
San Diego, California
EVERY TIME I SEE YOU FALLING, I GET DOWN ON MY KNEES AND PRAY...
VIOLET!
AAAA!
SORRY. C'MON, LET'S GO. SORRY.
CHRIST, HECTOR, ARE YOU ALL RIGHT? YOU SCARED ME!
YEAH, I'M FINE.
WHERE DO YOU WANNA GO?
NOT HOME. I DON'T WANNA GO HOME.
WELL, THAT KINDA ONLY LEAVES US THE ONE OPTION...

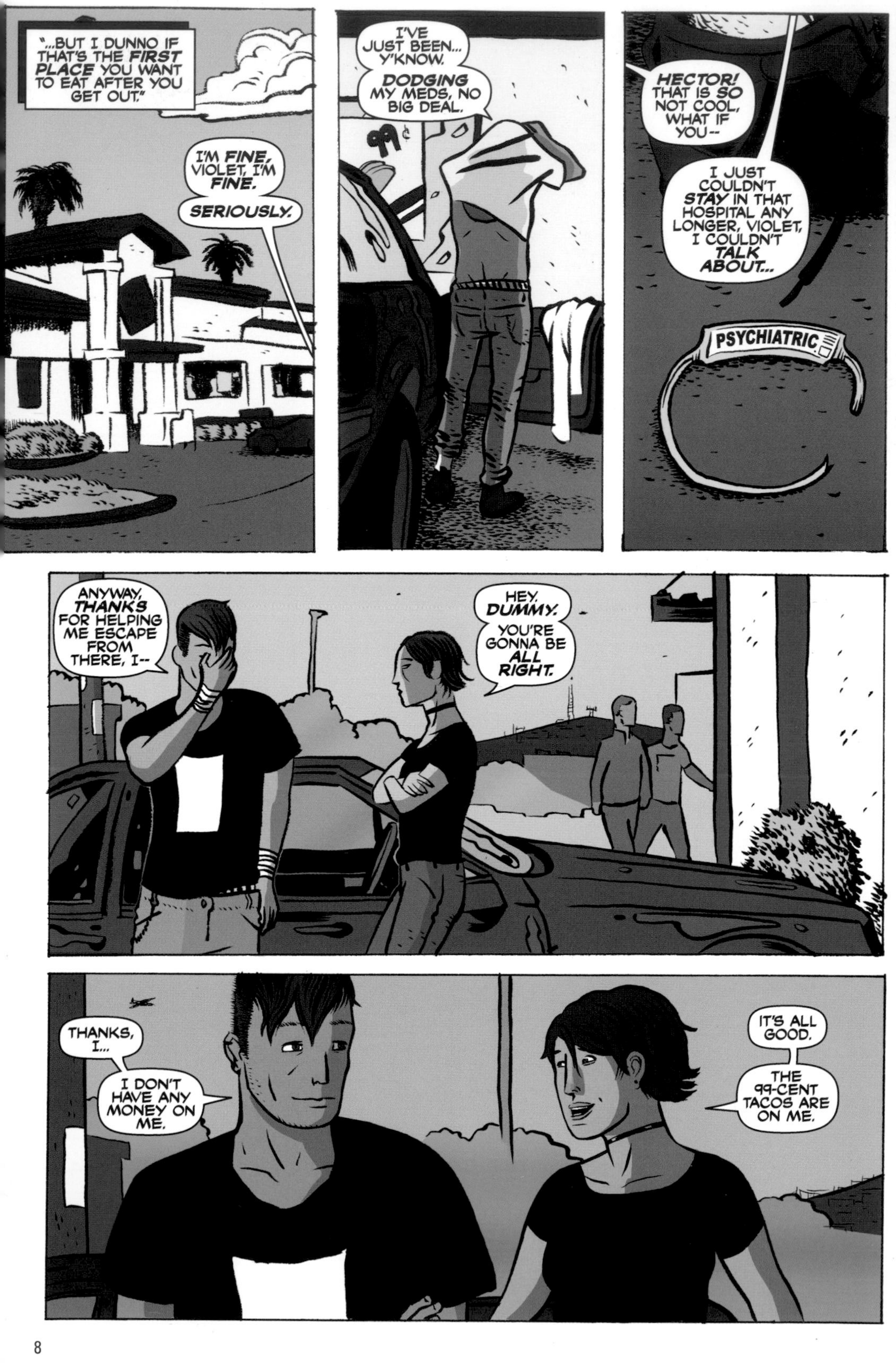
"...BUT I DUNNO IF THAT'S THE FIRST PLACE YOU WANT TO EAT AFTER YOU GET OUT."
I'M FINE, VIOLET, I'M FINE.
SERIOUSLY.
I'VE JUST BEEN... Y'KNOW.
DODGING MY MEDS, NO BIG DEAL.
99¢
HECTOR! THAT IS SO NOT COOL, WHAT IF YOU--
I JUST COULDN'T STAY IN THAT HOSPITAL ANY LONGER, VIOLET, I COULDN'T TALK ABOUT...
PSYCHIATRIC
ANYWAY, THANKS FOR HELPING ME ESCAPE FROM THERE, I--
HEY. DUMMY.
YOU'RE GONNA BE ALL RIGHT.
THANKS, I...
I DON'T HAVE ANY MONEY ON ME.
IT'S ALL GOOD.
THE 99-CENT TACOS ARE ON ME.

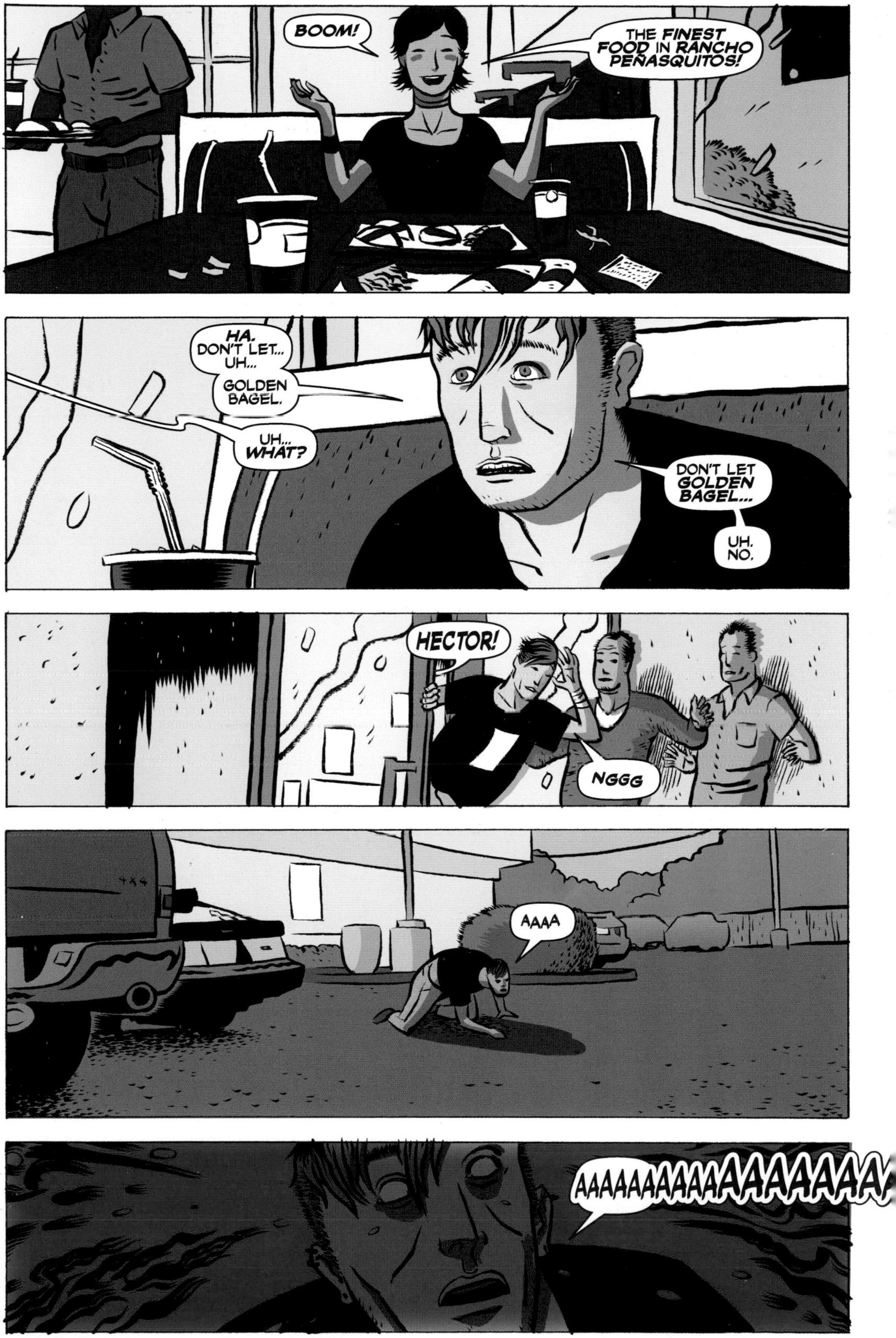
BOOM!
THE FINEST FOOD IN RANCHO PEÑASQUITOS!
HA. DON'T LET... UH...
GOLDEN BAGEL.
UH... WHAT?
DON'T LET GOLDEN BAGEL...
UH, NO.
HECTOR!
NGGG
AAAA
AAAAAAAAAAAAAAAAA

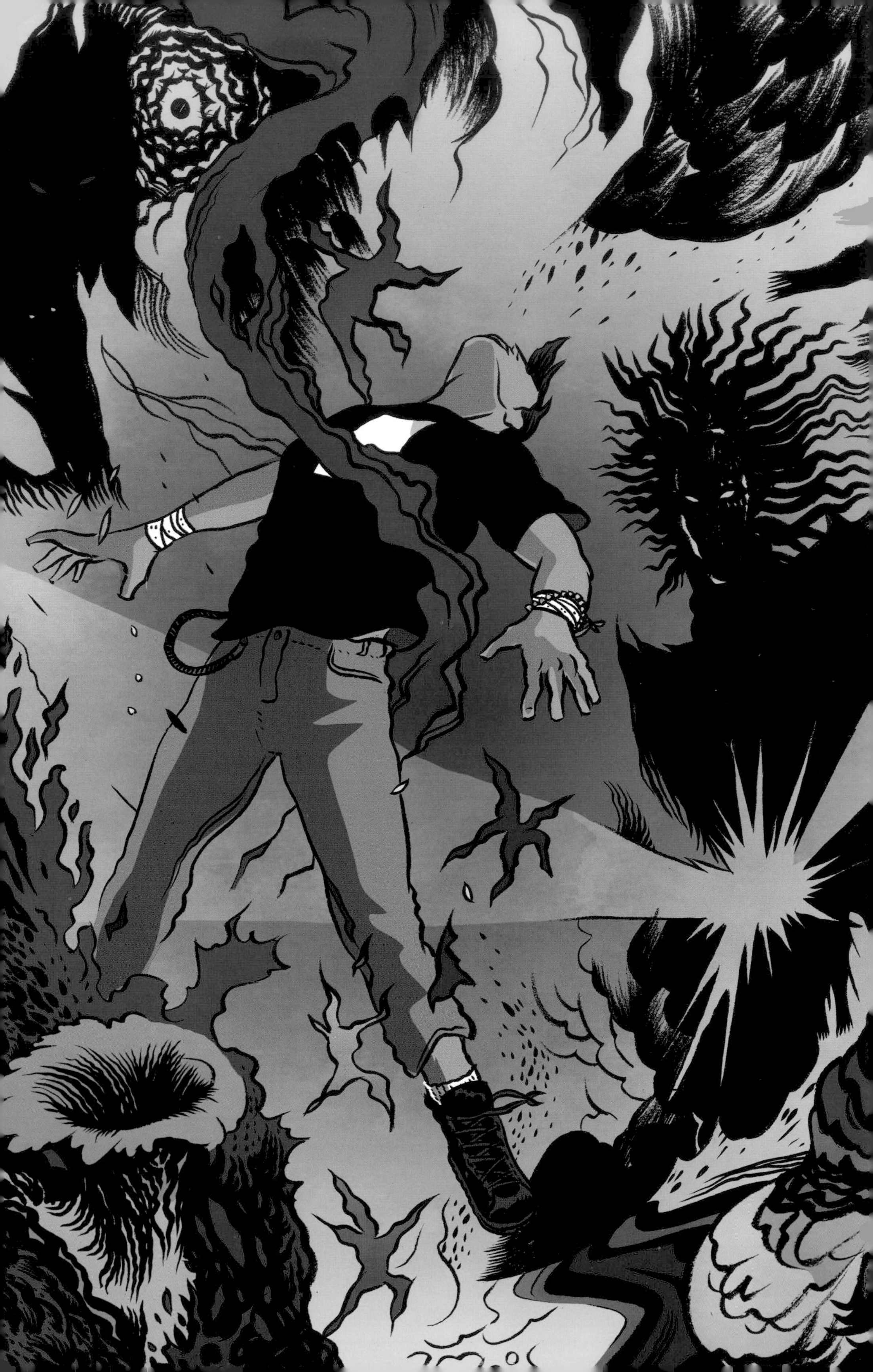

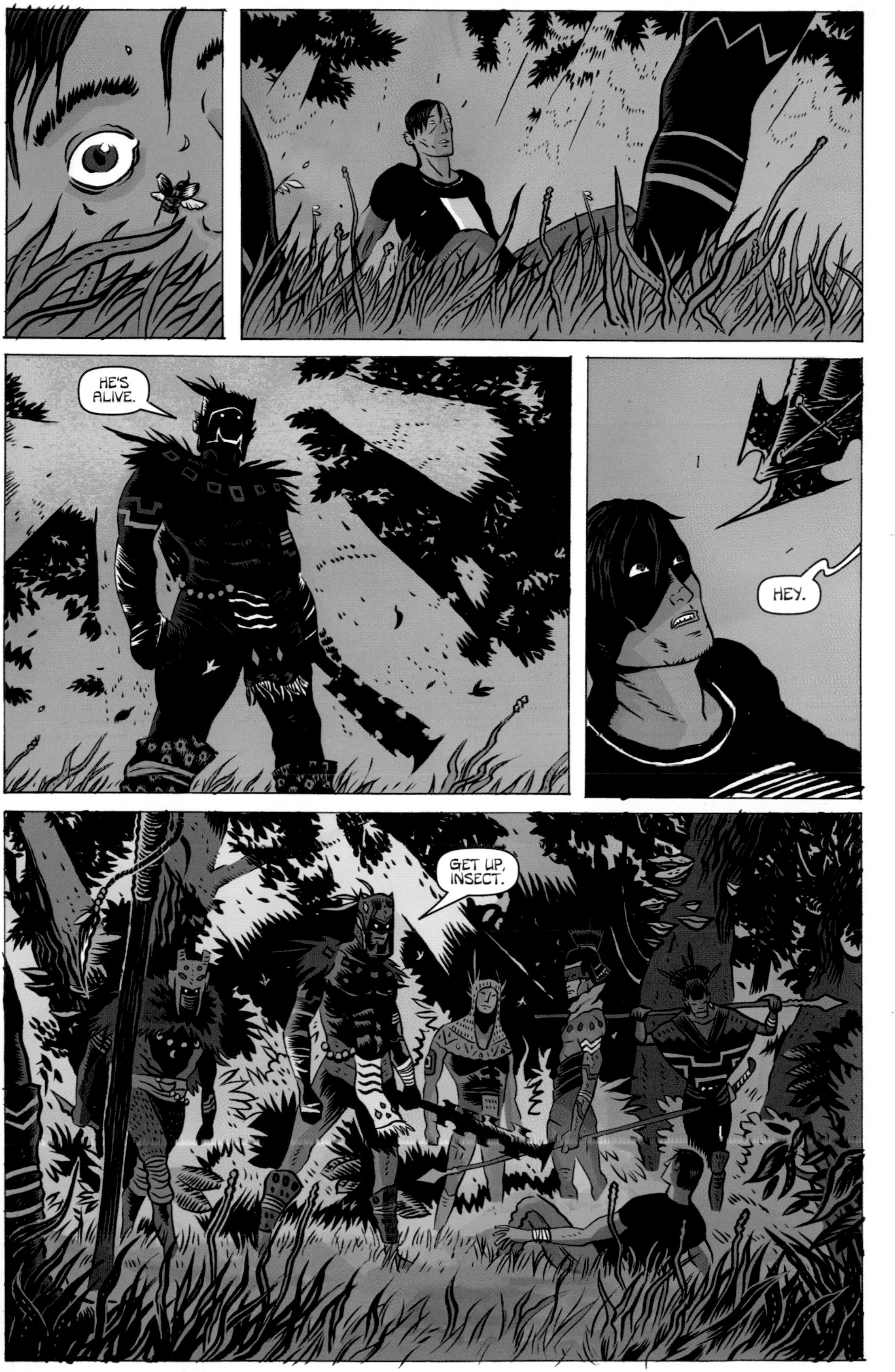
HE'S ALIVE.
HEY.
GET UP, INSECT.

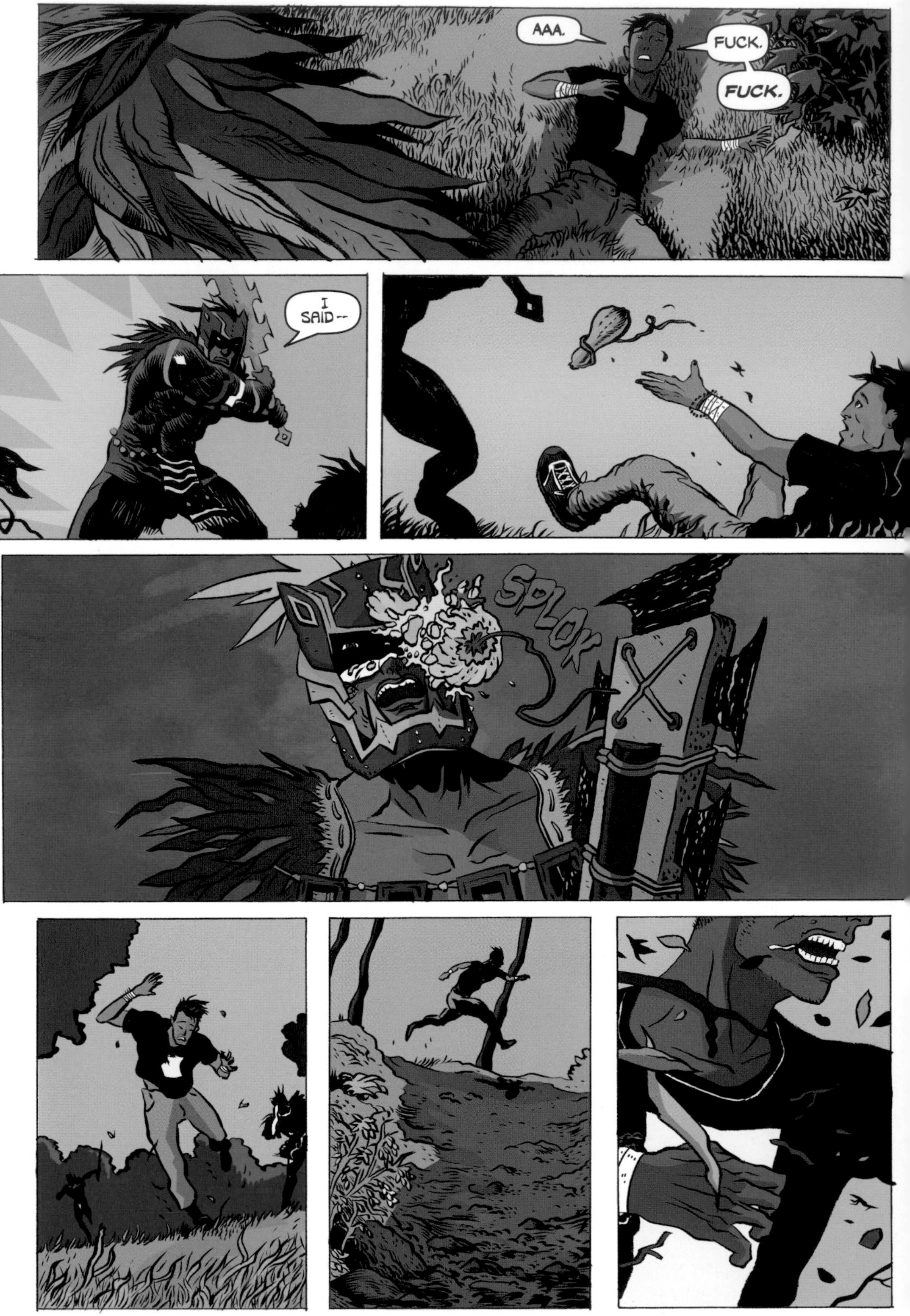
AAA.
FUCK.
FUCK.
I SAID--
SPLOK

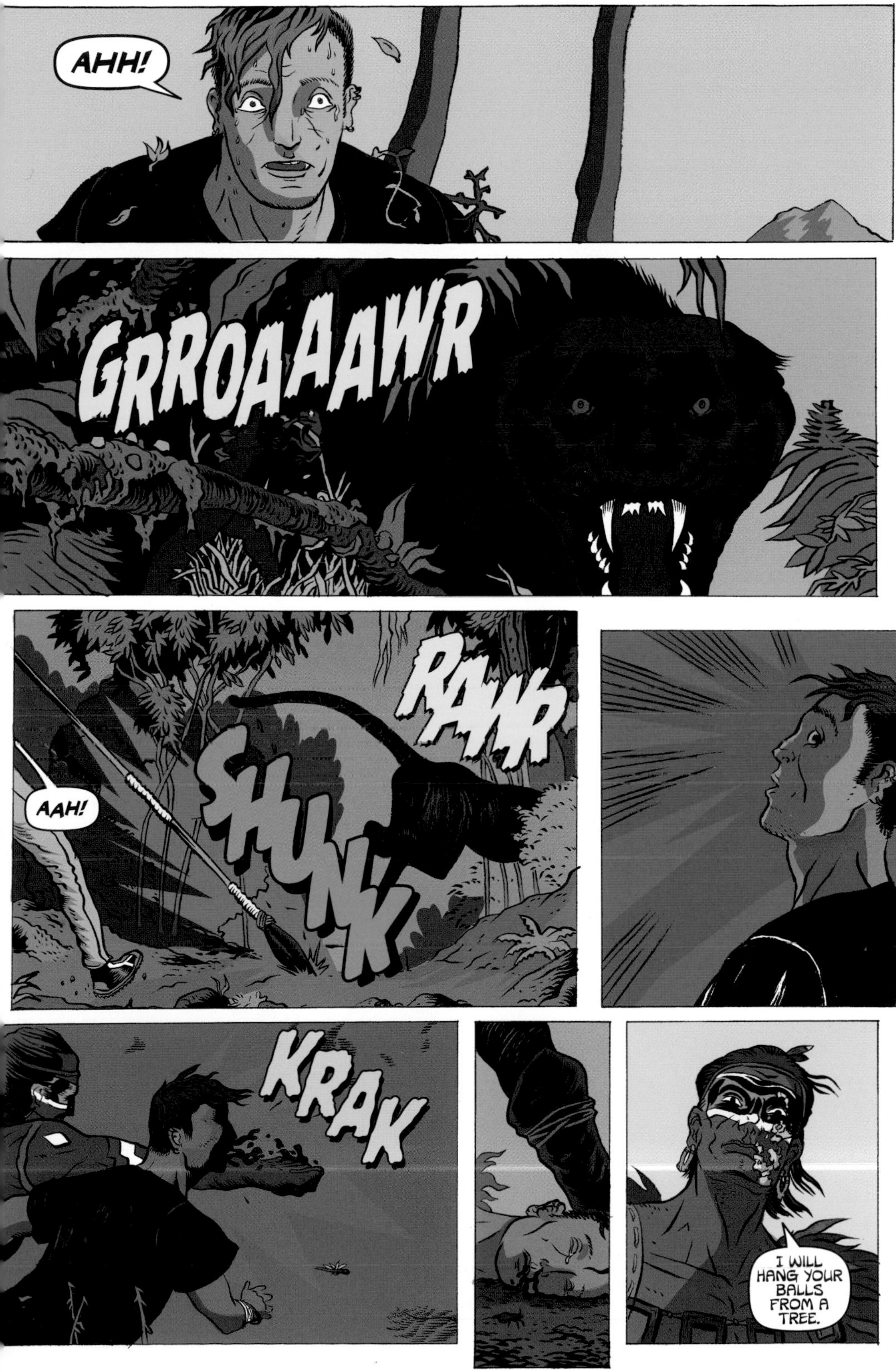
AHH!
GRROAAAWR
RAWR
SHUNK
AAH!
KRAK
I WILL HANG YOUR BALLS FROM A TREE.

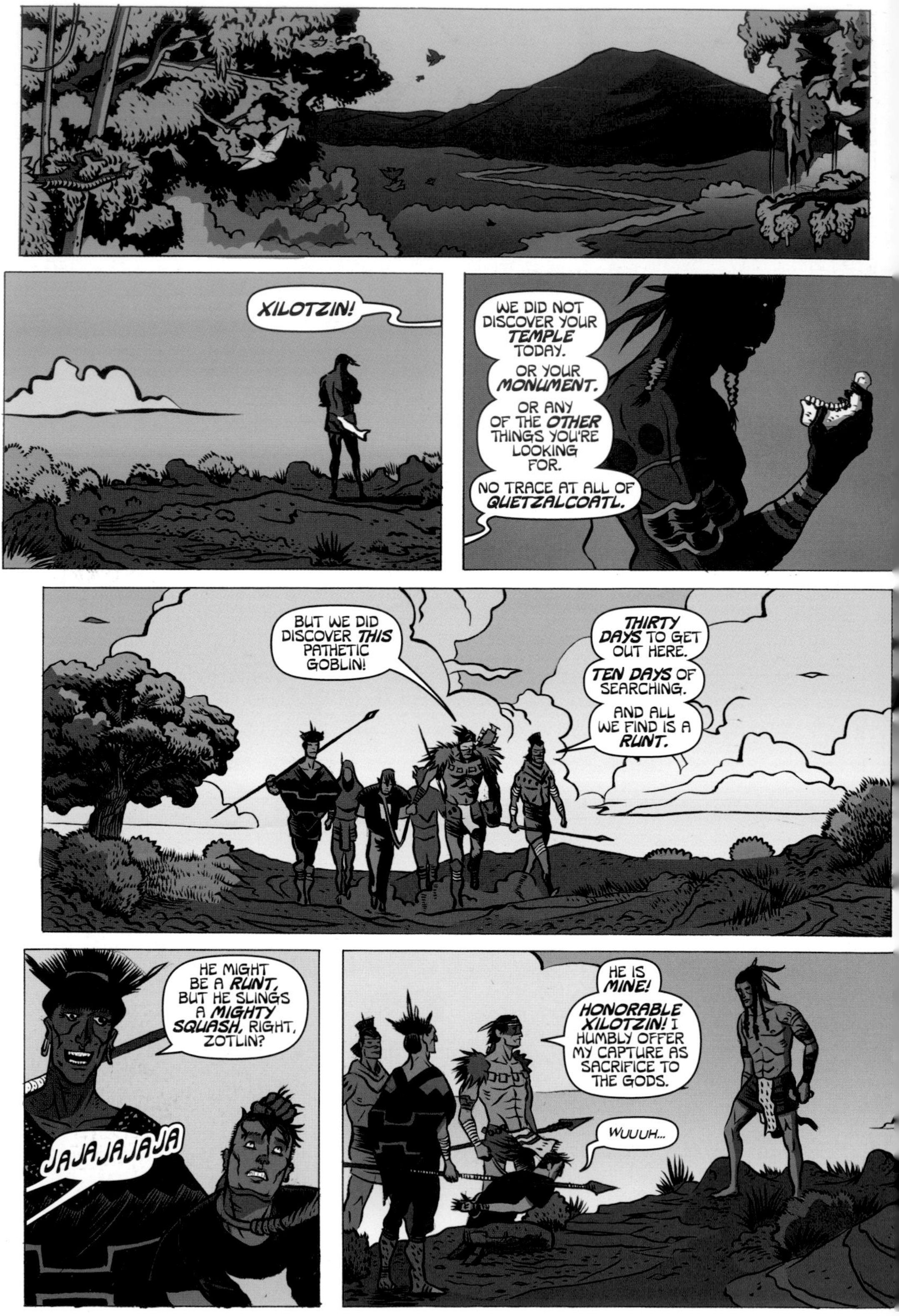
XILOTZIN!
WE DID NOT DISCOVER YOUR TEMPLE TODAY.
OR YOUR MONUMENT.
OR ANY OF THE OTHER THINGS YOU'RE LOOKING FOR.
NO TRACE AT ALL OF QUETZALCOATL.
BUT WE DID DISCOVER THIS PATHETIC GOBLIN!
THIRTY DAYS TO GET OUT HERE.
TEN DAYS OF SEARCHING.
AND ALL WE FIND IS A RUNT.
HE MIGHT BE A RUNT, BUT HE SLINGS A MIGHTY SQUASH, RIGHT, ZOTLIN?
JAJAJAJAJA
HE IS MINE!
HONORABLE XILOTZIN! I HUMBLY OFFER MY CAPTURE AS SACRIFICE TO THE GODS.
WUUUH...

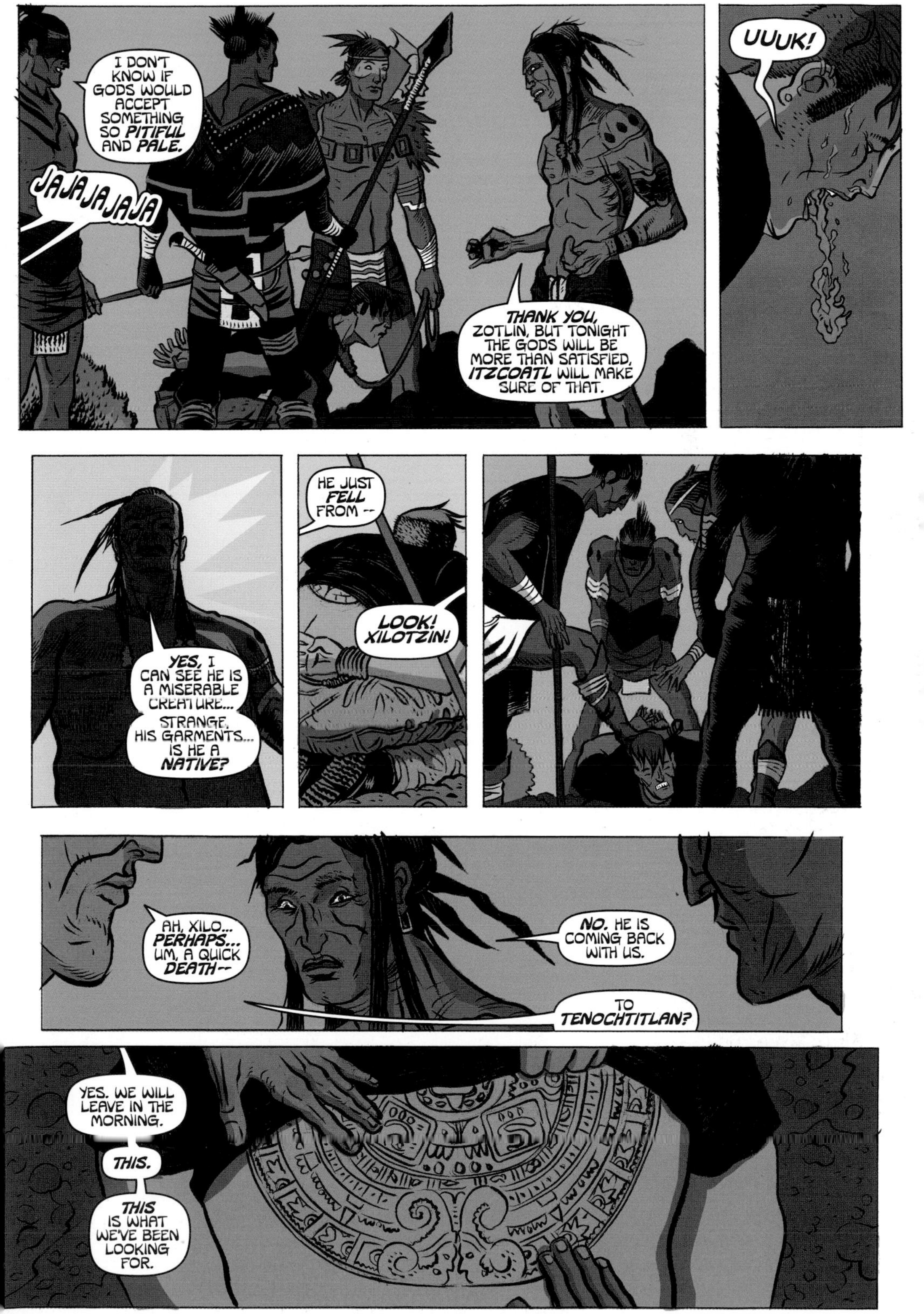
I DON'T KNOW IF GODS WOULD ACCEPT SOMETHING SO PITIFUL AND PALE.
JAJAJAJAJA
THANK YOU, ZOTLIN, BUT TONIGHT THE GODS WILL BE MORE THAN SATISFIED, ITZCOATL WILL MAKE SURE OF THAT.
UUUK!
YES, I CAN SEE HE IS A MISERABLE CREATURE... STRANGE, HIS GARMENTS... IS HE A NATIVE?
HE JUST FELL FROM --
LOOK! XILOTZIN!
AH, XILO... PERHAPS... UM, A QUICK DEATH--
NO. HE IS COMING BACK WITH US.
TO TENOCHTITLAN?
YES. WE WILL LEAVE IN THE MORNING.
THIS.
THIS IS WHAT WE'VE BEEN LOOKING FOR.

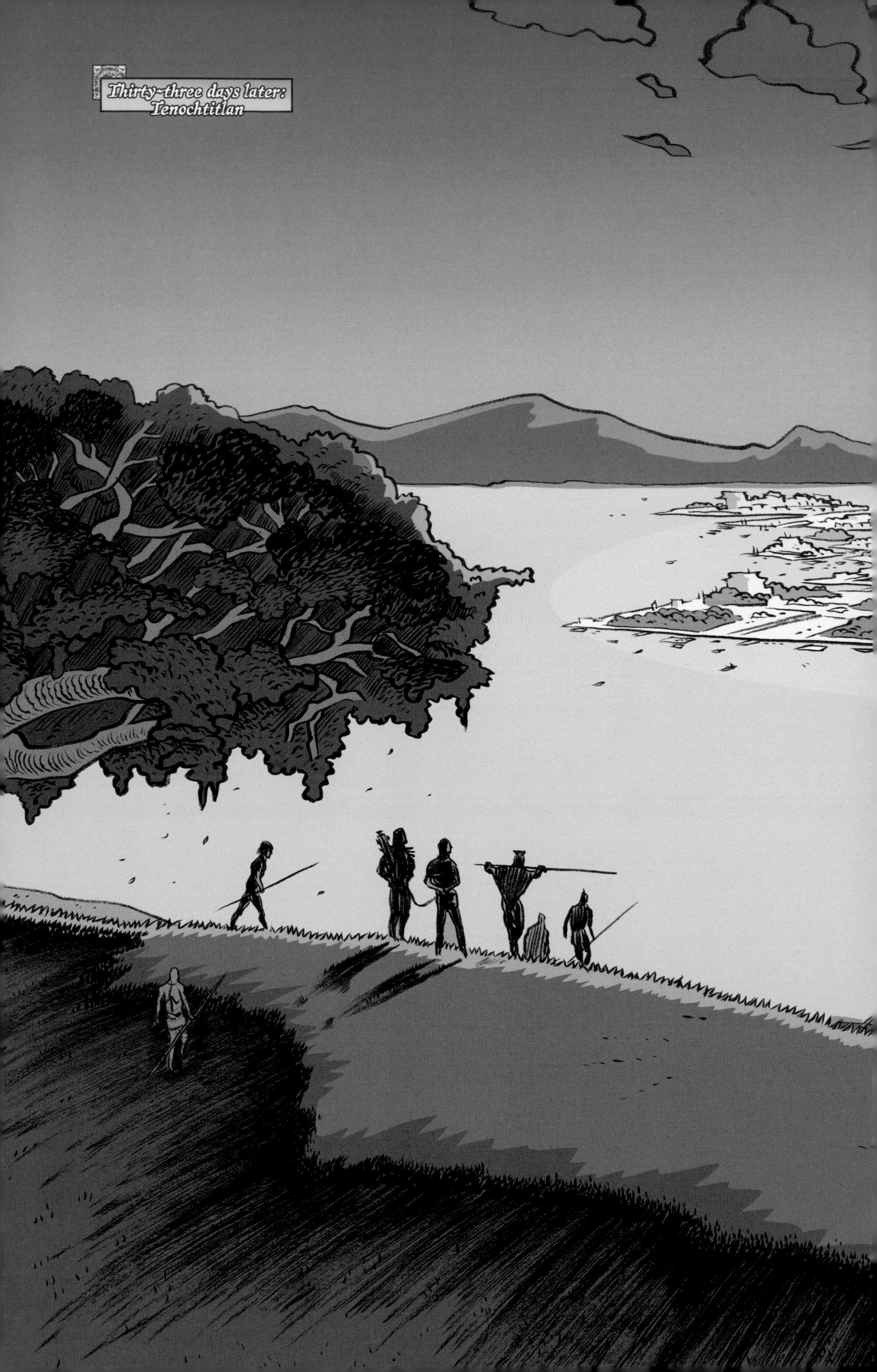
Thirty-three days later:
Tenochtitlan

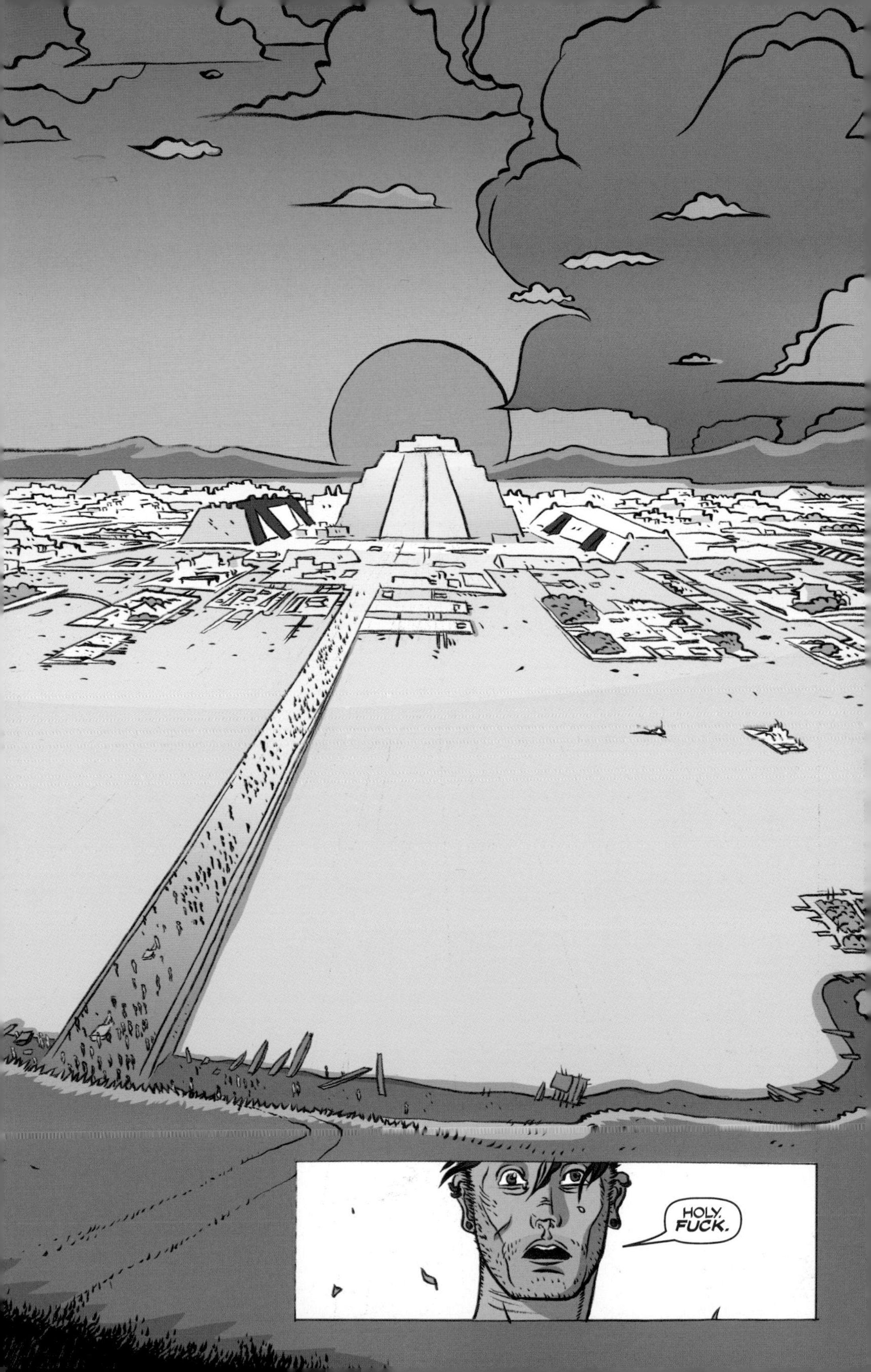
HOLY. FUCK.

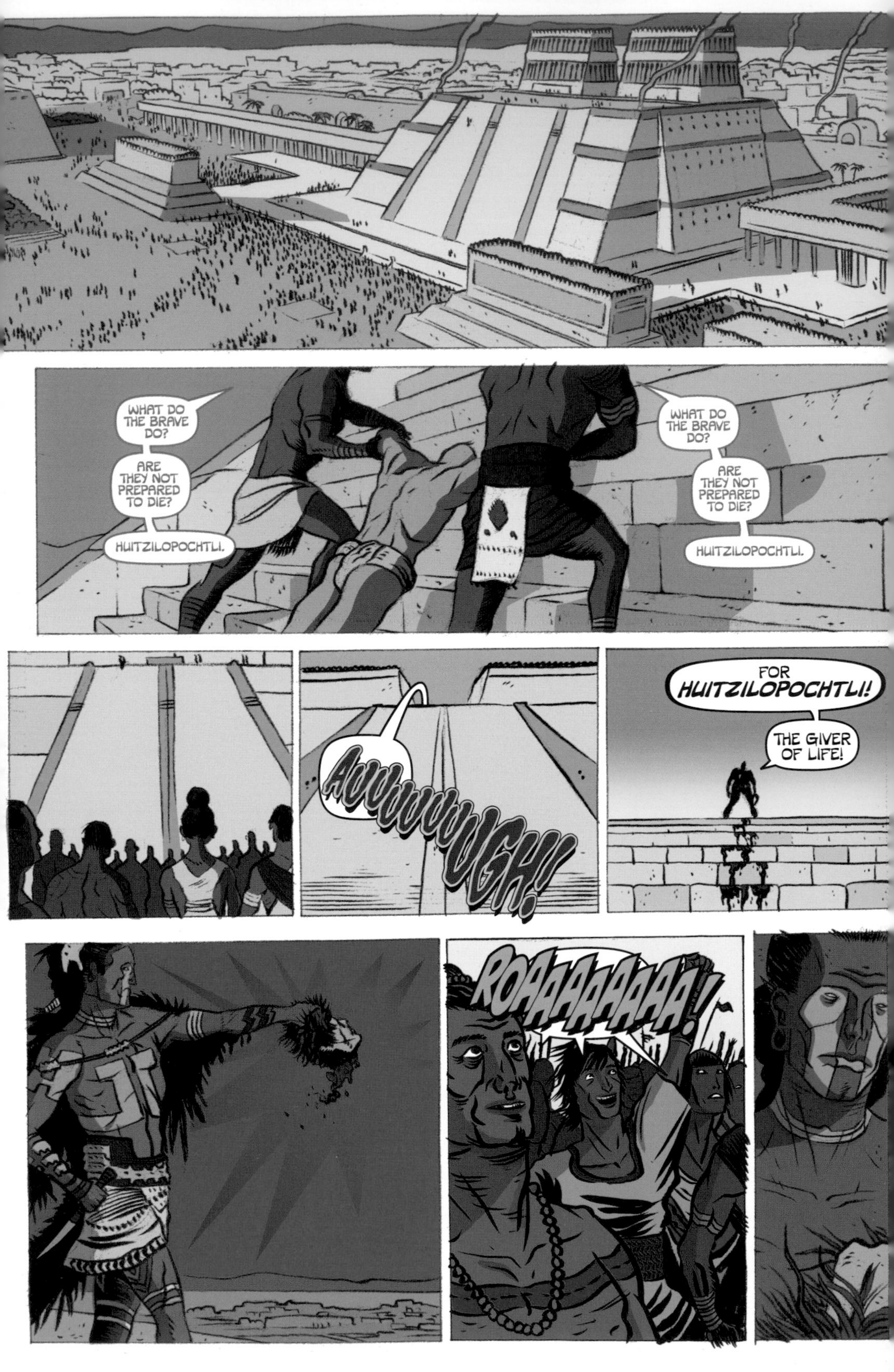

WHAT DO THE BRAVE DO?
ARE THEY NOT PREPARED TO DIE?
HUITZILOPOCHTLI.
WHAT DO THE BRAVE DO?
ARE THEY NOT PREPARED TO DIE?
HUITZILOPOCHTLI.
AUUUUUUUGH!
FOR HUITZILOPOCHTLI!
THE GIVER OF LIFE!
ROAAAAAAAA!

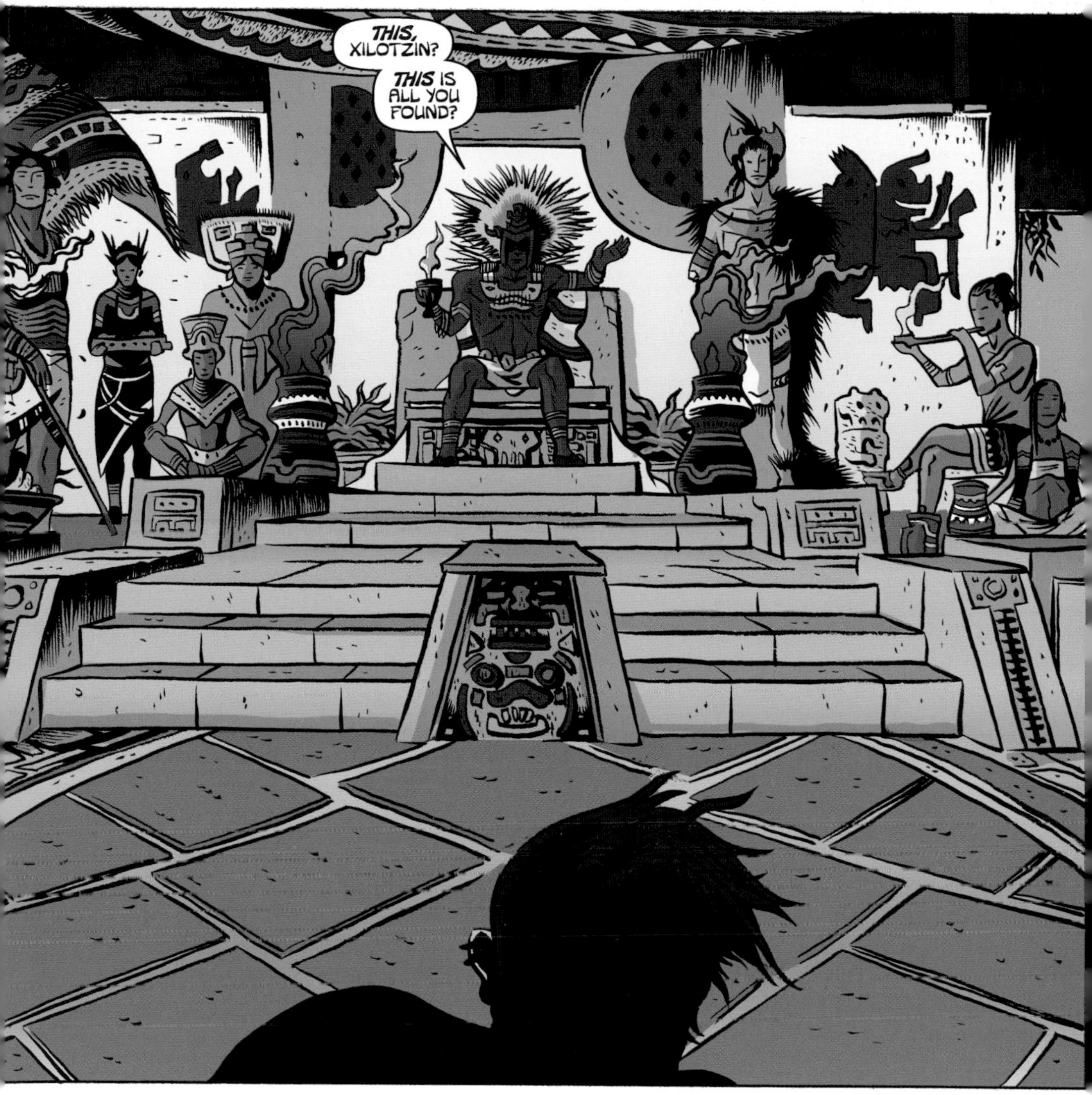
THIS, XILOTZIN?
THIS IS ALL YOU FOUND?

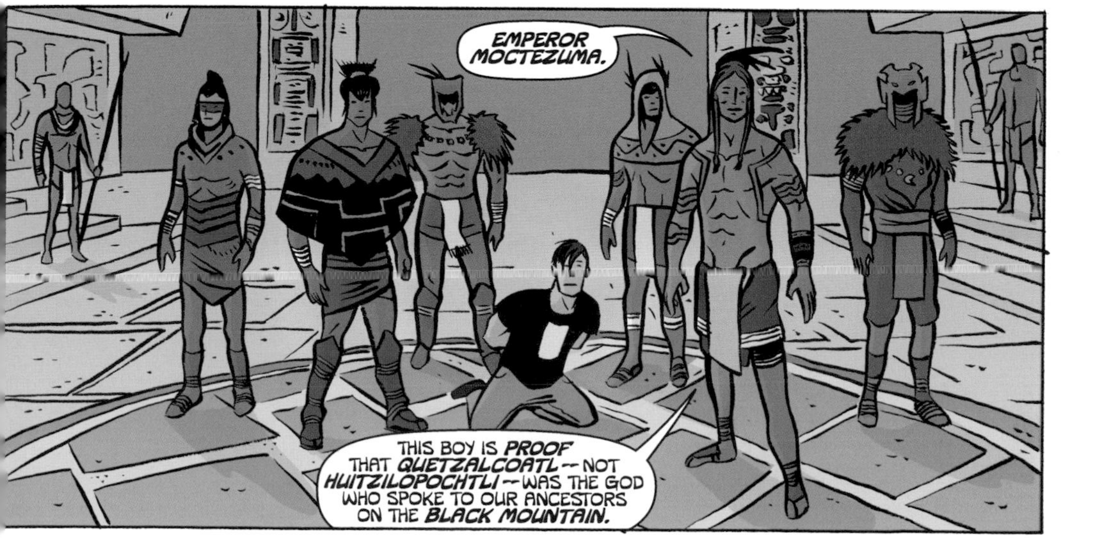
EMPEROR MOCTEZUMA.
THIS BOY IS PROOF THAT QUETZALCOATL -- NOT HUITZILOPOCHTLI -- WAS THE GOD WHO SPOKE TO OUR ANCESTORS ON THE BLACK MOUNTAIN.

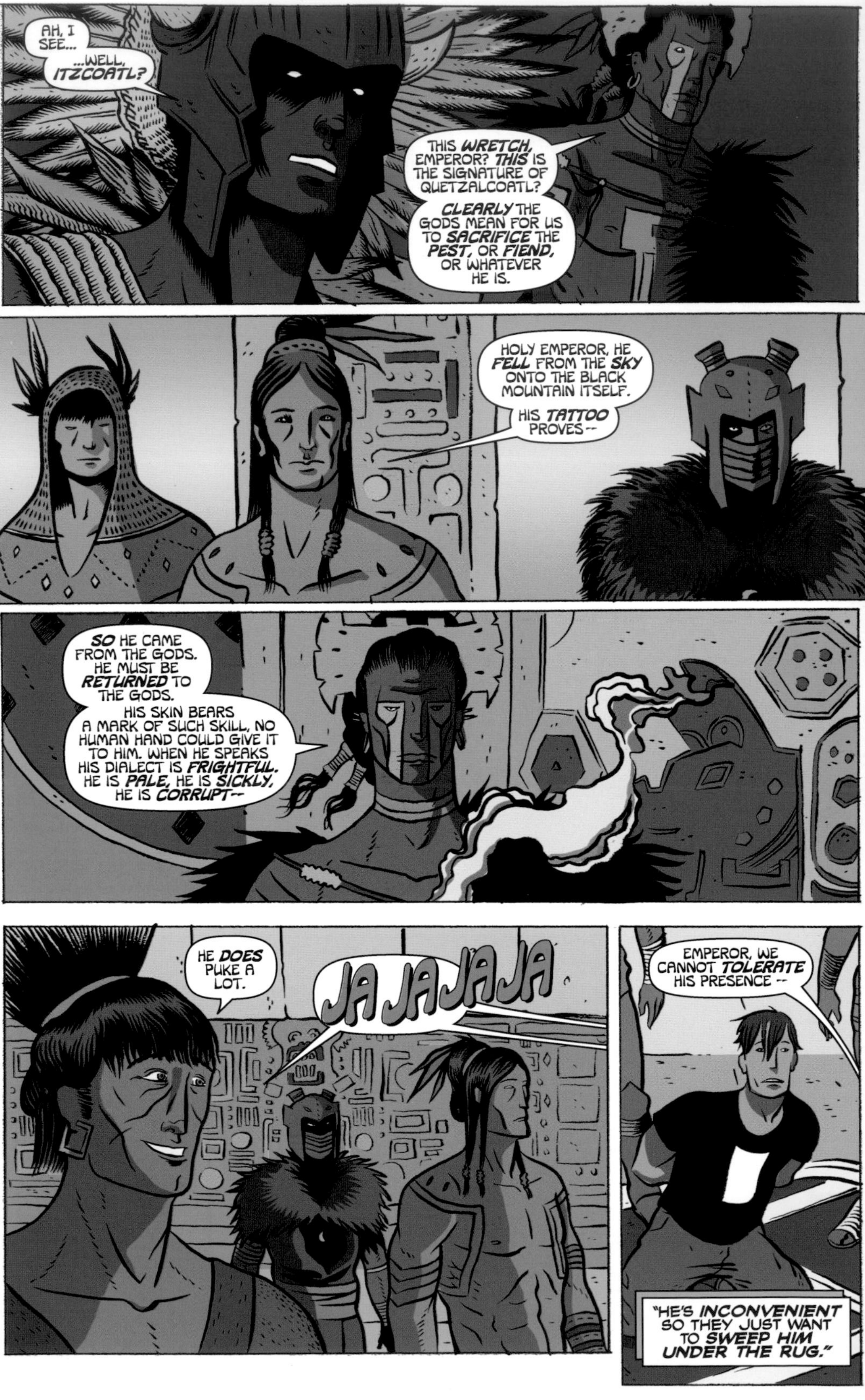
AH, I SEE...
...WELL, ITZCOATL?
THIS WRETCH, EMPEROR? THIS IS THE SIGNATURE OF QUETZALCOATL?
CLEARLY THE GODS MEAN FOR US TO SACRIFICE THE PEST, OR FIEND, OR WHATEVER HE IS.
HOLY EMPEROR, HE FELL FROM THE SKY ONTO THE BLACK MOUNTAIN ITSELF.
HIS TATTOO PROVES --
SO HE CAME FROM THE GODS. HE MUST BE RETURNED TO THE GODS.
HIS SKIN BEARS A MARK OF SUCH SKILL, NO HUMAN HAND COULD GIVE IT TO HIM. WHEN HE SPEAKS HIS DIALECT IS FRIGHTFUL. HE IS PALE, HE IS SICKLY, HE IS CORRUPT --
HE DOES PUKE A LOT.
JA JA JA JA
EMPEROR, WE CANNOT TOLERATE HIS PRESENCE --
"HE'S INCONVENIENT SO THEY JUST WANT TO SWEEP HIM UNDER THE RUG."

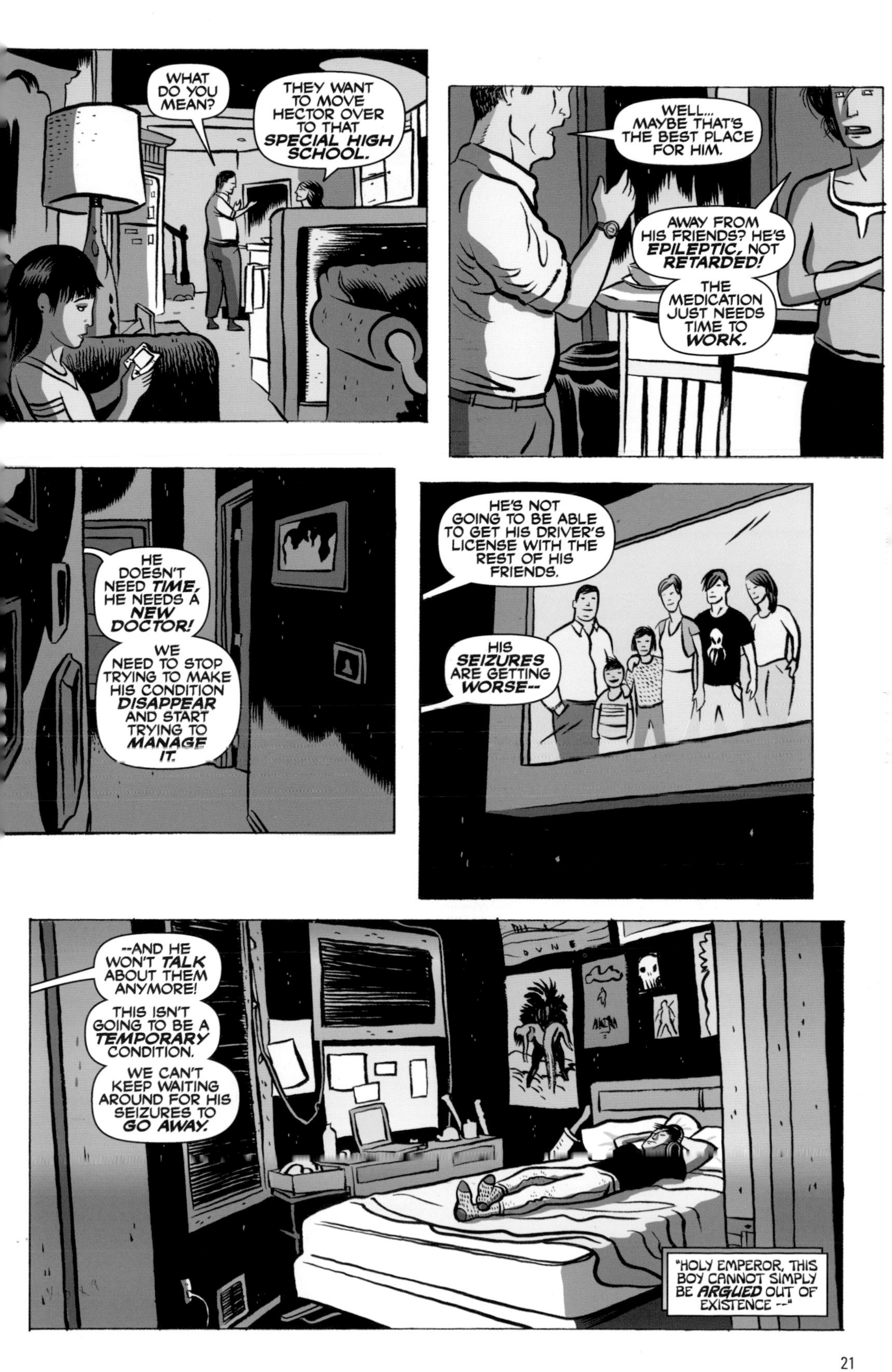
WHAT DO YOU MEAN?
THEY WANT TO MOVE HECTOR OVER TO THAT SPECIAL HIGH SCHOOL.
WELL... MAYBE THAT'S THE BEST PLACE FOR HIM.
AWAY FROM HIS FRIENDS? HE'S EPILEPTIC, NOT RETARDED!
THE MEDICATION JUST NEEDS TIME TO WORK.
HE DOESN'T NEED TIME, HE NEEDS A NEW DOCTOR!
WE NEED TO STOP TRYING TO MAKE HIS CONDITION DISAPPEAR AND START TRYING TO MANAGE IT.
HE'S NOT GOING TO BE ABLE TO GET HIS DRIVER'S LICENSE WITH THE REST OF HIS FRIENDS.
HIS SEIZURES ARE GETTING WORSE--
--AND HE WON'T TALK ABOUT THEM ANYMORE!
THIS ISN'T GOING TO BE A TEMPORARY CONDITION.
WE CAN'T KEEP WAITING AROUND FOR HIS SEIZURES TO GO AWAY.
"HOLY EMPEROR, THIS BOY CANNOT SIMPLY BE ARGUED OUT OF EXISTENCE --"

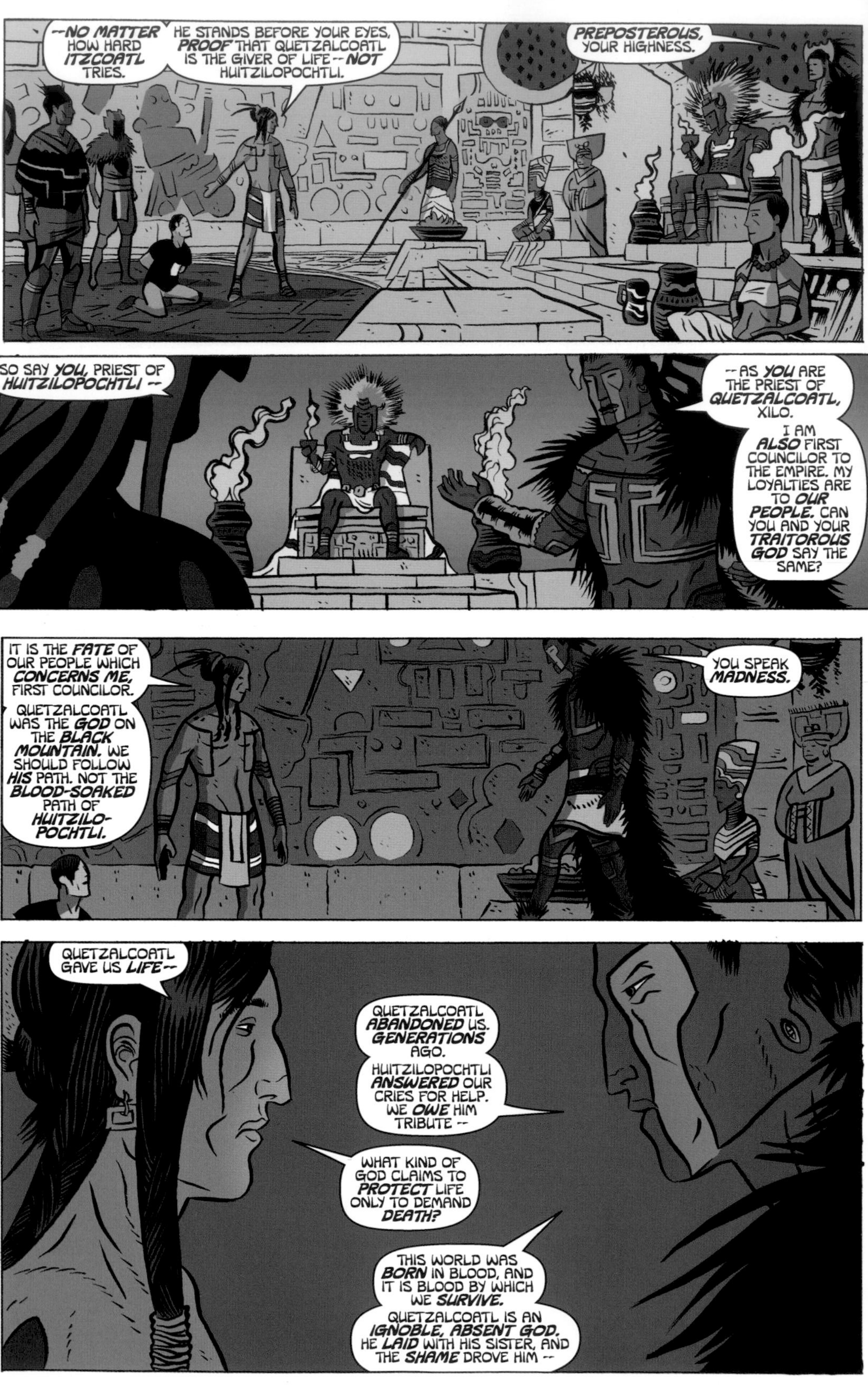
--NO MATTER HOW HARD ITZCOATL TRIES.
HE STANDS BEFORE YOUR EYES, PROOF THAT QUETZALCOATL IS THE GIVER OF LIFE--NOT HUITZILOPOCHTLI.
PREPOSTEROUS, YOUR HIGHNESS.
SO SAY YOU, PRIEST OF HUITZILOPOCHTLI --
--AS YOU ARE THE PRIEST OF QUETZALCOATL, XILO.
I AM ALSO FIRST COUNCILOR TO THE EMPIRE. MY LOYALTIES ARE TO OUR PEOPLE. CAN YOU AND YOUR TRAITOROUS GOD SAY THE SAME?
IT IS THE FATE OF OUR PEOPLE WHICH CONCERNS ME, FIRST COUNCILOR.
QUETZALCOATL WAS THE GOD ON THE BLACK MOUNTAIN. WE SHOULD FOLLOW HIS PATH. NOT THE BLOOD-SOAKED PATH OF HUITZILO-POCHTLI.
YOU SPEAK MADNESS.
QUETZALCOATL GAVE US LIFE--
QUETZALCOATL ABANDONED US. GENERATIONS AGO.
HUITZILOPOCHTLI ANSWERED OUR CRIES FOR HELP. WE OWE HIM TRIBUTE --
WHAT KIND OF GOD CLAIMS TO PROTECT LIFE ONLY TO DEMAND DEATH?
THIS WORLD WAS BORN IN BLOOD, AND IT IS BLOOD BY WHICH WE SURVIVE.
QUETZALCOATL IS AN IGNOBLE, ABSENT GOD. HE LAID WITH HIS SISTER, AND THE SHAME DROVE HIM --

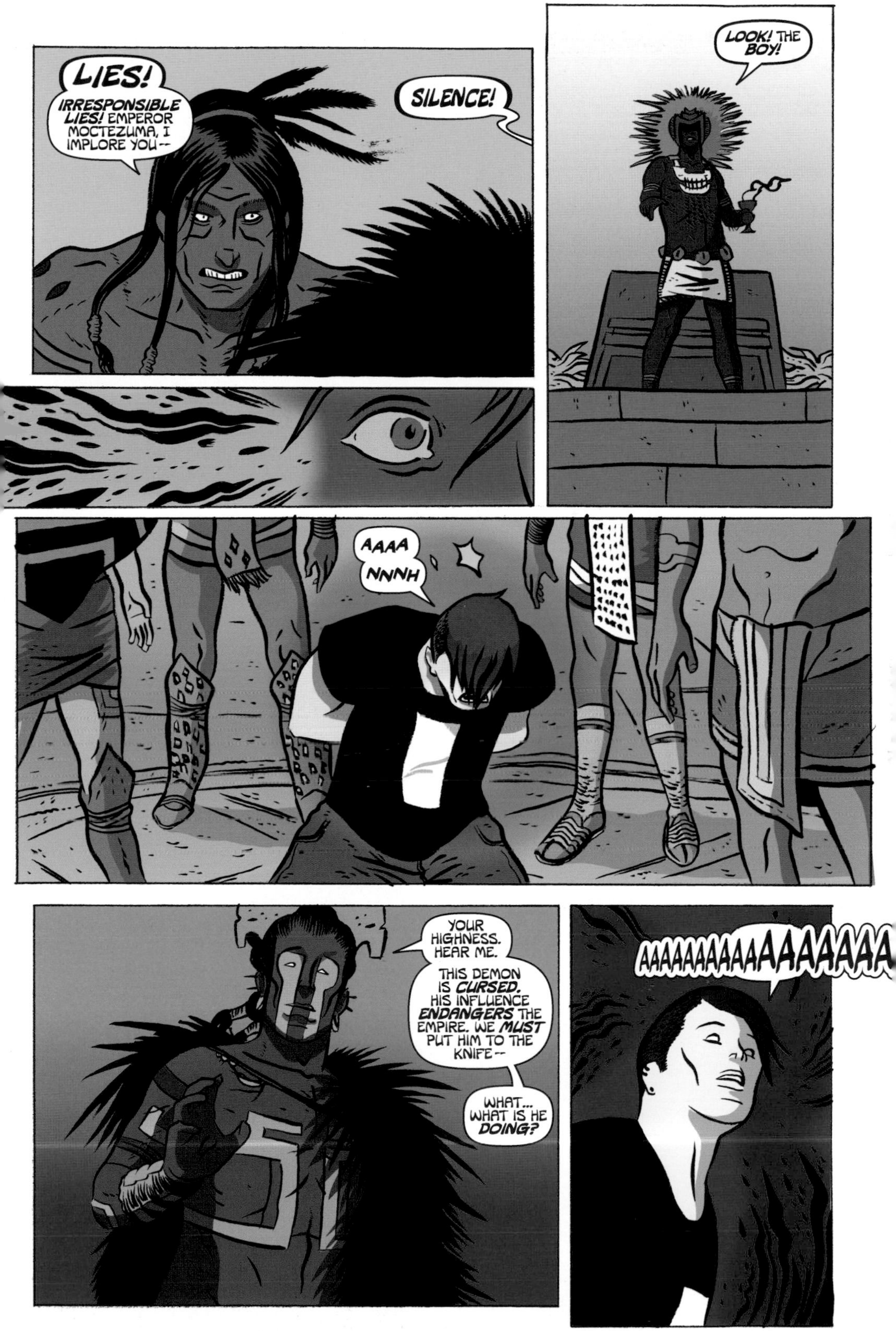
LIES! IRRESPONSIBLE LIES! EMPEROR MOCTEZUMA, I IMPLORE YOU--
SILENCE!
LOOK! THE BOY!
AAAA NNNH
YOUR HIGHNESS. HEAR ME.
THIS DEMON IS CURSED. HIS INFLUENCE ENDANGERS THE EMPIRE. WE MUST PUT HIM TO THE KNIFE--
WHAT... WHAT IS HE DOING?
AAAAAAAAAAAAAAAA

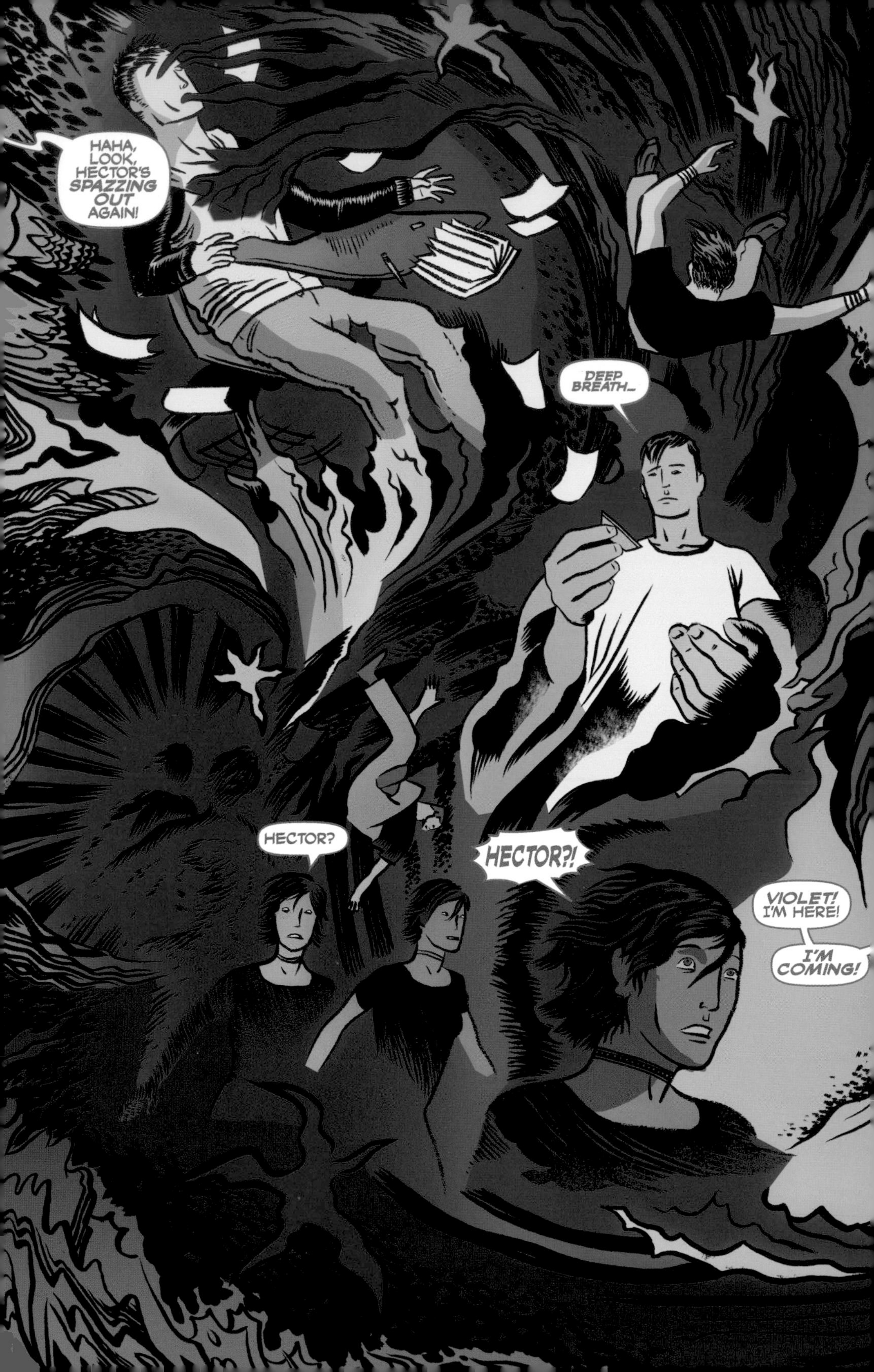
HAHA, LOOK, HECTOR'S SPAZZING OUT AGAIN!
DEEP BREATH...
HECTOR?
HECTOR?!
VIOLET! I'M HERE!
I'M COMING!

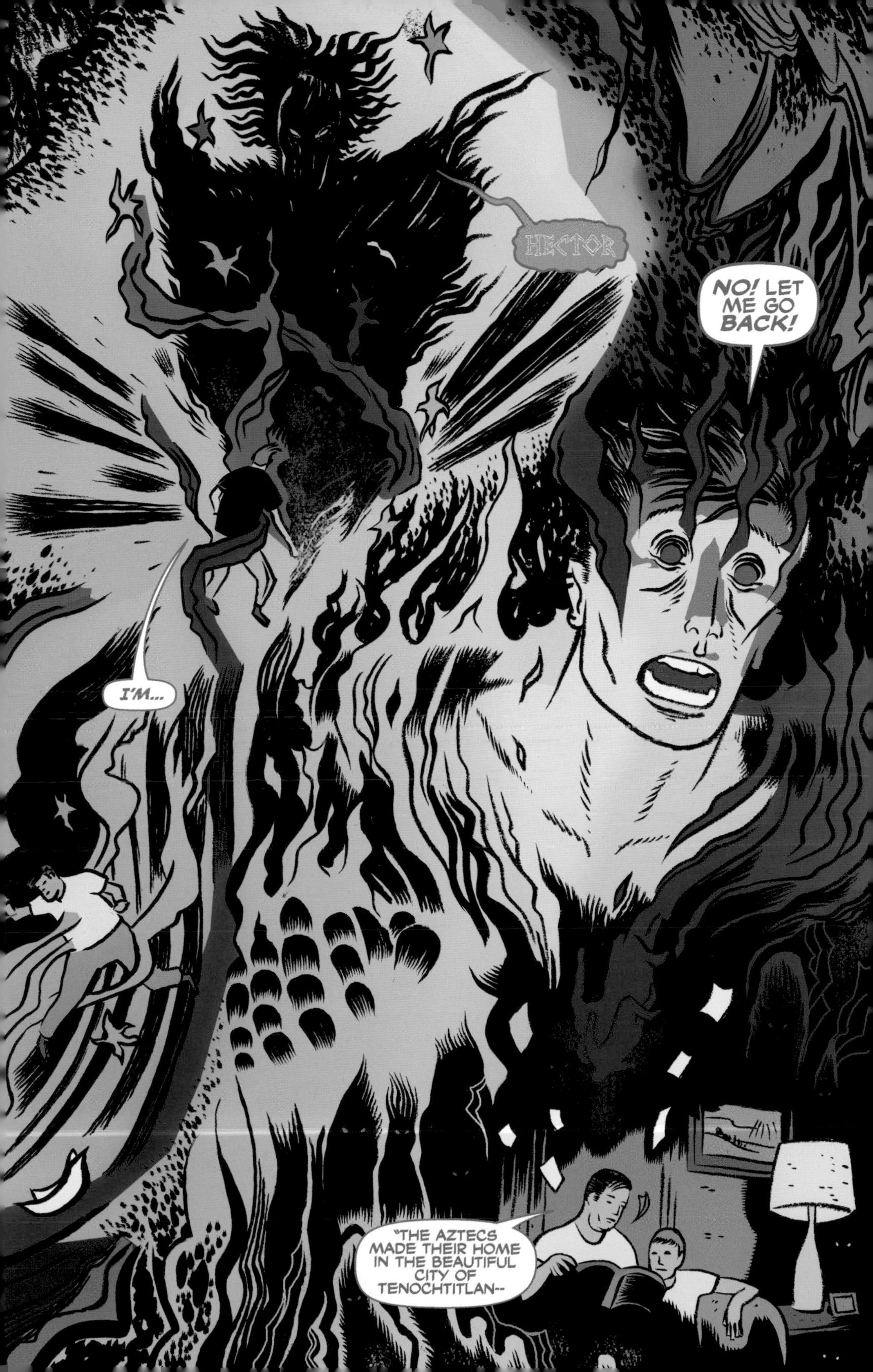
HECTOR
NO! LET ME GO BACK!
I'M...
"THE AZTECS MADE THEIR HOME IN THE BEAUTIFUL CITY OF TENOCHTITLAN--

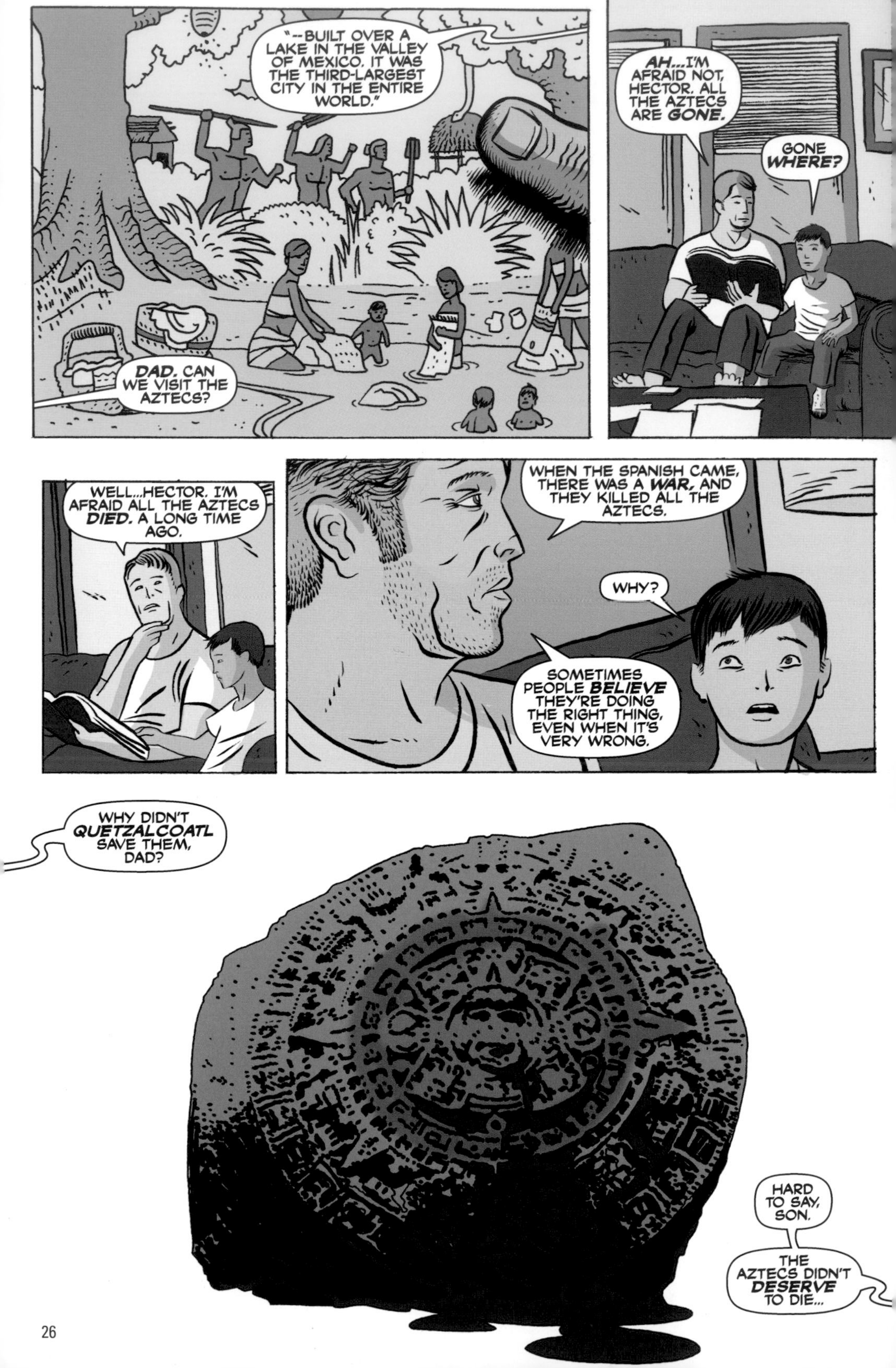
"--BUILT OVER A LAKE IN THE VALLEY OF MEXICO. IT WAS THE THIRD-LARGEST CITY IN THE ENTIRE WORLD."
DAD. CAN WE VISIT THE AZTECS?
AH...I'M AFRAID NOT, HECTOR. ALL THE AZTECS ARE GONE.
GONE WHERE?
WELL...HECTOR. I'M AFRAID ALL THE AZTECS DIED. A LONG TIME AGO.
WHEN THE SPANISH CAME, THERE WAS A WAR, AND THEY KILLED ALL THE AZTECS.
WHY?
SOMETIMES PEOPLE BELIEVE THEY'RE DOING THE RIGHT THING, EVEN WHEN IT'S VERY WRONG.
WHY DIDN'T QUETZALCOATL SAVE THEM, DAD?
HARD TO SAY, SON.
THE AZTECS DIDN'T DESERVE TO DIE...

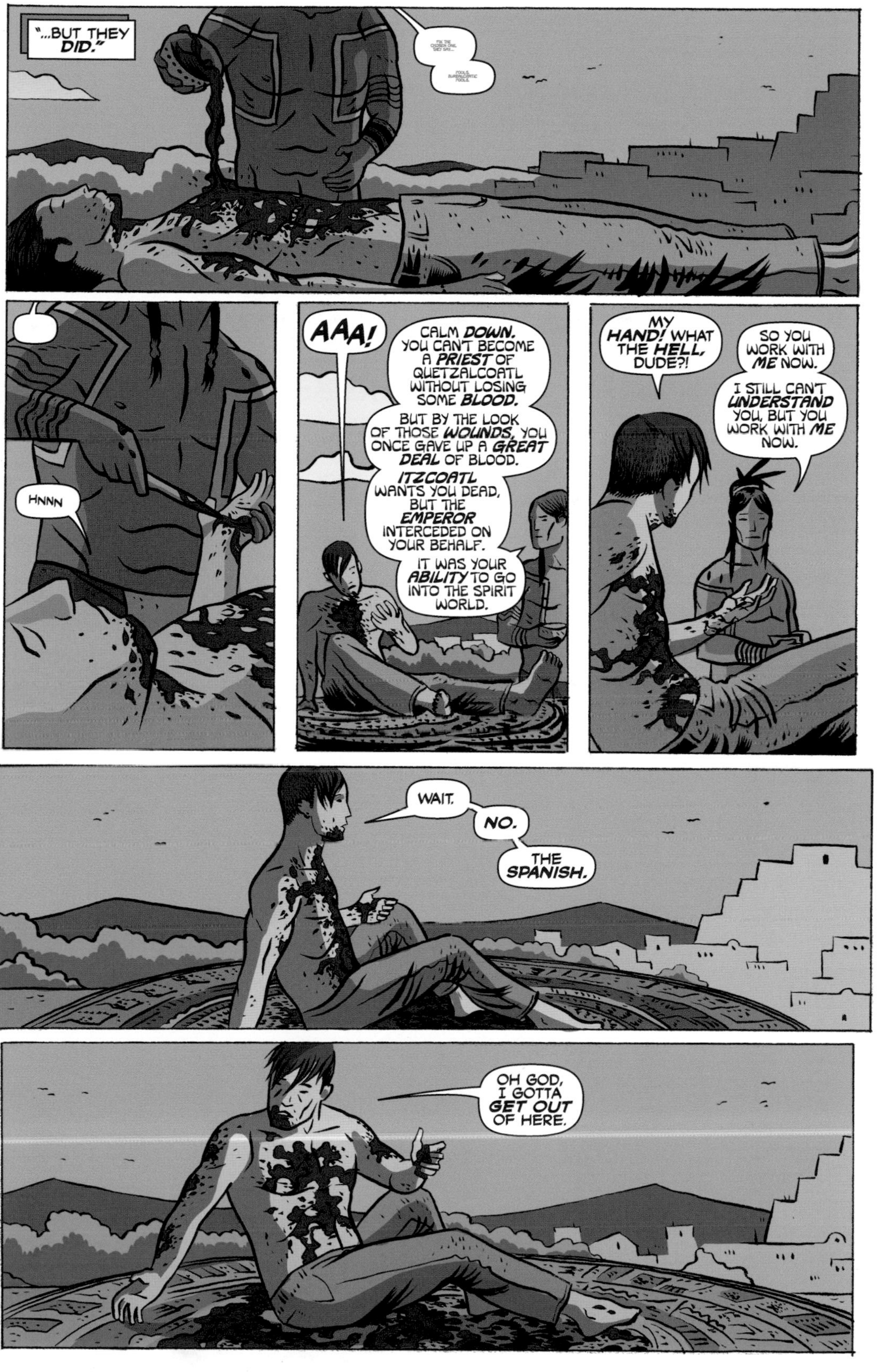
"...BUT THEY DID."
FIX THE CHOSEN ONE, THEY SAY...
FOOLS. BUREAUCRATIC FOOLS.
HNNN
AAA!
CALM DOWN. YOU CAN'T BECOME A PRIEST OF QUETZALCOATL WITHOUT LOSING SOME BLOOD.
BUT BY THE LOOK OF THOSE WOUNDS, YOU ONCE GAVE UP A GREAT DEAL OF BLOOD.
ITZCOATL WANTS YOU DEAD, BUT THE EMPEROR INTERCEDED ON YOUR BEHALF.
IT WAS YOUR ABILITY TO GO INTO THE SPIRIT WORLD.
MY HAND! WHAT THE HELL, DUDE?!
SO YOU WORK WITH ME NOW.
I STILL CAN'T UNDERSTAND YOU, BUT YOU WORK WITH ME NOW.
WAIT.
NO.
THE SPANISH.
OH GOD, I GOTTA GET OUT OF HERE.

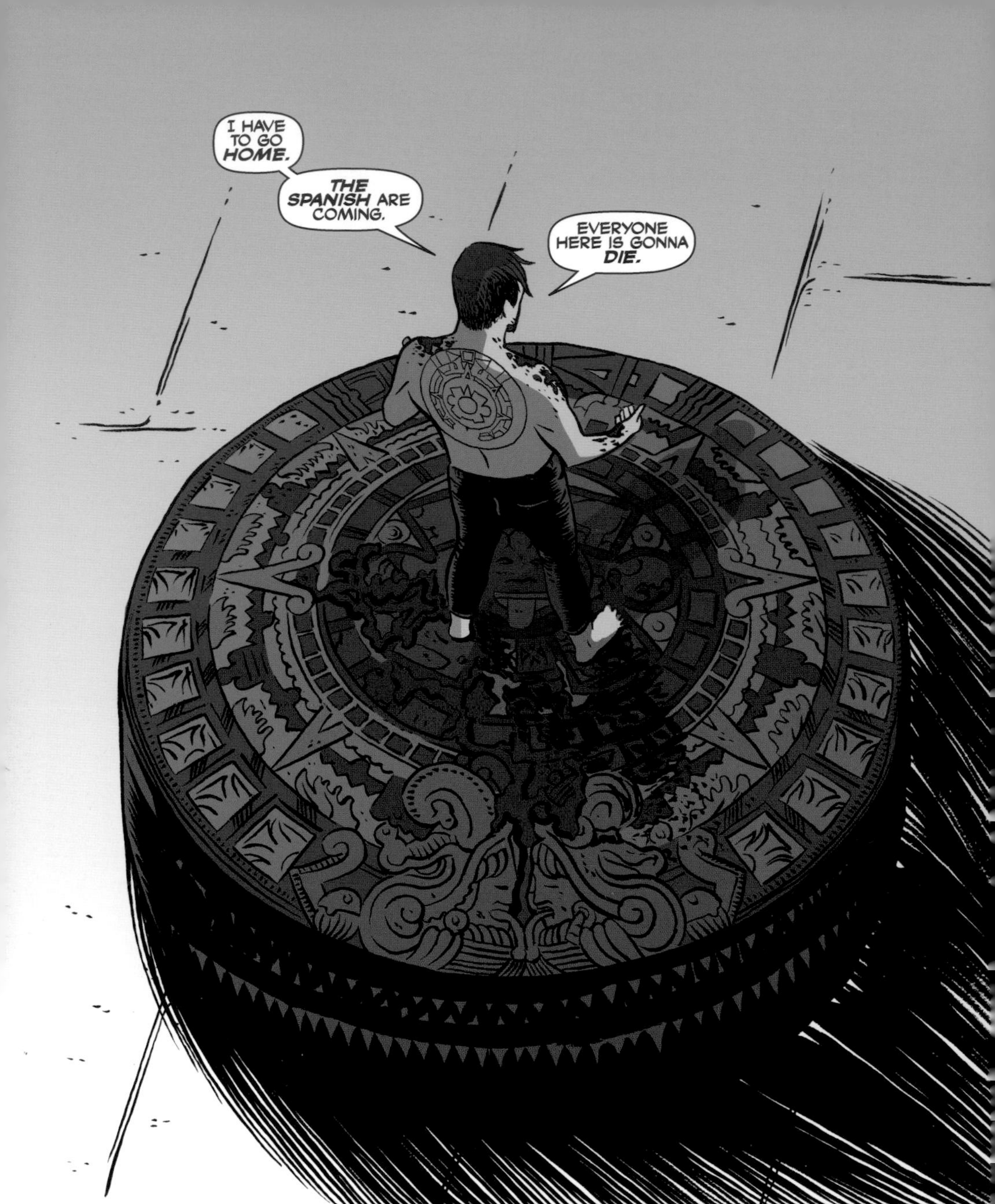
I HAVE TO GO HOME.
THE SPANISH ARE COMING.
EVERYONE HERE IS GONNA DIE.
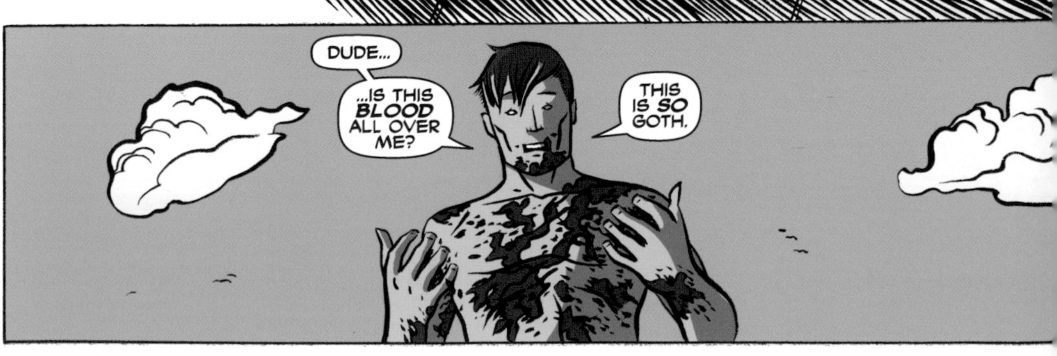
DUDE...
...IS THIS BLOOD ALL OVER ME?
THIS IS SO GOTH.

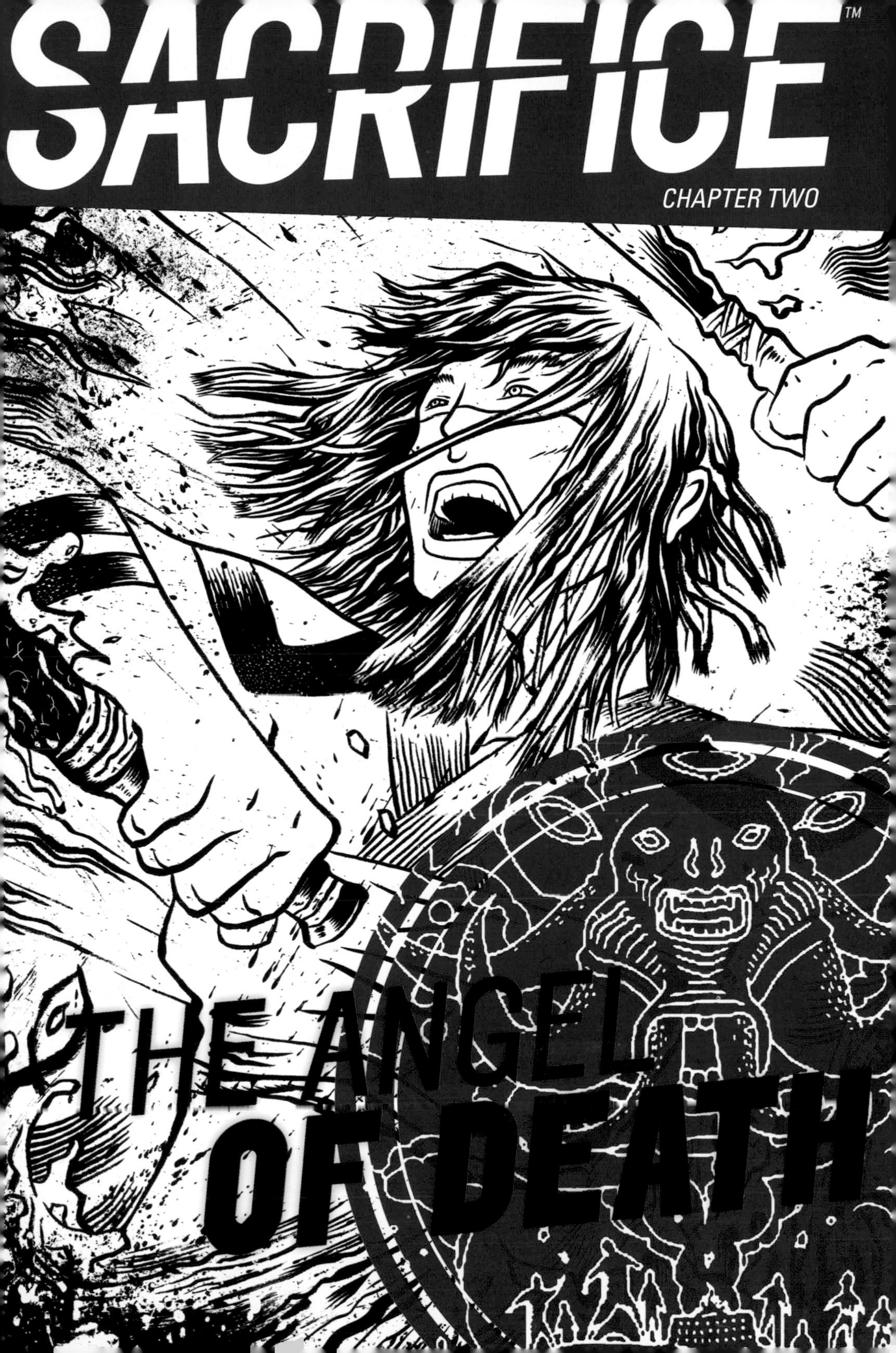
SACRIFICE™
CHAPTER TWO
THE ANGEL OF DEATH

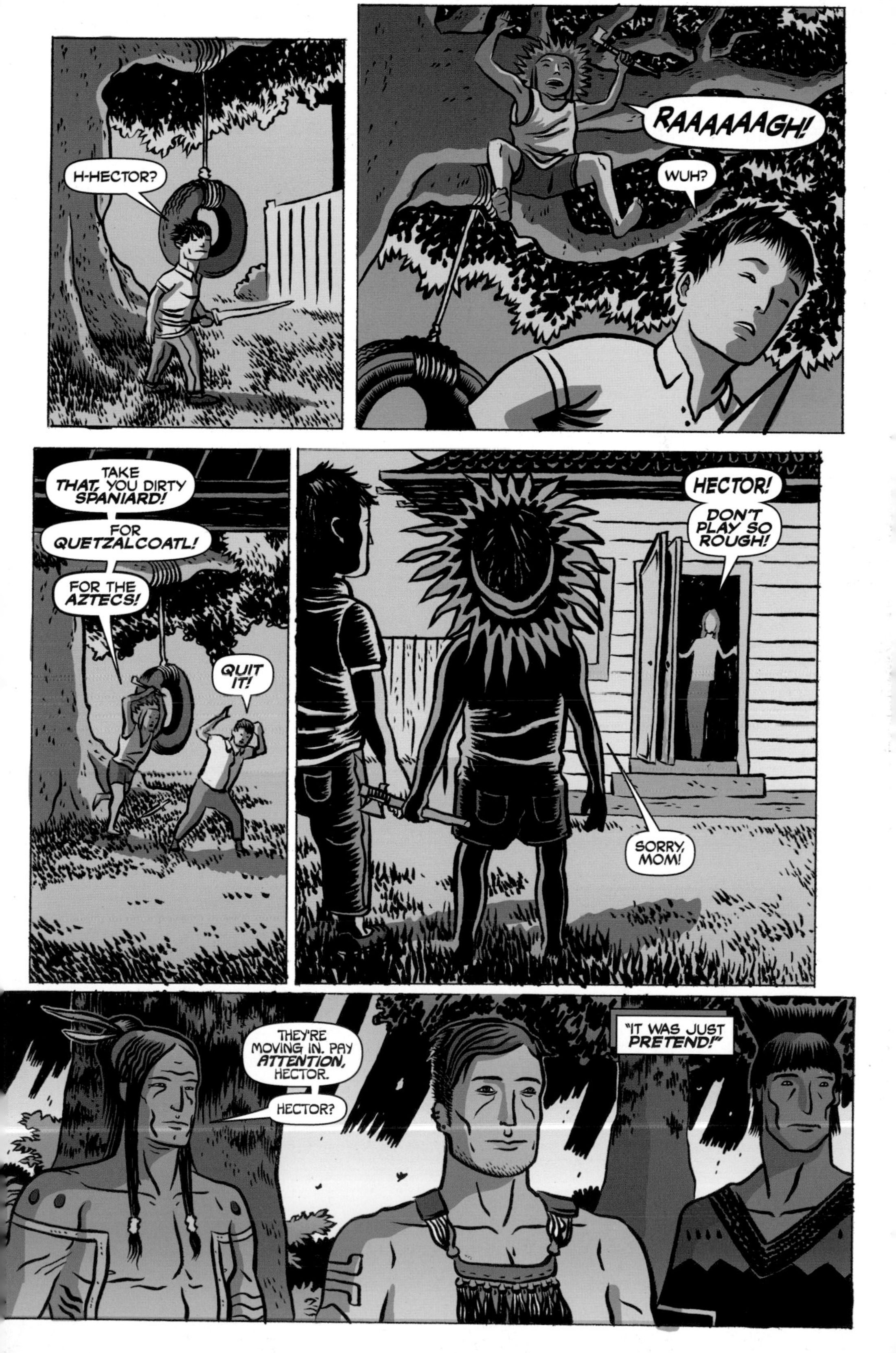
H-HECTOR?
RAAAAAAGH!
WUH?
TAKE THAT, YOU DIRTY SPANIARD!
FOR QUETZALCOATL!
FOR THE AZTECS!
QUIT IT!
HECTOR!
DON'T PLAY SO ROUGH!
SORRY, MOM!
THEY'RE MOVING IN. PAY ATTENTION, HECTOR.
HECTOR?
"IT WAS JUST PRETEND!"

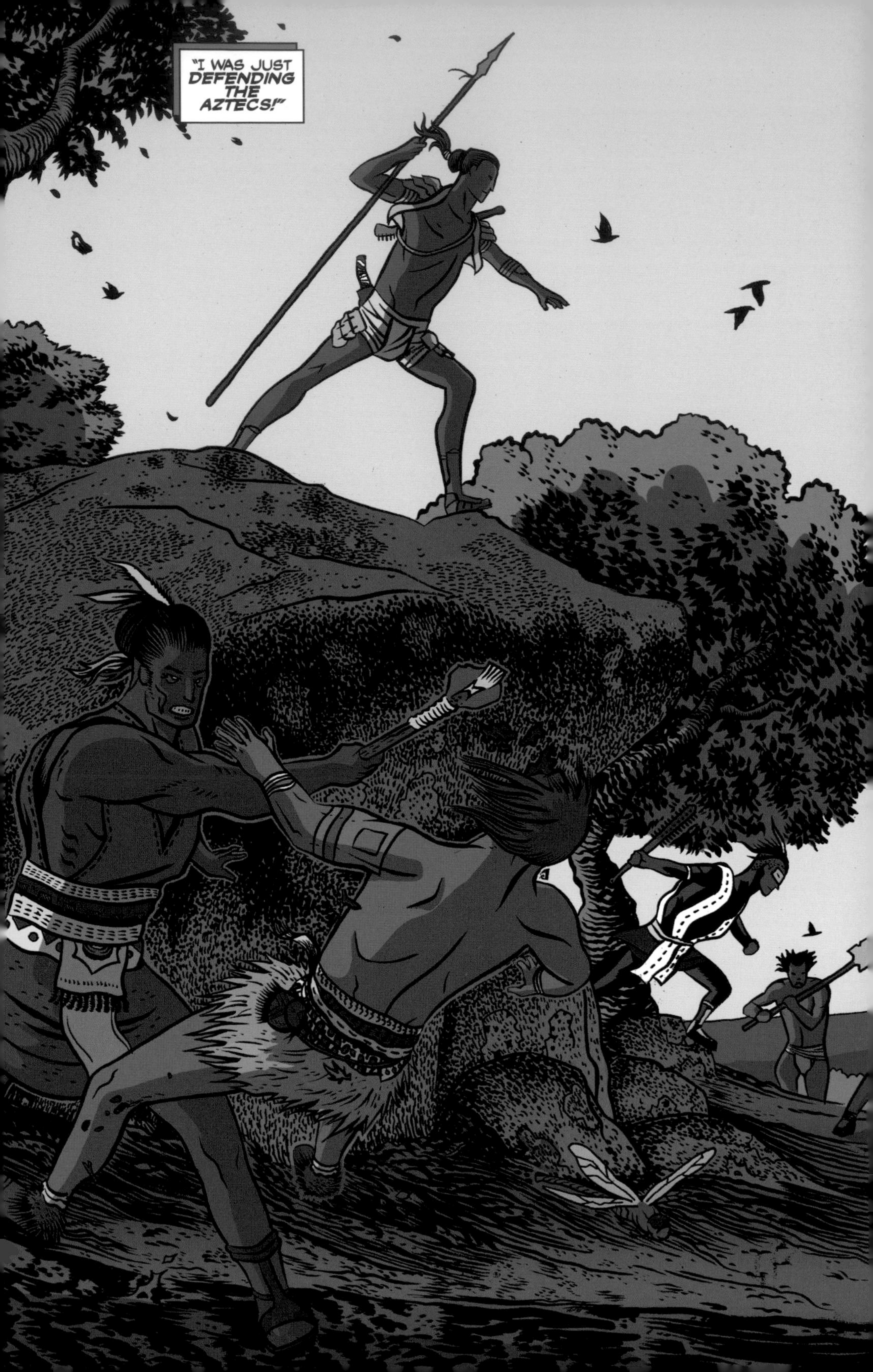
"I WAS JUST DEFENDING THE AZTECS!"

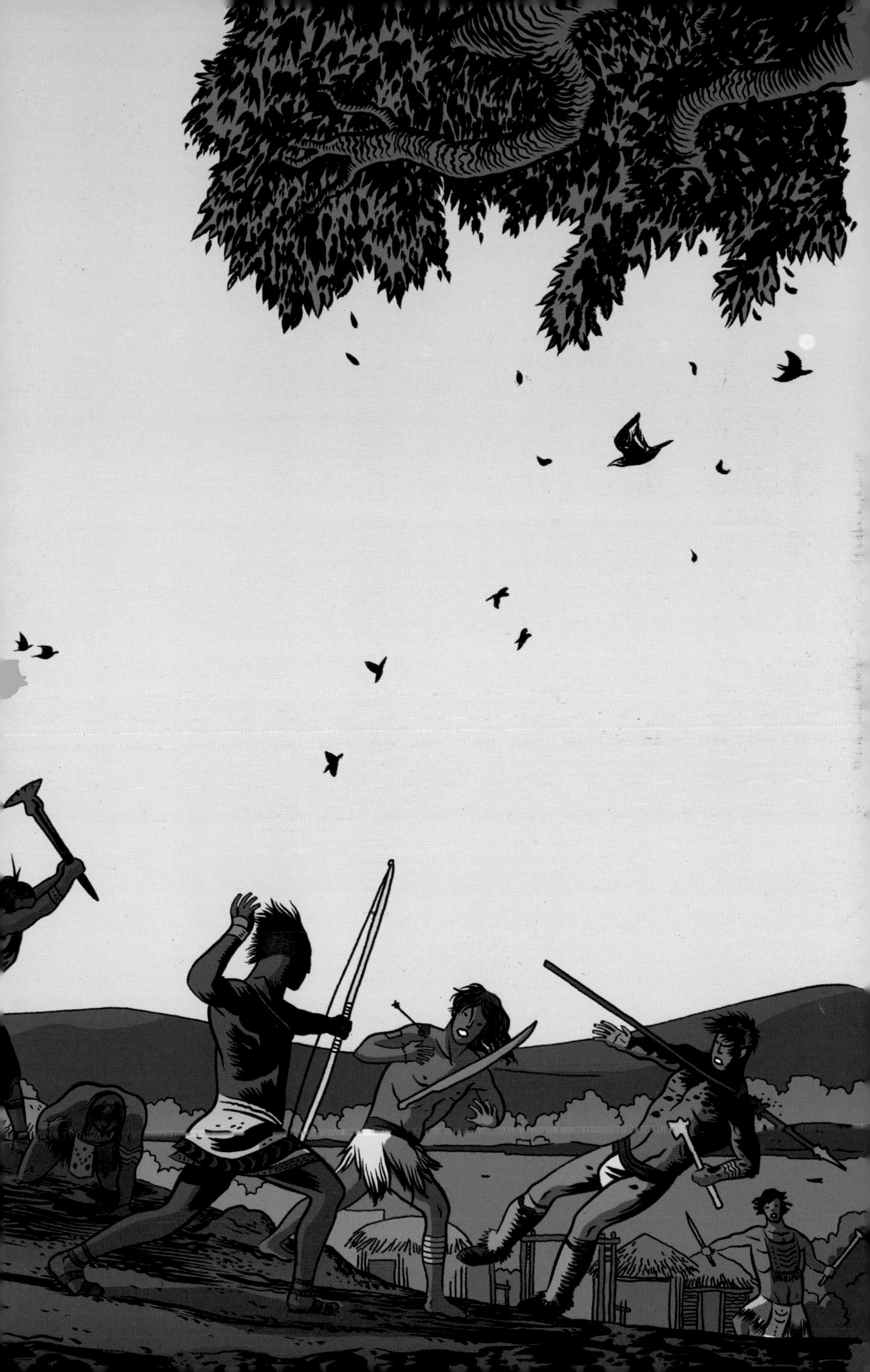

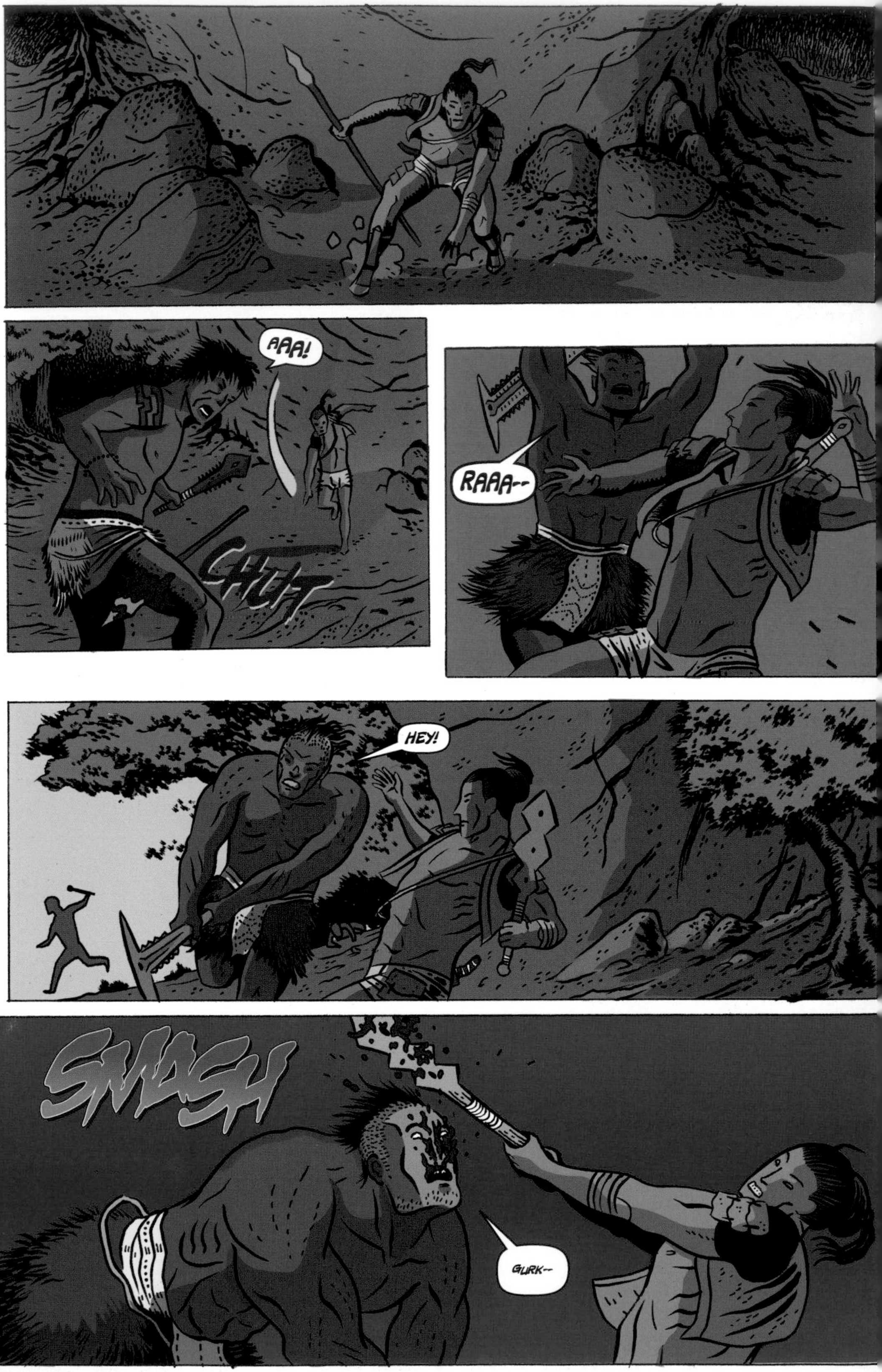
AAA!
CHUT
RAAA--
HEY!
SMASH
GURK--

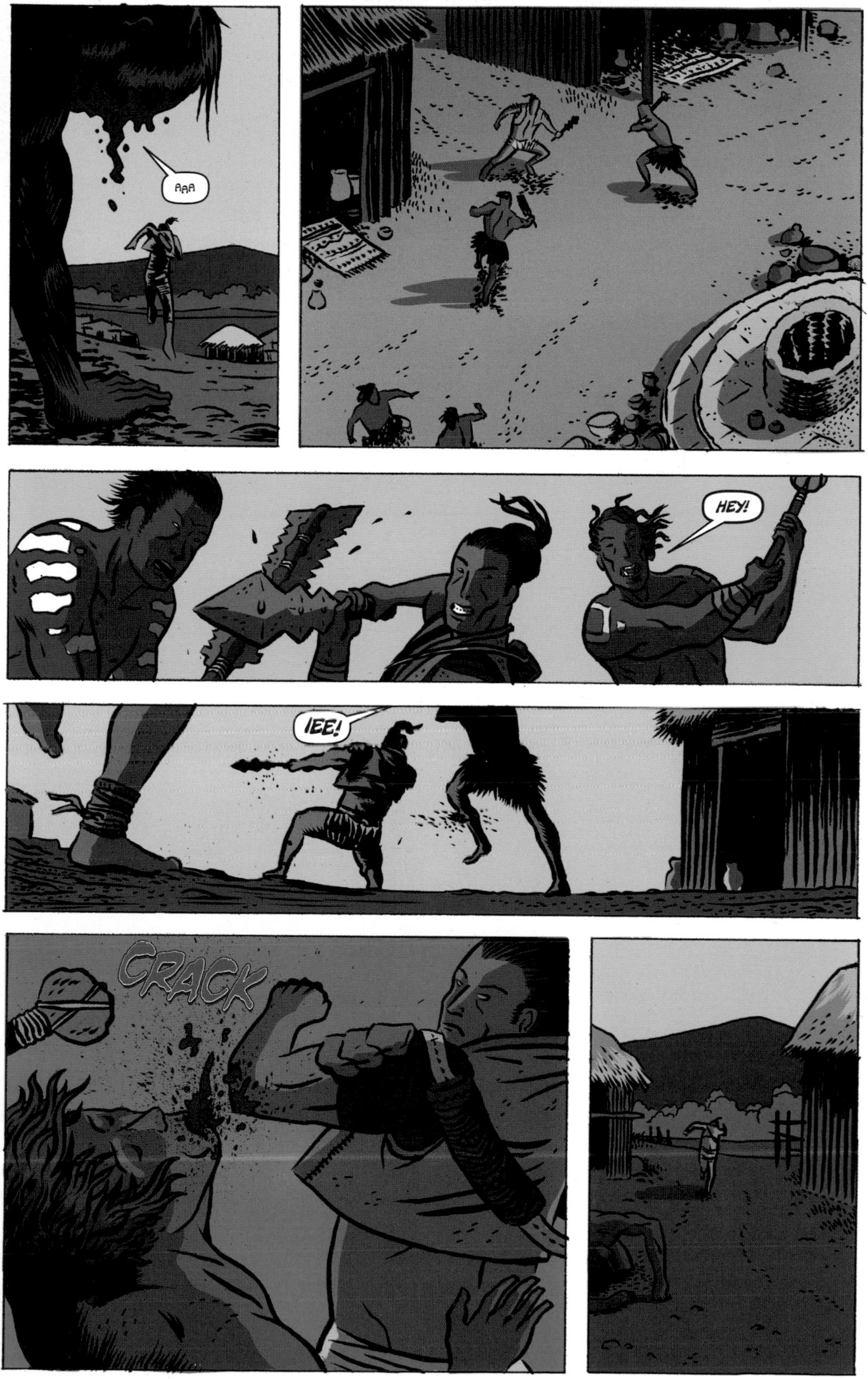
AAA
HEY!
IEE!
CRACK

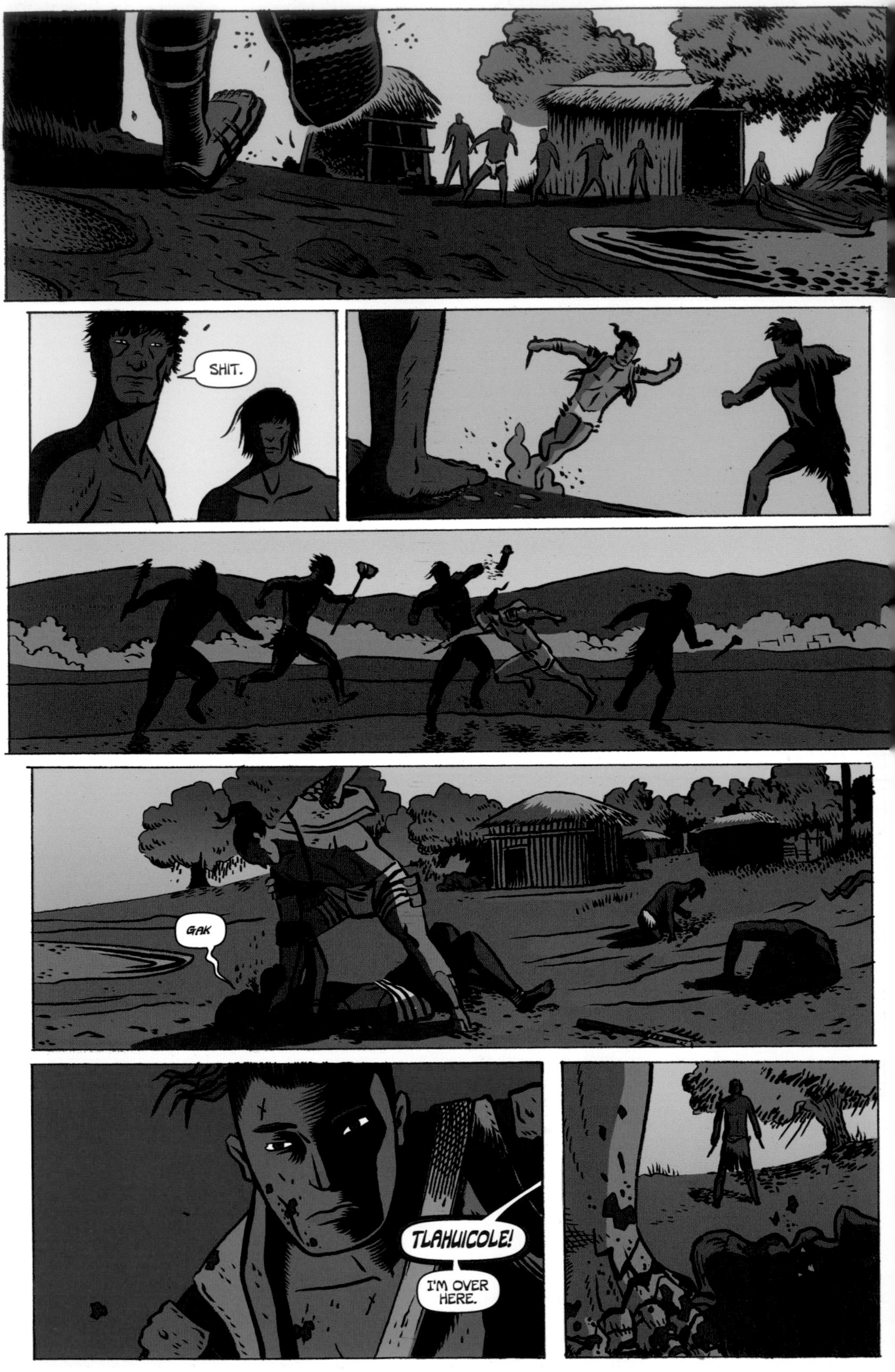
SHIT.
GAK
TLAHUICOLE!
I'M OVER HERE.

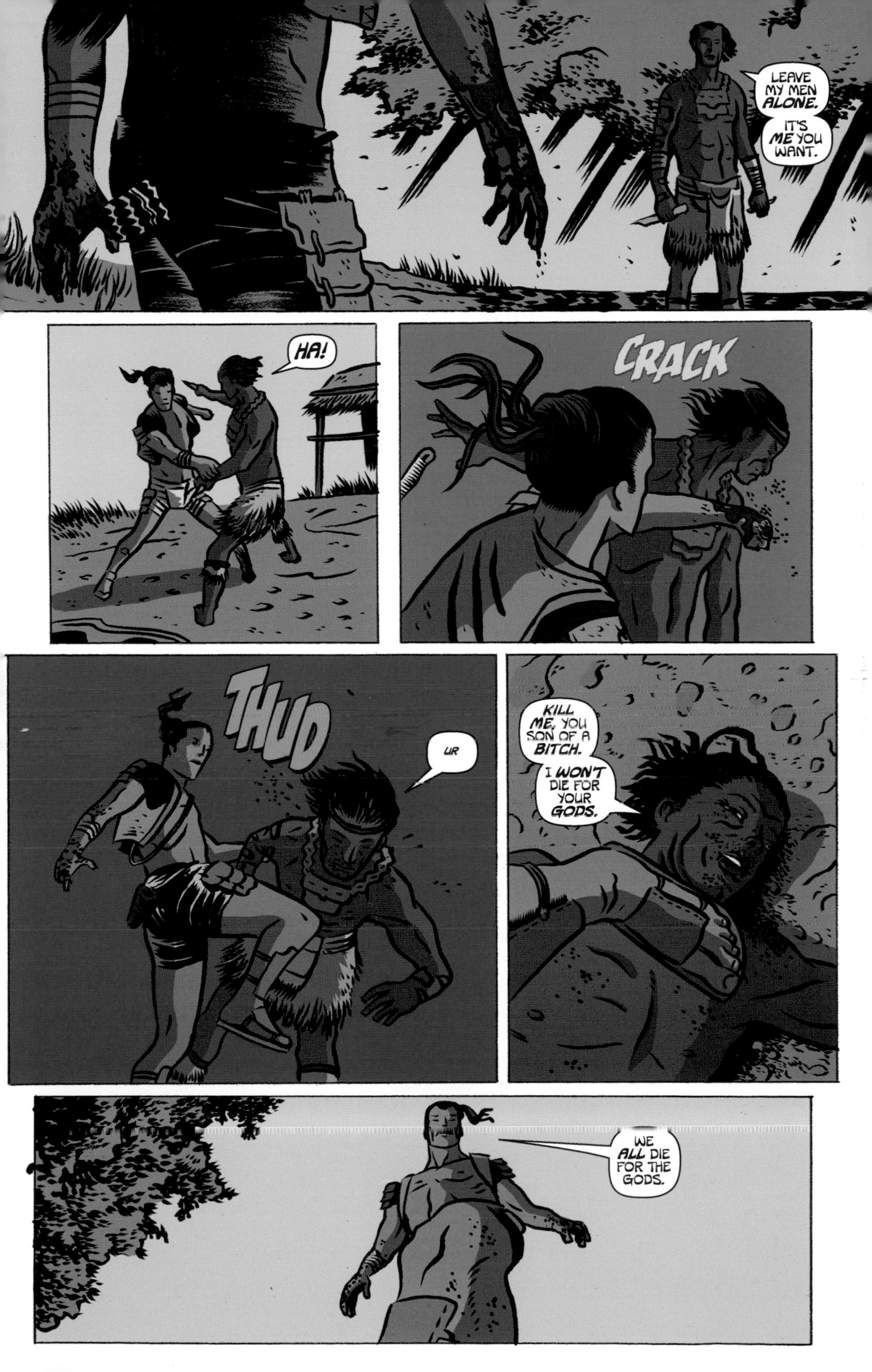

LEAVE MY MEN ALONE.
IT'S ME YOU WANT.
HA!
CRACK
THUD
UR
KILL ME, YOU SON OF A BITCH.
I WON'T DIE FOR YOUR GODS.
WE ALL DIE FOR THE GODS.

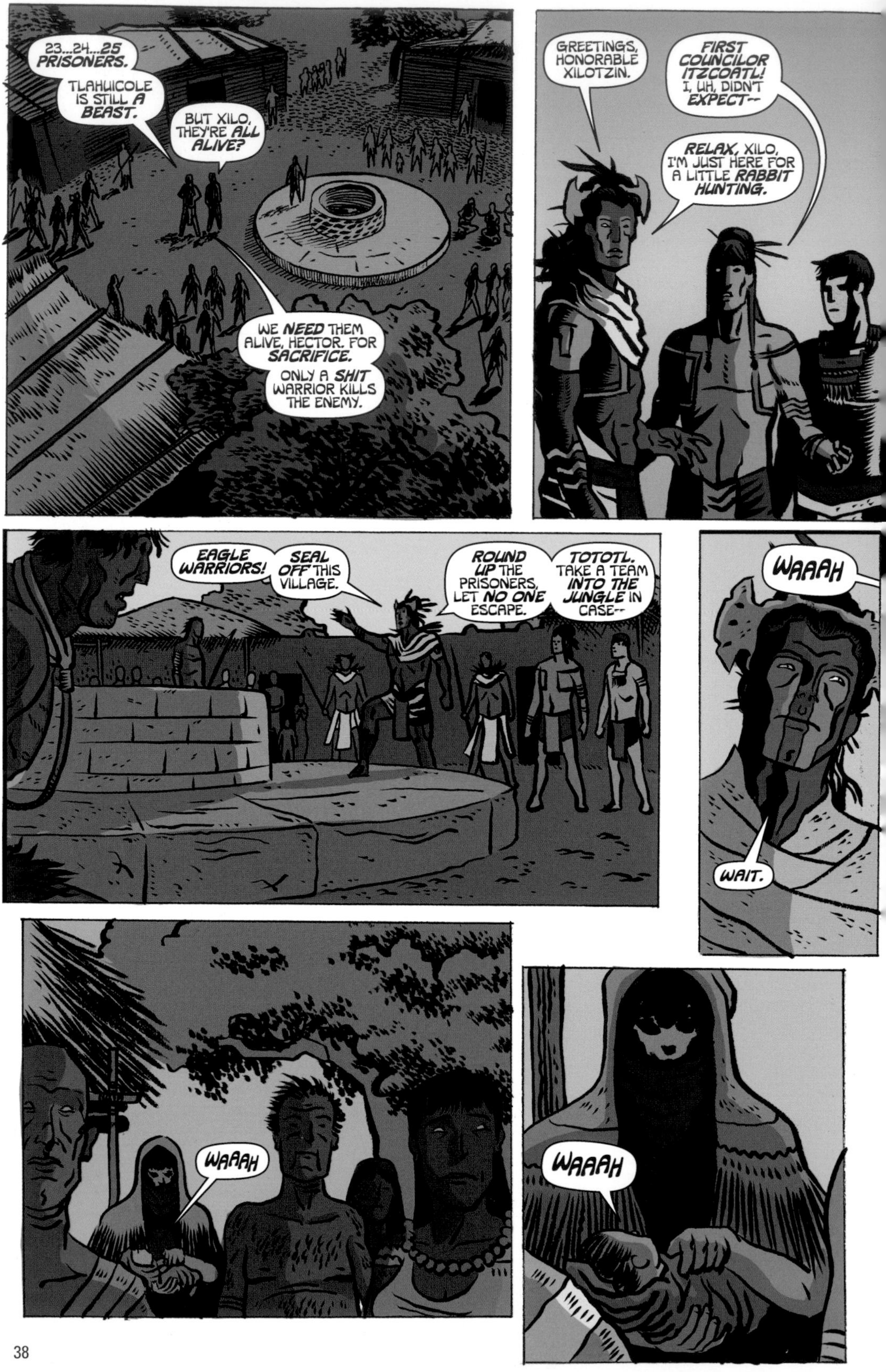
23...24...25 PRISONERS.
TLAHUICOLE IS STILL A BEAST.
BUT XILO, THEY'RE ALL ALIVE?
WE NEED THEM ALIVE, HECTOR. FOR SACRIFICE.
ONLY A SHIT WARRIOR KILLS THE ENEMY.
GREETINGS, HONORABLE XILOTZIN.
FIRST COUNCILOR ITZCOATL! I, UH, DIDN'T EXPECT--
RELAX, XILO, I'M JUST HERE FOR A LITTLE RABBIT HUNTING.
EAGLE WARRIORS!
SEAL OFF THIS VILLAGE.
ROUND UP THE PRISONERS, LET NO ONE ESCAPE.
TOTOTL. TAKE A TEAM INTO THE JUNGLE IN CASE--
WAAAH
WAIT.
WAAAH
WAAAH

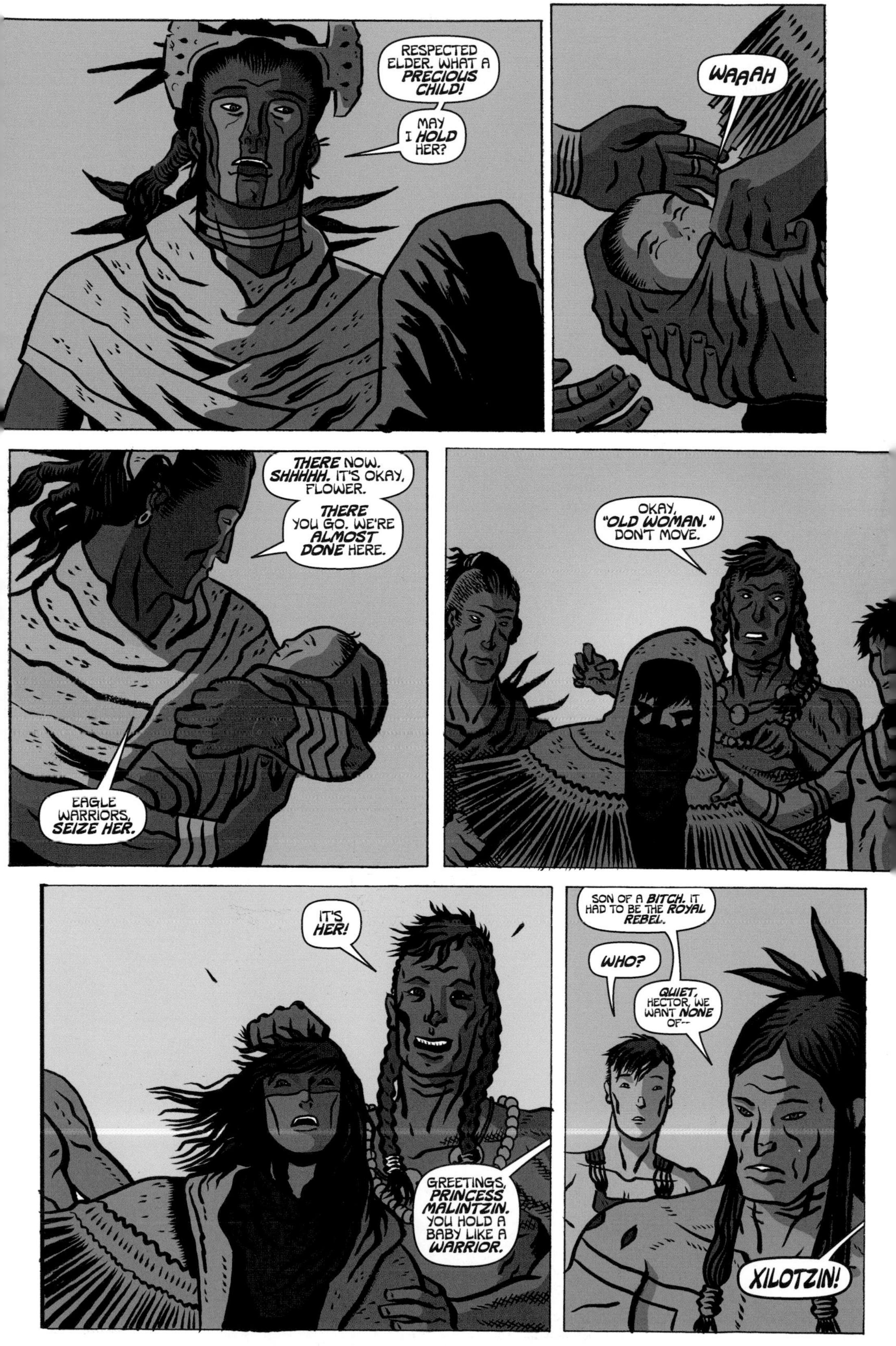
RESPECTED ELDER. WHAT A PRECIOUS CHILD!
MAY I HOLD HER?
WAAAH
THERE NOW. SHHHHH. IT'S OKAY, FLOWER.
THERE YOU GO. WE'RE ALMOST DONE HERE.
EAGLE WARRIORS, SEIZE HER.
OKAY, "OLD WOMAN." DON'T MOVE.
IT'S HER!
GREETINGS, PRINCESS MALINTZIN. YOU HOLD A BABY LIKE A WARRIOR.
SON OF A BITCH. IT HAD TO BE THE ROYAL REBEL.
WHO?
QUIET, HECTOR, WE WANT NONE OF--
XILOTZIN!

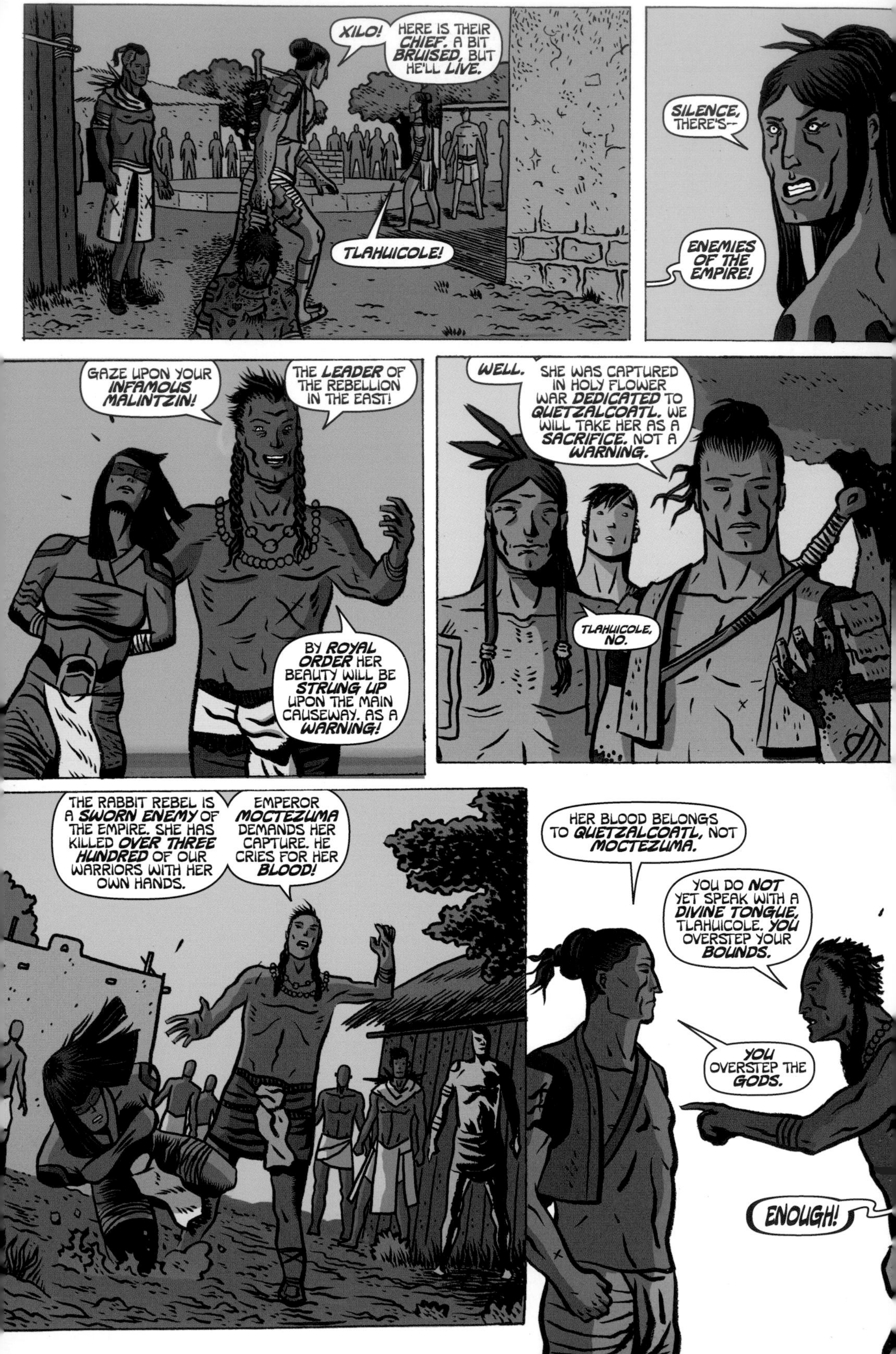
XILO!
HERE IS THEIR CHIEF. A BIT BRUISED, BUT HE'LL LIVE.
TLAHUICOLE!
SILENCE, THERE'S--
ENEMIES OF THE EMPIRE!
GAZE UPON YOUR INFAMOUS MALINTZIN!
THE LEADER OF THE REBELLION IN THE EAST!
BY ROYAL ORDER HER BEAUTY WILL BE STRUNG UP UPON THE MAIN CAUSEWAY. AS A WARNING!
WELL.
SHE WAS CAPTURED IN HOLY FLOWER WAR DEDICATED TO QUETZALCOATL. WE WILL TAKE HER AS A SACRIFICE. NOT A WARNING.
TLAHUICOLE, NO.
THE RABBIT REBEL IS A SWORN ENEMY OF THE EMPIRE. SHE HAS KILLED OVER THREE HUNDRED OF OUR WARRIORS WITH HER OWN HANDS.
EMPEROR MOCTEZUMA DEMANDS HER CAPTURE. HE CRIES FOR HER BLOOD!
HER BLOOD BELONGS TO QUETZALCOATL, NOT MOCTEZUMA.
YOU DO NOT YET SPEAK WITH A DIVINE TONGUE, TLAHUICOLE. YOU OVERSTEP YOUR BOUNDS.
YOU OVERSTEP THE GODS.
ENOUGH!

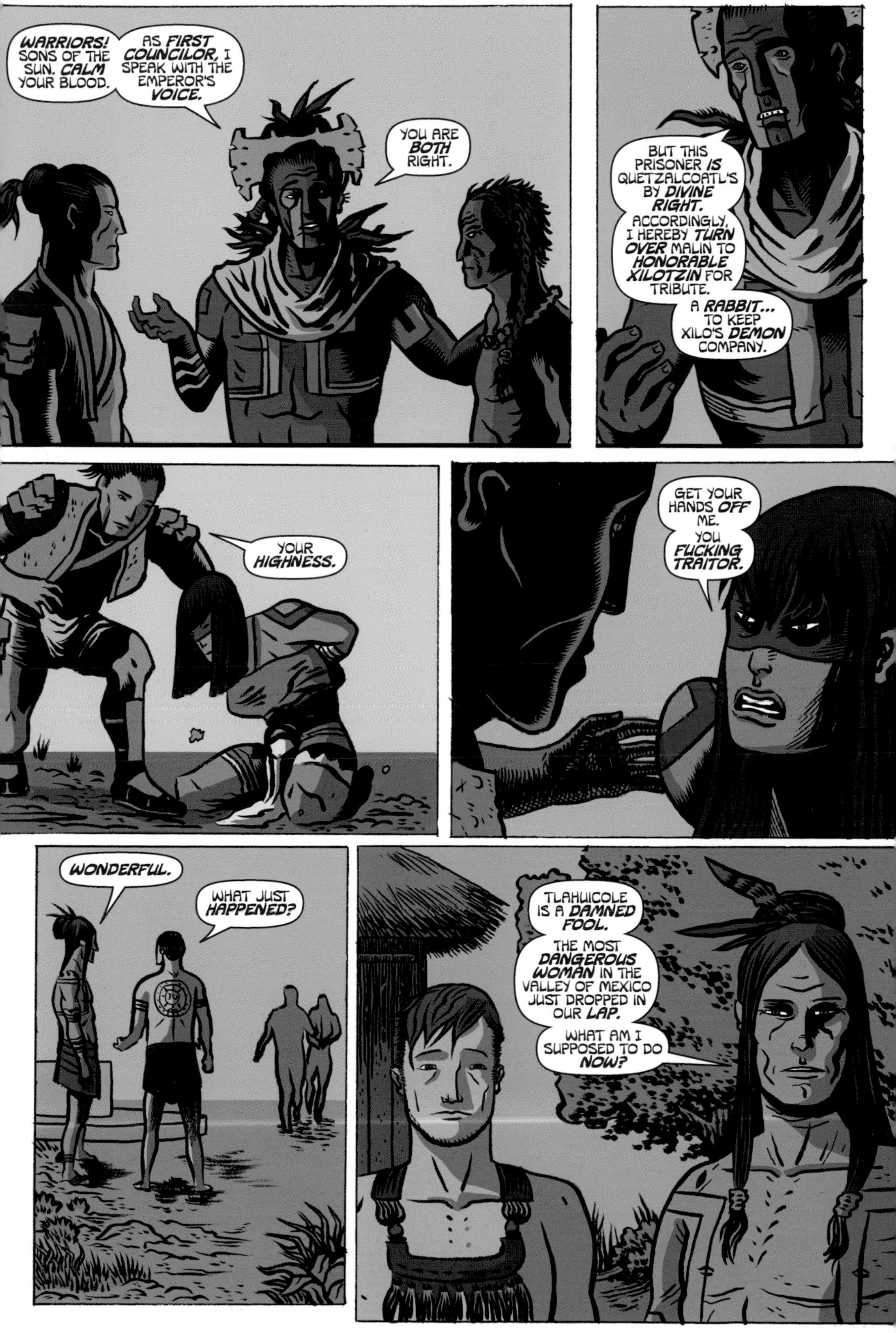
WARRIORS! SONS OF THE SUN. CALM YOUR BLOOD.
AS FIRST COUNCILOR, I SPEAK WITH THE EMPEROR'S VOICE.
YOU ARE BOTH RIGHT.
BUT THIS PRISONER IS QUETZALCOATL'S BY DIVINE RIGHT.
ACCORDINGLY, I HEREBY TURN OVER MALIN TO HONORABLE XILOTZIN FOR TRIBUTE.
A RABBIT... TO KEEP XILO'S DEMON COMPANY.
YOUR HIGHNESS.
GET YOUR HANDS OFF ME. YOU FUCKING TRAITOR.
WONDERFUL.
WHAT JUST HAPPENED?
TLAHUICOLE IS A DAMNED FOOL.
THE MOST DANGEROUS WOMAN IN THE VALLEY OF MEXICO JUST DROPPED IN OUR LAP.
WHAT AM I SUPPOSED TO DO NOW?

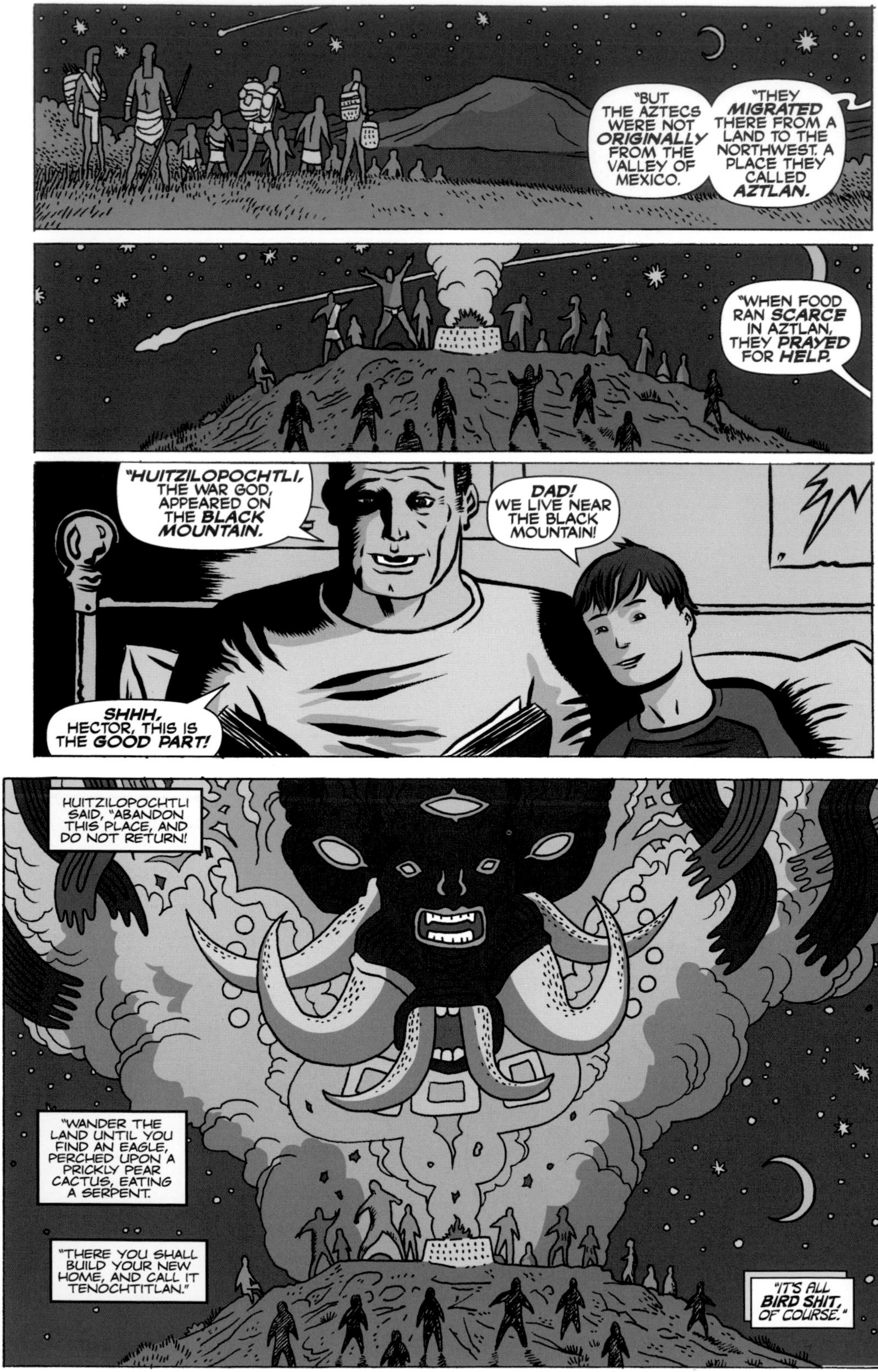
"BUT THE AZTECS WERE NOT ORIGINALLY FROM THE VALLEY OF MEXICO.
"THEY MIGRATED THERE FROM A LAND TO THE NORTHWEST. A PLACE THEY CALLED AZTLAN.
"WHEN FOOD RAN SCARCE IN AZTLAN, THEY PRAYED FOR HELP.
"HUITZILOPOCHTLI, THE WAR GOD, APPEARED ON THE BLACK MOUNTAIN.
DAD! WE LIVE NEAR THE BLACK MOUNTAIN!
SHHH, HECTOR, THIS IS THE GOOD PART!
HUITZILOPOCHTLI SAID, "ABANDON THIS PLACE, AND DO NOT RETURN!
"WANDER THE LAND UNTIL YOU FIND AN EAGLE, PERCHED UPON A PRICKLY PEAR CACTUS, EATING A SERPENT.
"THERE YOU SHALL BUILD YOUR NEW HOME, AND CALL IT TENOCHTITLAN."
"IT'S ALL BIRD SHIT, OF COURSE."

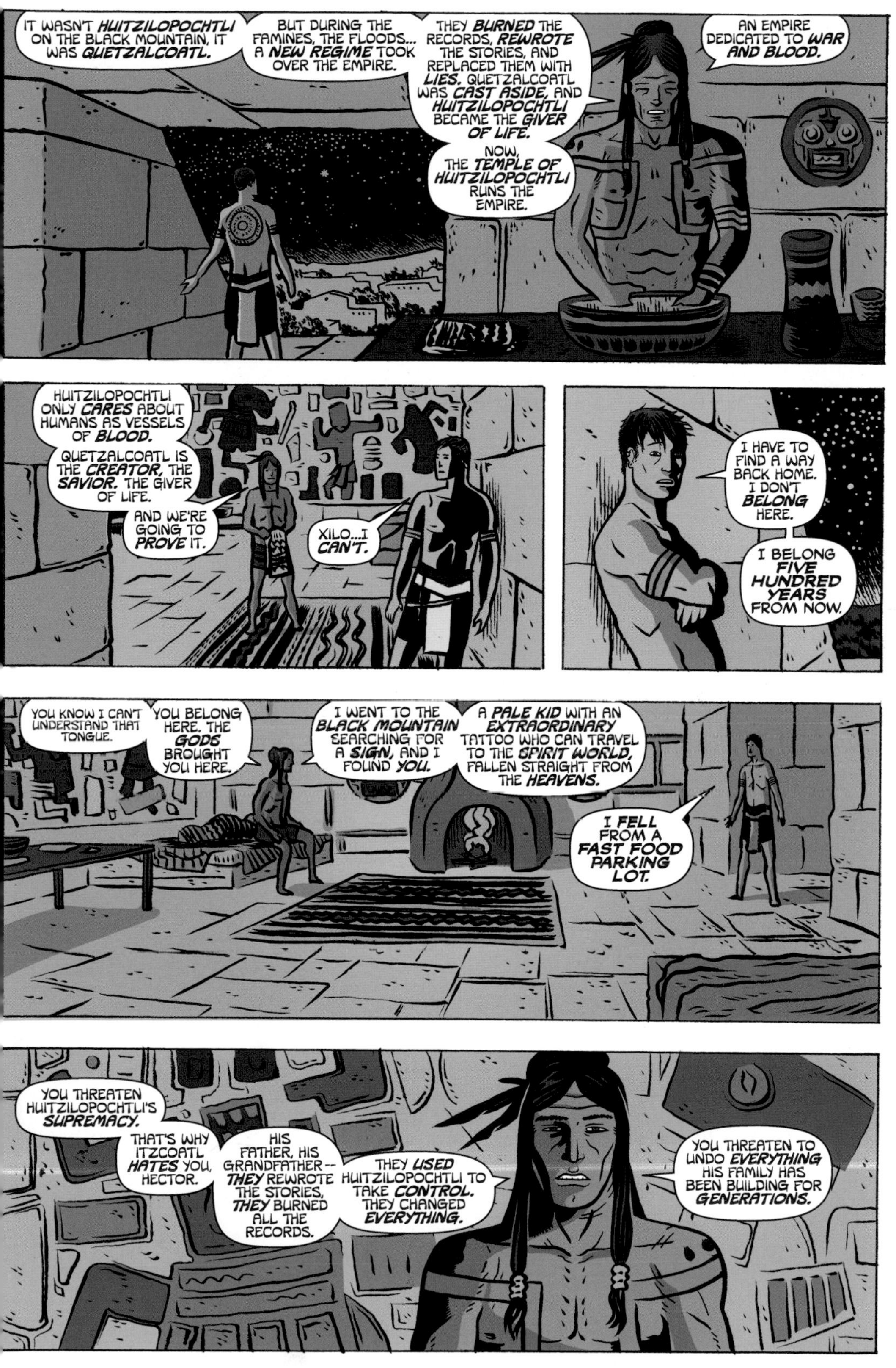
IT WASN'T HUITZILOPOCHTLI ON THE BLACK MOUNTAIN, IT WAS QUETZALCOATL.
BUT DURING THE FAMINES, THE FLOODS... A NEW REGIME TOOK OVER THE EMPIRE.
THEY BURNED THE RECORDS, REWROTE THE STORIES, AND REPLACED THEM WITH LIES. QUETZALCOATL WAS CAST ASIDE, AND HUITZILOPOCHTLI BECAME THE GIVER OF LIFE.
NOW, THE TEMPLE OF HUITZILOPOCHTLI RUNS THE EMPIRE.
AN EMPIRE DEDICATED TO WAR AND BLOOD.
HUITZILOPOCHTLI ONLY CARES ABOUT HUMANS AS VESSELS OF BLOOD.
QUETZALCOATL IS THE CREATOR, THE SAVIOR. THE GIVER OF LIFE.
AND WE'RE GOING TO PROVE IT.
XILO...I CAN'T.
I HAVE TO FIND A WAY BACK HOME. I DON'T BELONG HERE.
I BELONG FIVE HUNDRED YEARS FROM NOW.
YOU KNOW I CAN'T UNDERSTAND THAT TONGUE.
YOU BELONG HERE. THE GODS BROUGHT YOU HERE.
I WENT TO THE BLACK MOUNTAIN SEARCHING FOR A SIGN, AND I FOUND YOU.
A PALE KID WITH AN EXTRAORDINARY TATTOO WHO CAN TRAVEL TO THE SPIRIT WORLD, FALLEN STRAIGHT FROM THE HEAVENS.
I FELL FROM A FAST FOOD PARKING LOT.
YOU THREATEN HUITZILOPOCHTLI'S SUPREMACY.
THAT'S WHY ITZCOATL HATES YOU, HECTOR.
HIS FATHER, HIS GRANDFATHER -- THEY REWROTE THE STORIES, THEY BURNED ALL THE RECORDS.
THEY USED HUITZILOPOCHTLI TO TAKE CONTROL. THEY CHANGED EVERYTHING.
YOU THREATEN TO UNDO EVERYTHING HIS FAMILY HAS BEEN BUILDING FOR GENERATIONS.

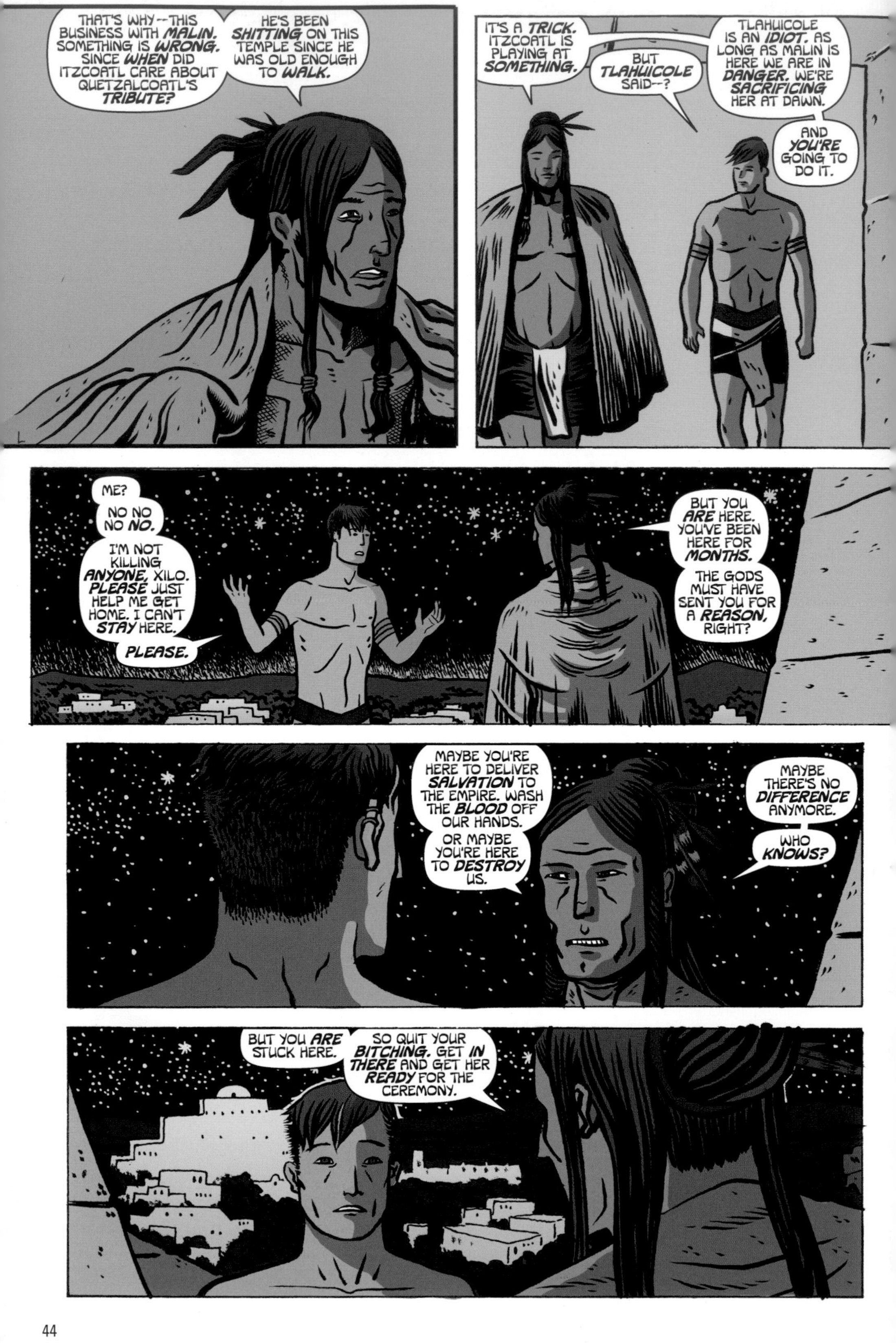
THAT'S WHY--THIS BUSINESS WITH MALIN. SOMETHING IS WRONG. SINCE WHEN DID ITZCOATL CARE ABOUT QUETZALCOATL'S TRIBUTE?
HE'S BEEN SHITTING ON THIS TEMPLE SINCE HE WAS OLD ENOUGH TO WALK.
IT'S A TRICK. ITZCOATL IS PLAYING AT SOMETHING.
BUT TLAHUICOLE SAID--?
TLAHUICOLE IS AN IDIOT. AS LONG AS MALIN IS HERE WE ARE IN DANGER. WE'RE SACRIFICING HER AT DAWN.
AND YOU'RE GOING TO DO IT.
ME?
NO NO NO NO.
I'M NOT KILLING ANYONE, XILO. PLEASE JUST HELP ME GET HOME. I CAN'T STAY HERE.
PLEASE.
BUT YOU ARE HERE. YOU'VE BEEN HERE FOR MONTHS.
THE GODS MUST HAVE SENT YOU FOR A REASON, RIGHT?
MAYBE YOU'RE HERE TO DELIVER SALVATION TO THE EMPIRE. WASH THE BLOOD OFF OUR HANDS.
OR MAYBE YOU'RE HERE TO DESTROY US.
MAYBE THERE'S NO DIFFERENCE ANYMORE.
WHO KNOWS?
BUT YOU ARE STUCK HERE.
SO QUIT YOUR BITCHING. GET IN THERE AND GET HER READY FOR THE CEREMONY.

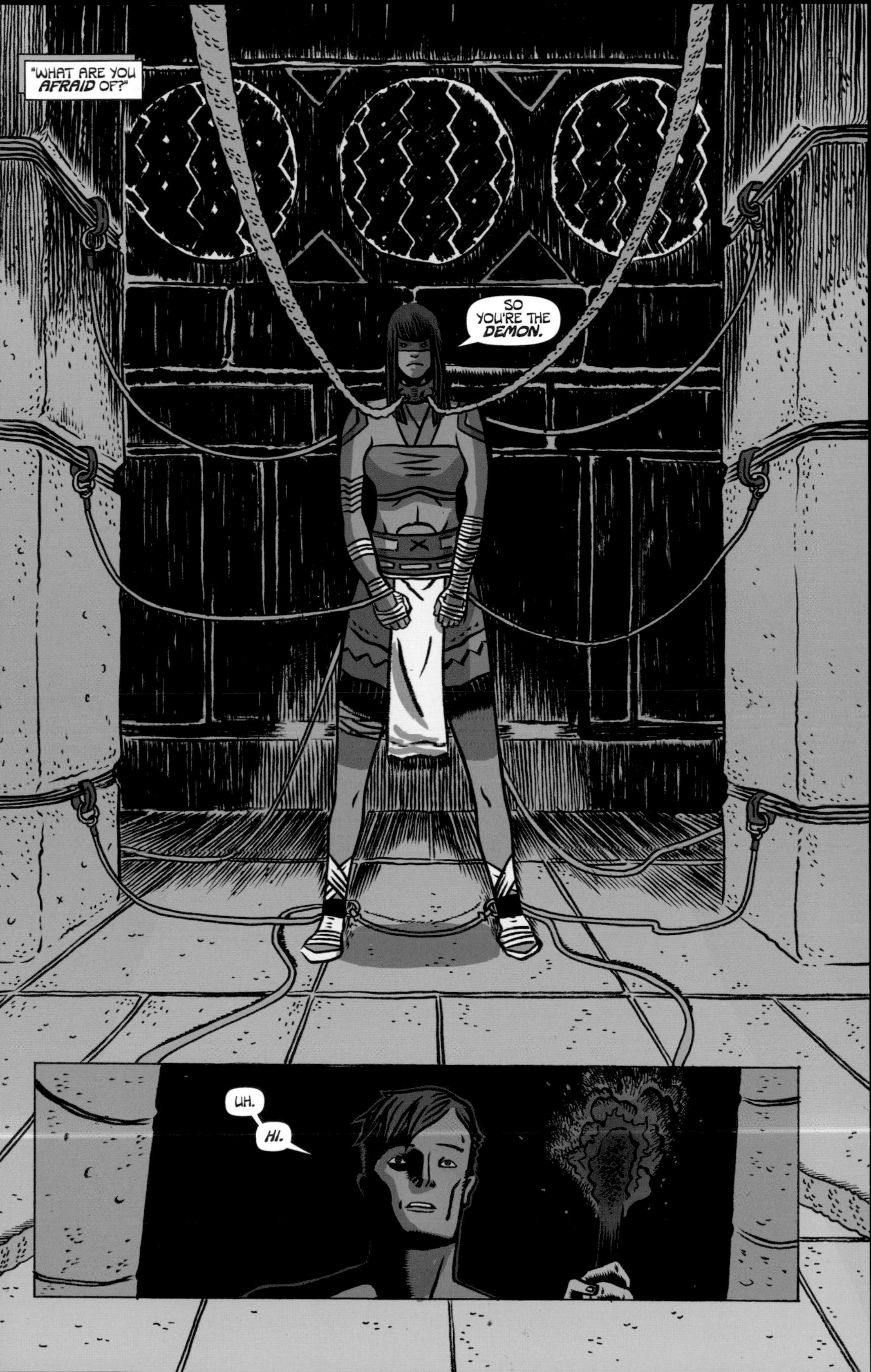
"WHAT ARE YOU AFRAID OF?"
SO YOU'RE THE DEMON.
UH.
HI.

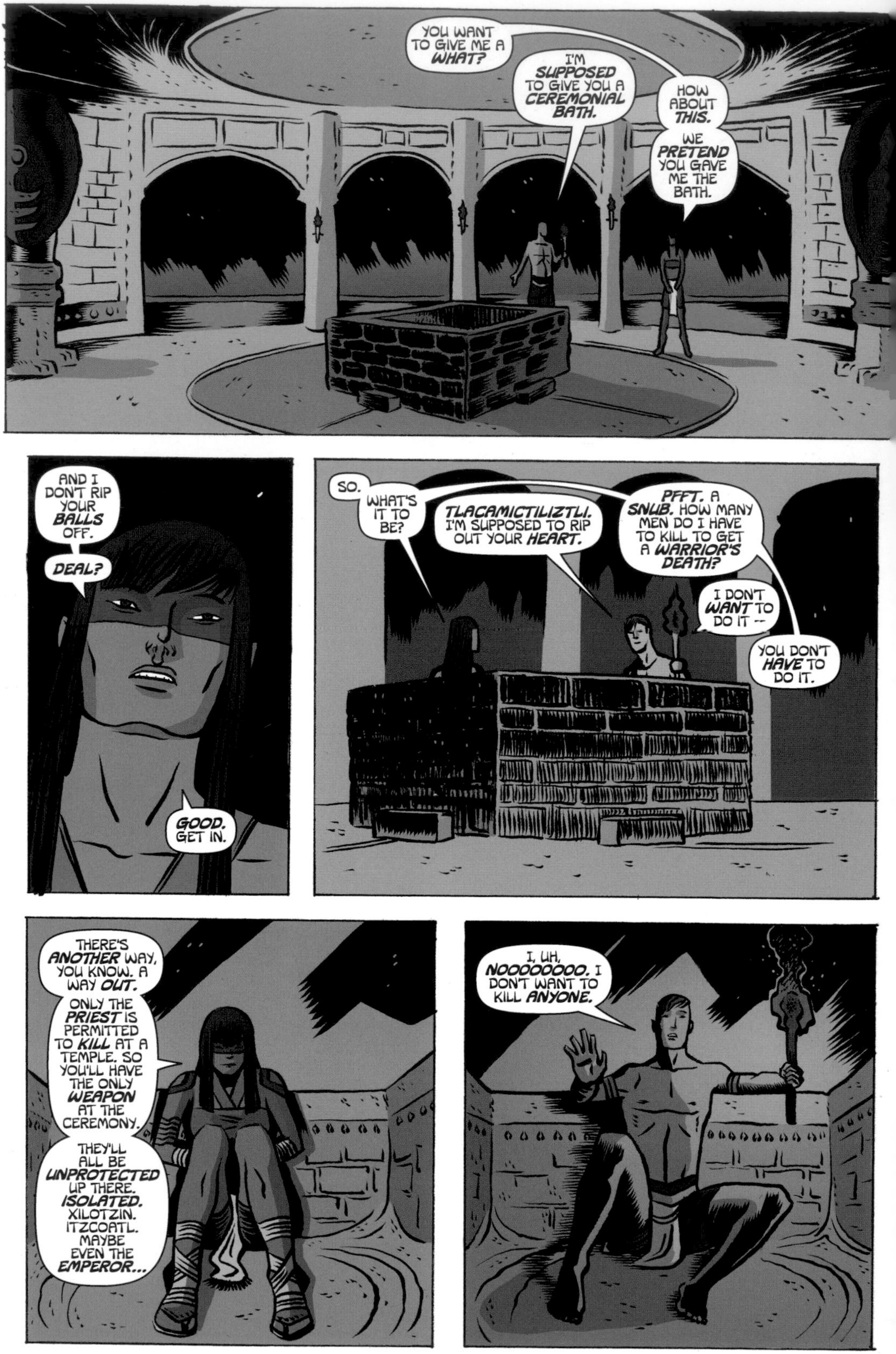
YOU WANT TO GIVE ME A WHAT?
I'M SUPPOSED TO GIVE YOU A CEREMONIAL BATH.
HOW ABOUT THIS.
WE PRETEND YOU GAVE ME THE BATH.
AND I DON'T RIP YOUR BALLS OFF.
DEAL?
GOOD. GET IN.
SO.
WHAT'S IT TO BE?
TLACAMICTILIZTLI. I'M SUPPOSED TO RIP OUT YOUR HEART.
PFFT. A SNUB. HOW MANY MEN DO I HAVE TO KILL TO GET A WARRIOR'S DEATH?
I DON'T WANT TO DO IT --
YOU DON'T HAVE TO DO IT.
THERE'S ANOTHER WAY, YOU KNOW. A WAY OUT.
ONLY THE PRIEST IS PERMITTED TO KILL AT A TEMPLE. SO YOU'LL HAVE THE ONLY WEAPON AT THE CEREMONY.
THEY'LL ALL BE UNPROTECTED UP THERE. ISOLATED. XILOTZIN. ITZCOATL. MAYBE EVEN THE EMPEROR...
I, UH, NOOOOOOOO. I DON'T WANT TO KILL ANYONE.

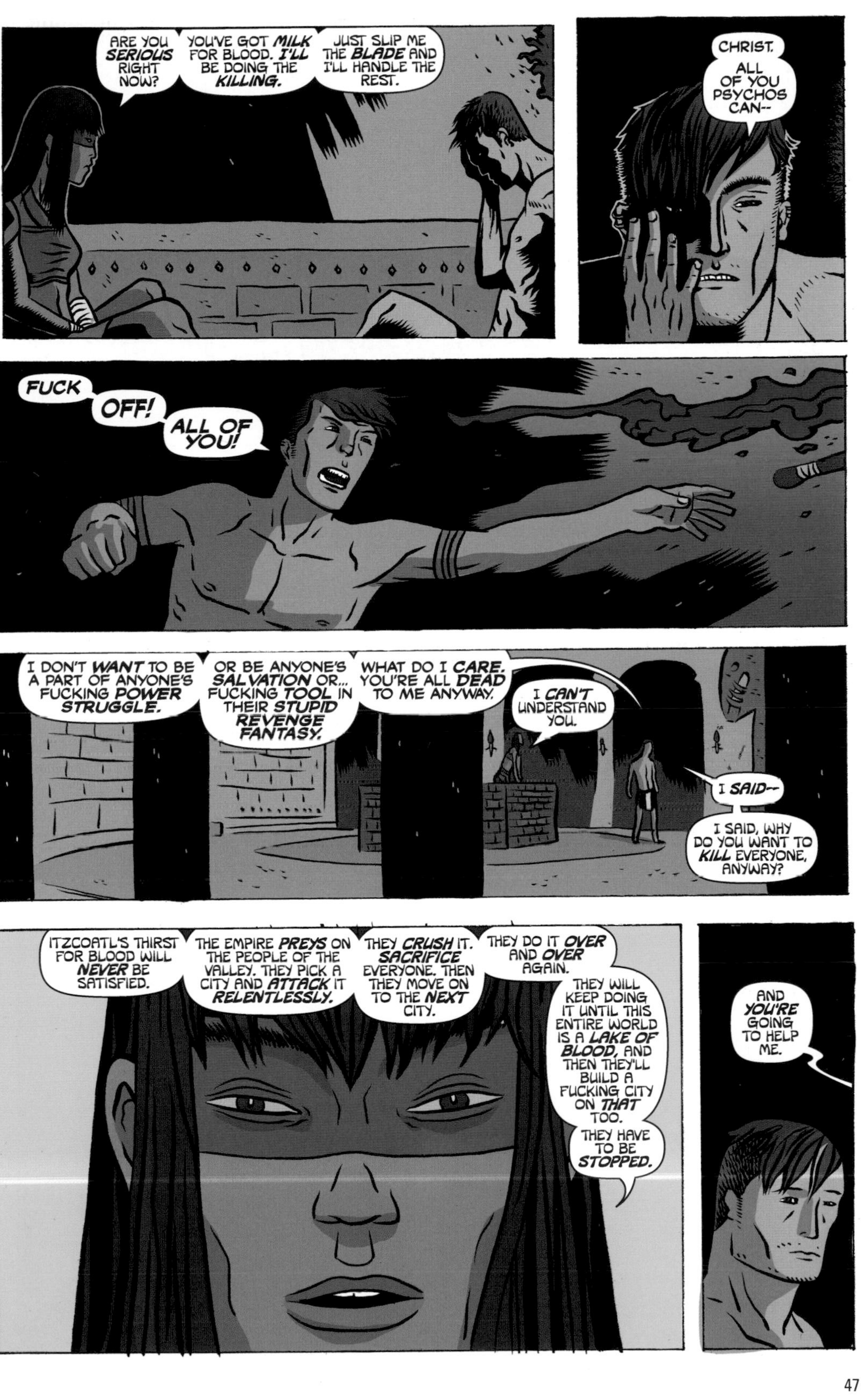
ARE YOU SERIOUS RIGHT NOW?
YOU'VE GOT MILK FOR BLOOD. I'LL BE DOING THE KILLING.
JUST SLIP ME THE BLADE AND I'LL HANDLE THE REST.
CHRIST. ALL OF YOU PSYCHOS CAN--
FUCK
OFF!
ALL OF YOU!
I DON'T WANT TO BE A PART OF ANYONE'S FUCKING POWER STRUGGLE.
OR BE ANYONE'S SALVATION OR... FUCKING TOOL IN THEIR STUPID REVENGE FANTASY.
WHAT DO I CARE. YOU'RE ALL DEAD TO ME ANYWAY.
I CAN'T UNDERSTAND YOU.
I SAID--
I SAID, WHY DO YOU WANT TO KILL EVERYONE, ANYWAY?
ITZCOATL'S THIRST FOR BLOOD WILL NEVER BE SATISFIED.
THE EMPIRE PREYS ON THE PEOPLE OF THE VALLEY. THEY PICK A CITY AND ATTACK IT RELENTLESSLY.
THEY CRUSH IT. SACRIFICE EVERYONE. THEN THEY MOVE ON TO THE NEXT CITY.
THEY DO IT OVER AND OVER AGAIN.
THEY WILL KEEP DOING IT UNTIL THIS ENTIRE WORLD IS A LAKE OF BLOOD, AND THEN THEY'LL BUILD A FUCKING CITY ON THAT TOO.
THEY HAVE TO BE STOPPED.
AND YOU'RE GOING TO HELP ME.

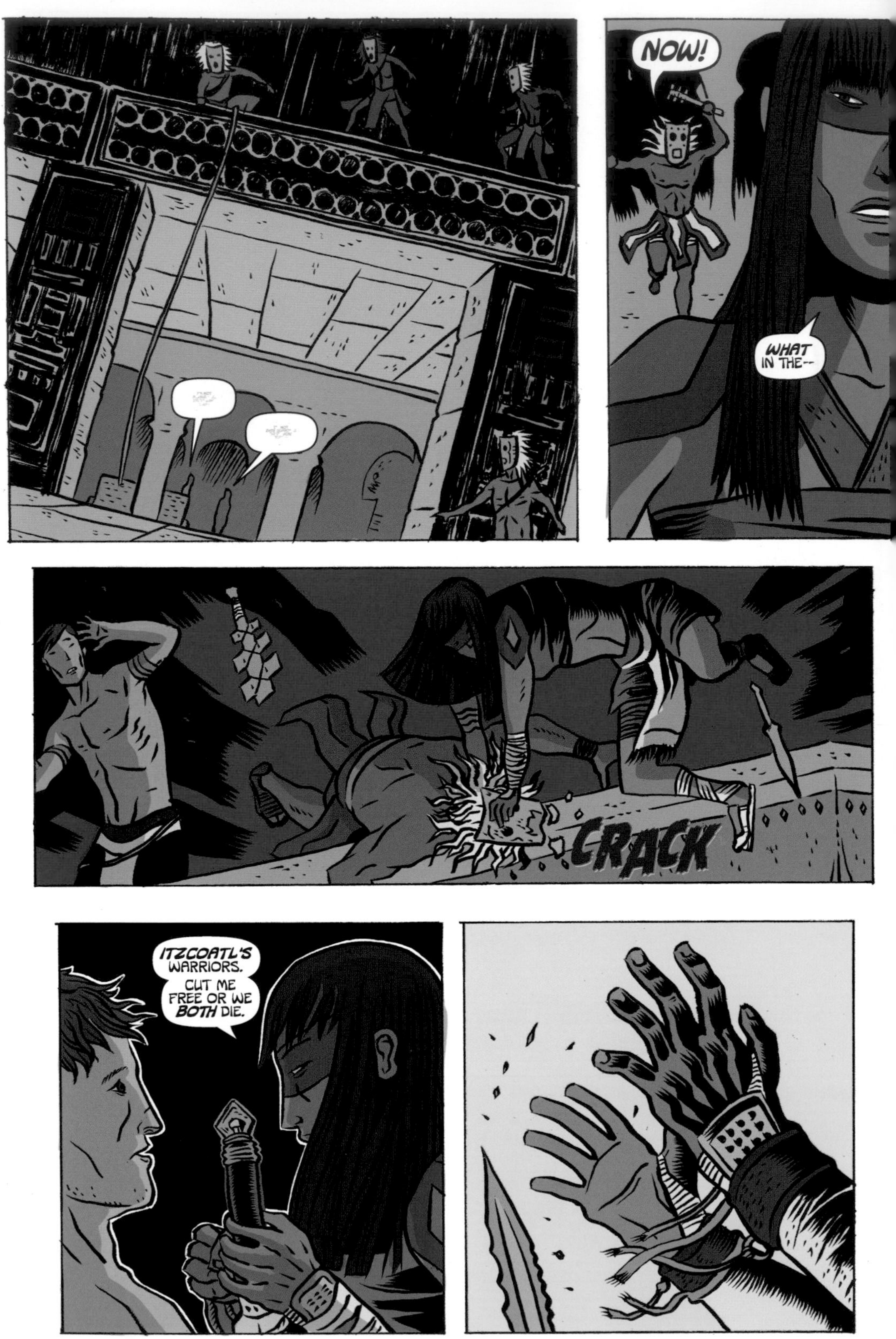
NOW!
WHAT IN THE--
CRACK
ITZCOATL'S WARRIORS. CUT ME FREE OR WE BOTH DIE.

HEY, SHITBLOOD!

RAAA--

UH

STOP!

THUD

AUGH!

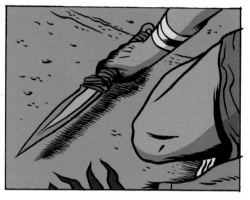

WAIT, I --

UT

TOTOTL, LOOK!

IT'S HER! THE RABBIT REBEL!

49

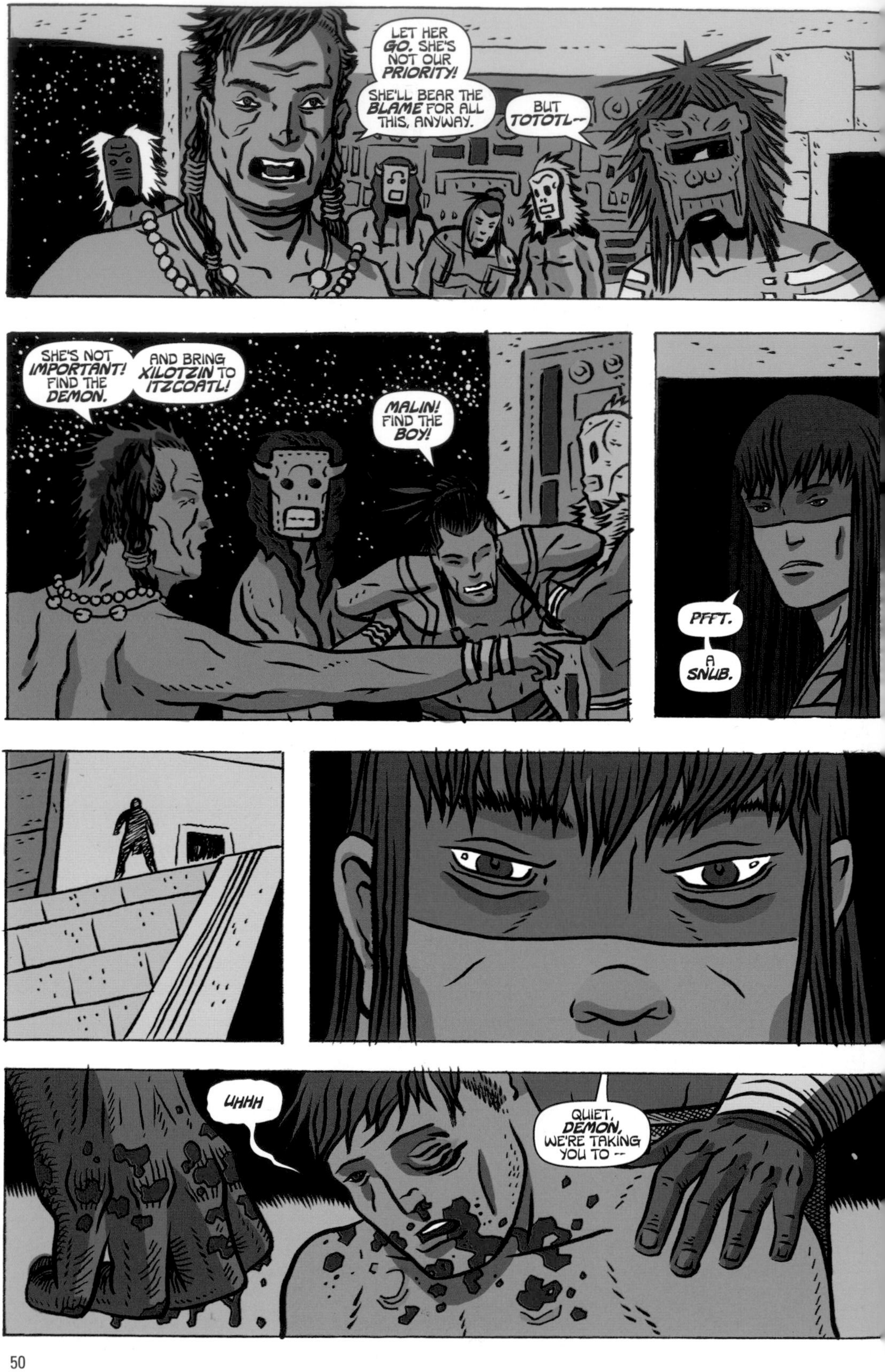

LET HER GO. SHE'S NOT OUR PRIORITY!
SHE'LL BEAR THE BLAME FOR ALL THIS, ANYWAY.
BUT TOTOTL--
SHE'S NOT IMPORTANT! FIND THE DEMON.
AND BRING XILOTZIN TO ITZCOATL!
MALIN! FIND THE BOY!
PFFT.
A SNUB.
UHHH
QUIET, DEMON, WE'RE TAKING YOU TO --

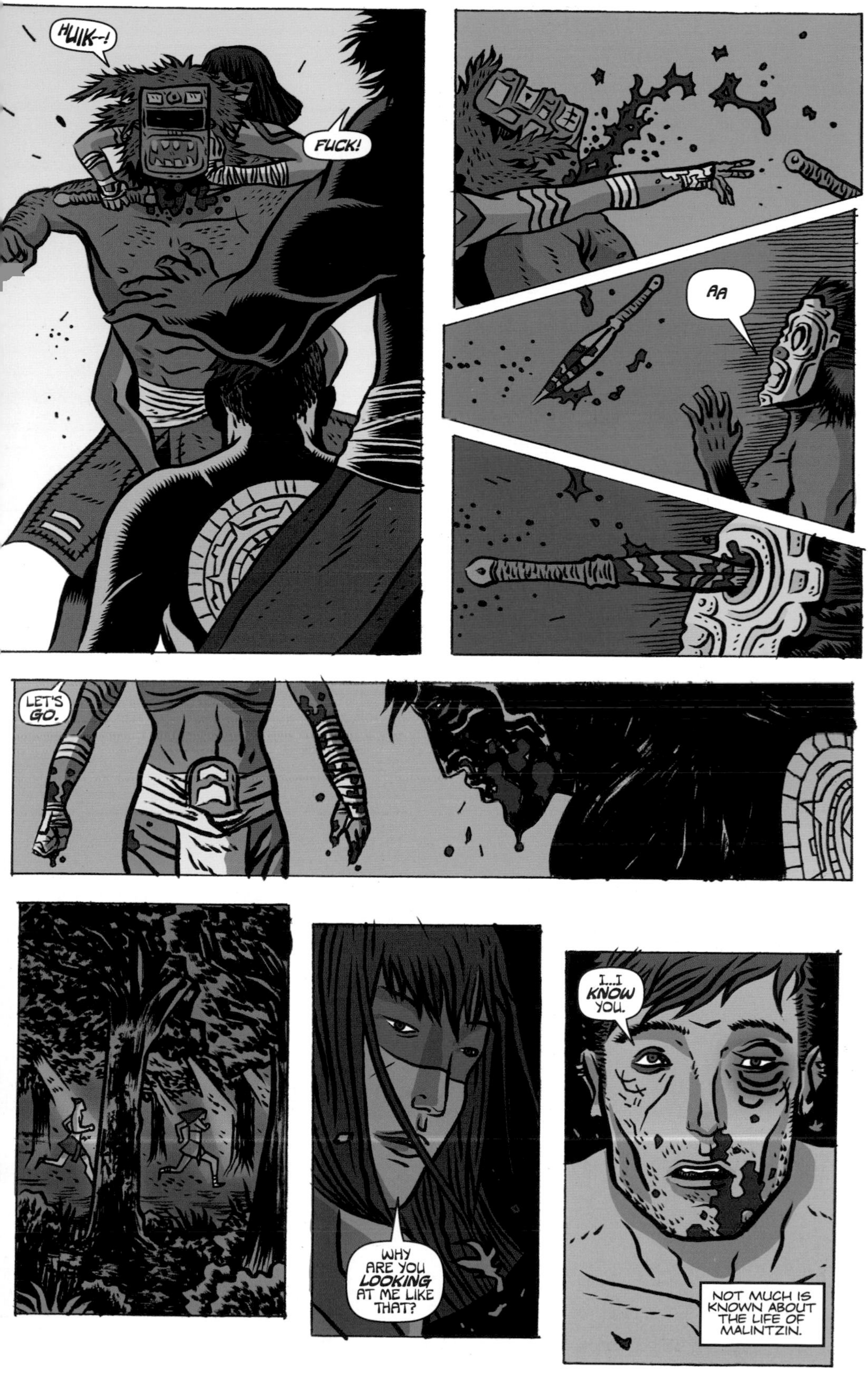
HUIK--!
FUCK!
AA
LET'S GO.
WHY ARE YOU LOOKING AT ME LIKE THAT?
I...I KNOW YOU.
NOT MUCH IS KNOWN ABOUT THE LIFE OF MALINTZIN.

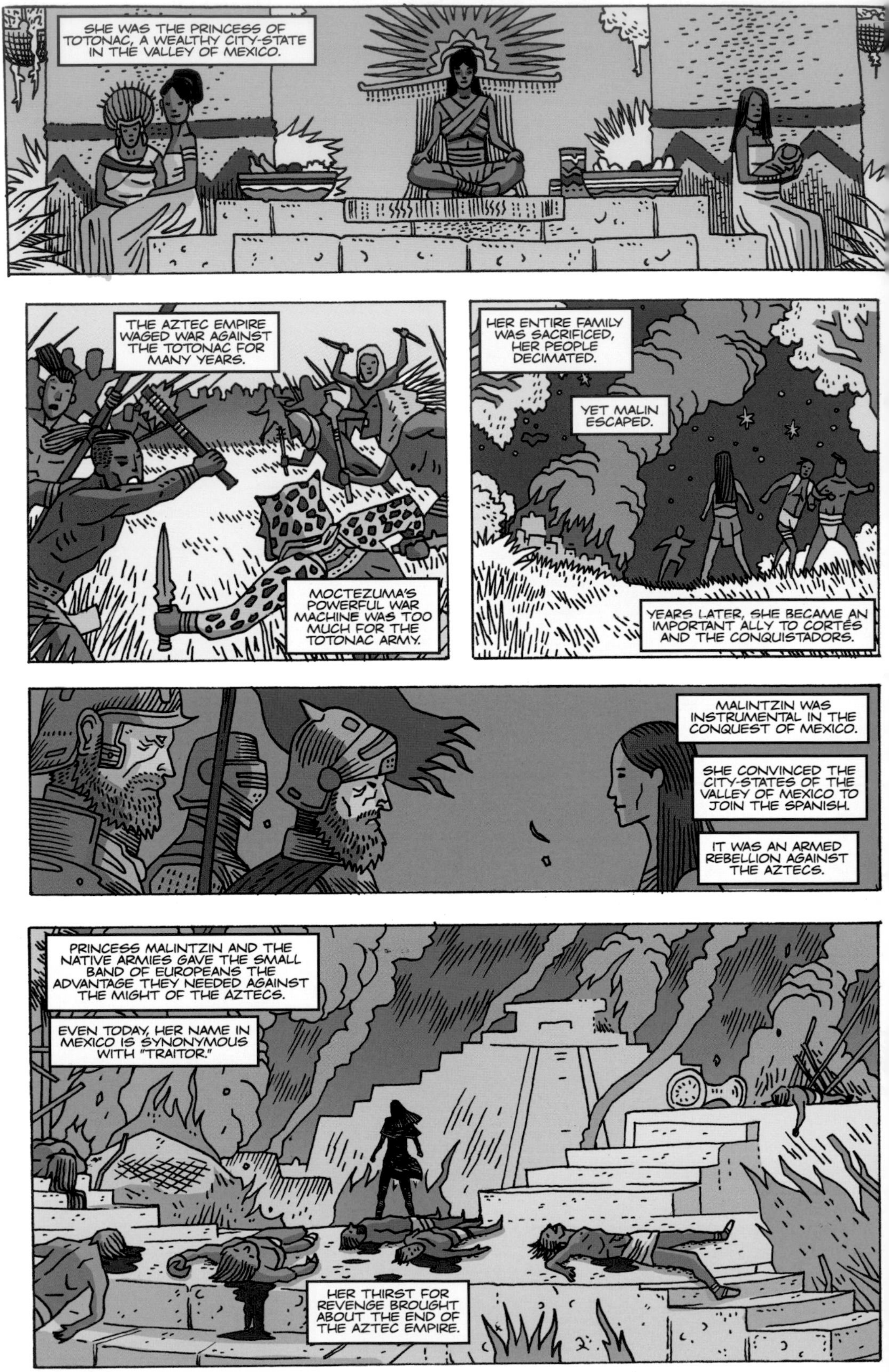
SHE WAS THE PRINCESS OF TOTONAC, A WEALTHY CITY-STATE IN THE VALLEY OF MEXICO.
THE AZTEC EMPIRE WAGED WAR AGAINST THE TOTONAC FOR MANY YEARS.
MOCTEZUMA'S POWERFUL WAR MACHINE WAS TOO MUCH FOR THE TOTONAC ARMY.
HER ENTIRE FAMILY WAS SACRIFICED, HER PEOPLE DECIMATED.
YET MALIN ESCAPED.
YEARS LATER, SHE BECAME AN IMPORTANT ALLY TO CORTÉS AND THE CONQUISTADORS.
MALINTZIN WAS INSTRUMENTAL IN THE CONQUEST OF MEXICO.
SHE CONVINCED THE CITY-STATES OF THE VALLEY OF MEXICO TO JOIN THE SPANISH.
IT WAS AN ARMED REBELLION AGAINST THE AZTECS.
PRINCESS MALINTZIN AND THE NATIVE ARMIES GAVE THE SMALL BAND OF EUROPEANS THE ADVANTAGE THEY NEEDED AGAINST THE MIGHT OF THE AZTECS.
EVEN TODAY, HER NAME IN MEXICO IS SYNONYMOUS WITH "TRAITOR."
HER THIRST FOR REVENGE BROUGHT ABOUT THE END OF THE AZTEC EMPIRE.

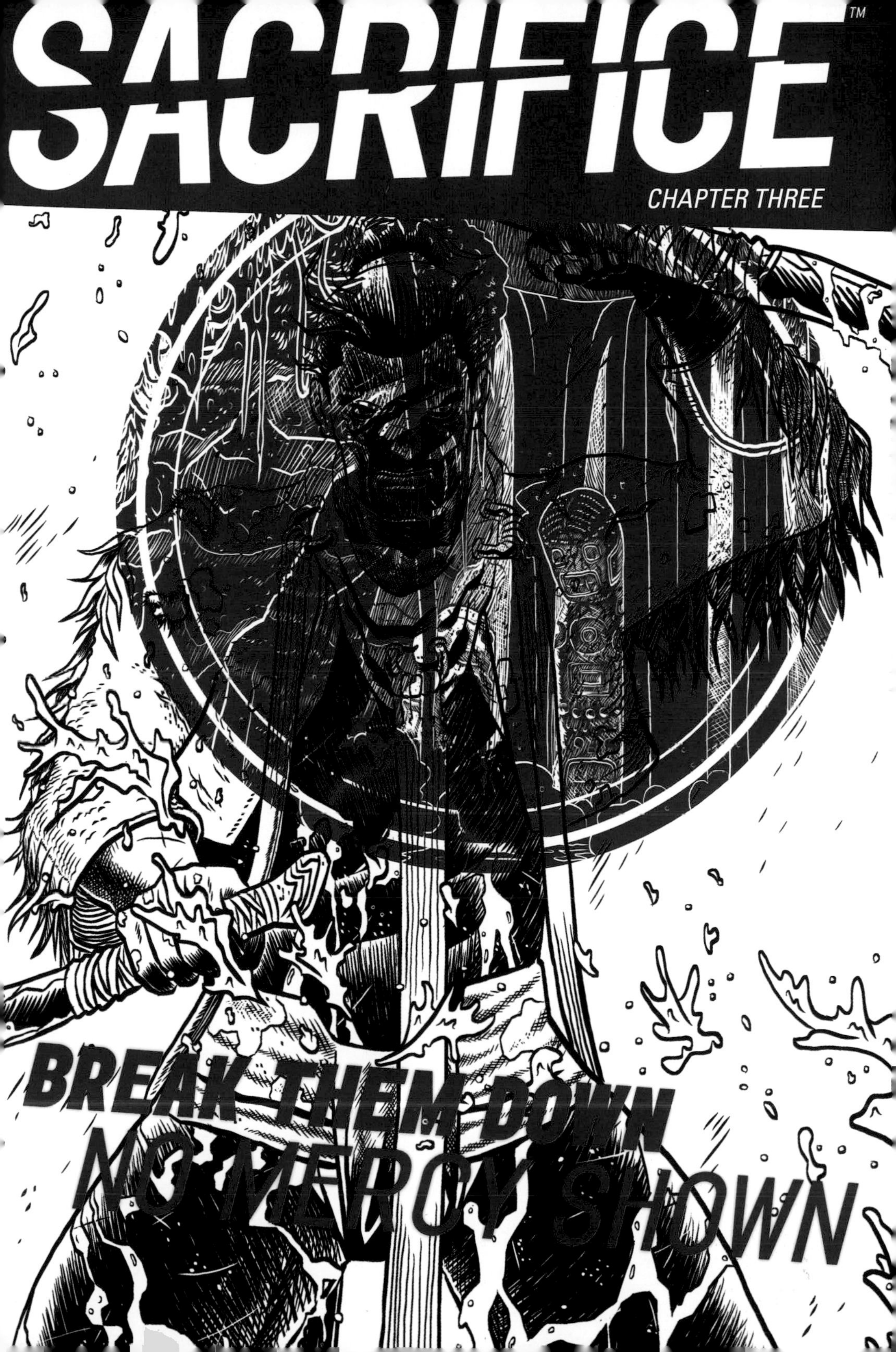
SACRIFICE™
CHAPTER THREE
BREAK THEM DOWN
NO MERCY SHOWN

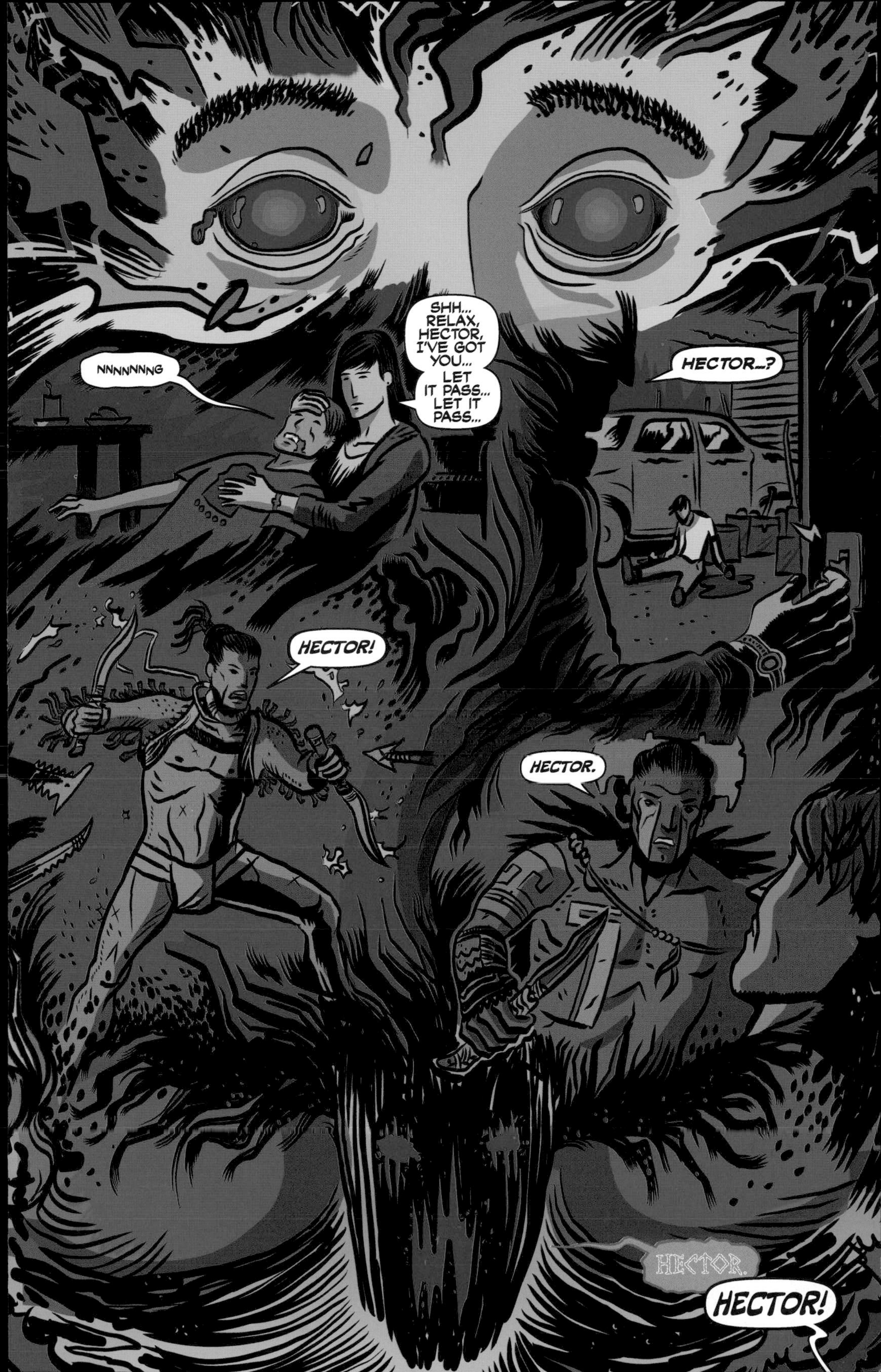
NNNNNNNG
SHH... RELAX, HECTOR, I'VE GOT YOU... LET IT PASS... LET IT PASS...
HECTOR...?
HECTOR!
HECTOR.
HECTOR.
HECTOR!

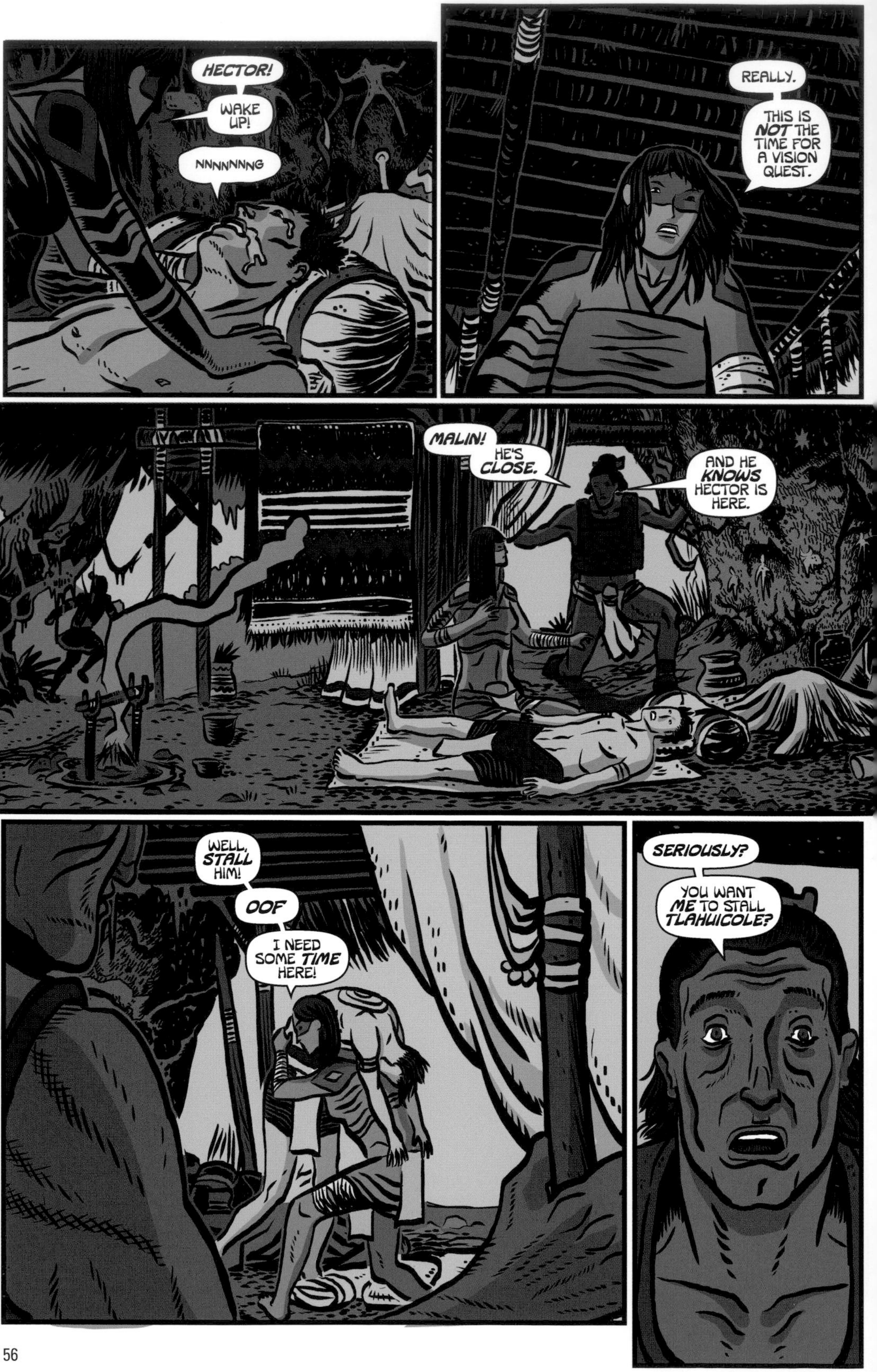

HECTOR!
WAKE UP!
NNNNNNNG
REALLY.
THIS IS NOT THE TIME FOR A VISION QUEST.
MALIN!
HE'S CLOSE.
AND HE KNOWS HECTOR IS HERE.
WELL, STALL HIM!
OOF
I NEED SOME TIME HERE!
SERIOUSLY?
YOU WANT ME TO STALL TLAHUICOLE?

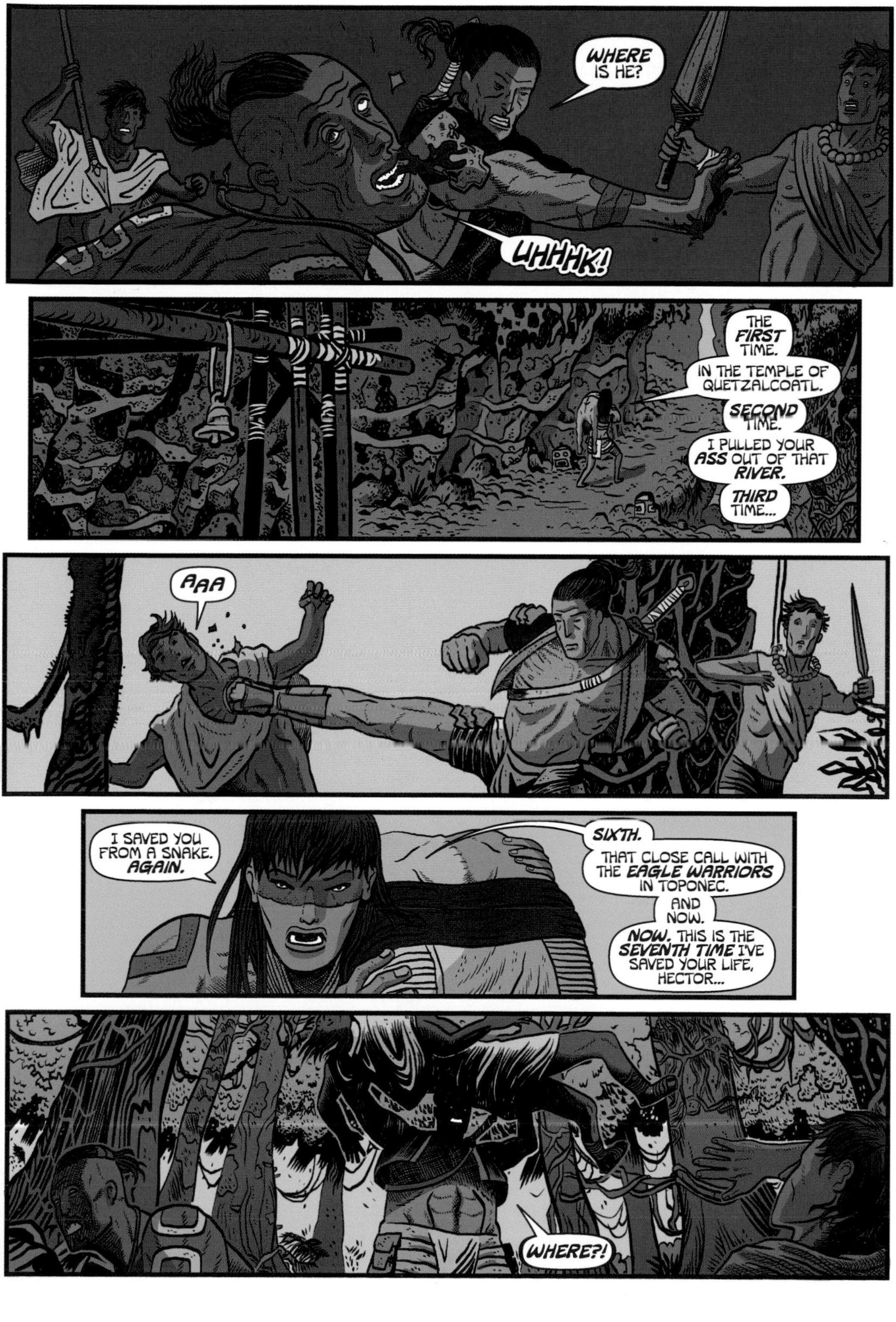

WHERE IS HE?
UHHHK!
THE FIRST TIME.
IN THE TEMPLE OF QUETZALCOATL.
SECOND TIME.
I PULLED YOUR ASS OUT OF THAT RIVER.
THIRD TIME...
AAA
I SAVED YOU FROM A SNAKE. AGAIN.
SIXTH.
THAT CLOSE CALL WITH THE EAGLE WARRIORS IN TOPONEC.
AND NOW.
NOW. THIS IS THE SEVENTH TIME I'VE SAVED YOUR LIFE, HECTOR...
WHERE?!

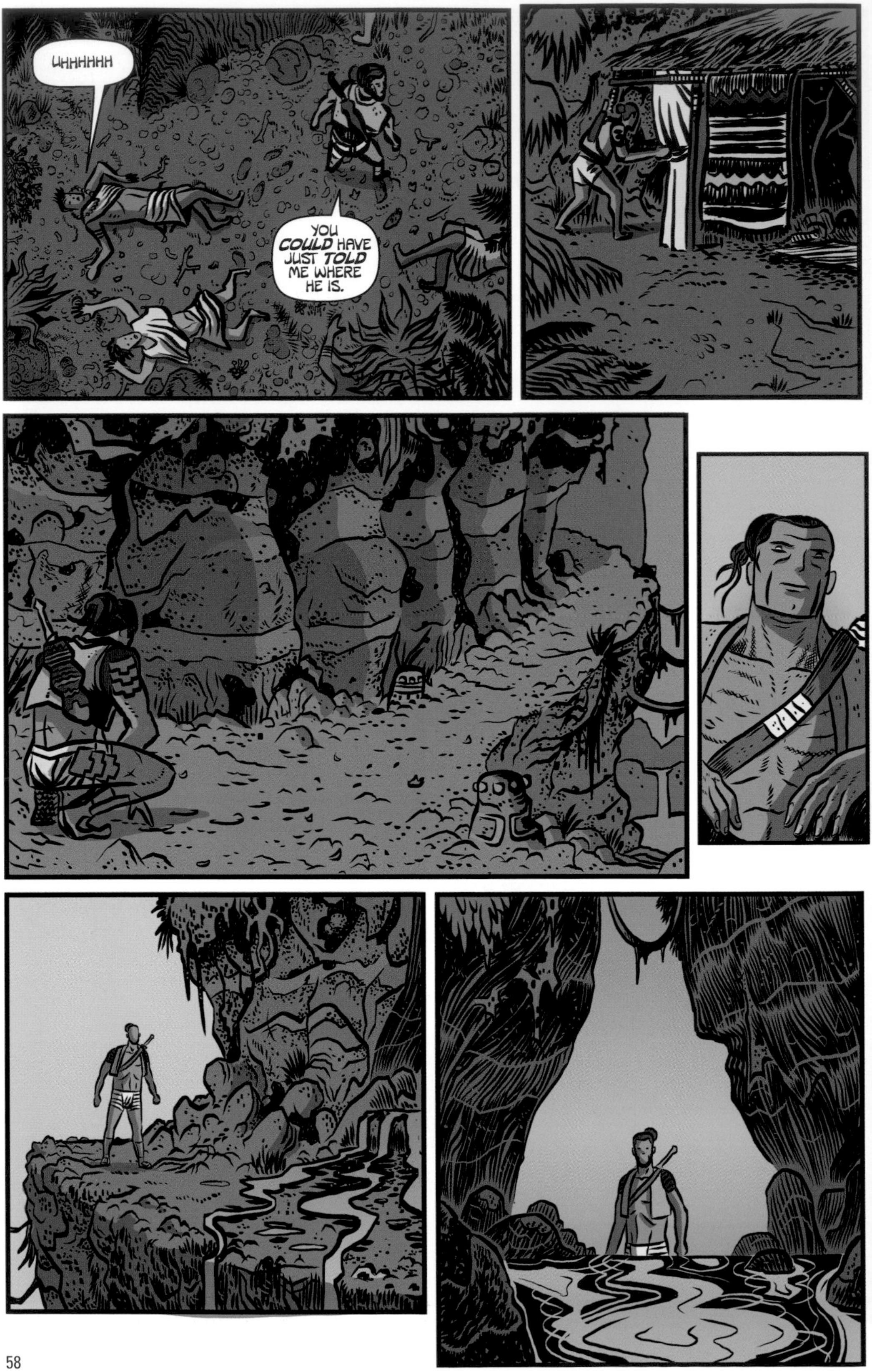
UHHHHHH
YOU COULD HAVE JUST TOLD ME WHERE HE IS.

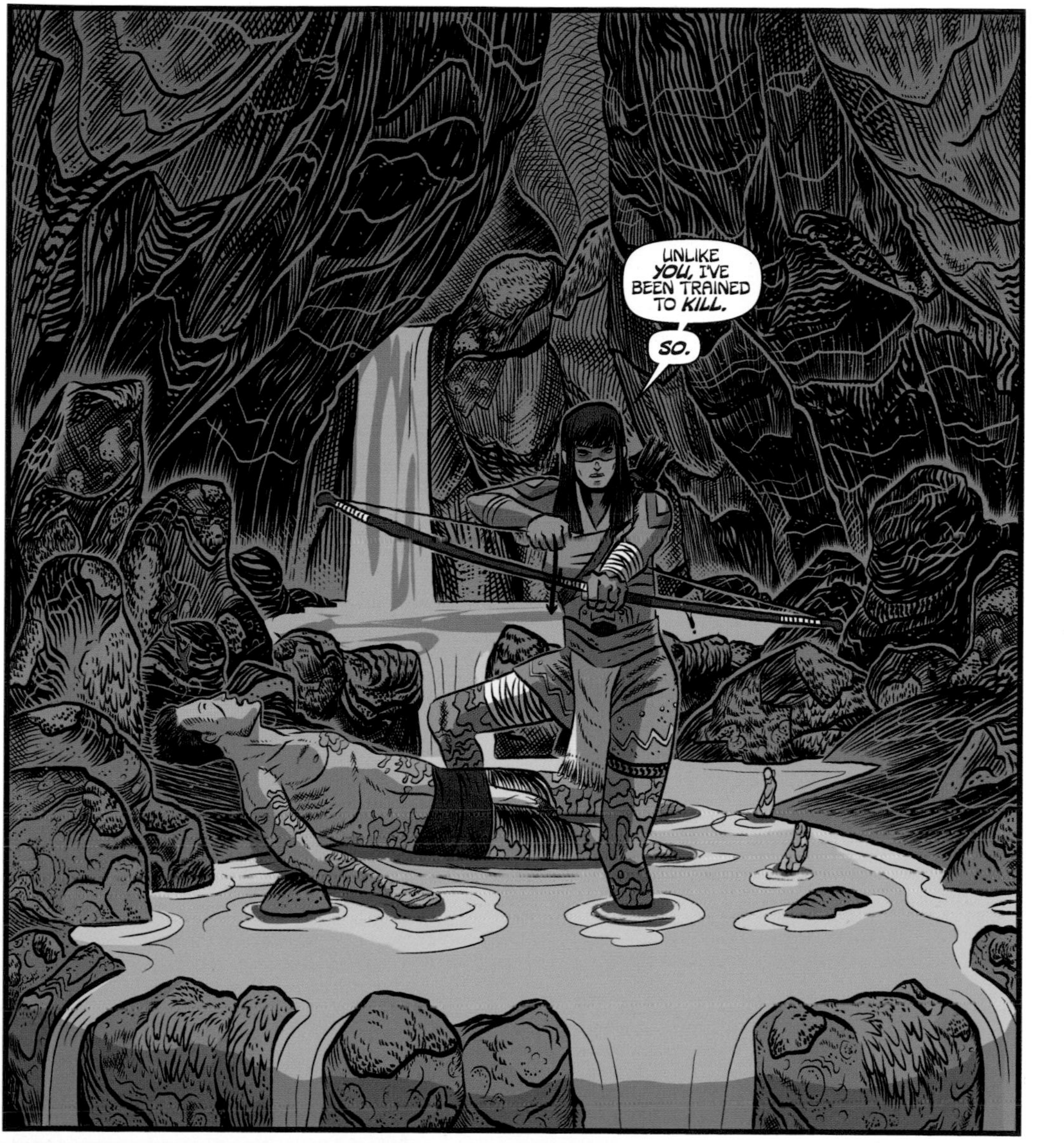
UNLIKE YOU, I'VE BEEN TRAINED TO KILL.
SO.

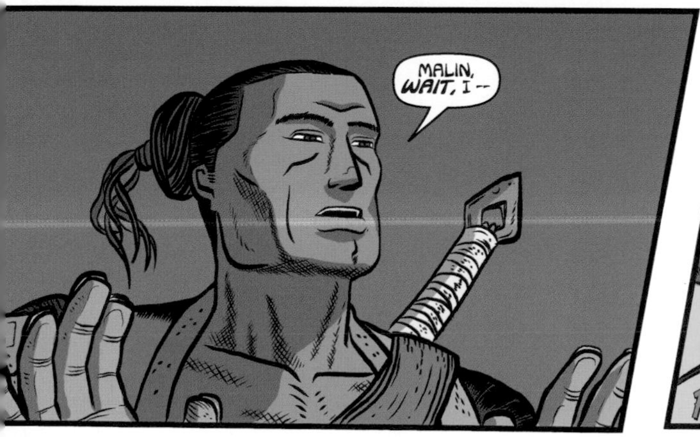
MALIN, WAIT, I --

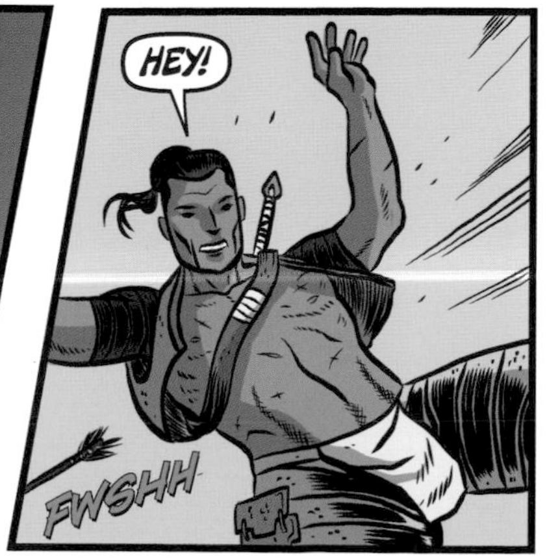
HEY!
FWSHH

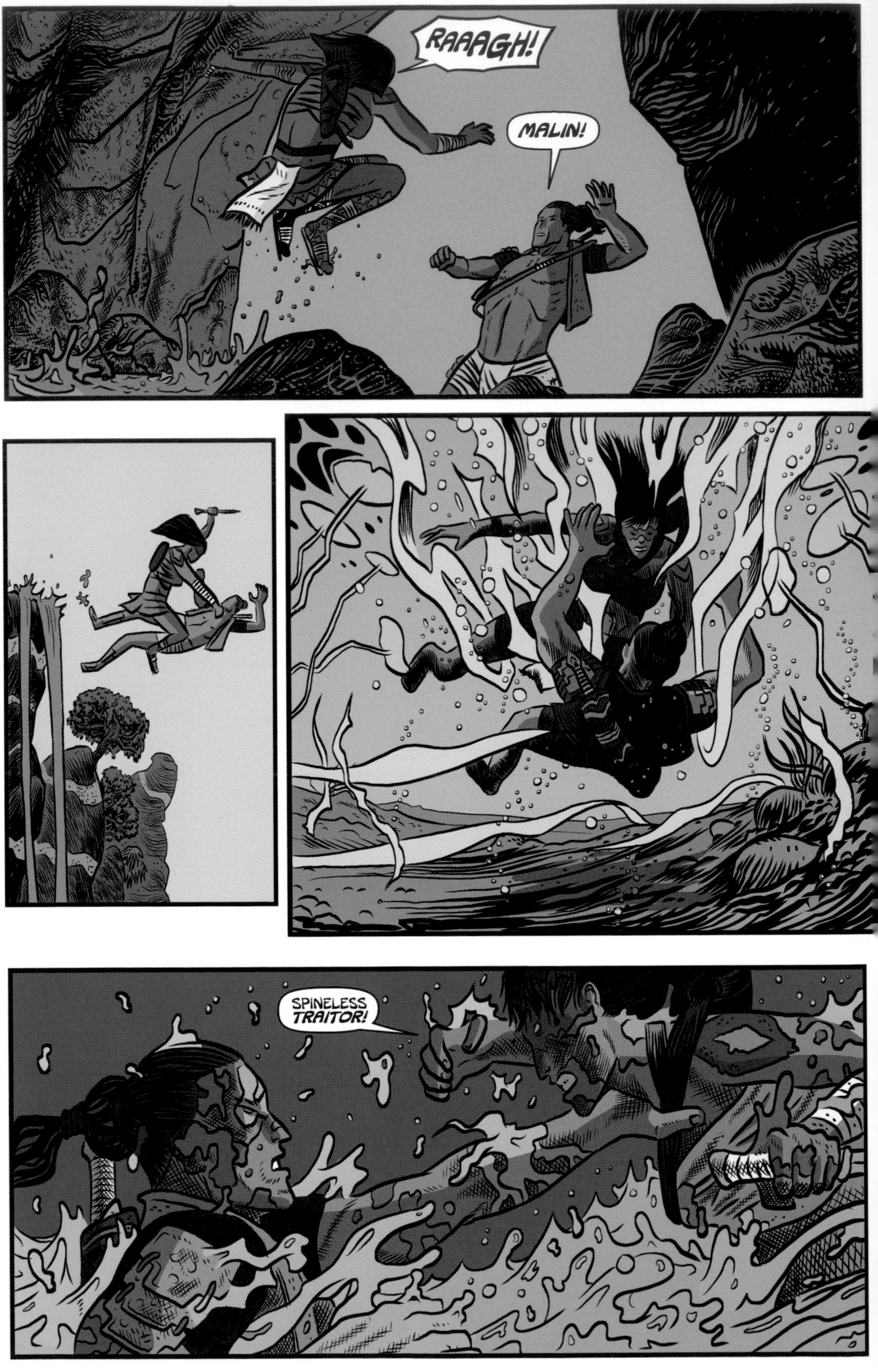
RAAAGH!
MALIN!
SPINELESS TRAITOR!

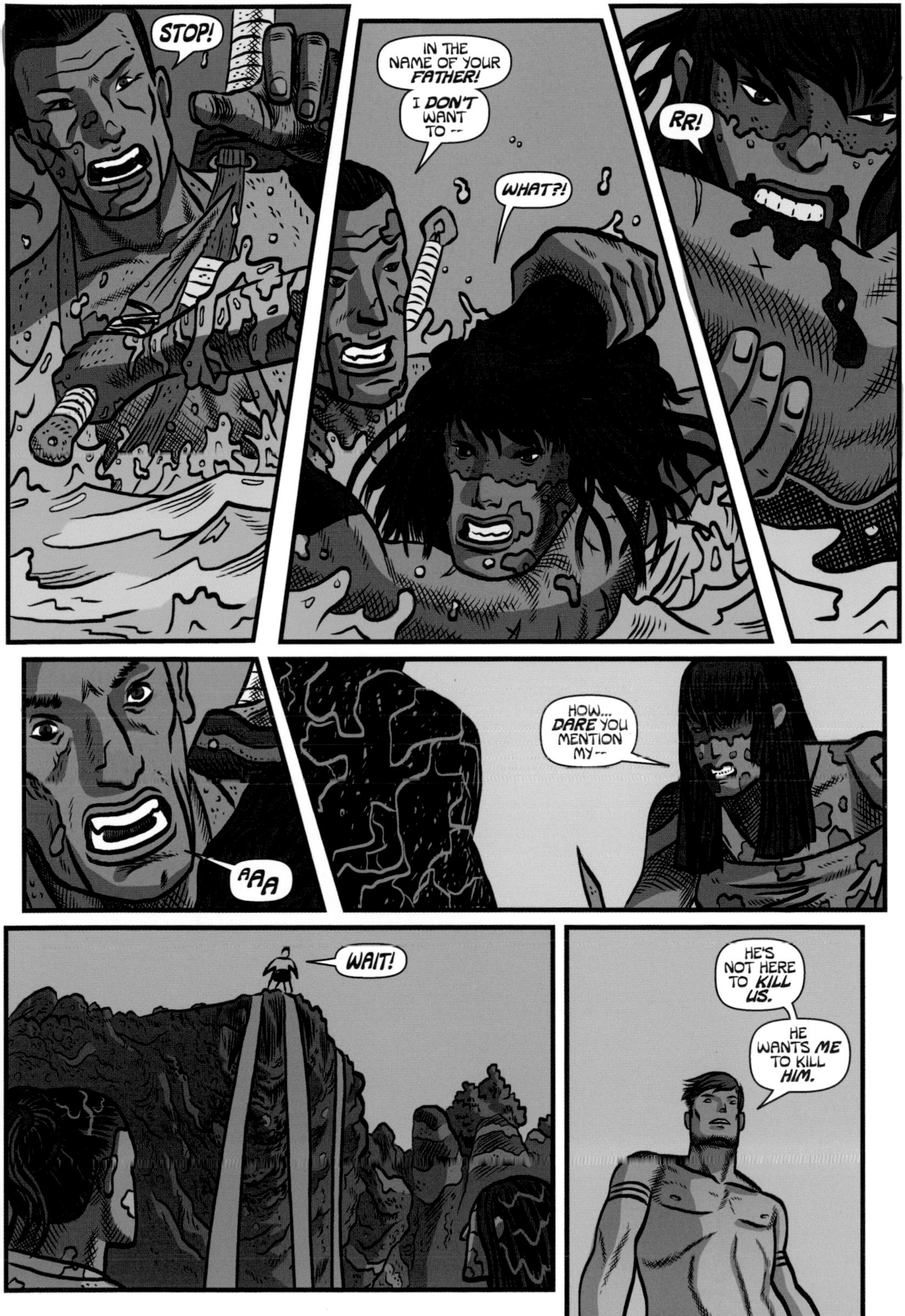
STOP!
IN THE NAME OF YOUR FATHER!
I DON'T WANT TO --
WHAT?!
RR!
AAA
HOW... DARE YOU MENTION MY--
WAIT!
HE'S NOT HERE TO KILL US.
HE WANTS ME TO KILL HIM.

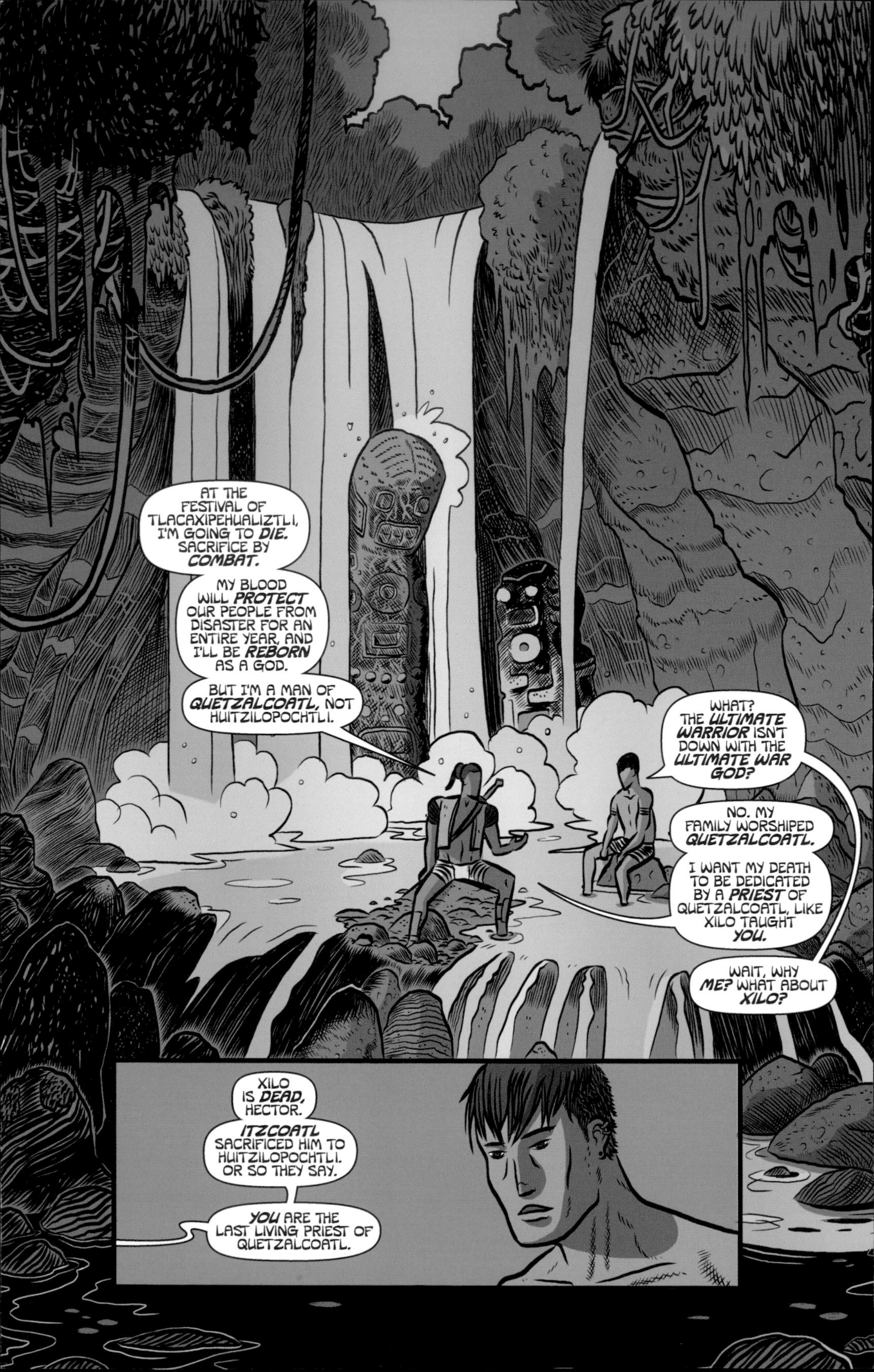
AT THE FESTIVAL OF TLACAXIPEHUALIZTLI, I'M GOING TO DIE. SACRIFICE BY COMBAT.
MY BLOOD WILL PROTECT OUR PEOPLE FROM DISASTER FOR AN ENTIRE YEAR, AND I'LL BE REBORN AS A GOD.
BUT I'M A MAN OF QUETZALCOATL, NOT HUITZILOPOCHTLI.
WHAT? THE ULTIMATE WARRIOR ISN'T DOWN WITH THE ULTIMATE WAR GOD?
NO. MY FAMILY WORSHIPED QUETZALCOATL.
I WANT MY DEATH TO BE DEDICATED BY A PRIEST OF QUETZALCOATL, LIKE XILO TAUGHT YOU.
WAIT, WHY ME? WHAT ABOUT XILO?
XILO IS DEAD, HECTOR.
ITZCOATL SACRIFICED HIM TO HUITZILOPOCHTLI. OR SO THEY SAY.
YOU ARE THE LAST LIVING PRIEST OF QUETZALCOATL.

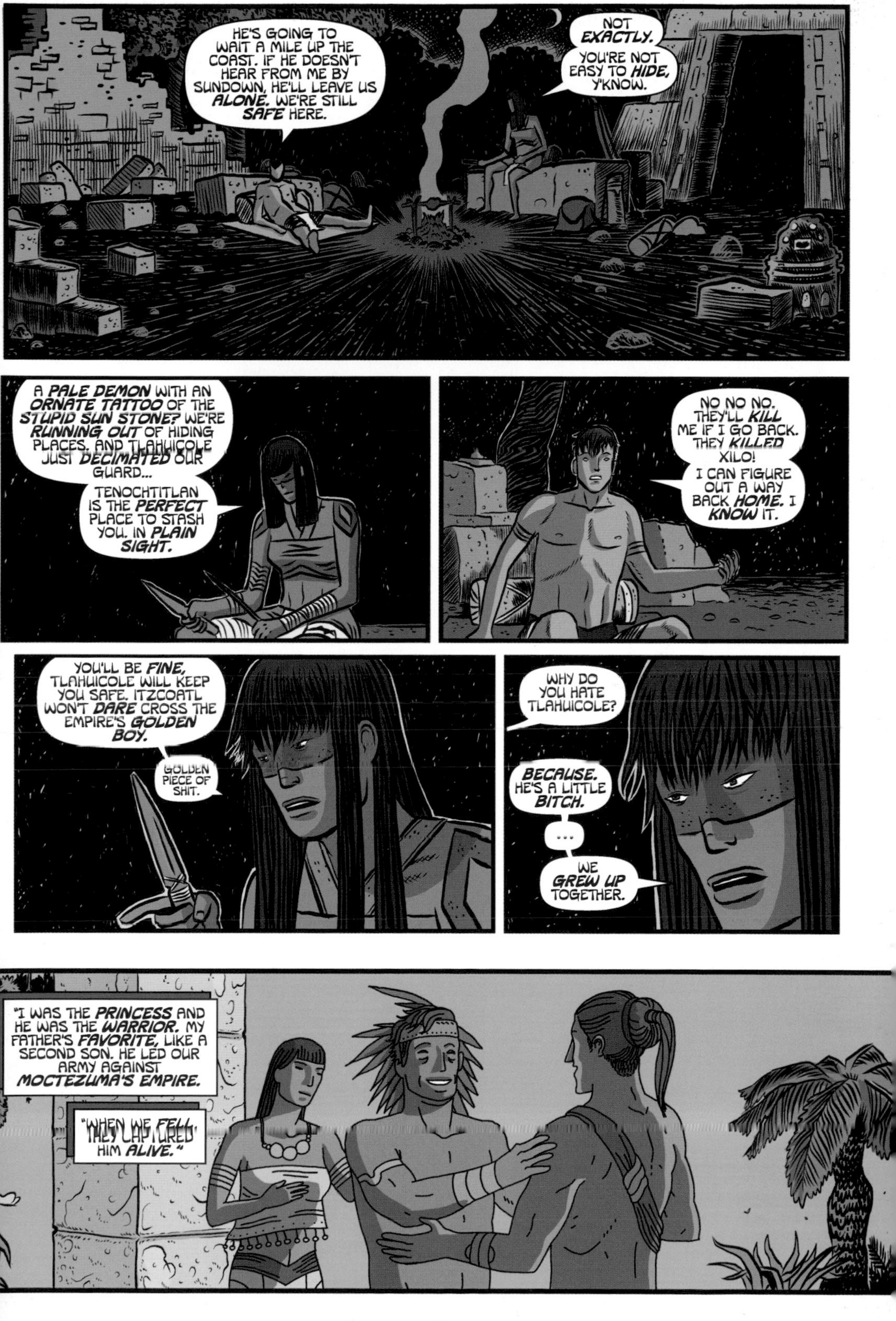

HE'S GOING TO WAIT A MILE UP THE COAST. IF HE DOESN'T HEAR FROM ME BY SUNDOWN, HE'LL LEAVE US ALONE. WE'RE STILL SAFE HERE.
NOT EXACTLY.
YOU'RE NOT EASY TO HIDE, Y'KNOW.
A PALE DEMON WITH AN ORNATE TATTOO OF THE STUPID SUN STONE? WE'RE RUNNING OUT OF HIDING PLACES. AND TLAHUICOLE JUST DECIMATED OUR GUARD...
TENOCHTITLAN IS THE PERFECT PLACE TO STASH YOU. IN PLAIN SIGHT.
NO NO NO. THEY'LL KILL ME IF I GO BACK. THEY KILLED XILO!
I CAN FIGURE OUT A WAY BACK HOME. I KNOW IT.
YOU'LL BE FINE, TLAHUICOLE WILL KEEP YOU SAFE. ITZCOATL WON'T DARE CROSS THE EMPIRE'S GOLDEN BOY.
GOLDEN PIECE OF SHIT.
WHY DO YOU HATE TLAHUICOLE?
BECAUSE. HE'S A LITTLE BITCH.
...
WE GREW UP TOGETHER.
"I WAS THE PRINCESS AND HE WAS THE WARRIOR. MY FATHER'S FAVORITE, LIKE A SECOND SON. HE LED OUR ARMY AGAINST MOCTEZUMA'S EMPIRE.
"WHEN WE FELL, THEY CAPTURED HIM ALIVE."

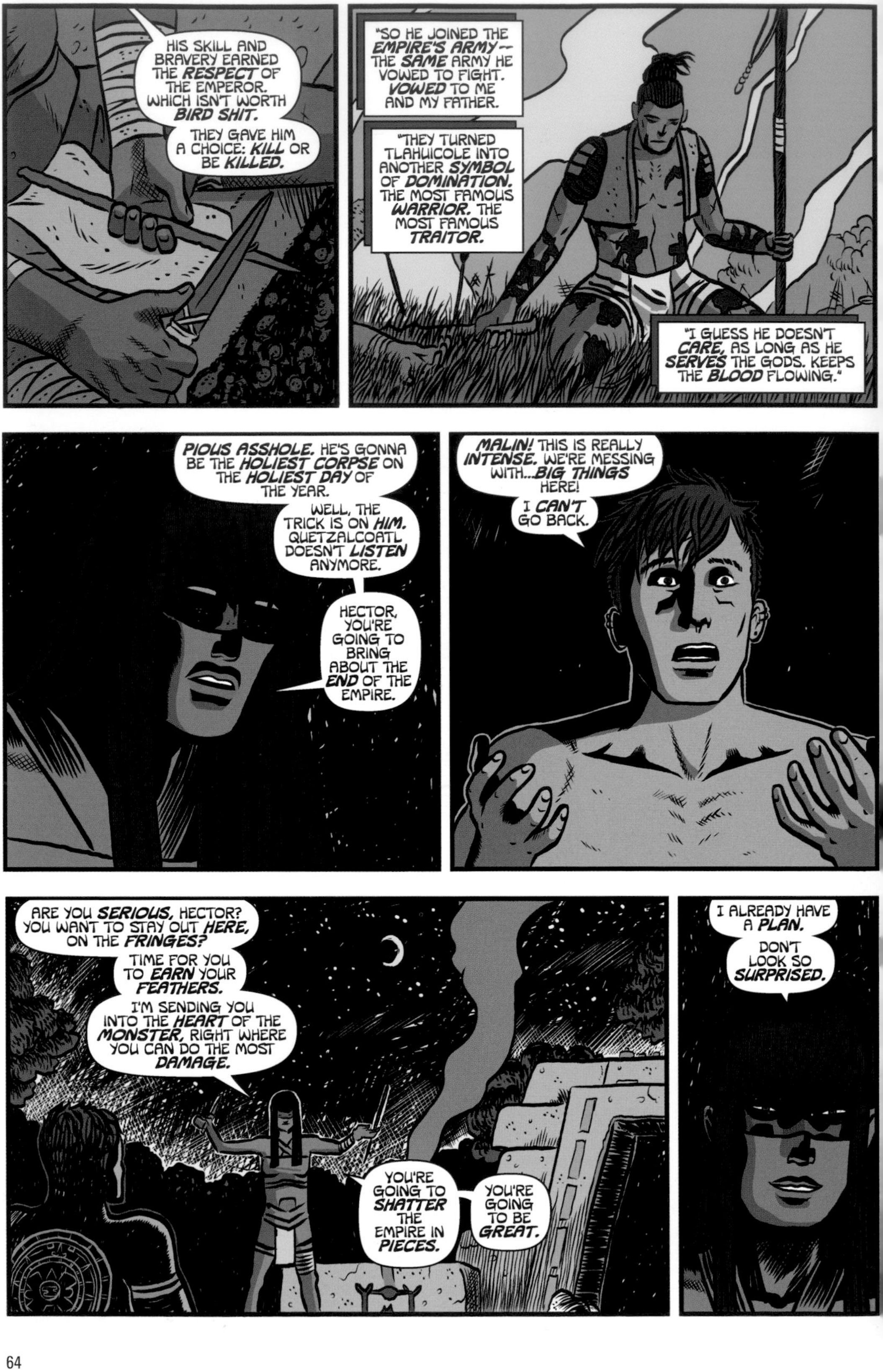
HIS SKILL AND BRAVERY EARNED THE RESPECT OF THE EMPEROR. WHICH ISN'T WORTH BIRD SHIT.
THEY GAVE HIM A CHOICE: KILL OR BE KILLED.
"SO HE JOINED THE EMPIRE'S ARMY-- THE SAME ARMY HE VOWED TO FIGHT. VOWED TO ME AND MY FATHER.
"THEY TURNED TLAHUICOLE INTO ANOTHER SYMBOL OF DOMINATION. THE MOST FAMOUS WARRIOR. THE MOST FAMOUS TRAITOR.
"I GUESS HE DOESN'T CARE, AS LONG AS HE SERVES THE GODS. KEEPS THE BLOOD FLOWING."
PIOUS ASSHOLE. HE'S GONNA BE THE HOLIEST CORPSE ON THE HOLIEST DAY OF THE YEAR.
WELL, THE TRICK IS ON HIM. QUETZALCOATL DOESN'T LISTEN ANYMORE.
HECTOR, YOU'RE GOING TO BRING ABOUT THE END OF THE EMPIRE.
MALIN! THIS IS REALLY INTENSE. WE'RE MESSING WITH...BIG THINGS HERE!
I CAN'T GO BACK.
ARE YOU SERIOUS, HECTOR? YOU WANT TO STAY OUT HERE, ON THE FRINGES?
TIME FOR YOU TO EARN YOUR FEATHERS.
I'M SENDING YOU INTO THE HEART OF THE MONSTER, RIGHT WHERE YOU CAN DO THE MOST DAMAGE.
YOU'RE GOING TO SHATTER THE EMPIRE IN PIECES.
YOU'RE GOING TO BE GREAT.
I ALREADY HAVE A PLAN.
DON'T LOOK SO SURPRISED.

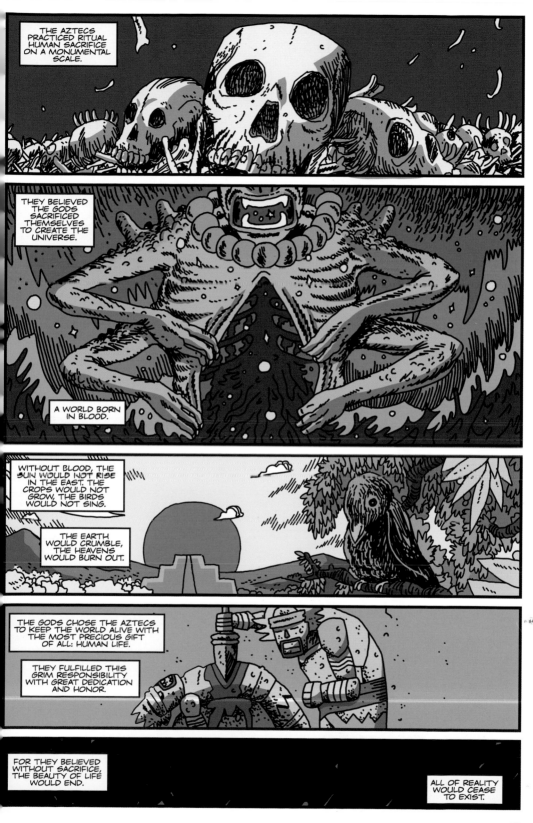

THE AZTECS PRACTICED RITUAL HUMAN SACRIFICE ON A MONUMENTAL SCALE.

THEY BELIEVED THE GODS SACRIFICED THEMSELVES TO CREATE THE UNIVERSE.

A WORLD BORN IN BLOOD.

WITHOUT BLOOD, THE SUN WOULD NOT RISE IN THE EAST. THE CROPS WOULD NOT GROW, THE BIRDS WOULD NOT SING.

THE EARTH WOULD CRUMBLE, THE HEAVENS WOULD BURN OUT.

THE GODS CHOSE THE AZTECS TO KEEP THE WORLD ALIVE WITH THE MOST PRECIOUS GIFT OF ALL: HUMAN LIFE.

THEY FULFILLED THIS GRIM RESPONSIBILITY WITH GREAT DEDICATION AND HONOR.

FOR THEY BELIEVED WITHOUT SACRIFICE, THE BEAUTY OF LIFE WOULD END.

ALL OF REALITY WOULD CEASE TO EXIST.

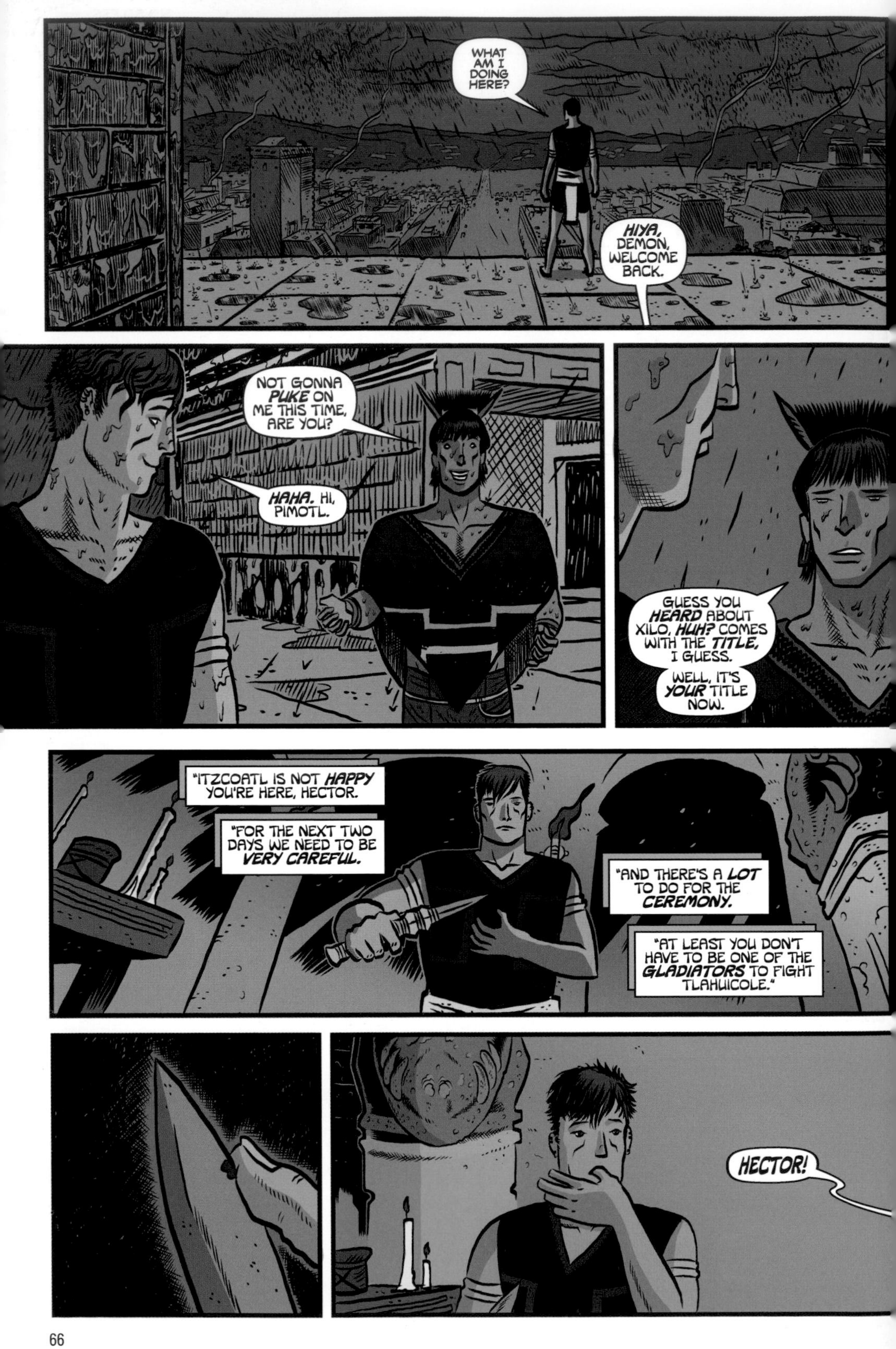

WHAT AM I DOING HERE?
HIYA, DEMON, WELCOME BACK.
NOT GONNA PUKE ON ME THIS TIME, ARE YOU?
HAHA. HI, PIMOTL.
GUESS YOU HEARD ABOUT XILO, HUH? COMES WITH THE TITLE, I GUESS.
WELL, IT'S YOUR TITLE NOW.
"ITZCOATL IS NOT HAPPY YOU'RE HERE, HECTOR.
"FOR THE NEXT TWO DAYS WE NEED TO BE VERY CAREFUL.
"AND THERE'S A LOT TO DO FOR THE CEREMONY.
"AT LEAST YOU DON'T HAVE TO BE ONE OF THE GLADIATORS TO FIGHT TLAHUICOLE."
HECTOR!

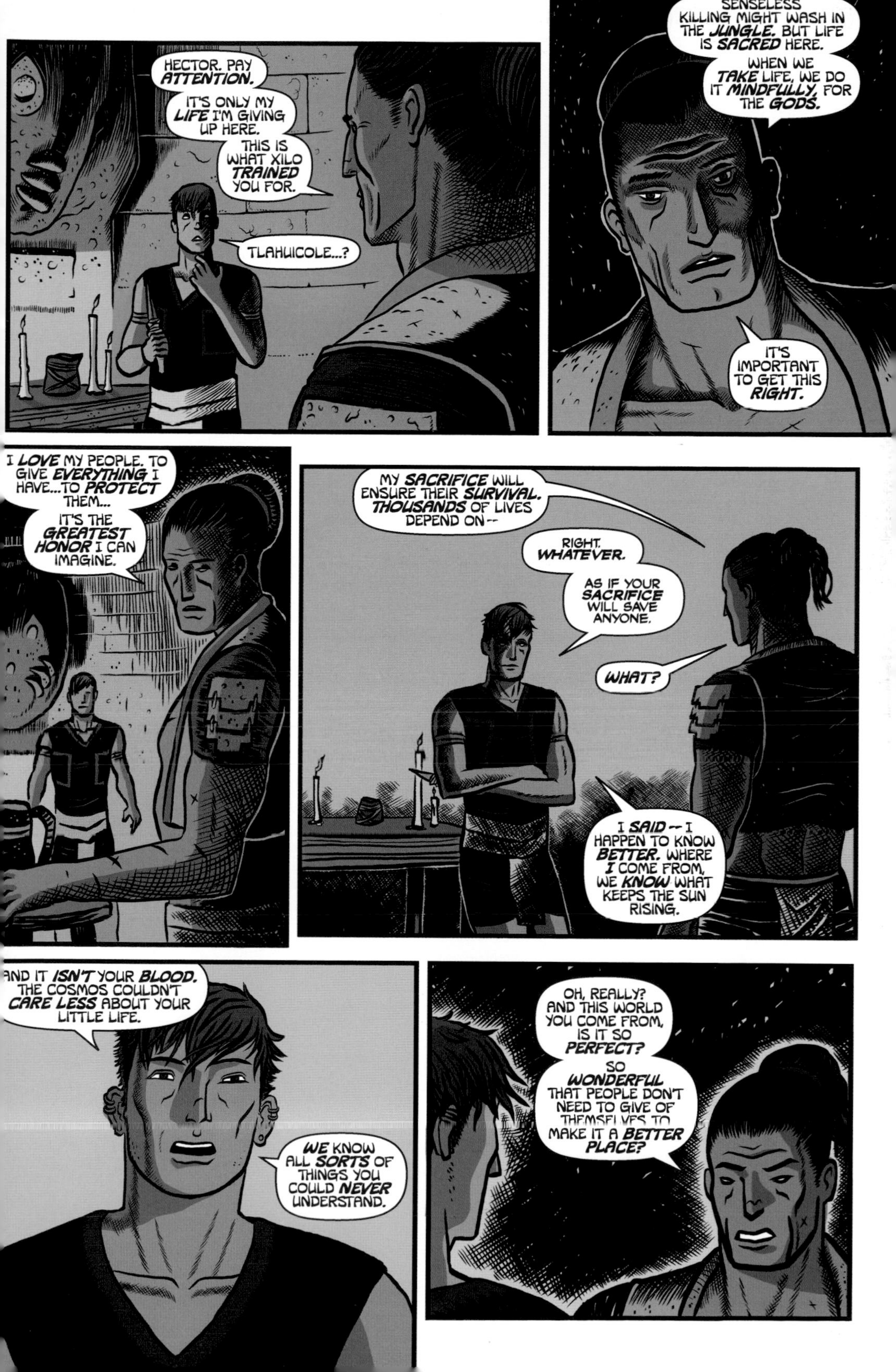
HECTOR. PAY ATTENTION.
IT'S ONLY MY LIFE I'M GIVING UP HERE.
THIS IS WHAT XILO TRAINED YOU FOR.
TLAHUICOLE...?
SENSELESS KILLING MIGHT WASH IN THE JUNGLE. BUT LIFE IS SACRED HERE.
WHEN WE TAKE LIFE, WE DO IT MINDFULLY, FOR THE GODS.
IT'S IMPORTANT TO GET THIS RIGHT.
I LOVE MY PEOPLE. TO GIVE EVERYTHING I HAVE...TO PROTECT THEM...
IT'S THE GREATEST HONOR I CAN IMAGINE.
MY SACRIFICE WILL ENSURE THEIR SURVIVAL. THOUSANDS OF LIVES DEPEND ON--
RIGHT. WHATEVER.
AS IF YOUR SACRIFICE WILL SAVE ANYONE.
WHAT?
I SAID -- I HAPPEN TO KNOW BETTER. WHERE I COME FROM, WE KNOW WHAT KEEPS THE SUN RISING.
AND IT ISN'T YOUR BLOOD. THE COSMOS COULDN'T CARE LESS ABOUT YOUR LITTLE LIFE.
WE KNOW ALL SORTS OF THINGS YOU COULD NEVER UNDERSTAND.
OH, REALLY? AND THIS WORLD YOU COME FROM, IS IT SO PERFECT?
SO WONDERFUL THAT PEOPLE DON'T NEED TO GIVE OF THEMSELVES TO MAKE IT A BETTER PLACE?

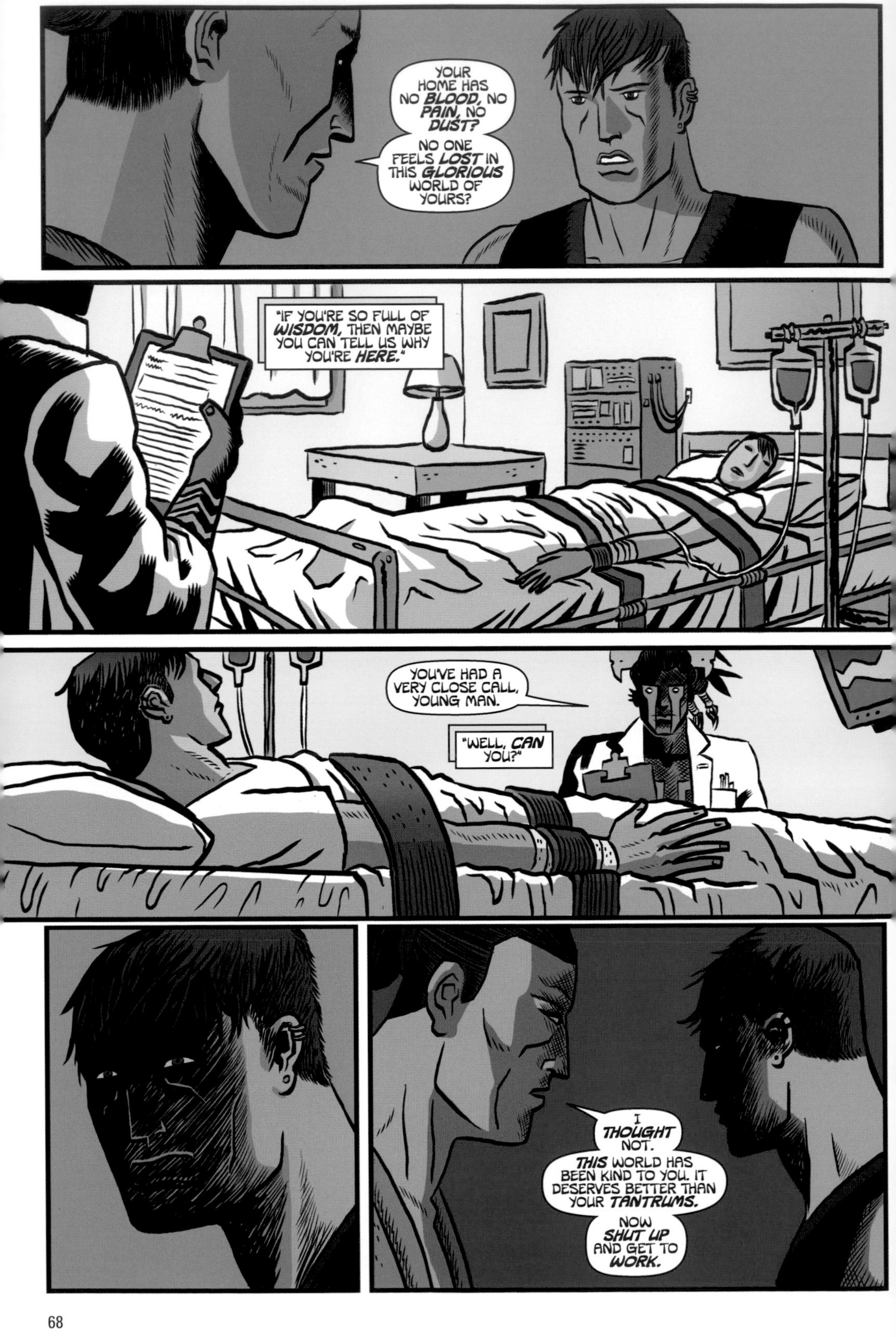
YOUR HOME HAS NO BLOOD, NO PAIN, NO DUST?
NO ONE FEELS LOST IN THIS GLORIOUS WORLD OF YOURS?
"IF YOU'RE SO FULL OF WISDOM, THEN MAYBE YOU CAN TELL US WHY YOU'RE HERE."
YOU'VE HAD A VERY CLOSE CALL, YOUNG MAN.
"WELL, CAN YOU?"
I THOUGHT NOT.
THIS WORLD HAS BEEN KIND TO YOU. IT DESERVES BETTER THAN YOUR TANTRUMS.
NOW SHUT UP AND GET TO WORK.

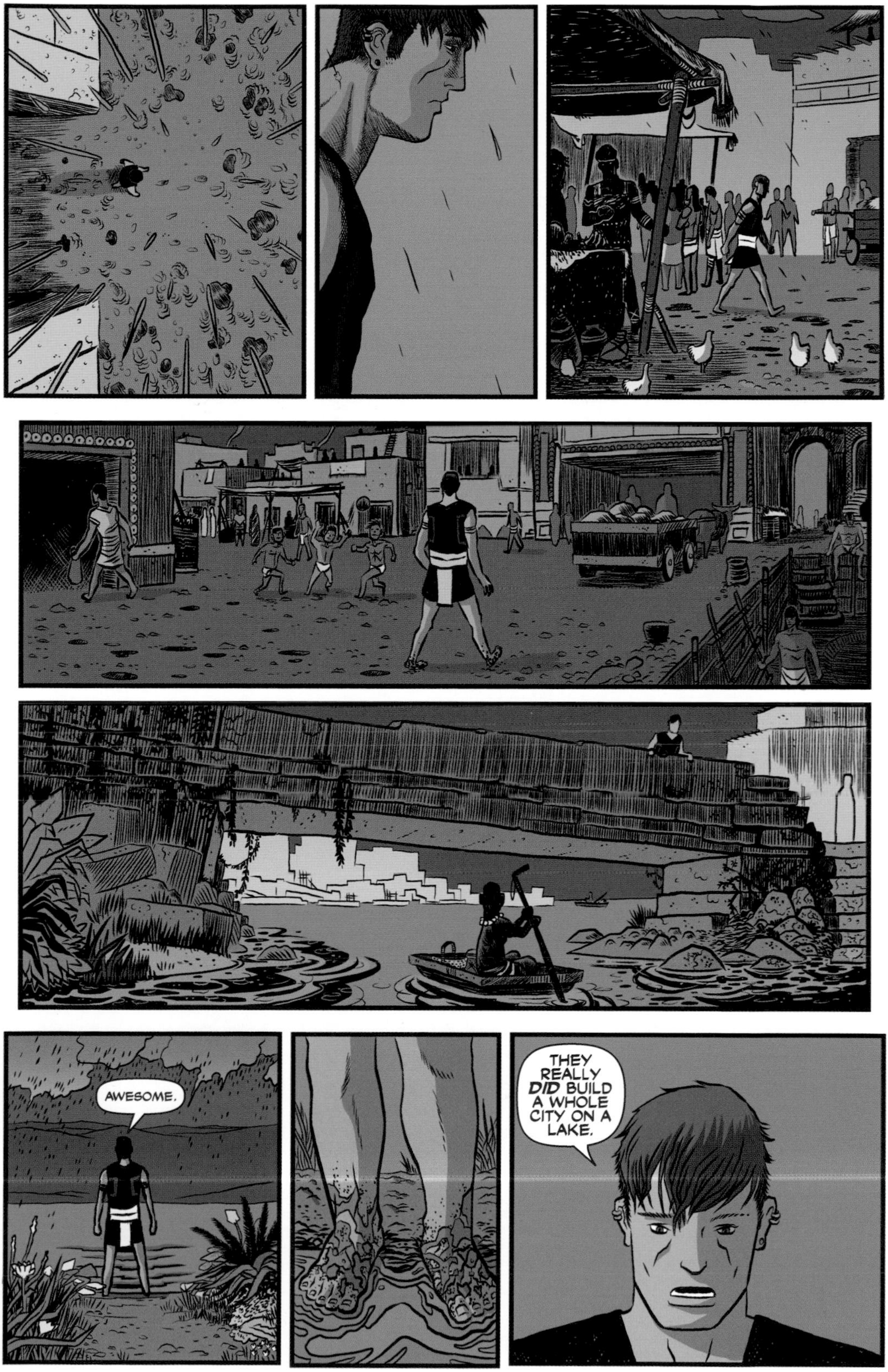
AWESOME.
THEY REALLY DID BUILD A WHOLE CITY ON A LAKE.

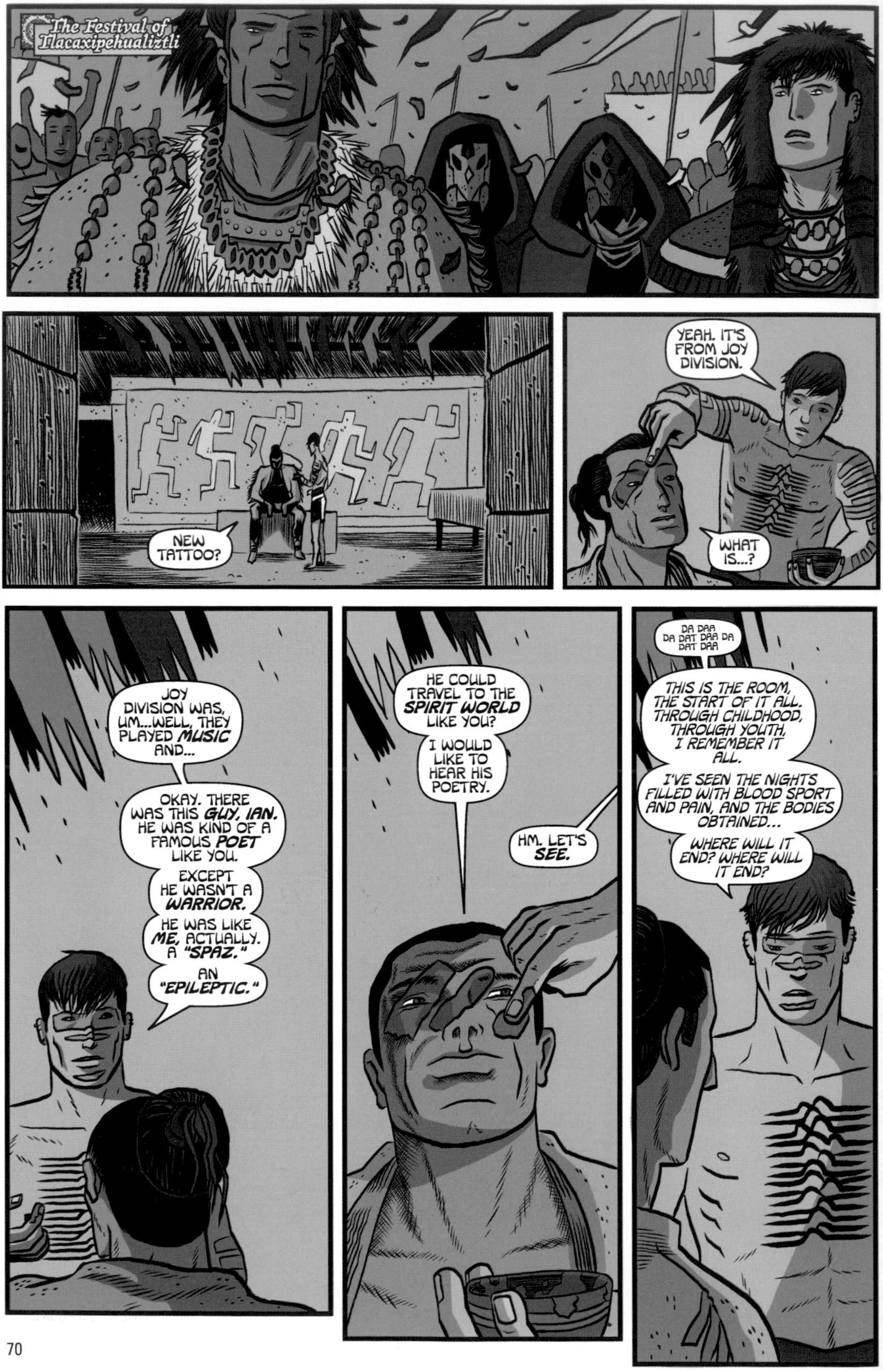

The Festival of Tlacaxipehualiztli
NEW TATTOO?
YEAH. IT'S FROM JOY DIVISION.
WHAT IS...?
JOY DIVISION WAS, UM...WELL, THEY PLAYED MUSIC AND...
OKAY. THERE WAS THIS GUY, IAN. HE WAS KIND OF A FAMOUS POET LIKE YOU.
EXCEPT HE WASN'T A WARRIOR.
HE WAS LIKE ME, ACTUALLY. A "SPAZ."
AN "EPILEPTIC."
HE COULD TRAVEL TO THE SPIRIT WORLD LIKE YOU?
I WOULD LIKE TO HEAR HIS POETRY.
HM. LET'S SEE.
DA DAA DA DAT DAA DA DAT DAA
THIS IS THE ROOM, THE START OF IT ALL, THROUGH CHILDHOOD, THROUGH YOUTH, I REMEMBER IT ALL.
I'VE SEEN THE NIGHTS FILLED WITH BLOOD SPORT AND PAIN, AND THE BODIES OBTAINED...
WHERE WILL IT END? WHERE WILL IT END?

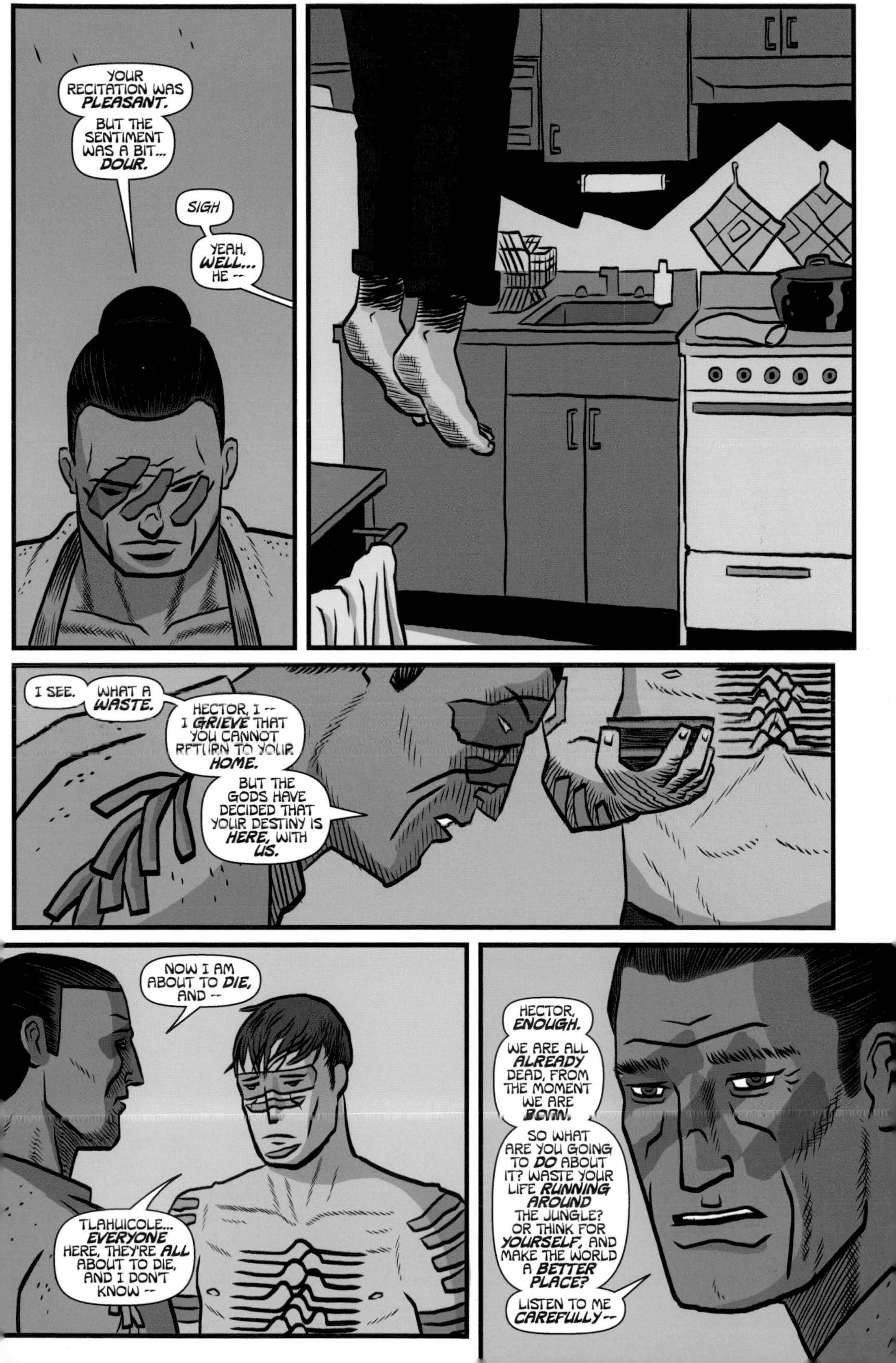
YOUR RECITATION WAS PLEASANT.
BUT THE SENTIMENT WAS A BIT... DOUR.
SIGH
YEAH, WELL... HE --
I SEE.
WHAT A WASTE.
HECTOR, I -- I GRIEVE THAT YOU CANNOT RETURN TO YOUR HOME.
BUT THE GODS HAVE DECIDED THAT YOUR DESTINY IS HERE, WITH US.
NOW I AM ABOUT TO DIE, AND --
TLAHUICOLE... EVERYONE HERE, THEY'RE ALL ABOUT TO DIE, AND I DON'T KNOW --
HECTOR, ENOUGH.
WE ARE ALL ALREADY DEAD, FROM THE MOMENT WE ARE BORN.
SO WHAT ARE YOU GOING TO DO ABOUT IT? WASTE YOUR LIFE RUNNING AROUND THE JUNGLE? OR THINK FOR YOURSELF, AND MAKE THE WORLD A BETTER PLACE?
LISTEN TO ME CAREFULLY--

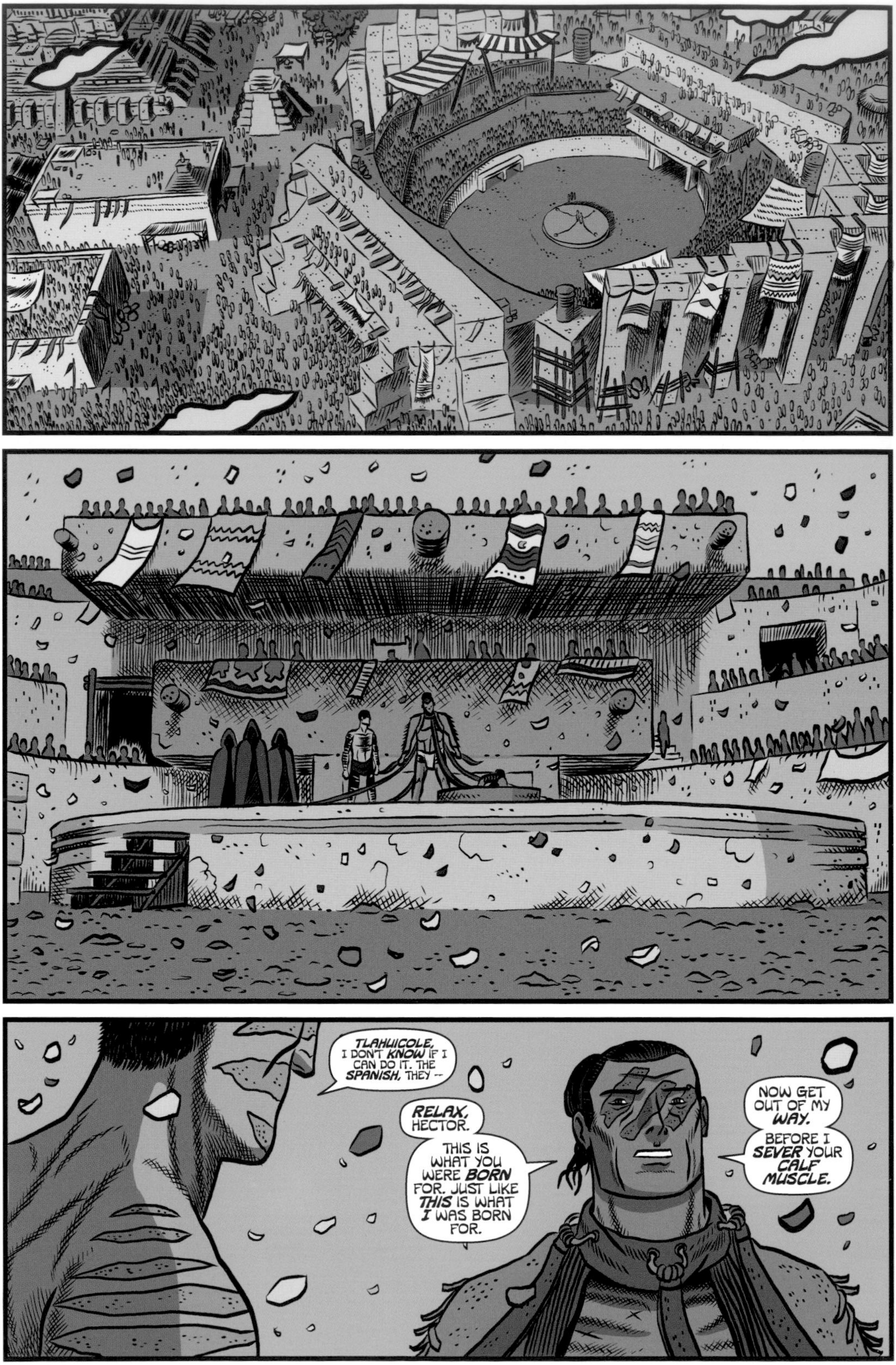
TLAHUICOLE, I DON'T KNOW IF I CAN DO IT. THE SPANISH, THEY --
RELAX, HECTOR.
THIS IS WHAT YOU WERE BORN FOR. JUST LIKE THIS IS WHAT I WAS BORN FOR.
NOW GET OUT OF MY WAY.
BEFORE I SEVER YOUR CALF MUSCLE.

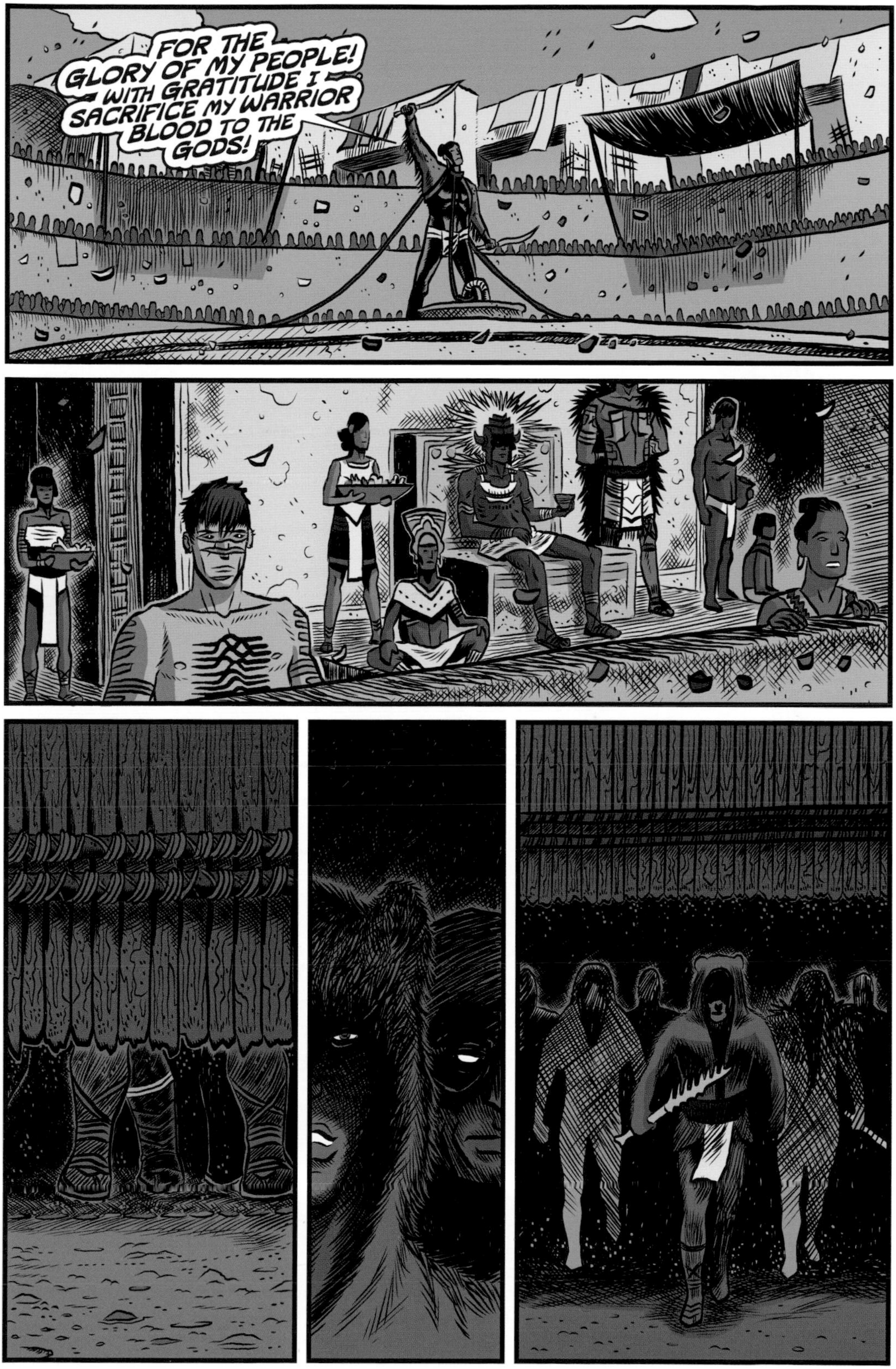
FOR THE GLORY OF MY PEOPLE! WITH GRATITUDE I SACRIFICE MY WARRIOR BLOOD TO THE GODS!

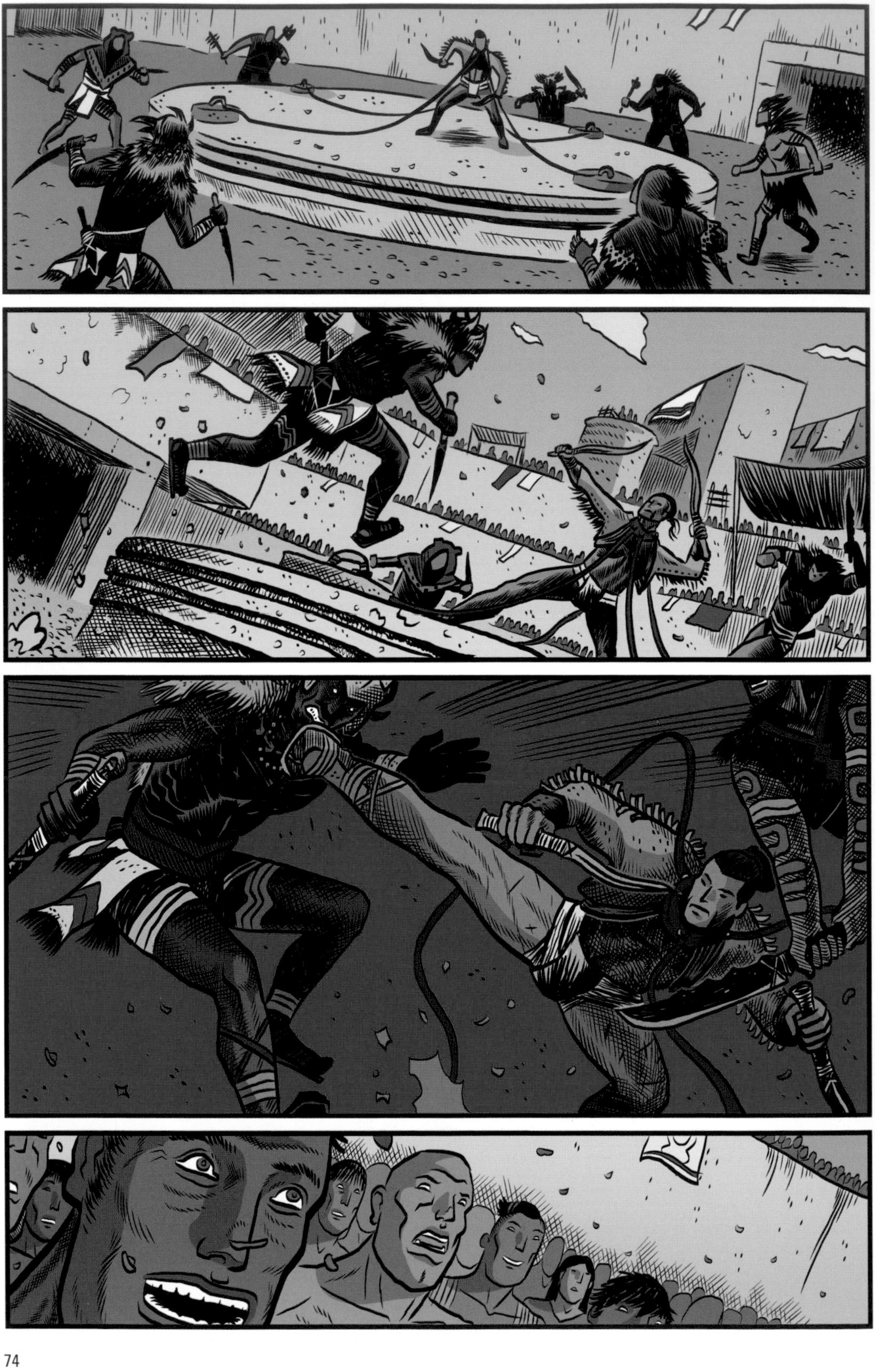

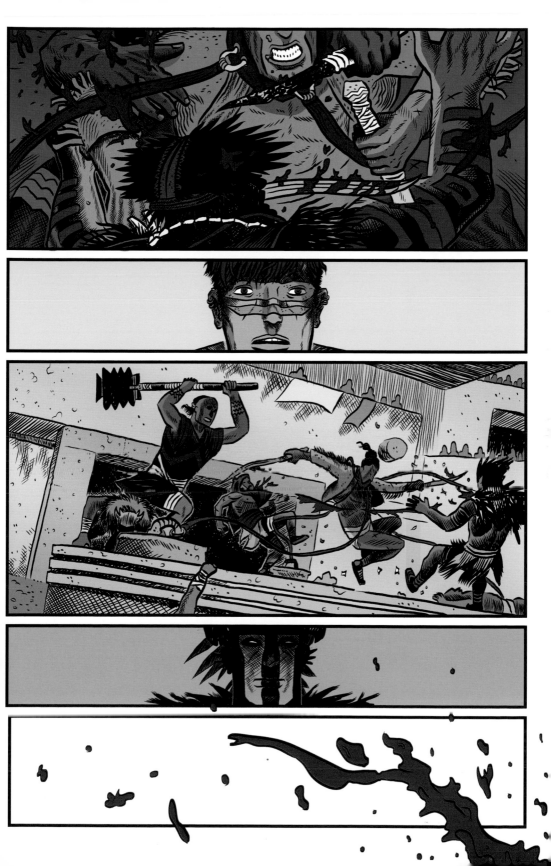

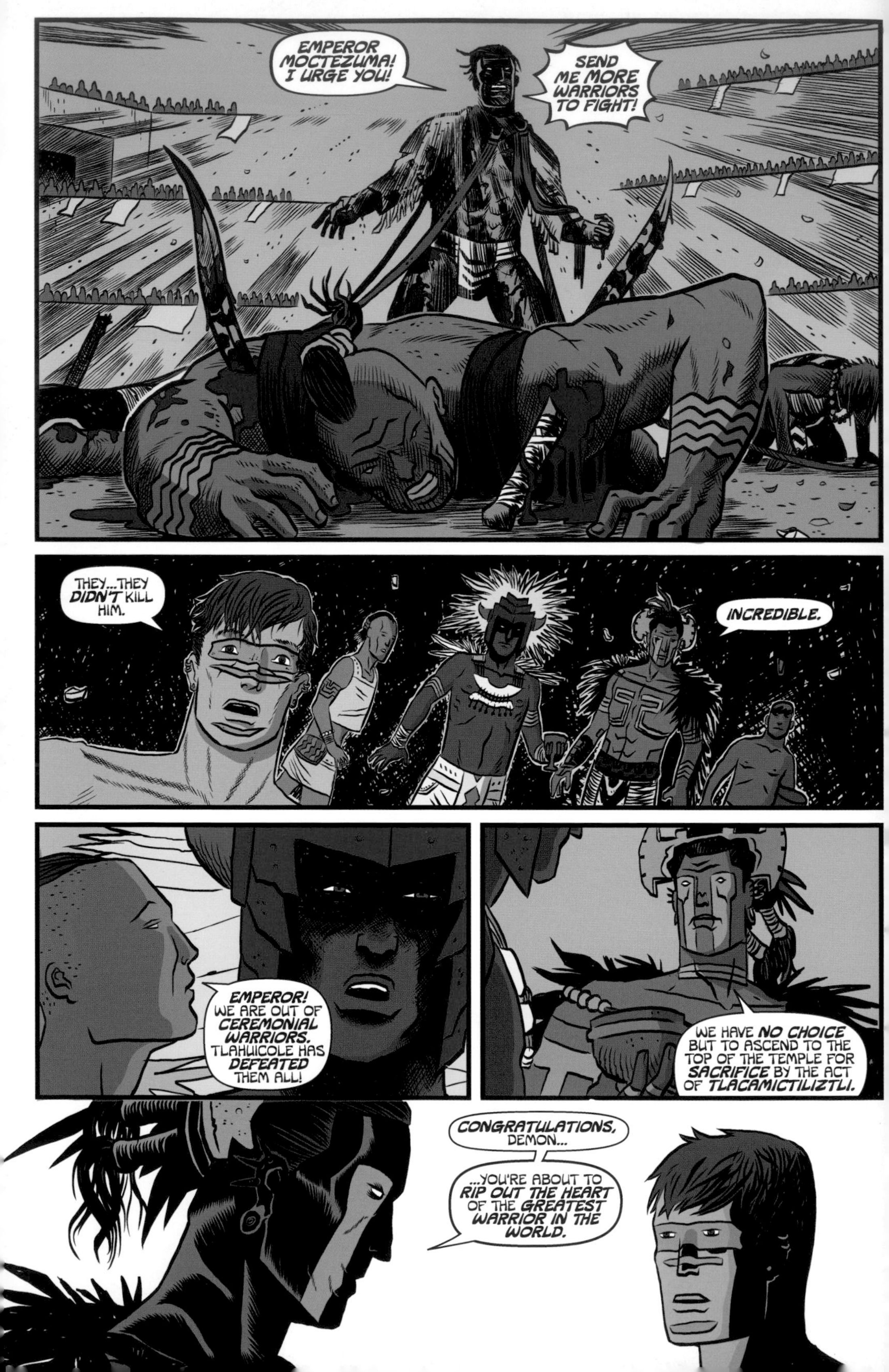
EMPEROR MOCTEZUMA! I URGE YOU!
SEND ME MORE WARRIORS TO FIGHT!
THEY... THEY DIDN'T KILL HIM.
INCREDIBLE.
EMPEROR! WE ARE OUT OF CEREMONIAL WARRIORS. TLAHUICOLE HAS DEFEATED THEM ALL!
WE HAVE NO CHOICE BUT TO ASCEND TO THE TOP OF THE TEMPLE FOR SACRIFICE BY THE ACT OF TLACAMICTILIZTLI.
CONGRATULATIONS, DEMON...
...YOU'RE ABOUT TO RIP OUT THE HEART OF THE GREATEST WARRIOR IN THE WORLD.

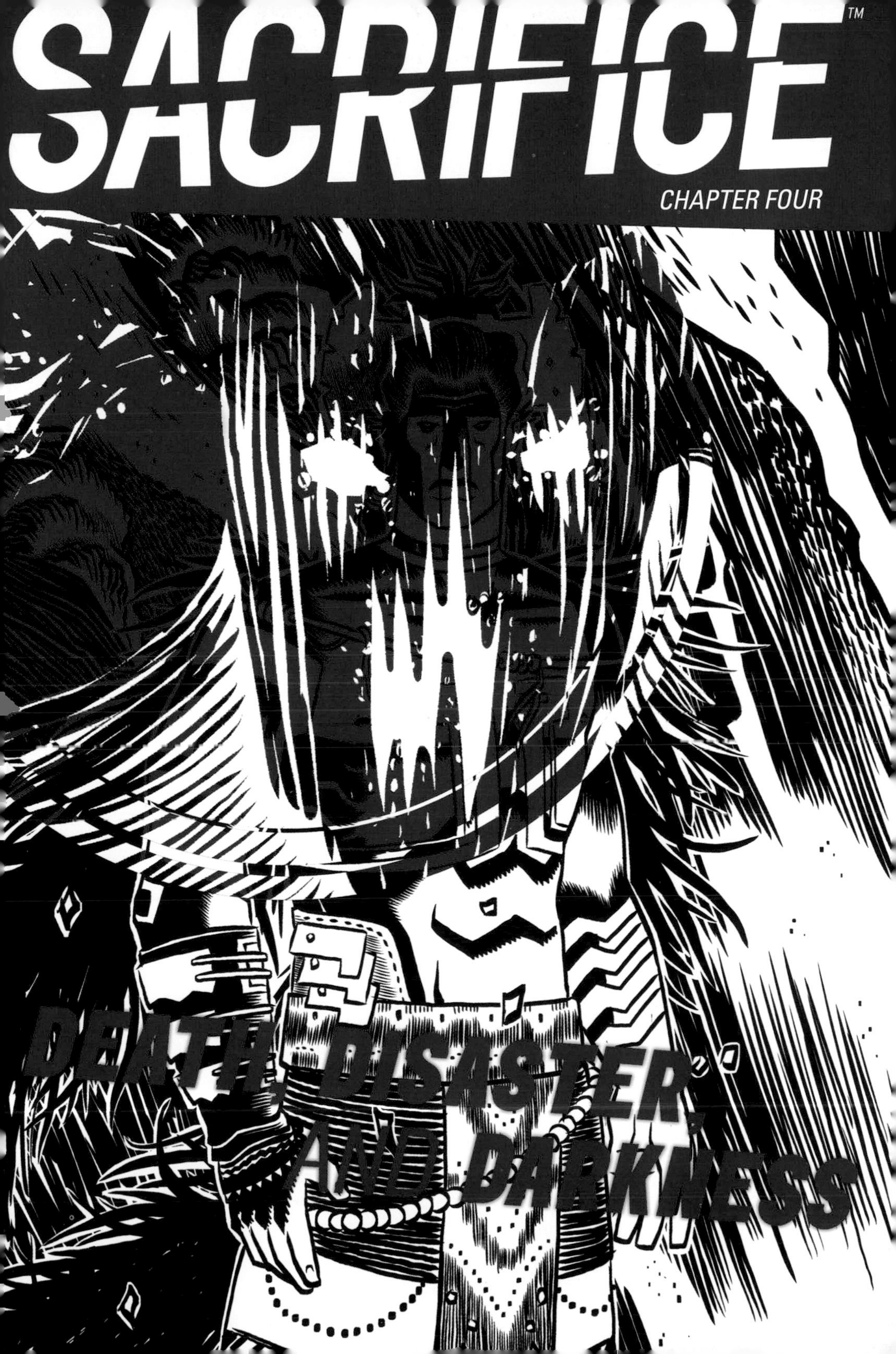
SACRIFICE™
CHAPTER FOUR
DEATH, DISASTER, AND DARKNESS

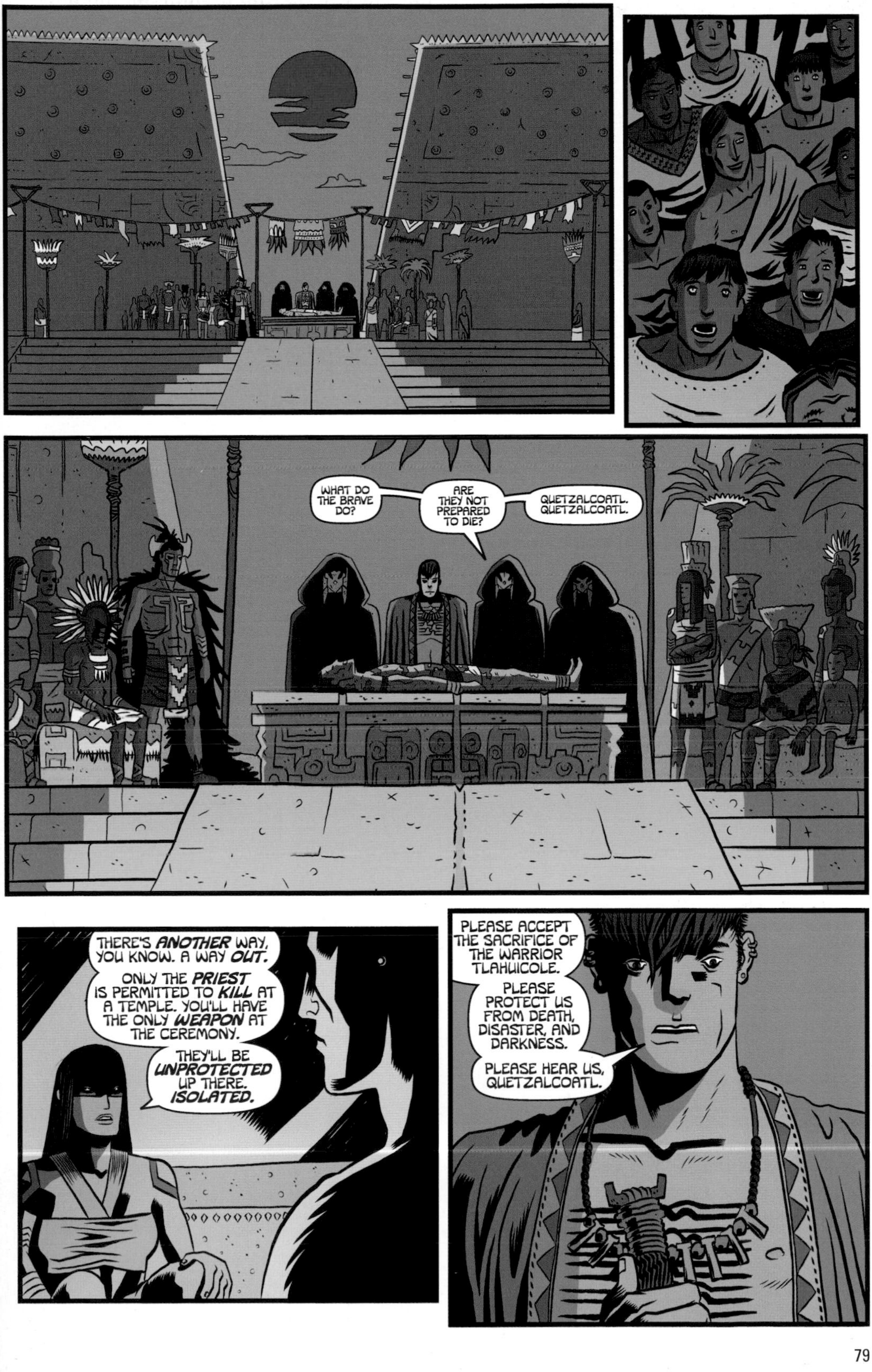
WHAT DO THE BRAVE DO?
ARE THEY NOT PREPARED TO DIE?
QUETZALCOATL. QUETZALCOATL.
THERE'S **ANOTHER** WAY, YOU KNOW. A WAY **OUT.**
ONLY THE **PRIEST** IS PERMITTED TO **KILL** AT A TEMPLE. YOU'LL HAVE THE ONLY **WEAPON** AT THE CEREMONY.
THEY'LL BE **UNPROTECTED** UP THERE. **ISOLATED.**
PLEASE ACCEPT THE SACRIFICE OF THE WARRIOR TLAHUICOLE.
PLEASE PROTECT US FROM DEATH, DISASTER, AND DARKNESS.
PLEASE HEAR US, QUETZALCOATL.

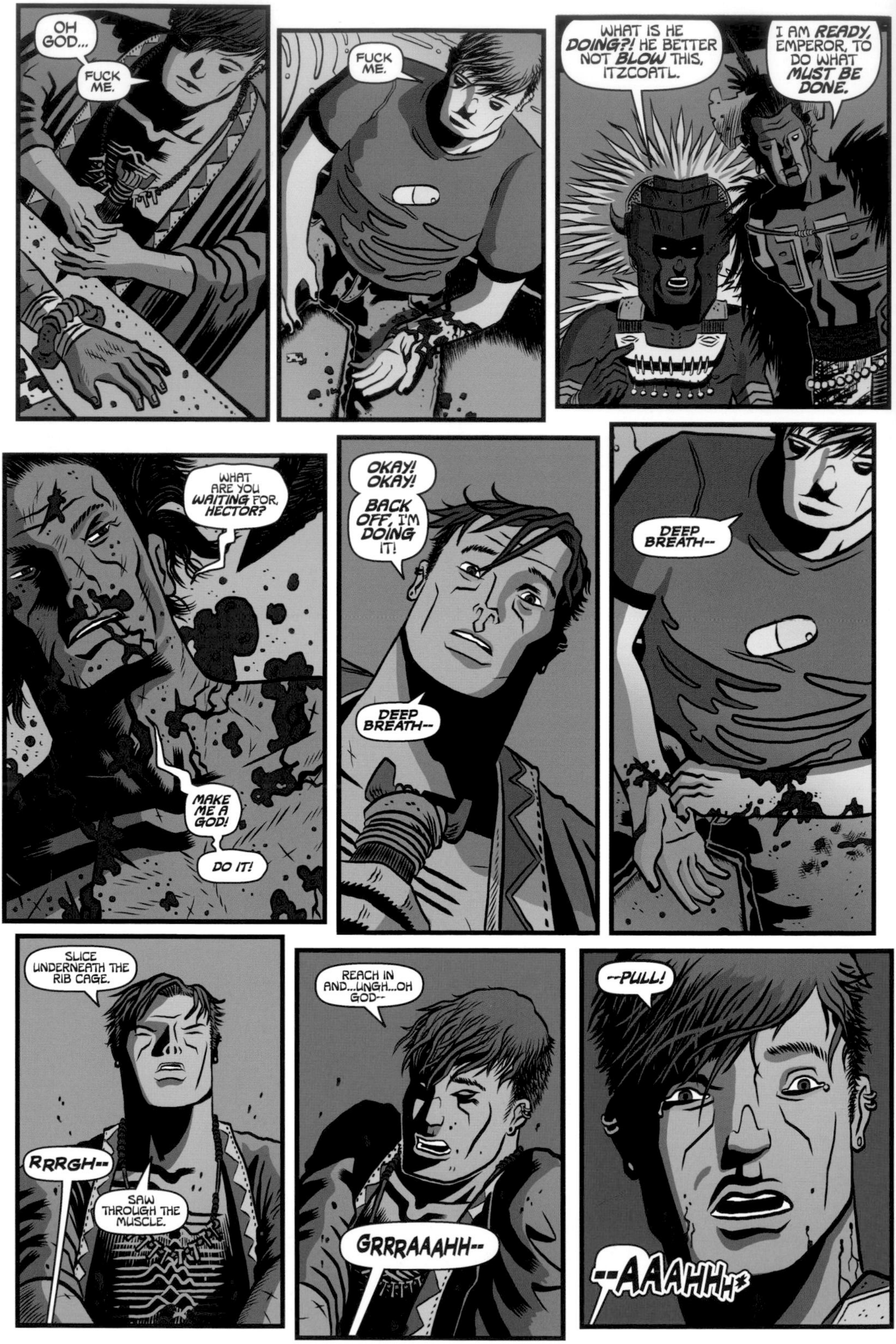
OH GOD...
FUCK ME.
FUCK ME.
WHAT IS HE DOING?! HE BETTER NOT BLOW THIS, ITZCOATL.
I AM READY, EMPEROR, TO DO WHAT MUST BE DONE.
WHAT ARE YOU WAITING FOR, HECTOR?
MAKE ME A GOD!
DO IT!
OKAY! OKAY!
BACK OFF, I'M DOING IT!
DEEP BREATH--
DEEP BREATH--
SLICE UNDERNEATH THE RIB CAGE.
RRRGH--
SAW THROUGH THE MUSCLE.
REACH IN AND...UNGH...OH GOD--
GRRRAAAHH--
--PULL!
--AAAHHH

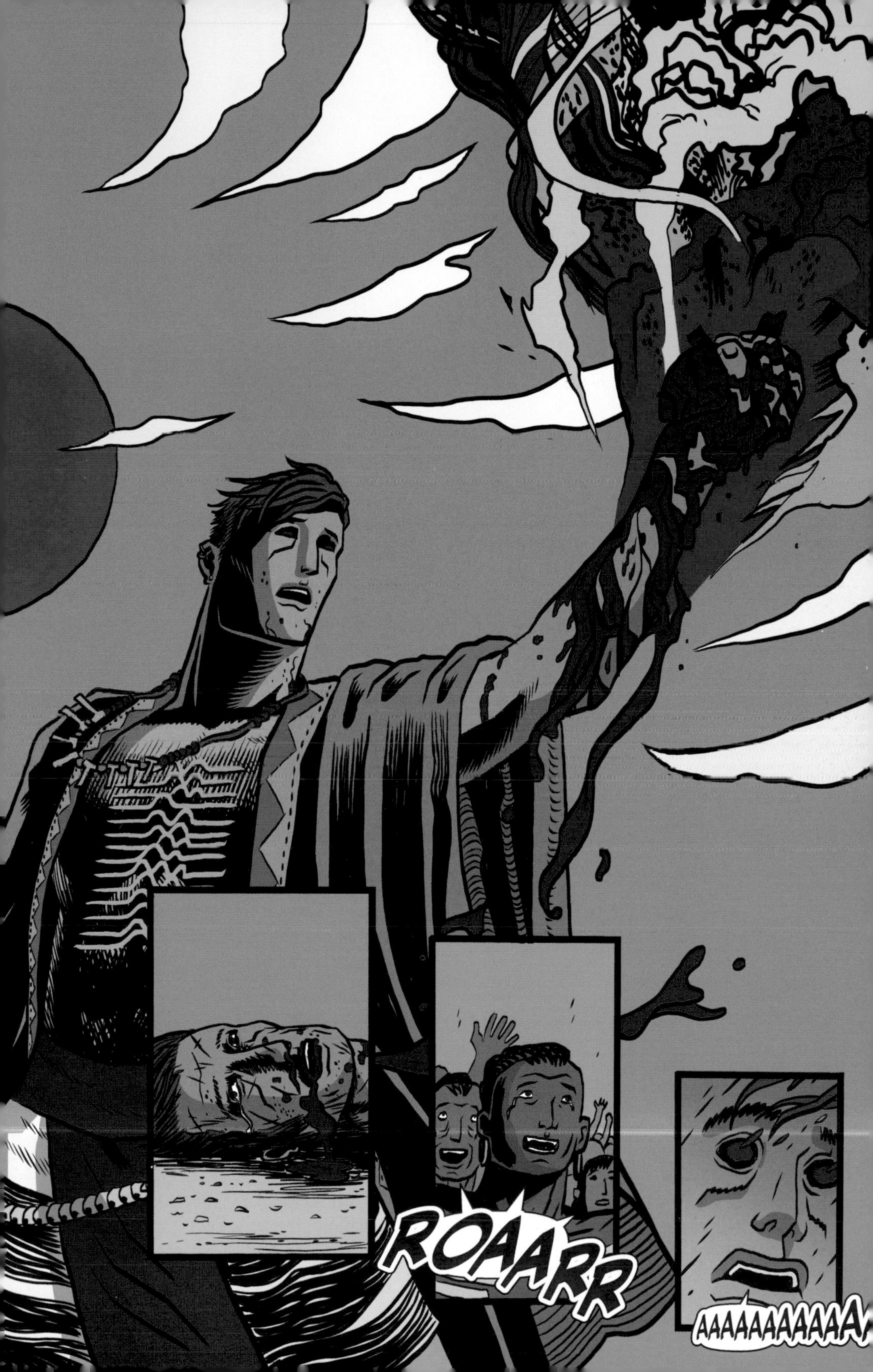

ROAARR
AAAAAAAAAAAA

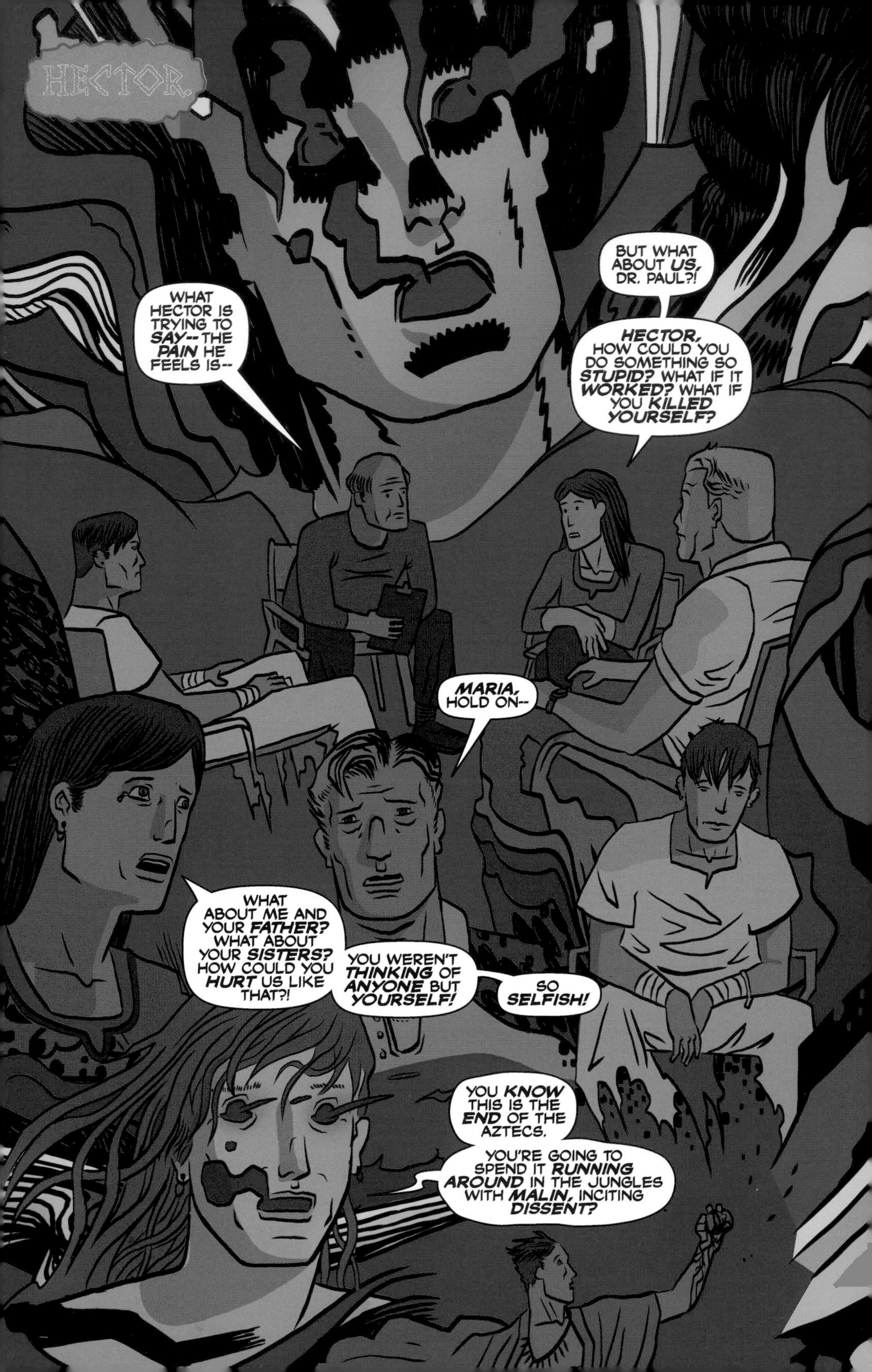
HECTOR.
WHAT HECTOR IS TRYING TO SAY-- THE PAIN HE FEELS IS--
BUT WHAT ABOUT US, DR. PAUL?!
HECTOR, HOW COULD YOU DO SOMETHING SO STUPID? WHAT IF IT WORKED? WHAT IF YOU KILLED YOURSELF?
MARIA, HOLD ON--
WHAT ABOUT ME AND YOUR FATHER? WHAT ABOUT YOUR SISTERS? HOW COULD YOU HURT US LIKE THAT?!
YOU WEREN'T THINKING OF ANYONE BUT YOURSELF!
SO SELFISH!
YOU KNOW THIS IS THE END OF THE AZTECS.
YOU'RE GOING TO SPEND IT RUNNING AROUND IN THE JUNGLES WITH MALIN, INCITING DISSENT?

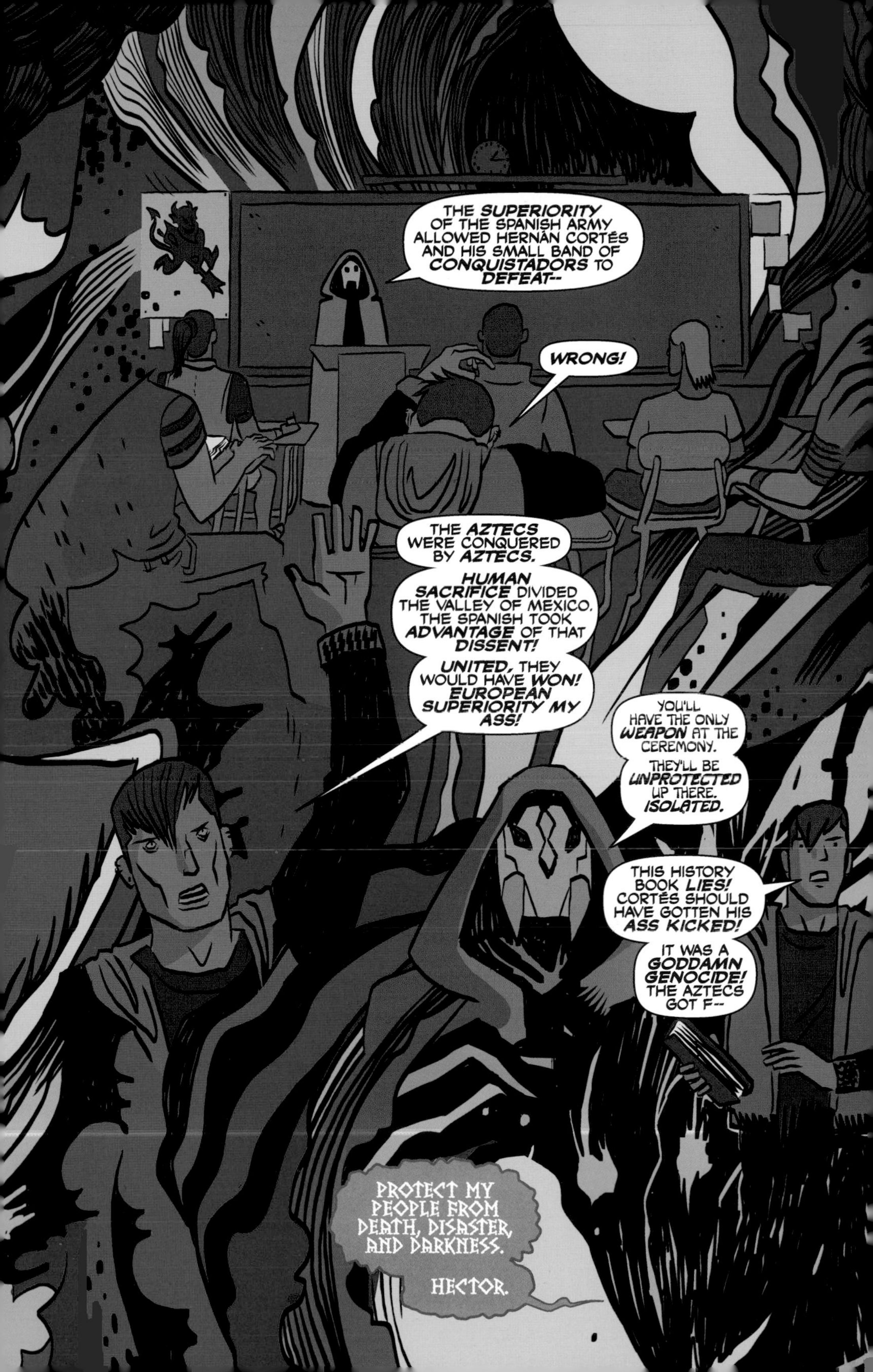
THE SUPERIORITY OF THE SPANISH ARMY ALLOWED HERNÁN CORTÉS AND HIS SMALL BAND OF CONQUISTADORS TO DEFEAT--
WRONG!
THE AZTECS WERE CONQUERED BY AZTECS.
HUMAN SACRIFICE DIVIDED THE VALLEY OF MEXICO. THE SPANISH TOOK ADVANTAGE OF THAT DISSENT!
UNITED, THEY WOULD HAVE WON! EUROPEAN SUPERIORITY MY ASS!
YOU'LL HAVE THE ONLY WEAPON AT THE CEREMONY.
THEY'LL BE UNPROTECTED UP THERE. ISOLATED.
THIS HISTORY BOOK LIES! CORTÉS SHOULD HAVE GOTTEN HIS ASS KICKED!
IT WAS A GODDAMN GENOCIDE! THE AZTECS GOT F--
PROTECT MY PEOPLE FROM DEATH, DISASTER, AND DARKNESS.
HECTOR.

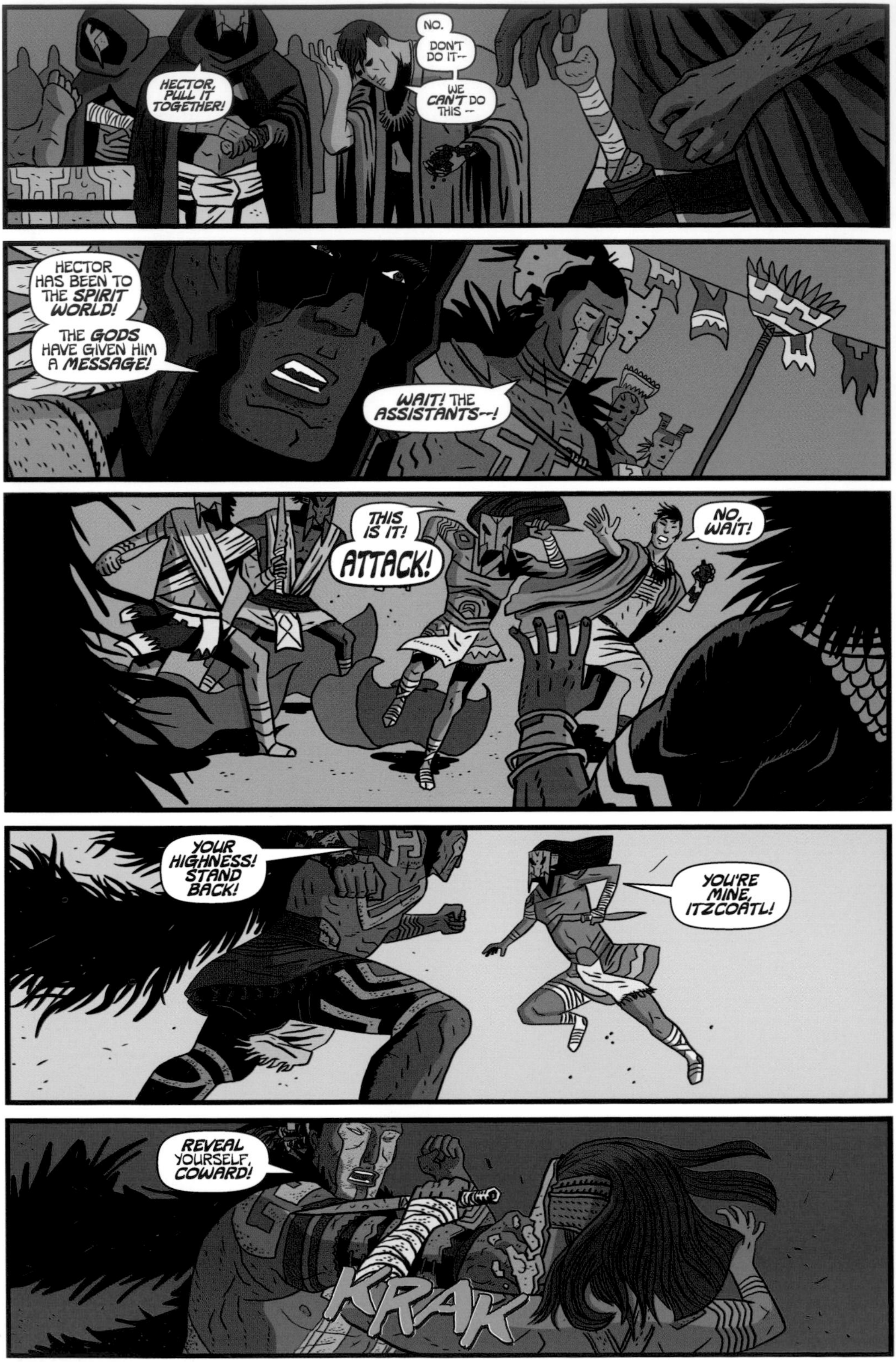

NO.
DON'T DO IT--
HECTOR, PULL IT TOGETHER!
WE CAN'T DO THIS --
HECTOR HAS BEEN TO THE SPIRIT WORLD!
THE GODS HAVE GIVEN HIM A MESSAGE!
WAIT! THE ASSISTANTS--!
THIS IS IT!
ATTACK!
NO, WAIT!
YOUR HIGHNESS! STAND BACK!
YOU'RE MINE, ITZCOATL!
REVEAL YOURSELF, COWARD!
KRAK

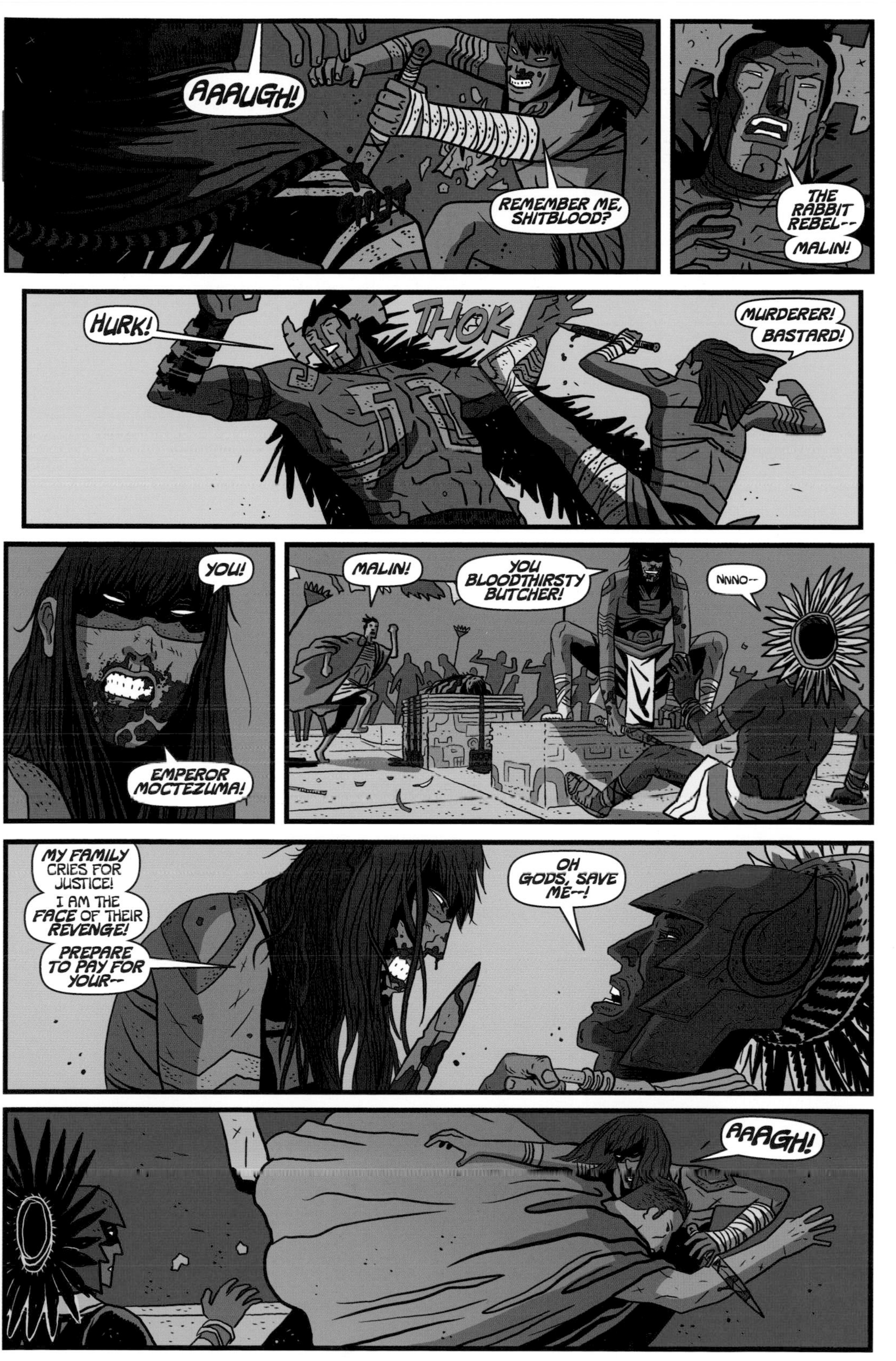
AAAUGH!
CHUT
REMEMBER ME, SHITBLOOD?
THE RABBIT REBEL--
MALIN!
HURK!
THOK
MURDERER! BASTARD!
YOU!
EMPEROR MOCTEZUMA!
MALIN!
YOU BLOODTHIRSTY BUTCHER!
NNNO--
MY FAMILY CRIES FOR JUSTICE!
I AM THE FACE OF THEIR REVENGE!
PREPARE TO PAY FOR YOUR--
OH GODS, SAVE ME--!
AAAGH!

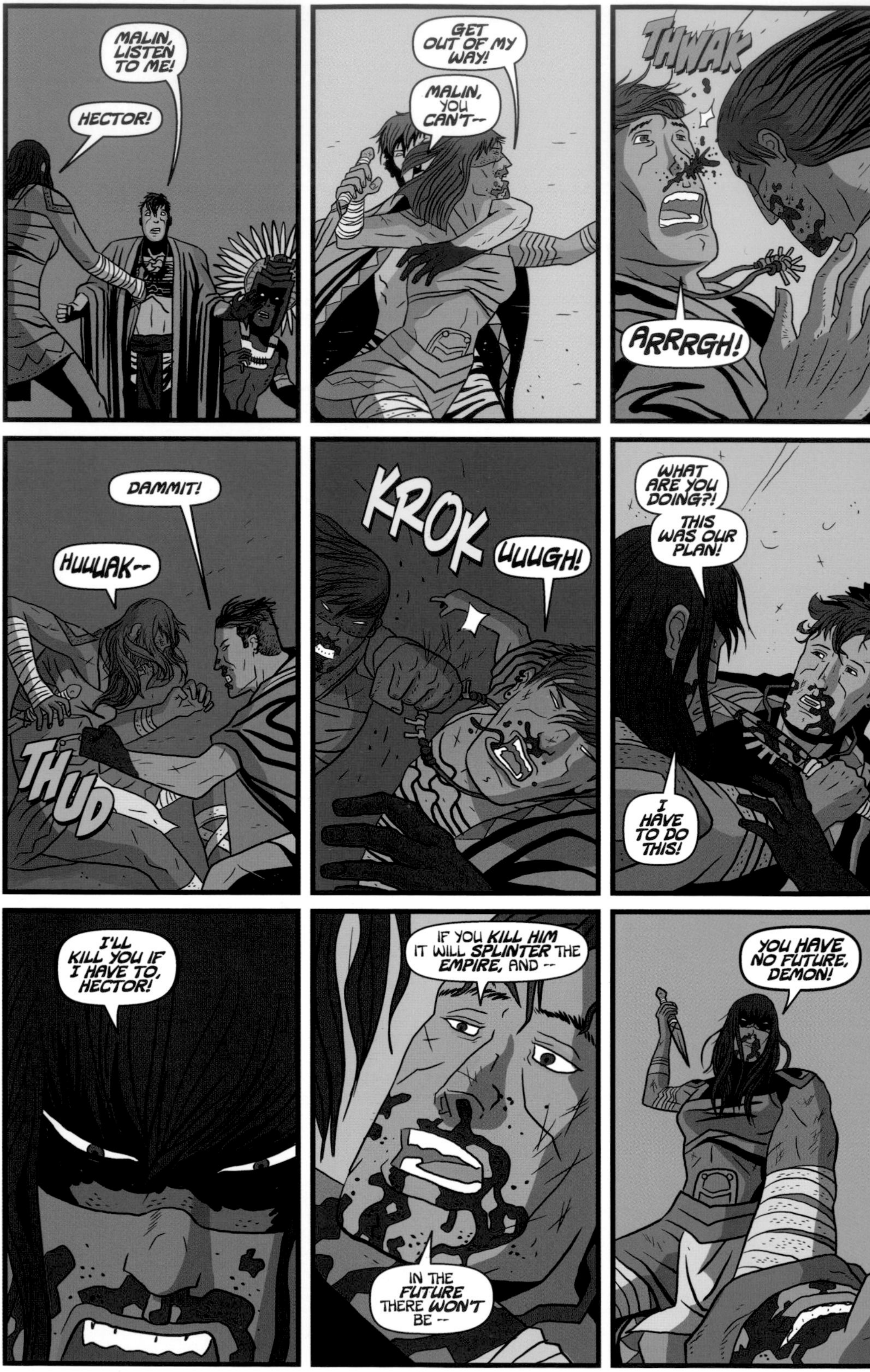
MALIN, LISTEN TO ME!
HECTOR!
GET OUT OF MY WAY!
MALIN, YOU CAN'T--
THWAK
ARRRGH!
DAMMIT!
HUUUAK--
THUD
KROK
UUUGH!
WHAT ARE YOU DOING?! THIS WAS OUR PLAN!
I HAVE TO DO THIS!
I'LL KILL YOU IF I HAVE TO, HECTOR!
IF YOU KILL HIM IT WILL SPLINTER THE EMPIRE, AND --
IN THE FUTURE THERE WON'T BE --
YOU HAVE NO FUTURE, DEMON!

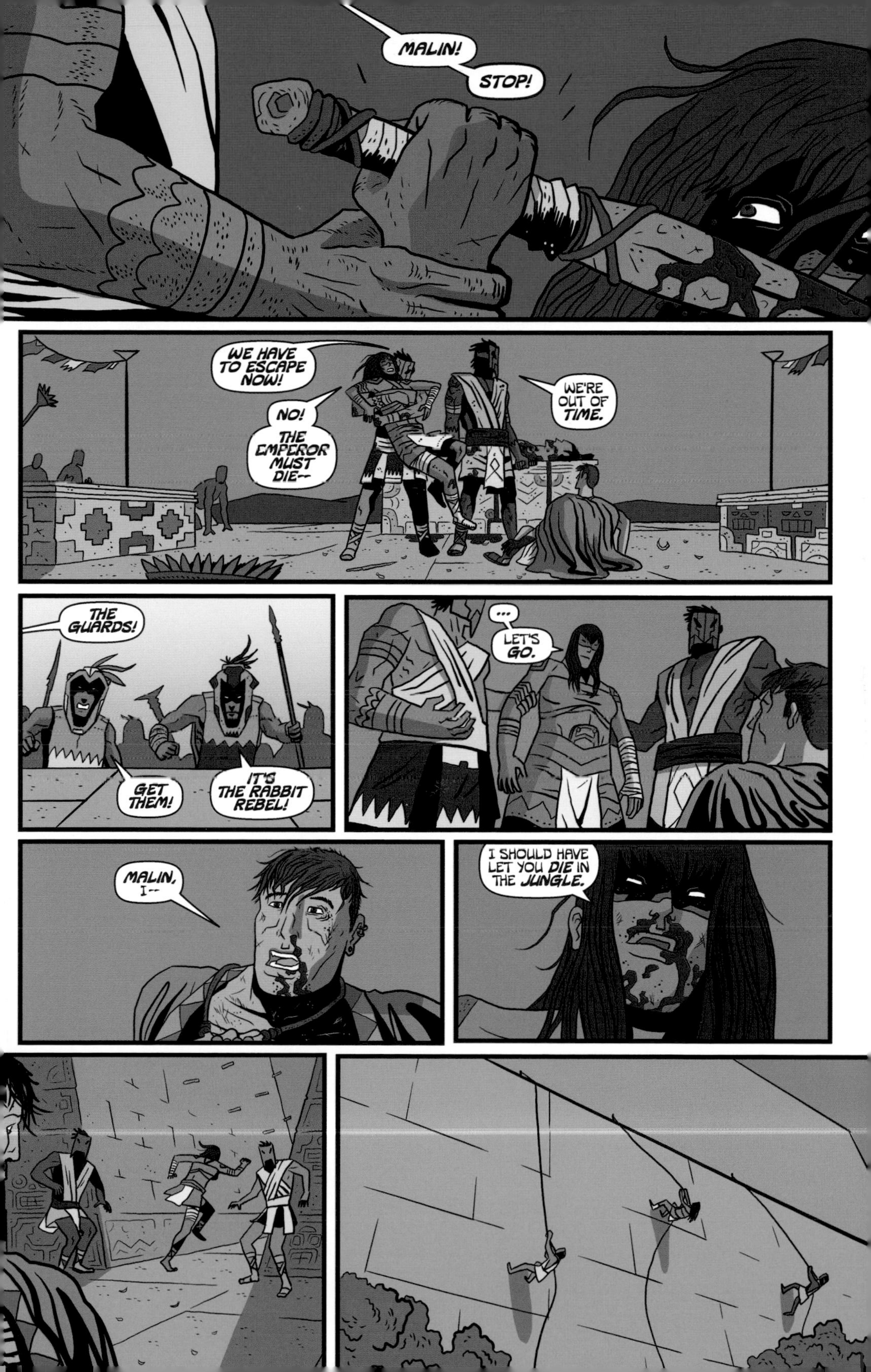

MALIN!
STOP!
WE HAVE TO ESCAPE NOW!
NO! THE EMPEROR MUST DIE--
WE'RE OUT OF TIME.
THE GUARDS!
GET THEM!
IT'S THE RABBIT REBEL!
...
LET'S GO.
MALIN, I--
I SHOULD HAVE LET YOU DIE IN THE JUNGLE.

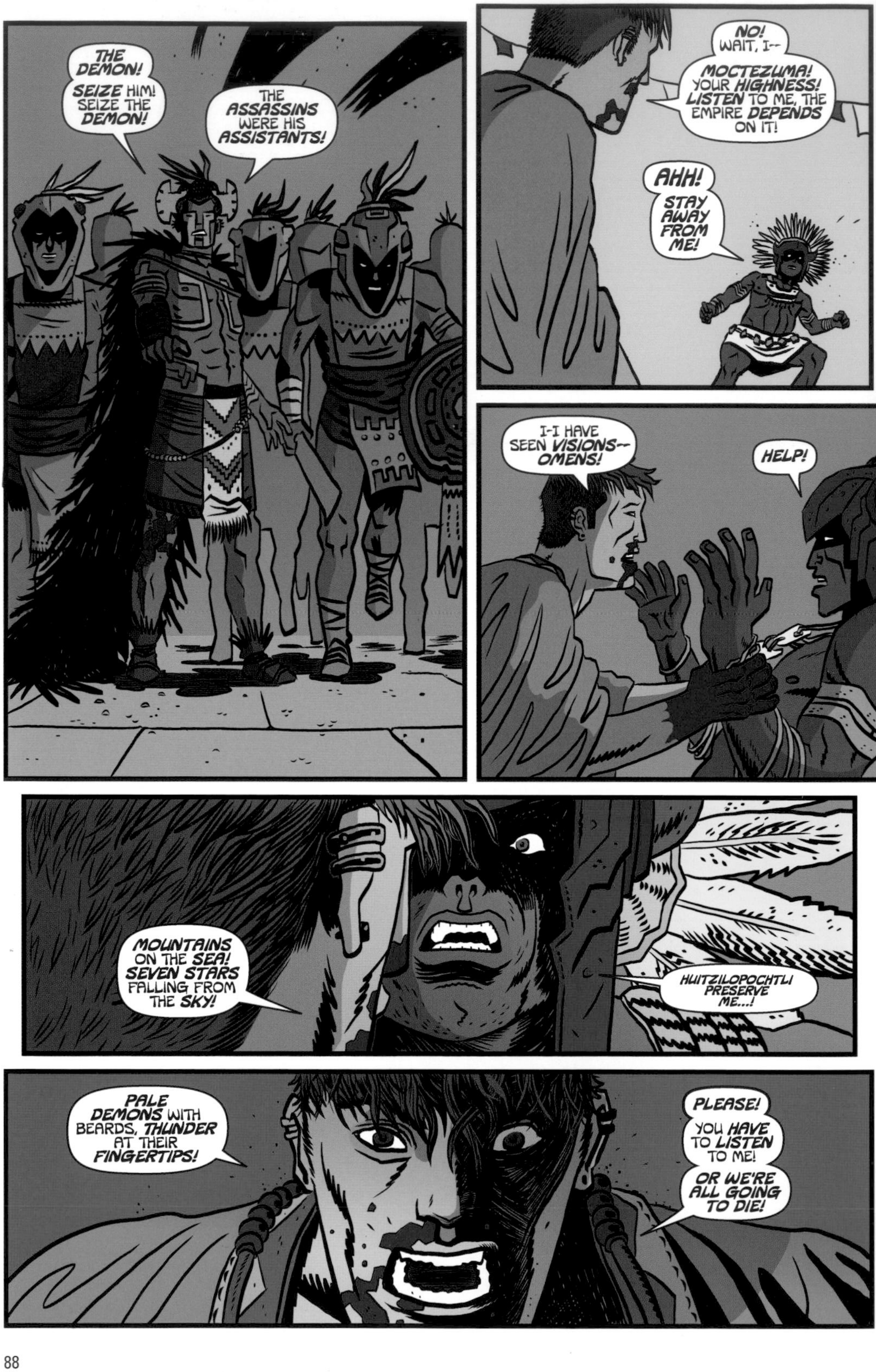
THE DEMON! SEIZE HIM! SEIZE THE DEMON!
THE ASSASSINS WERE HIS ASSISTANTS!
NO! WAIT, I--
MOCTEZUMA! YOUR HIGHNESS! LISTEN TO ME, THE EMPIRE DEPENDS ON IT!
AHH! STAY AWAY FROM ME!
I-I HAVE SEEN VISIONS--OMENS!
HELP!
MOUNTAINS ON THE SEA! SEVEN STARS FALLING FROM THE SKY!
HUITZILOPOCHTLI PRESERVE ME...!
PALE DEMONS WITH BEARDS, THUNDER AT THEIR FINGERTIPS!
PLEASE!
YOU HAVE TO LISTEN TO ME!
OR WE'RE ALL GOING TO DIE!

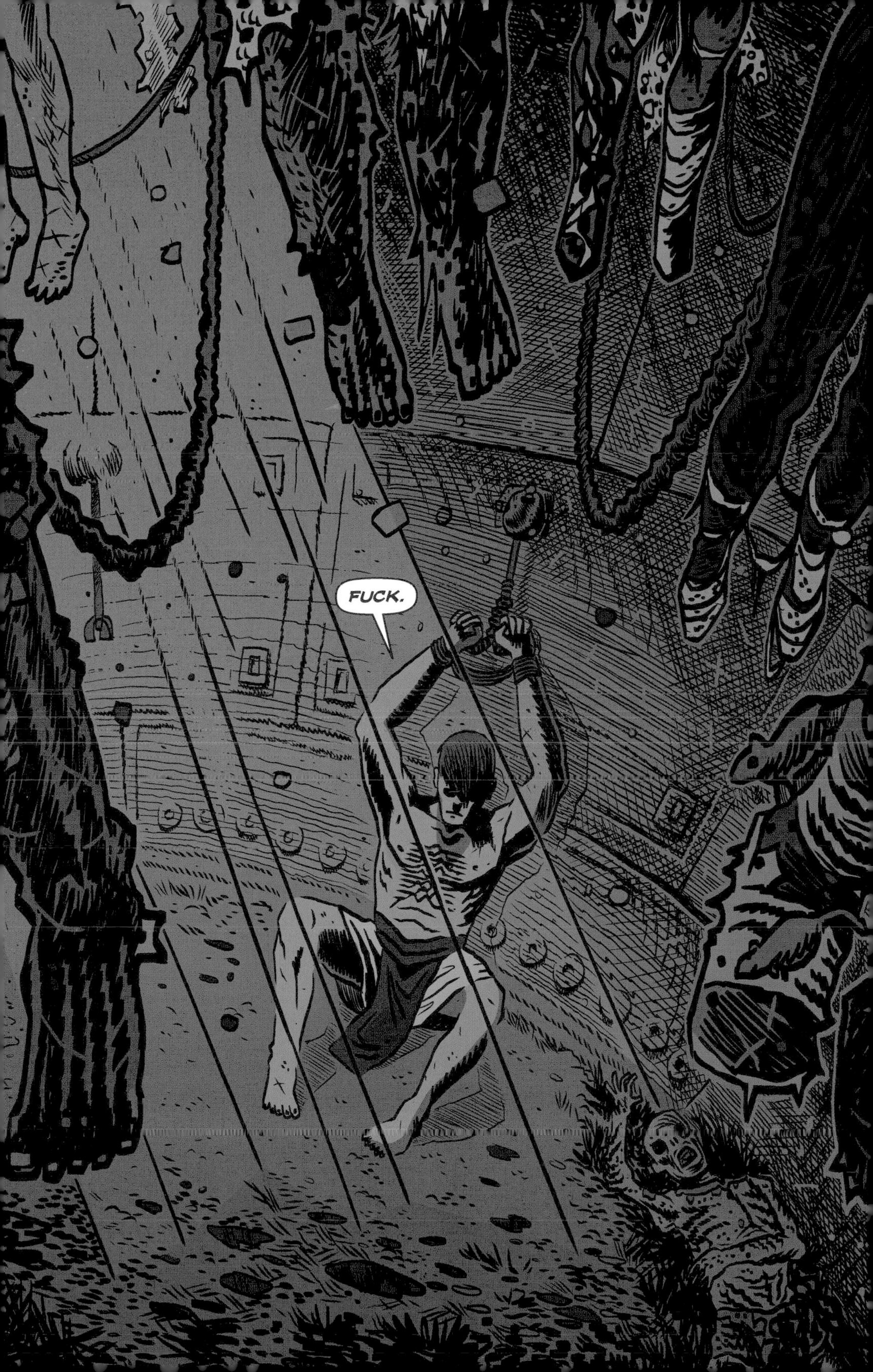
FUCK.

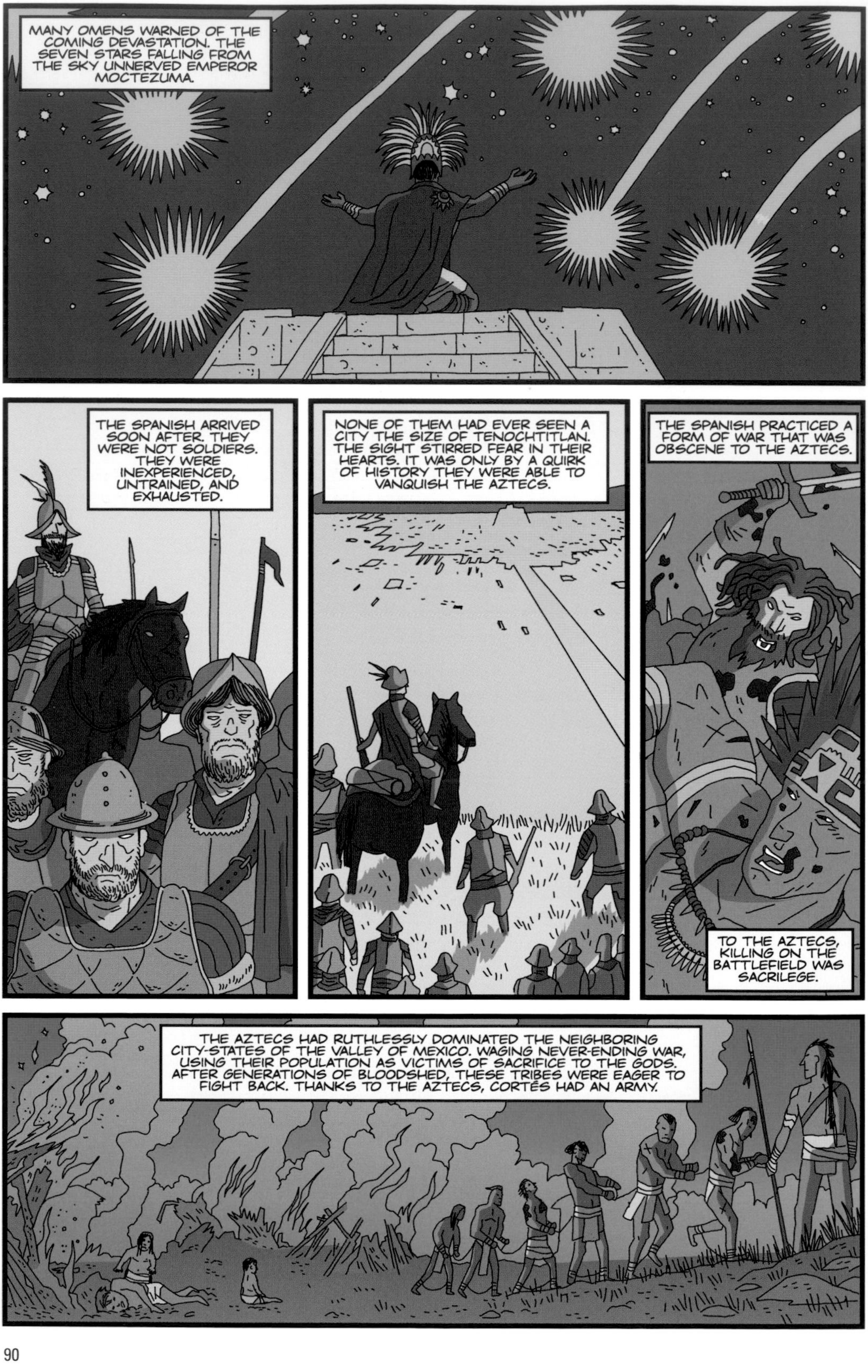
MANY OMENS WARNED OF THE COMING DEVASTATION. THE SEVEN STARS FALLING FROM THE SKY UNNERVED EMPEROR MOCTEZUMA.
THE SPANISH ARRIVED SOON AFTER. THEY WERE NOT SOLDIERS. THEY WERE INEXPERIENCED, UNTRAINED, AND EXHAUSTED.
NONE OF THEM HAD EVER SEEN A CITY THE SIZE OF TENOCHTITLAN. THE SIGHT STIRRED FEAR IN THEIR HEARTS. IT WAS ONLY BY A QUIRK OF HISTORY THEY WERE ABLE TO VANQUISH THE AZTECS.
THE SPANISH PRACTICED A FORM OF WAR THAT WAS OBSCENE TO THE AZTECS.
TO THE AZTECS, KILLING ON THE BATTLEFIELD WAS SACRILEGE.
THE AZTECS HAD RUTHLESSLY DOMINATED THE NEIGHBORING CITY-STATES OF THE VALLEY OF MEXICO. WAGING NEVER-ENDING WAR, USING THEIR POPULATION AS VICTIMS OF SACRIFICE TO THE GODS. AFTER GENERATIONS OF BLOODSHED, THESE TRIBES WERE EAGER TO FIGHT BACK. THANKS TO THE AZTECS, CORTÉS HAD AN ARMY.

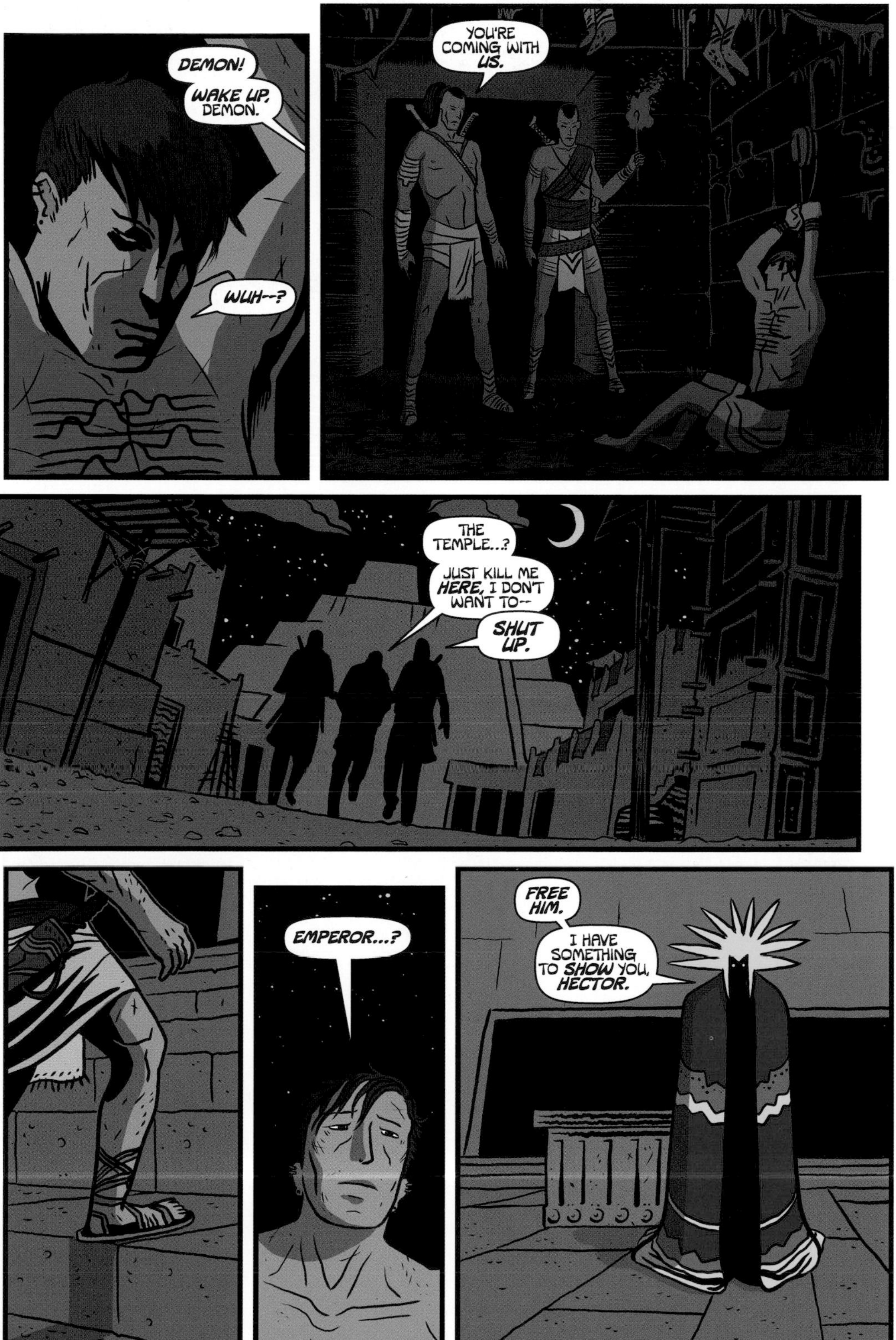
DEMON!
WAKE UP, DEMON.
WUH--?
YOU'RE COMING WITH US.
THE TEMPLE...?
JUST KILL ME HERE, I DON'T WANT TO--
SHUT UP.
EMPEROR...?
FREE HIM.
I HAVE SOMETHING TO SHOW YOU, HECTOR.

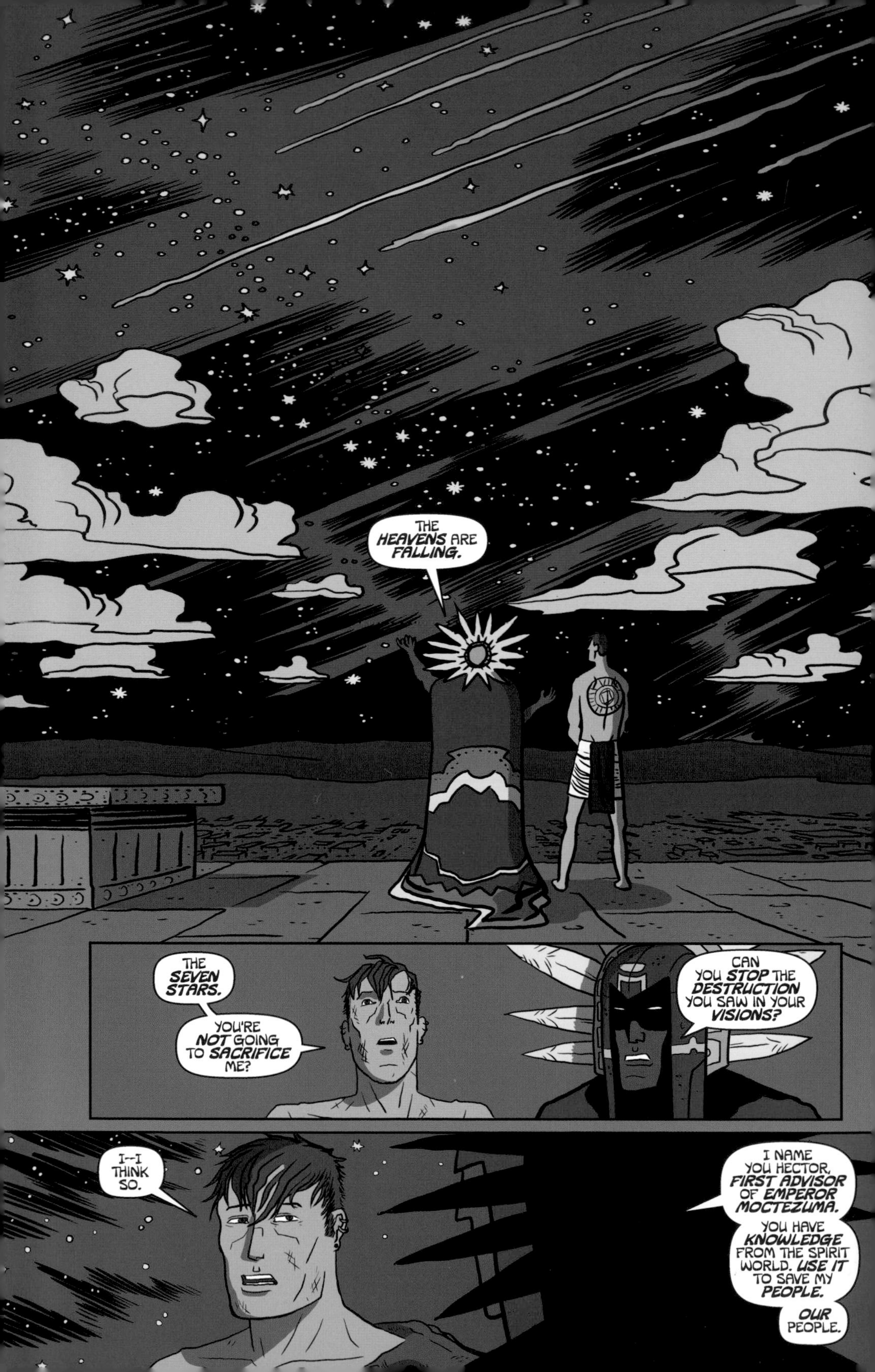

THE HEAVENS ARE FALLING.
THE SEVEN STARS.
YOU'RE NOT GOING TO SACRIFICE ME?
CAN YOU STOP THE DESTRUCTION YOU SAW IN YOUR VISIONS?
I--I THINK SO.
I NAME YOU HECTOR, FIRST ADVISOR OF EMPEROR MOCTEZUMA.
YOU HAVE KNOWLEDGE FROM THE SPIRIT WORLD. USE IT TO SAVE MY PEOPLE.
OUR PEOPLE.

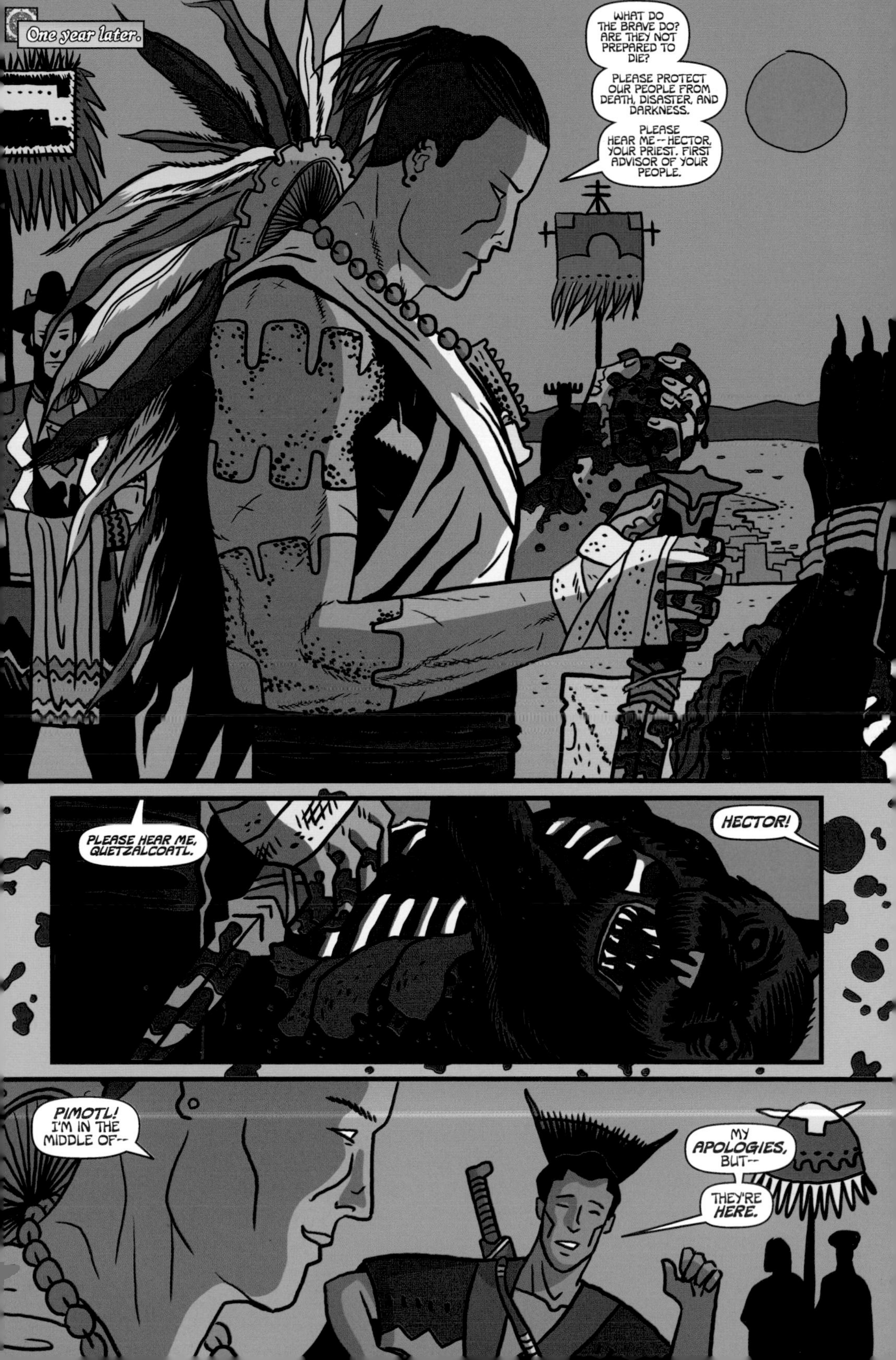
One year later.
WHAT DO THE BRAVE DO? ARE THEY NOT PREPARED TO DIE?
PLEASE PROTECT OUR PEOPLE FROM DEATH, DISASTER, AND DARKNESS.
PLEASE HEAR ME--HECTOR, YOUR PRIEST. FIRST ADVISOR OF YOUR PEOPLE.
PLEASE HEAR ME, QUETZALCOATL.
HECTOR!
PIMOTL! I'M IN THE MIDDLE OF--
MY APOLOGIES, BUT--
THEY'RE HERE.

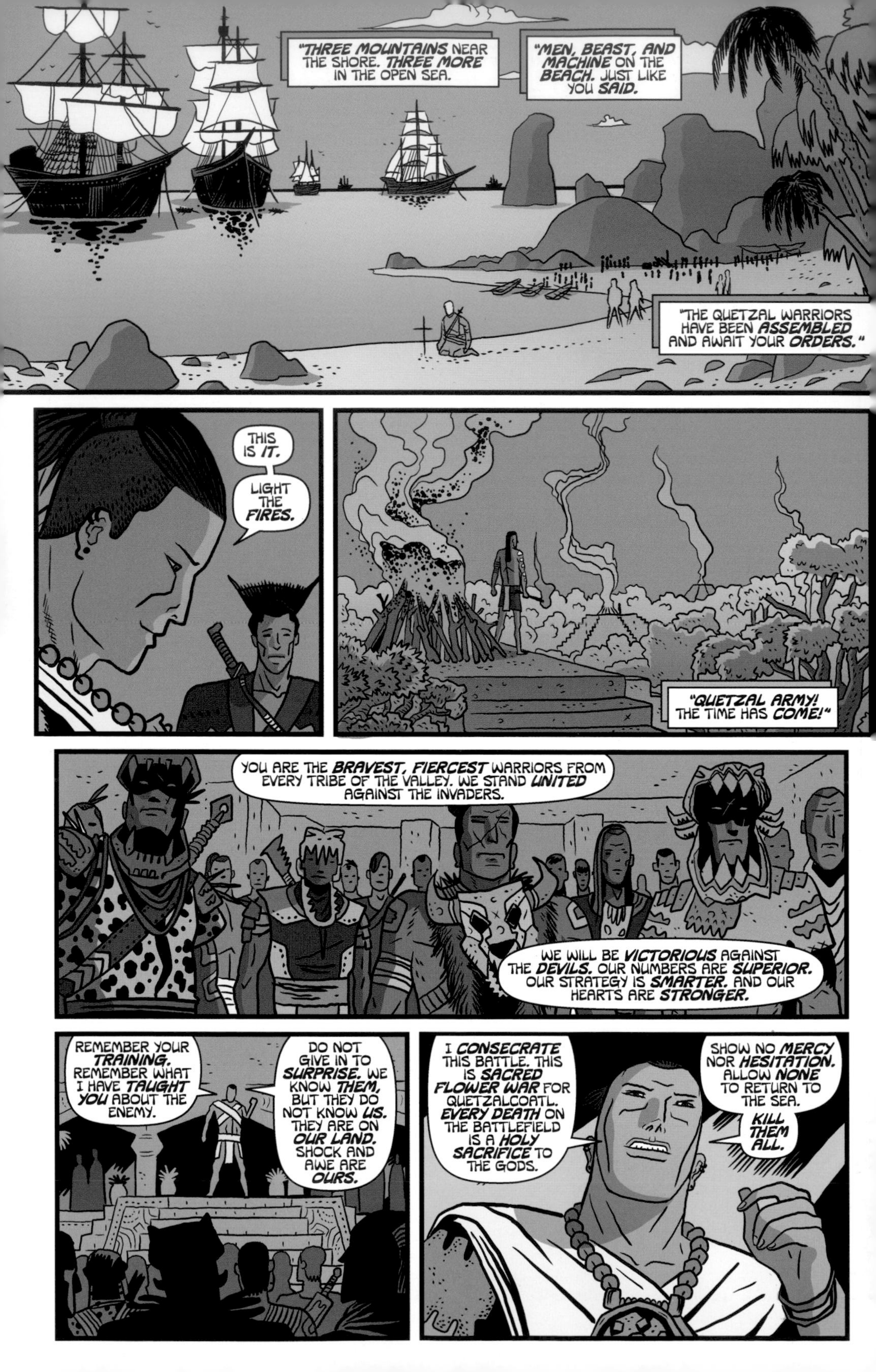
"THREE MOUNTAINS NEAR THE SHORE. THREE MORE IN THE OPEN SEA.
"MEN, BEAST, AND MACHINE ON THE BEACH. JUST LIKE YOU SAID.
"THE QUETZAL WARRIORS HAVE BEEN ASSEMBLED AND AWAIT YOUR ORDERS."
THIS IS IT.
LIGHT THE FIRES.
"QUETZAL ARMY! THE TIME HAS COME!"
YOU ARE THE BRAVEST, FIERCEST WARRIORS FROM EVERY TRIBE OF THE VALLEY. WE STAND UNITED AGAINST THE INVADERS.
WE WILL BE VICTORIOUS AGAINST THE DEVILS. OUR NUMBERS ARE SUPERIOR. OUR STRATEGY IS SMARTER. AND OUR HEARTS ARE STRONGER.
REMEMBER YOUR TRAINING. REMEMBER WHAT I HAVE TAUGHT YOU ABOUT THE ENEMY.
DO NOT GIVE IN TO SURPRISE. WE KNOW THEM, BUT THEY DO NOT KNOW US. THEY ARE ON OUR LAND. SHOCK AND AWE ARE OURS.
I CONSECRATE THIS BATTLE. THIS IS SACRED FLOWER WAR FOR QUETZALCOATL. EVERY DEATH ON THE BATTLEFIELD IS A HOLY SACRIFICE TO THE GODS.
SHOW NO MERCY NOR HESITATION. ALLOW NONE TO RETURN TO THE SEA.
KILL THEM ALL.

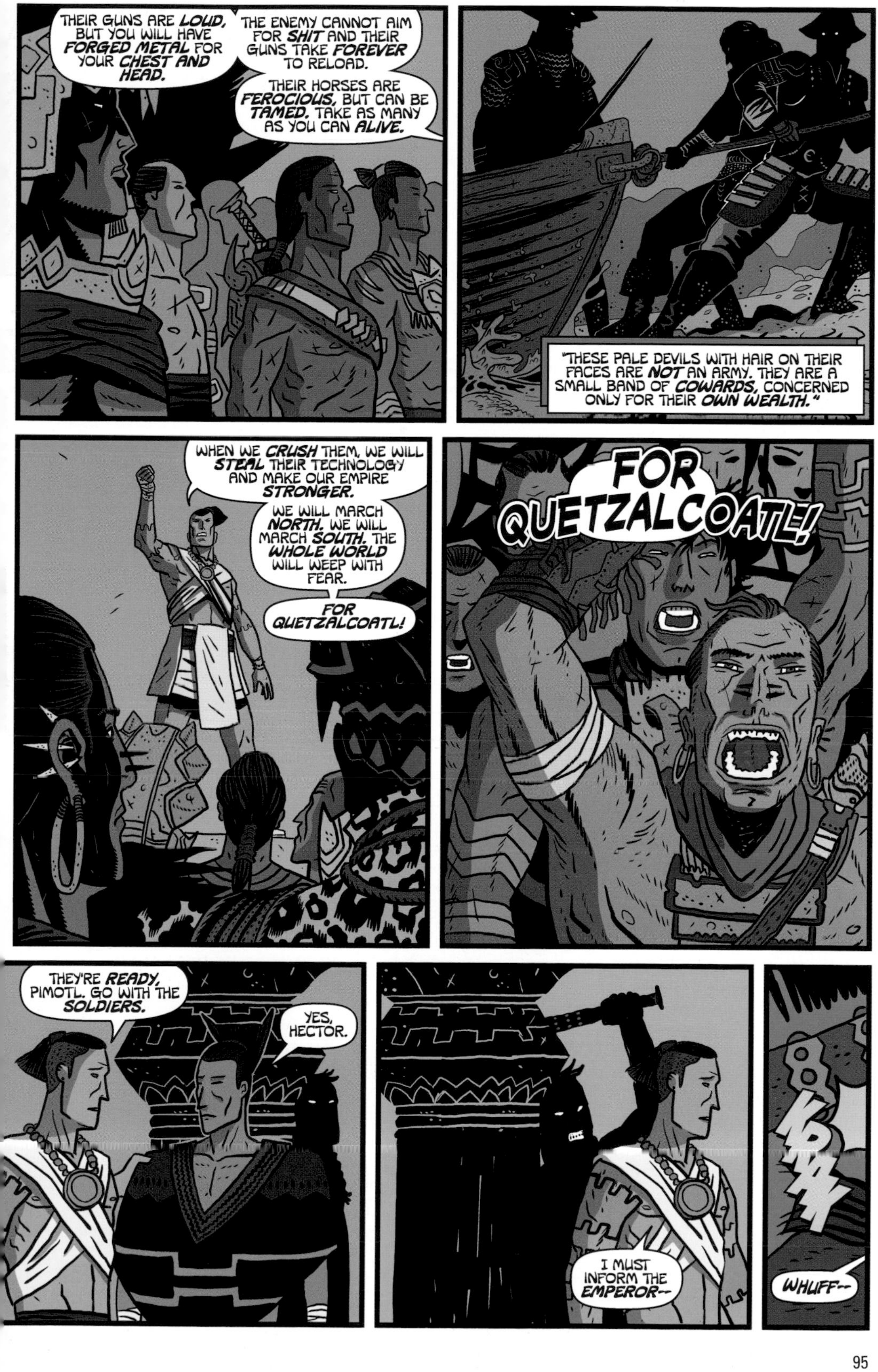
THEIR GUNS ARE LOUD, BUT YOU WILL HAVE FORGED METAL FOR YOUR CHEST AND HEAD.
THE ENEMY CANNOT AIM FOR SHIT AND THEIR GUNS TAKE FOREVER TO RELOAD.
THEIR HORSES ARE FEROCIOUS, BUT CAN BE TAMED. TAKE AS MANY AS YOU CAN ALIVE.
"THESE PALE DEVILS WITH HAIR ON THEIR FACES ARE NOT AN ARMY. THEY ARE A SMALL BAND OF COWARDS, CONCERNED ONLY FOR THEIR OWN WEALTH."
WHEN WE CRUSH THEM, WE WILL STEAL THEIR TECHNOLOGY AND MAKE OUR EMPIRE STRONGER.
WE WILL MARCH NORTH. WE WILL MARCH SOUTH. THE WHOLE WORLD WILL WEEP WITH FEAR.
FOR QUETZALCOATL!
FOR QUETZALCOATL!
THEY'RE READY, PIMOTL. GO WITH THE SOLDIERS.
YES, HECTOR.
I MUST INFORM THE EMPEROR--
KRAK
WHUFF--

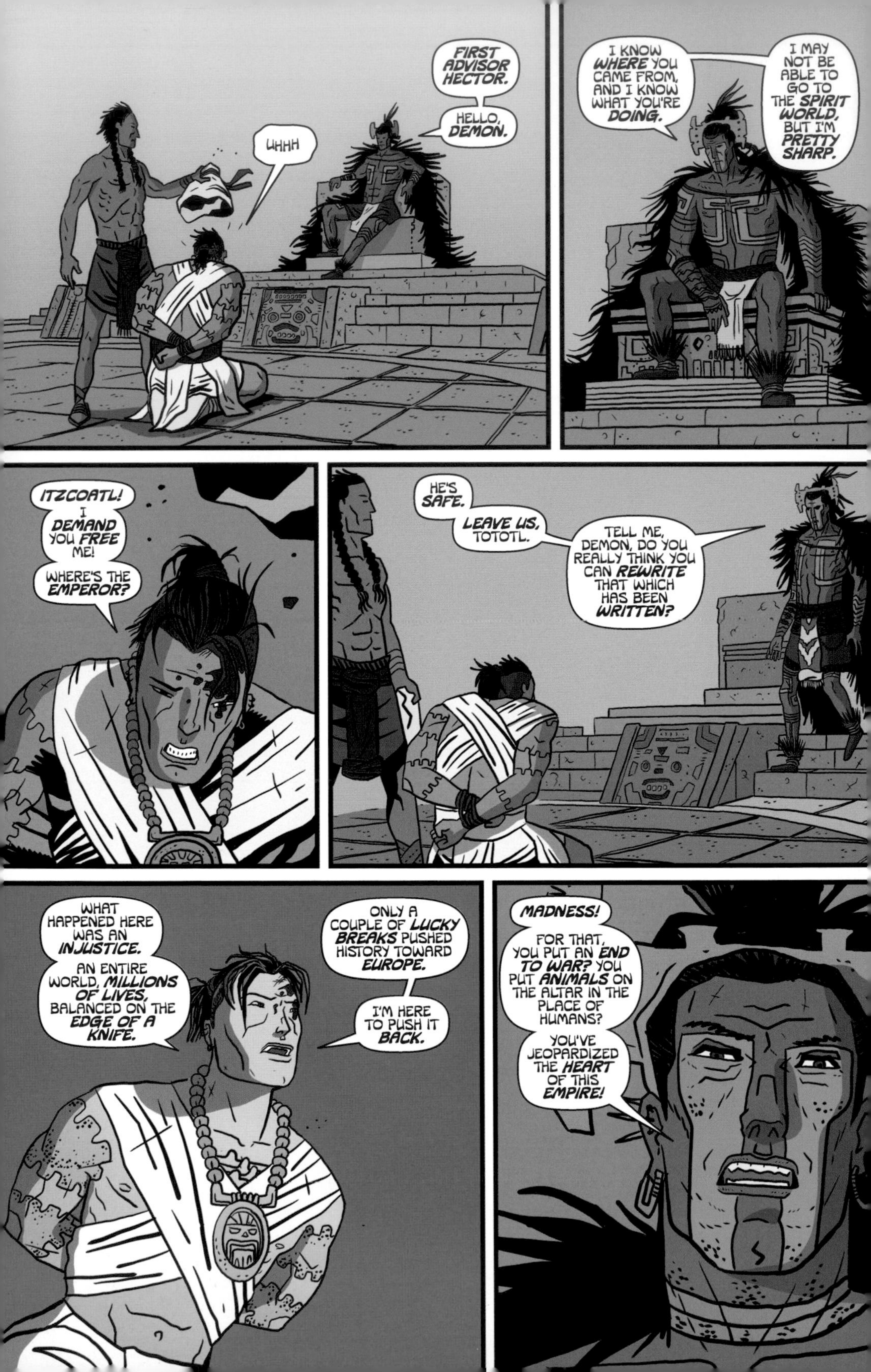
UHHH
FIRST ADVISOR HECTOR.
HELLO, DEMON.
I KNOW WHERE YOU CAME FROM, AND I KNOW WHAT YOU'RE DOING.
I MAY NOT BE ABLE TO GO TO THE SPIRIT WORLD, BUT I'M PRETTY SHARP.
ITZCOATL! I DEMAND YOU FREE ME!
WHERE'S THE EMPEROR?
HE'S SAFE.
LEAVE US, TOTOTL.
TELL ME, DEMON, DO YOU REALLY THINK YOU CAN REWRITE THAT WHICH HAS BEEN WRITTEN?
WHAT HAPPENED HERE WAS AN INJUSTICE.
AN ENTIRE WORLD, MILLIONS OF LIVES, BALANCED ON THE EDGE OF A KNIFE.
ONLY A COUPLE OF LUCKY BREAKS PUSHED HISTORY TOWARD EUROPE.
I'M HERE TO PUSH IT BACK.
MADNESS!
FOR THAT, YOU PUT AN END TO WAR? YOU PUT ANIMALS ON THE ALTAR IN THE PLACE OF HUMANS?
YOU'VE JEOPARDIZED THE HEART OF THIS EMPIRE!

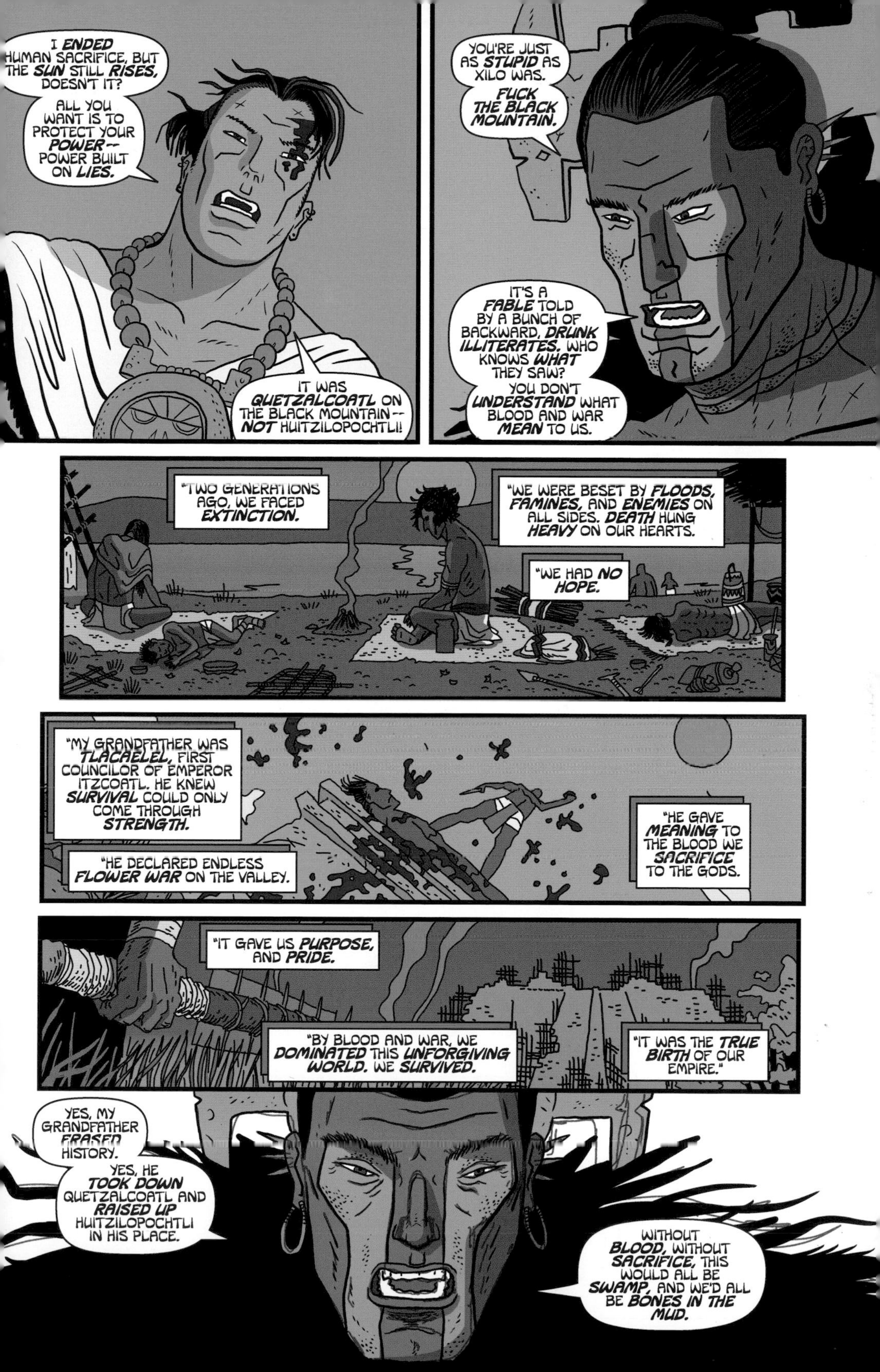
I ENDED HUMAN SACRIFICE, BUT THE SUN STILL RISES, DOESN'T IT?
ALL YOU WANT IS TO PROTECT YOUR POWER-- POWER BUILT ON LIES.
IT WAS QUETZALCOATL ON THE BLACK MOUNTAIN-- NOT HUITZILOPOCHTLI!
YOU'RE JUST AS STUPID AS XILO WAS.
FUCK THE BLACK MOUNTAIN.
IT'S A FABLE TOLD BY A BUNCH OF BACKWARD, DRUNK ILLITERATES. WHO KNOWS WHAT THEY SAW?
YOU DON'T UNDERSTAND WHAT BLOOD AND WAR MEAN TO US.
"TWO GENERATIONS AGO, WE FACED EXTINCTION.
"WE WERE BESET BY FLOODS, FAMINES, AND ENEMIES ON ALL SIDES. DEATH HUNG HEAVY ON OUR HEARTS.
"WE HAD NO HOPE.
"MY GRANDFATHER WAS TLACAELEL, FIRST COUNCILOR OF EMPEROR ITZCOATL. HE KNEW SURVIVAL COULD ONLY COME THROUGH STRENGTH.
"HE DECLARED ENDLESS FLOWER WAR ON THE VALLEY.
"HE GAVE MEANING TO THE BLOOD WE SACRIFICE TO THE GODS.
"IT GAVE US PURPOSE, AND PRIDE.
"BY BLOOD AND WAR, WE DOMINATED THIS UNFORGIVING WORLD. WE SURVIVED.
"IT WAS THE TRUE BIRTH OF OUR EMPIRE."
YES, MY GRANDFATHER ERASED HISTORY.
YES, HE TOOK DOWN QUETZALCOATL AND RAISED UP HUITZILOPOCHTLI IN HIS PLACE.
WITHOUT BLOOD, WITHOUT SACRIFICE, THIS WOULD ALL BE SWAMP, AND WE'D ALL BE BONES IN THE MUD.

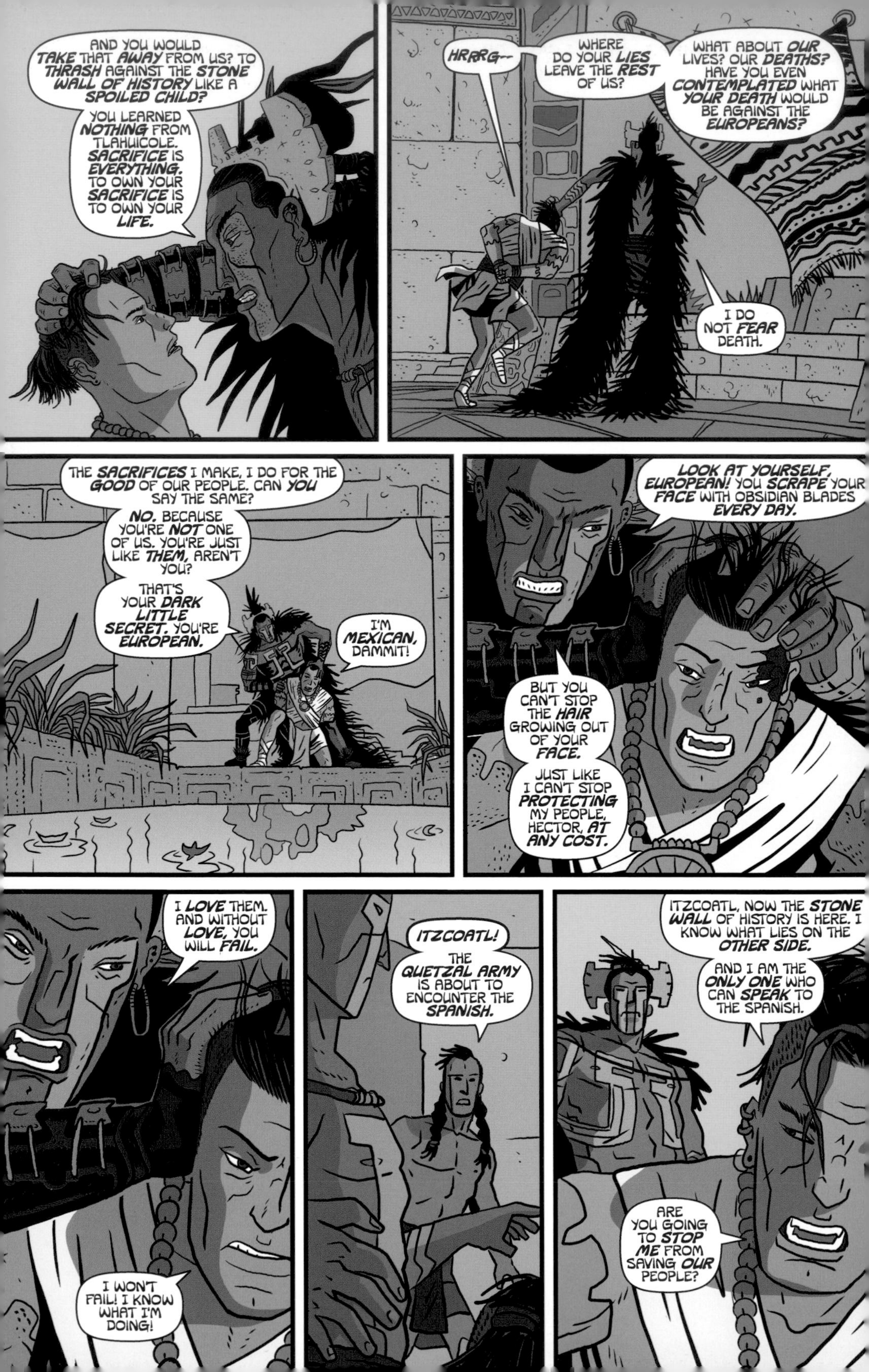
AND YOU WOULD TAKE THAT AWAY FROM US? TO THRASH AGAINST THE STONE WALL OF HISTORY LIKE A SPOILED CHILD?
YOU LEARNED NOTHING FROM TLAHUICOLE. SACRIFICE IS EVERYTHING. TO OWN YOUR SACRIFICE IS TO OWN YOUR LIFE.
HRRRG--
WHERE DO YOUR LIES LEAVE THE REST OF US?
WHAT ABOUT OUR LIVES? OUR DEATHS? HAVE YOU EVEN CONTEMPLATED WHAT YOUR DEATH WOULD BE AGAINST THE EUROPEANS?
I DO NOT FEAR DEATH.
THE SACRIFICES I MAKE, I DO FOR THE GOOD OF OUR PEOPLE. CAN YOU SAY THE SAME?
NO. BECAUSE YOU'RE NOT ONE OF US. YOU'RE JUST LIKE THEM, AREN'T YOU?
THAT'S YOUR DARK LITTLE SECRET. YOU'RE EUROPEAN.
I'M MEXICAN, DAMMIT!
LOOK AT YOURSELF, EUROPEAN! YOU SCRAPE YOUR FACE WITH OBSIDIAN BLADES EVERY DAY.
BUT YOU CAN'T STOP THE HAIR GROWING OUT OF YOUR FACE.
JUST LIKE I CAN'T STOP PROTECTING MY PEOPLE, HECTOR, AT ANY COST.
I LOVE THEM. AND WITHOUT LOVE, YOU WILL FAIL.
I WON'T FAIL! I KNOW WHAT I'M DOING!
ITZCOATL!
THE QUETZAL ARMY IS ABOUT TO ENCOUNTER THE SPANISH.
ITZCOATL, NOW THE STONE WALL OF HISTORY IS HERE. I KNOW WHAT LIES ON THE OTHER SIDE.
AND I AM THE ONLY ONE WHO CAN SPEAK TO THE SPANISH.
ARE YOU GOING TO STOP ME FROM SAVING OUR PEOPLE?

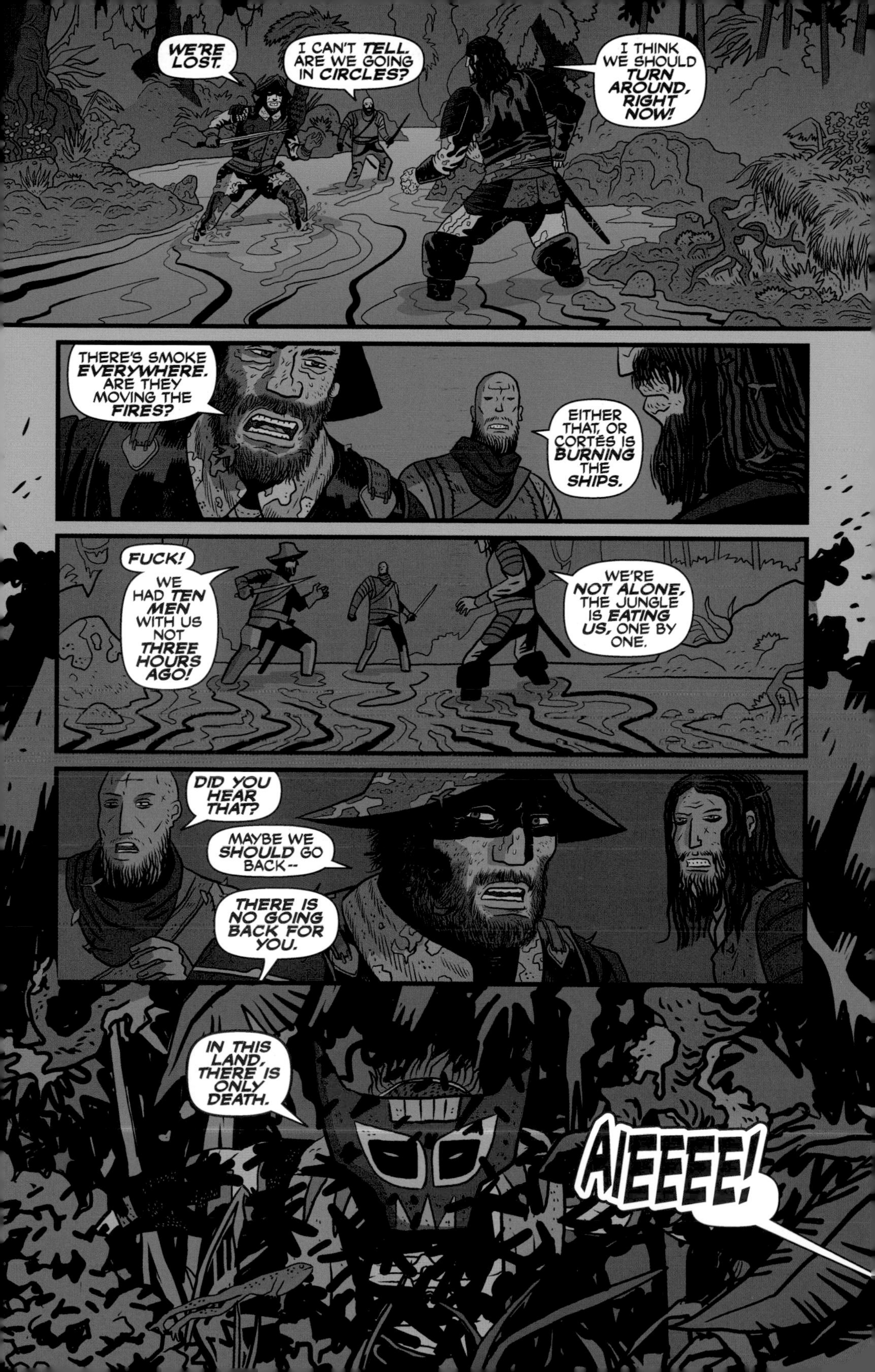
WE'RE LOST.
I CAN'T TELL. ARE WE GOING IN CIRCLES?
I THINK WE SHOULD TURN AROUND, RIGHT NOW!
THERE'S SMOKE EVERYWHERE. ARE THEY MOVING THE FIRES?
EITHER THAT, OR CORTÉS IS BURNING THE SHIPS.
FUCK! WE HAD TEN MEN WITH US NOT THREE HOURS AGO!
WE'RE NOT ALONE, THE JUNGLE IS EATING US, ONE BY ONE.
DID YOU HEAR THAT?
MAYBE WE SHOULD GO BACK--
THERE IS NO GOING BACK FOR YOU.
IN THIS LAND, THERE IS ONLY DEATH.
AIEEEE!

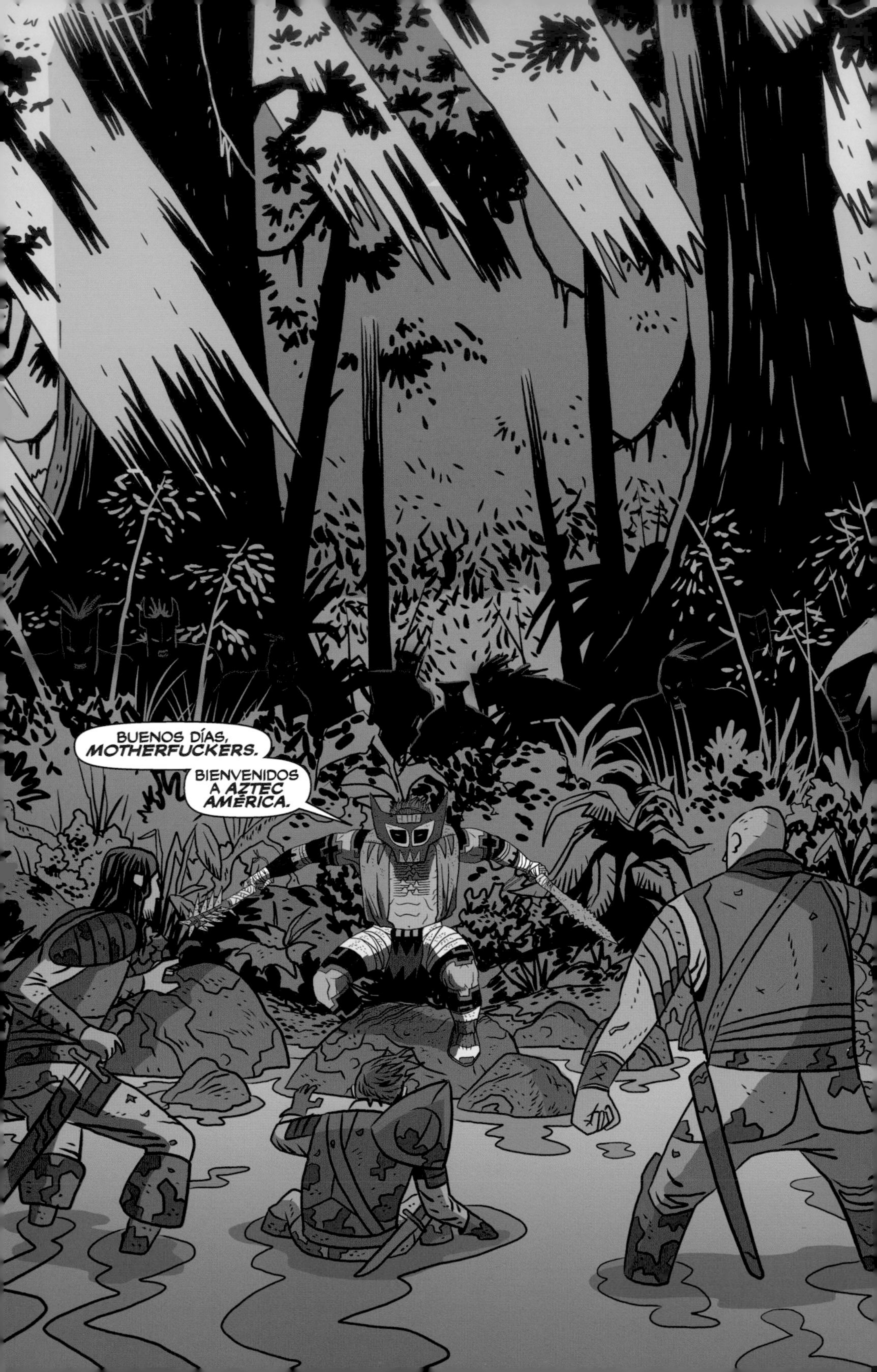
BUENOS DÍAS, MOTHERFUCKERS.
BIENVENIDOS A AZTEC AMÉRICA.

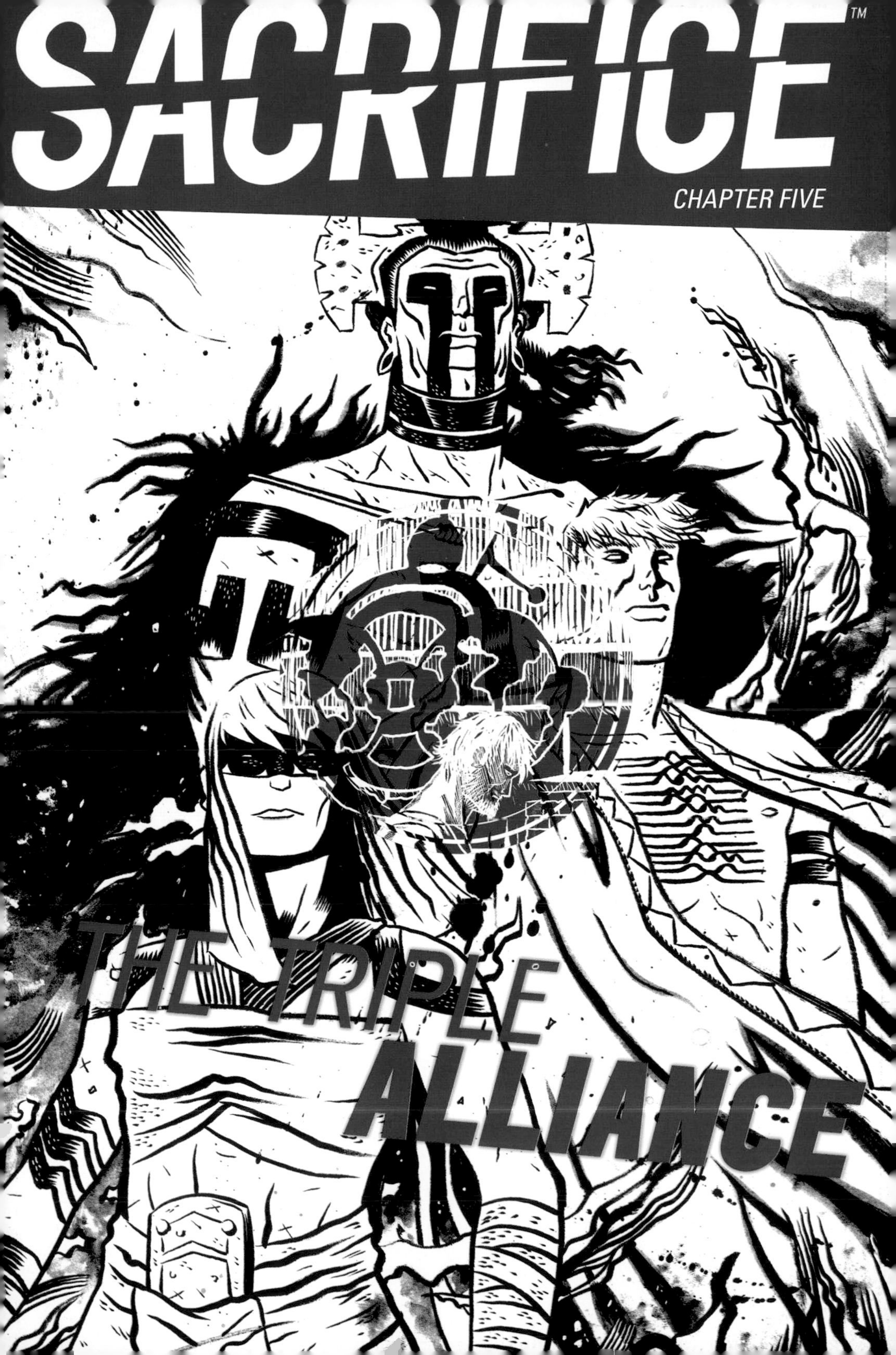

SACRIFICE™
CHAPTER FIVE
THE TRIPLE ALLIANCE

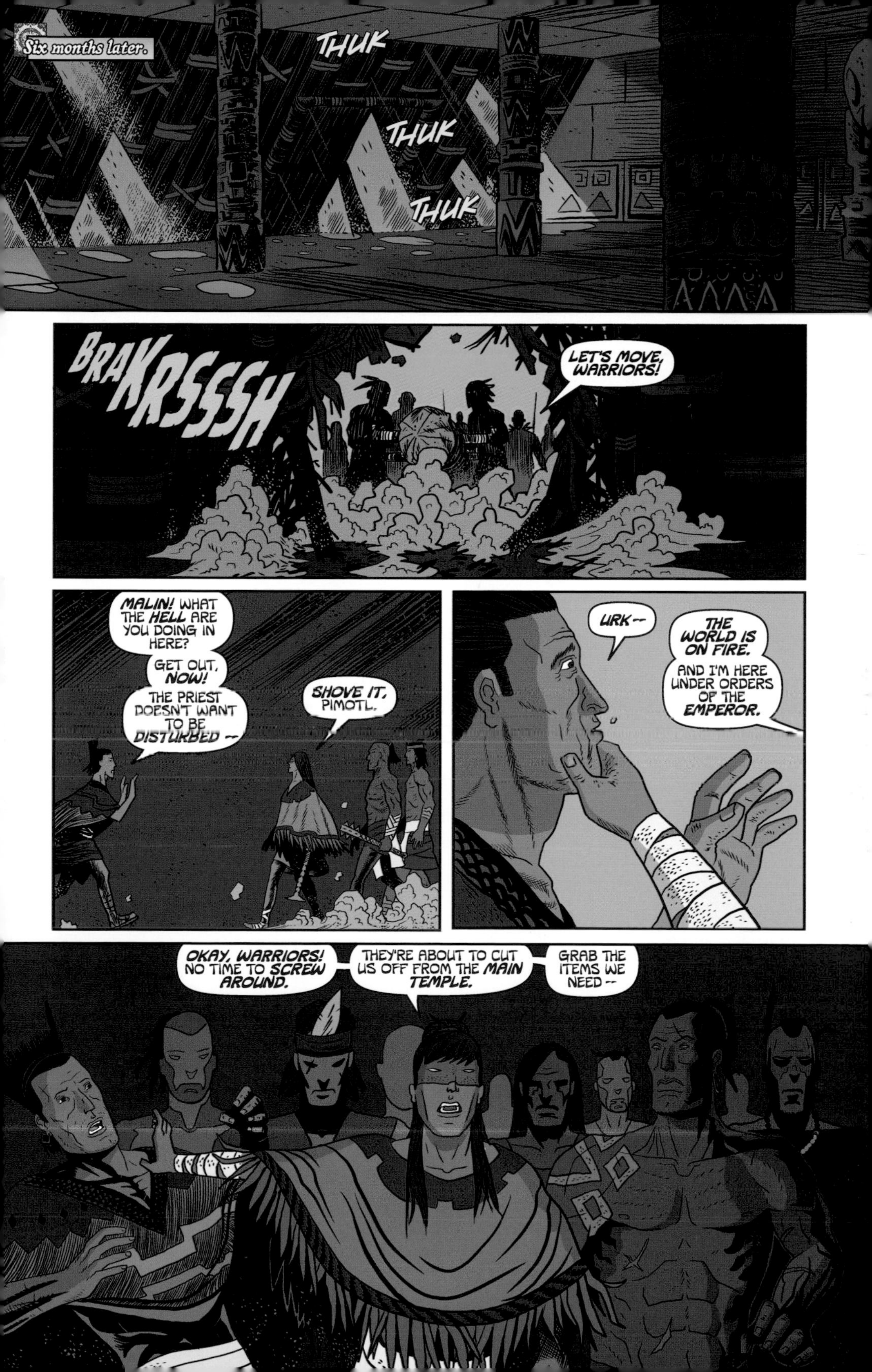
Six months later.
THUK
THUK
THUK
BRAKRSSSH
LET'S MOVE, WARRIORS!
MALIN! WHAT THE HELL ARE YOU DOING IN HERE?
GET OUT, NOW!
THE PRIEST DOESN'T WANT TO BE DISTURBED --
SHOVE IT, PIMOTL.
URK --
THE WORLD IS ON FIRE.
AND I'M HERE UNDER ORDERS OF THE EMPEROR.
OKAY, WARRIORS! NO TIME TO SCREW AROUND.
THEY'RE ABOUT TO CUT US OFF FROM THE MAIN TEMPLE.
GRAB THE ITEMS WE NEED --

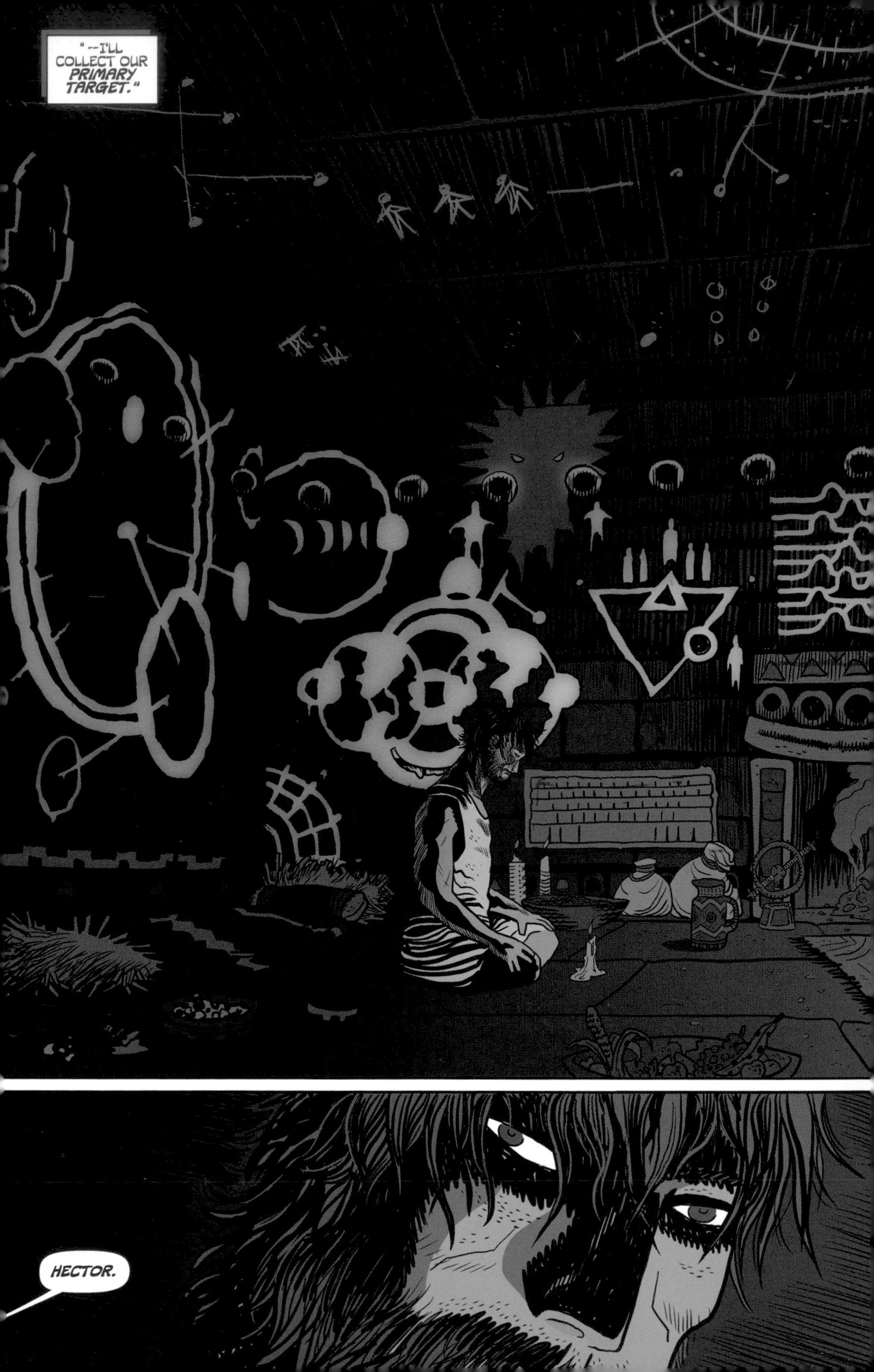
"--I'LL COLLECT OUR PRIMARY TARGET."
HECTOR.

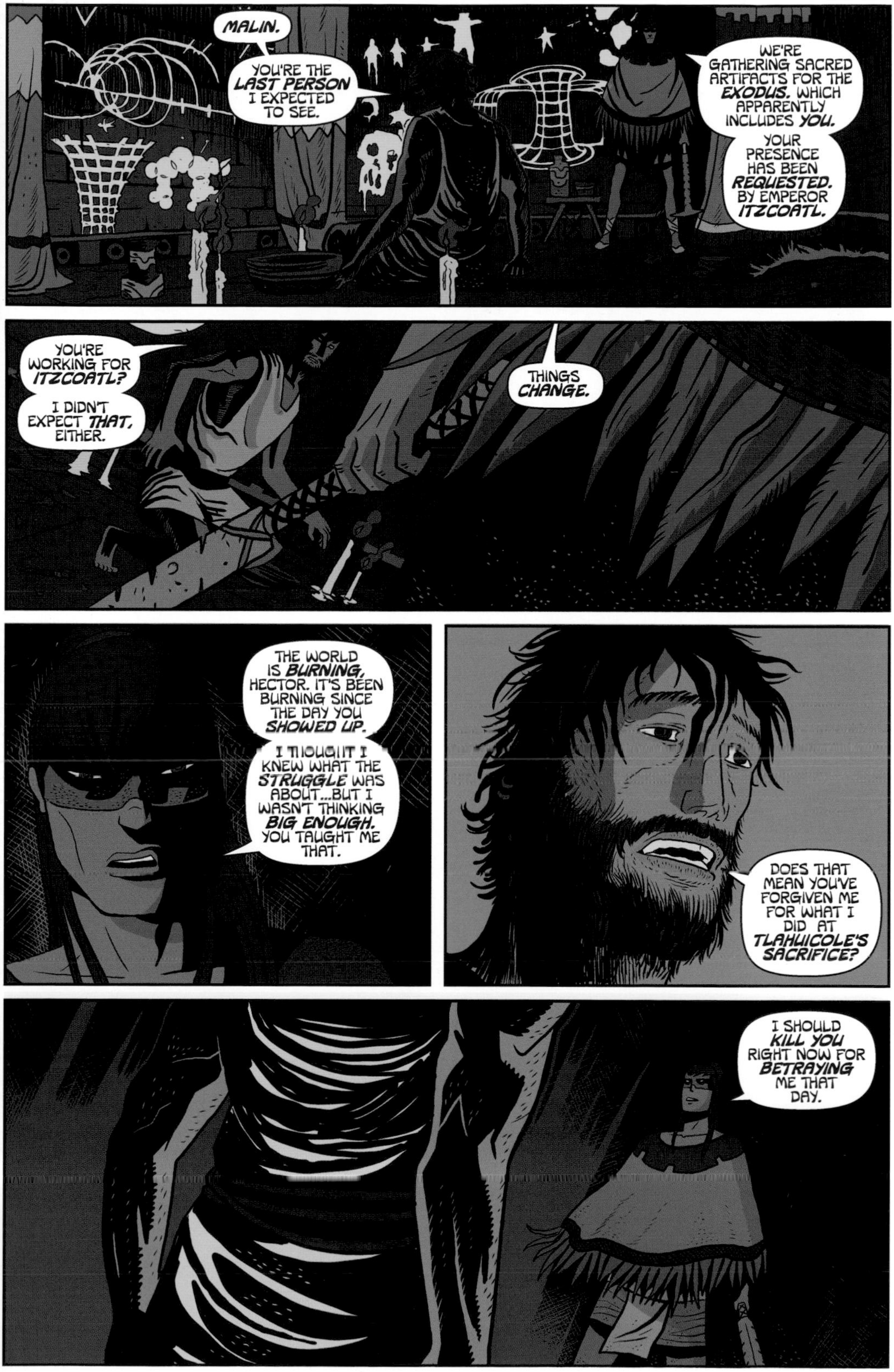
MALIN.
YOU'RE THE LAST PERSON I EXPECTED TO SEE.
WE'RE GATHERING SACRED ARTIFACTS FOR THE EXODUS. WHICH APPARENTLY INCLUDES YOU.
YOUR PRESENCE HAS BEEN REQUESTED. BY EMPEROR ITZCOATL.
YOU'RE WORKING FOR ITZCOATL?
I DIDN'T EXPECT THAT, EITHER.
THINGS CHANGE.
THE WORLD IS BURNING, HECTOR. IT'S BEEN BURNING SINCE THE DAY YOU SHOWED UP.
I THOUGHT I KNEW WHAT THE STRUGGLE WAS ABOUT...BUT I WASN'T THINKING BIG ENOUGH. YOU TAUGHT ME THAT.
DOES THAT MEAN YOU'VE FORGIVEN ME FOR WHAT I DID AT TLAHUICOLE'S SACRIFICE?
I SHOULD KILL YOU RIGHT NOW FOR BETRAYING ME THAT DAY.

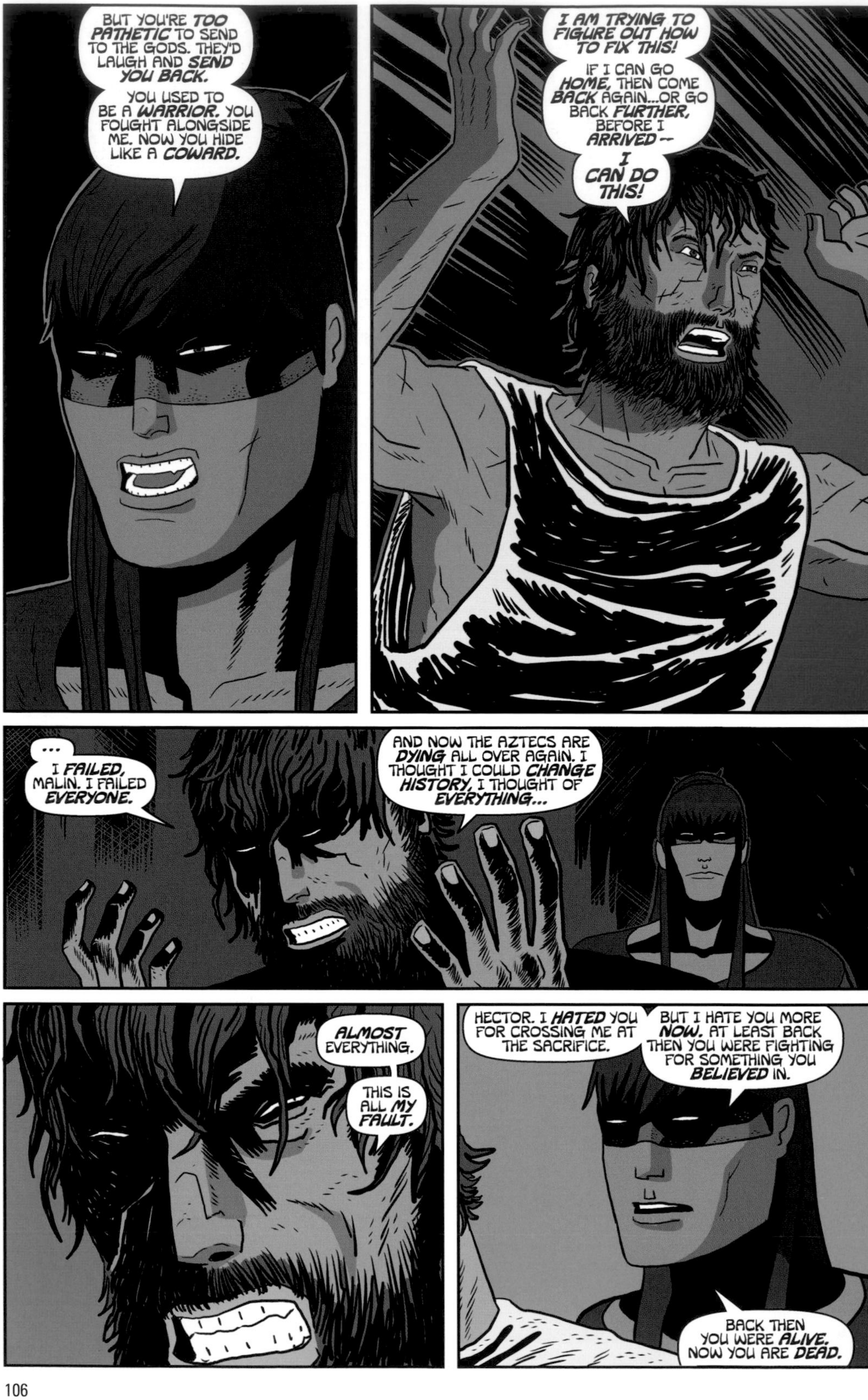
BUT YOU'RE TOO PATHETIC TO SEND TO THE GODS. THEY'D LAUGH AND SEND YOU BACK.
YOU USED TO BE A WARRIOR. YOU FOUGHT ALONGSIDE ME. NOW YOU HIDE LIKE A COWARD.
I AM TRYING TO FIGURE OUT HOW TO FIX THIS!
IF I CAN GO HOME, THEN COME BACK AGAIN...OR GO BACK FURTHER, BEFORE I ARRIVED --
I CAN DO THIS!
...
I FAILED, MALIN. I FAILED EVERYONE.
AND NOW THE AZTECS ARE DYING ALL OVER AGAIN. I THOUGHT I COULD CHANGE HISTORY, I THOUGHT OF EVERYTHING...
ALMOST EVERYTHING.
THIS IS ALL MY FAULT.
HECTOR. I HATED YOU FOR CROSSING ME AT THE SACRIFICE.
BUT I HATE YOU MORE NOW. AT LEAST BACK THEN YOU WERE FIGHTING FOR SOMETHING YOU BELIEVED IN.
BACK THEN YOU WERE ALIVE. NOW YOU ARE DEAD.

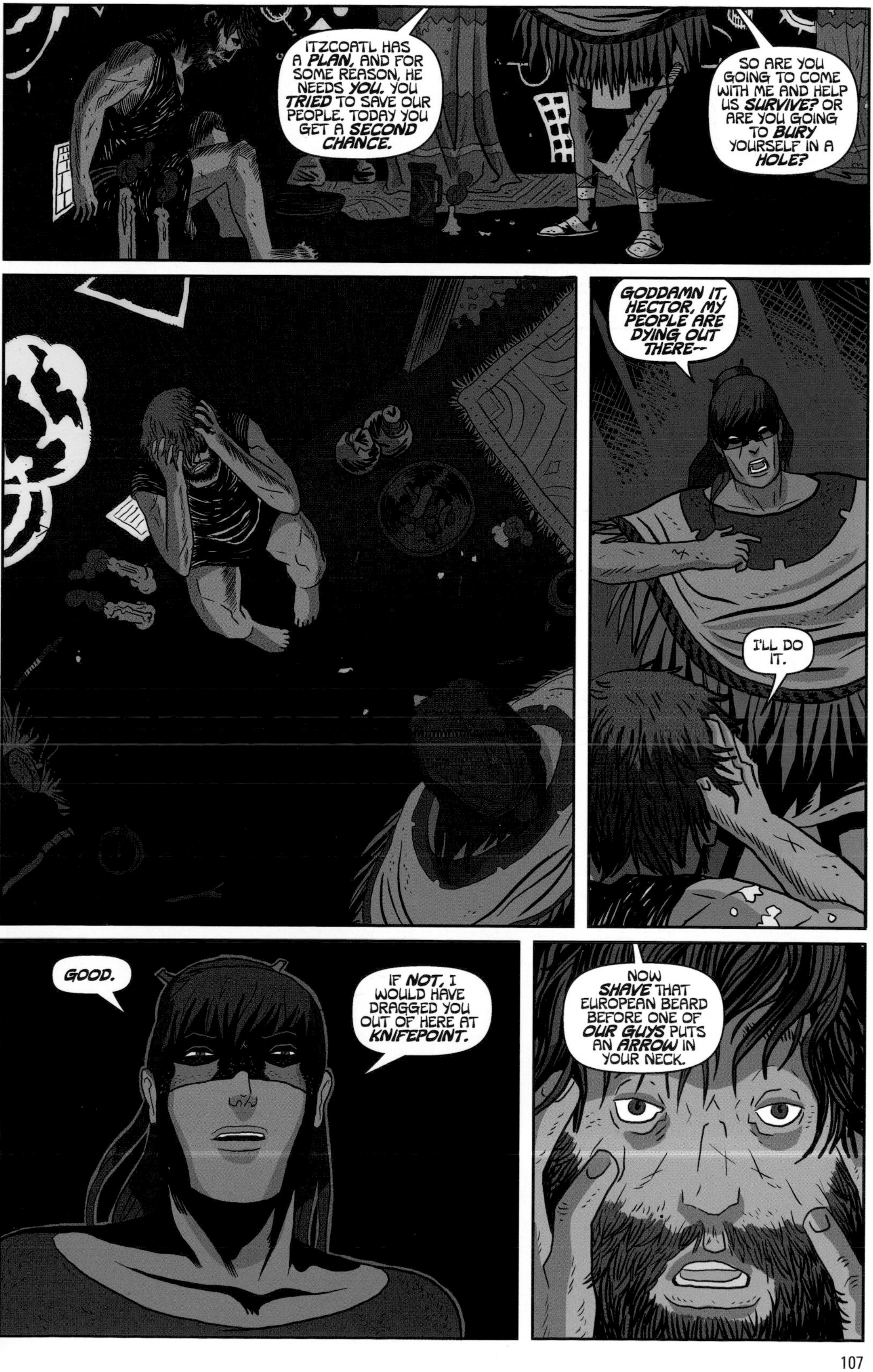
ITZCOATL HAS A PLAN, AND FOR SOME REASON, HE NEEDS YOU. YOU TRIED TO SAVE OUR PEOPLE. TODAY YOU GET A SECOND CHANCE.
SO ARE YOU GOING TO COME WITH ME AND HELP US SURVIVE? OR ARE YOU GOING TO BURY YOURSELF IN A HOLE?
GODDAMN IT, HECTOR, MY PEOPLE ARE DYING OUT THERE--
I'LL DO IT.
GOOD.
IF NOT, I WOULD HAVE DRAGGED YOU OUT OF HERE AT KNIFEPOINT.
NOW SHAVE THAT EUROPEAN BEARD BEFORE ONE OF OUR GUYS PUTS AN ARROW IN YOUR NECK.

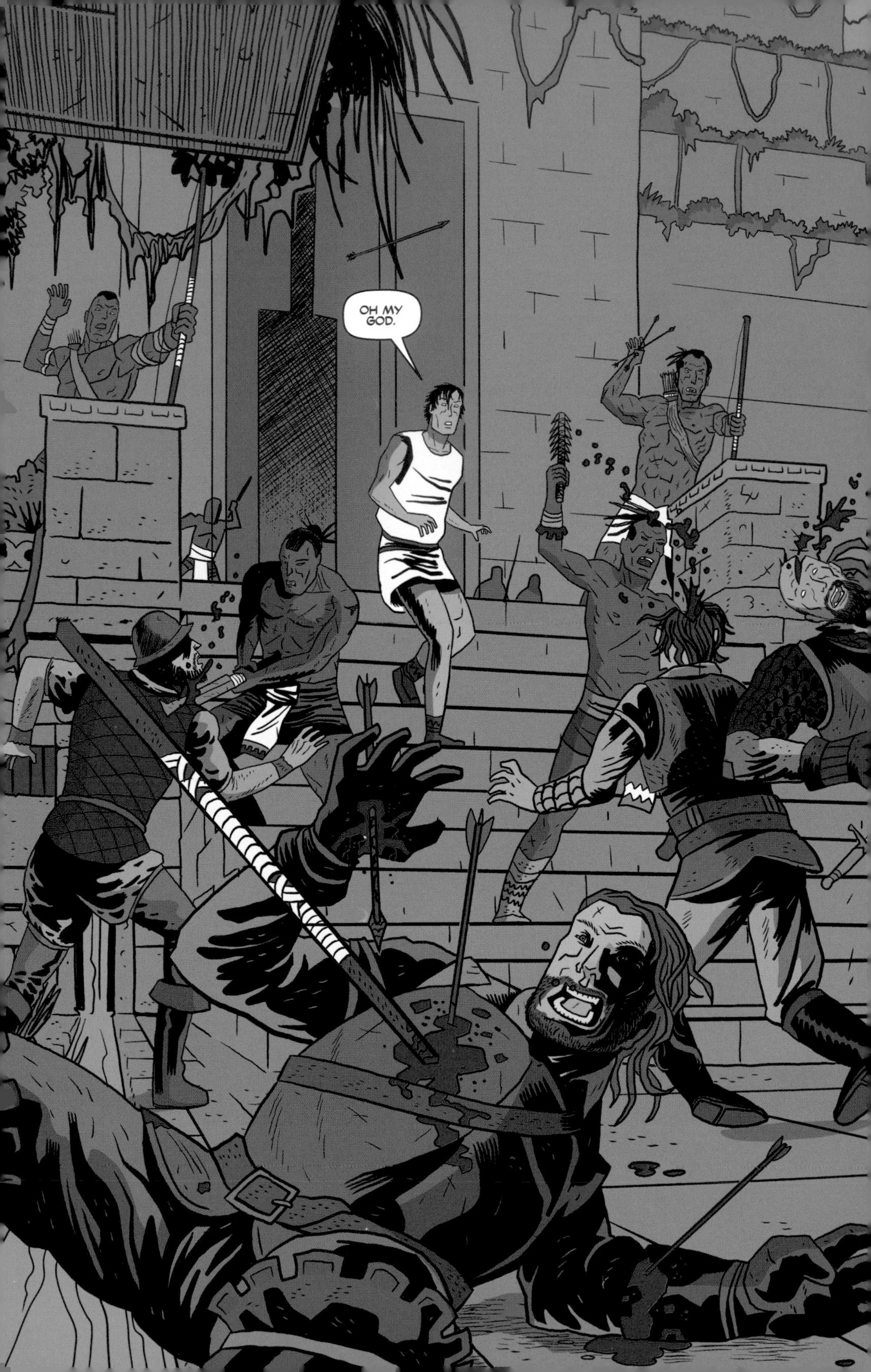
OH MY GOD.

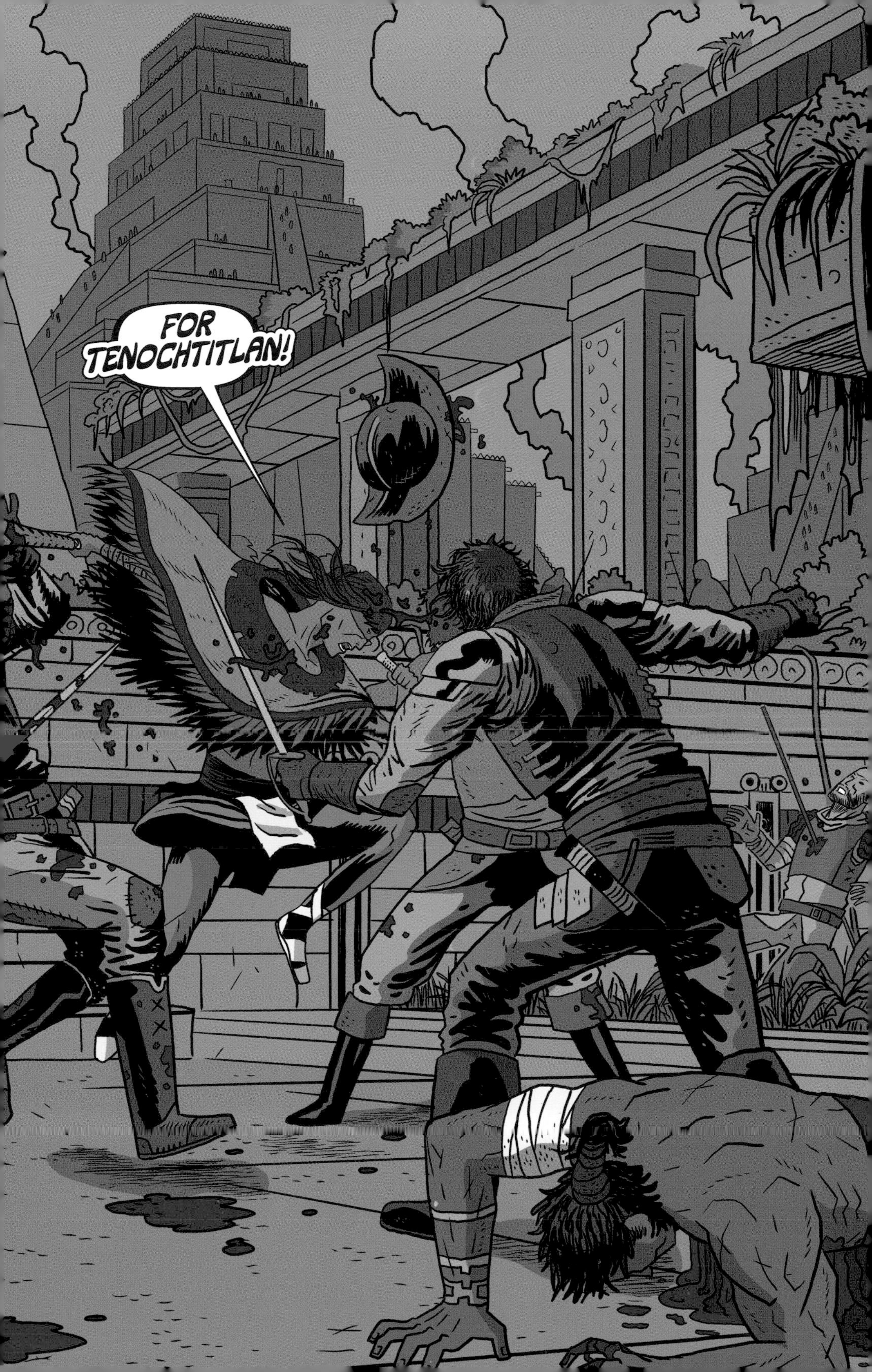
FOR TENOCHTITLAN!

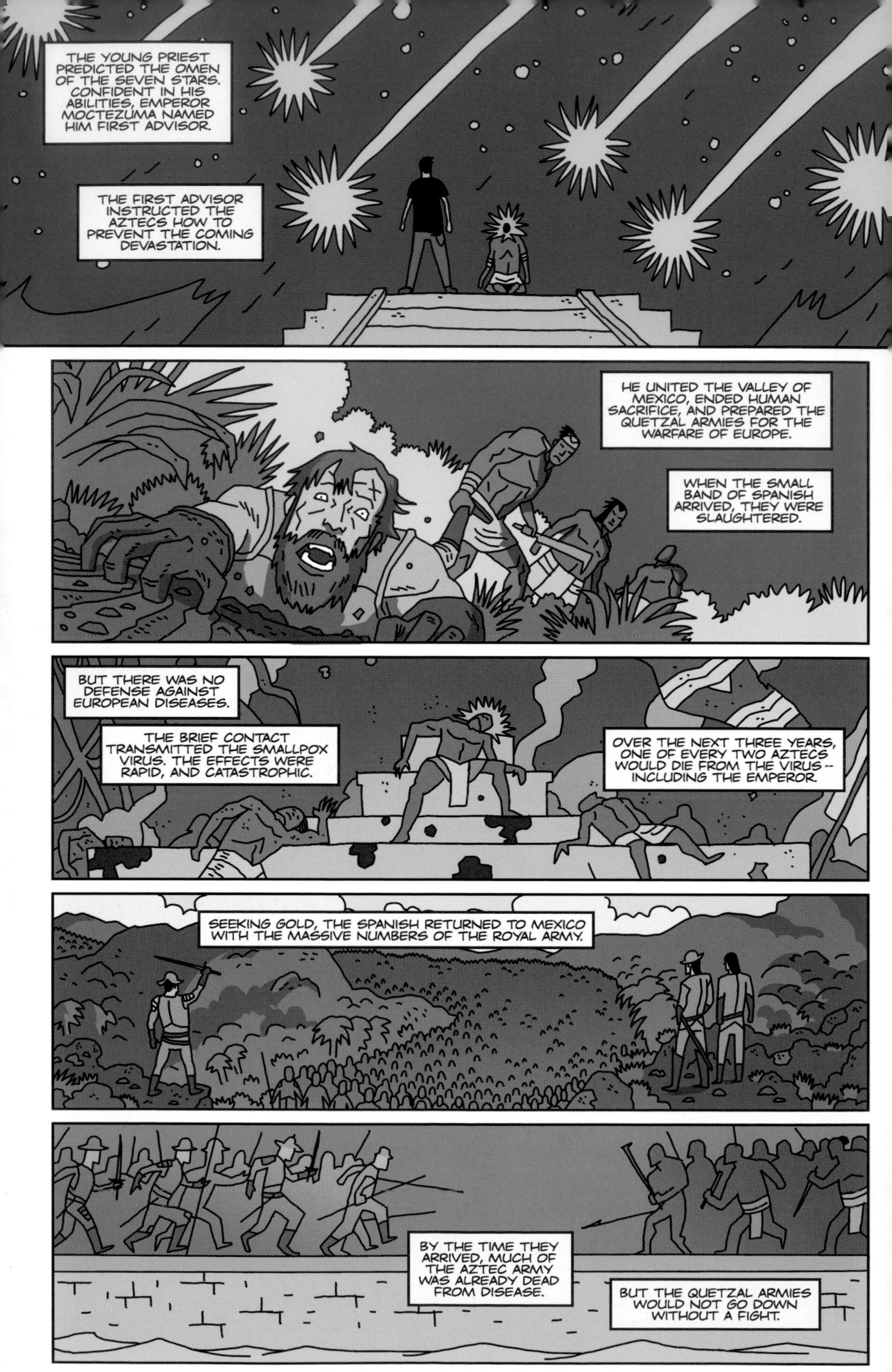
THE YOUNG PRIEST PREDICTED THE OMEN OF THE SEVEN STARS. CONFIDENT IN HIS ABILITIES, EMPEROR MOCTEZUMA NAMED HIM FIRST ADVISOR.
THE FIRST ADVISOR INSTRUCTED THE AZTECS HOW TO PREVENT THE COMING DEVASTATION.
HE UNITED THE VALLEY OF MEXICO, ENDED HUMAN SACRIFICE, AND PREPARED THE QUETZAL ARMIES FOR THE WARFARE OF EUROPE.
WHEN THE SMALL BAND OF SPANISH ARRIVED, THEY WERE SLAUGHTERED.
BUT THERE WAS NO DEFENSE AGAINST EUROPEAN DISEASES.
THE BRIEF CONTACT TRANSMITTED THE SMALLPOX VIRUS. THE EFFECTS WERE RAPID, AND CATASTROPHIC.
OVER THE NEXT THREE YEARS, ONE OF EVERY TWO AZTECS WOULD DIE FROM THE VIRUS -- INCLUDING THE EMPEROR.
SEEKING GOLD, THE SPANISH RETURNED TO MEXICO WITH THE MASSIVE NUMBERS OF THE ROYAL ARMY.
BY THE TIME THEY ARRIVED, MUCH OF THE AZTEC ARMY WAS ALREADY DEAD FROM DISEASE.
BUT THE QUETZAL ARMIES WOULD NOT GO DOWN WITHOUT A FIGHT.

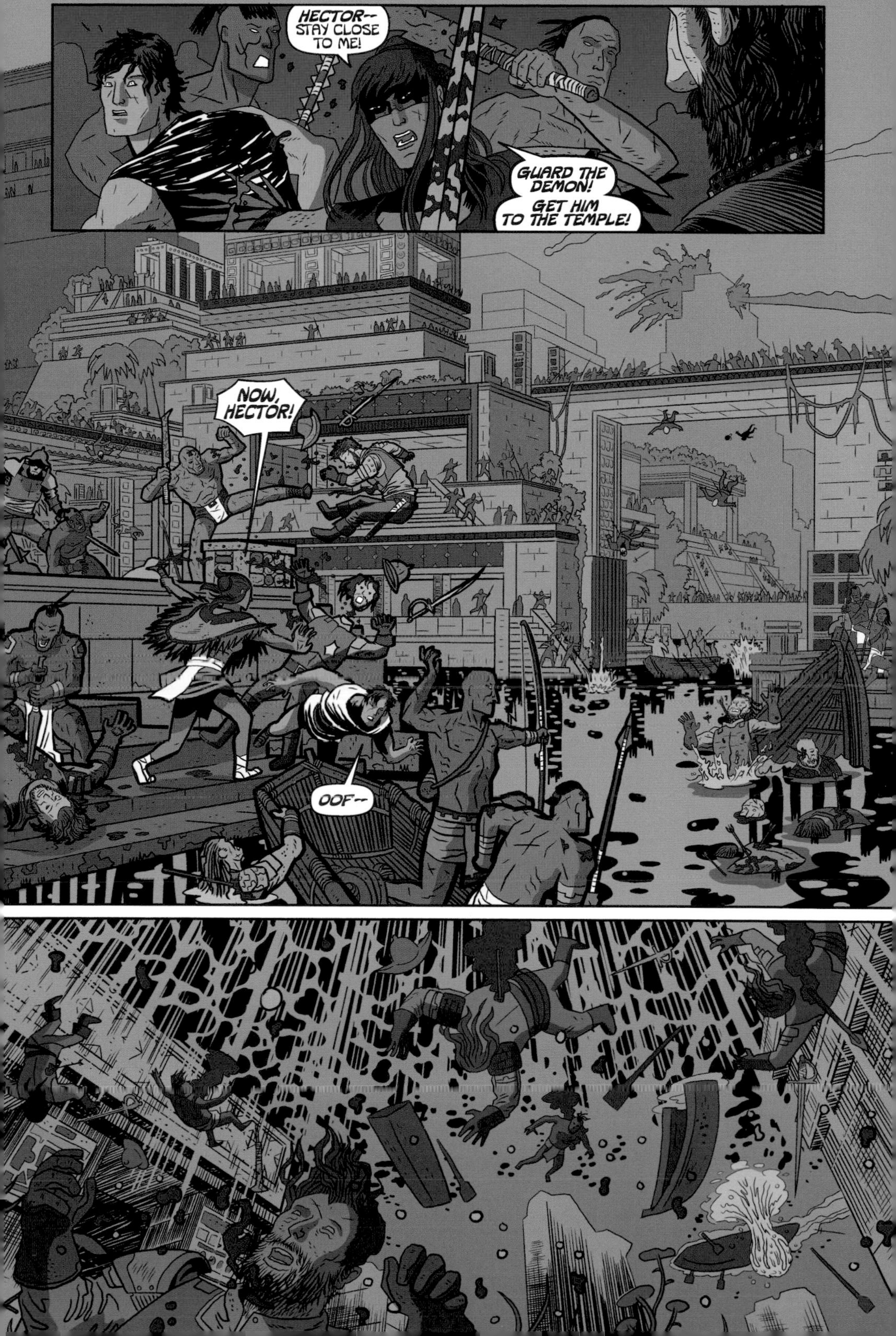
HECTOR-- STAY CLOSE TO ME!
GUARD THE DEMON! GET HIM TO THE TEMPLE!
NOW, HECTOR!
OOF--

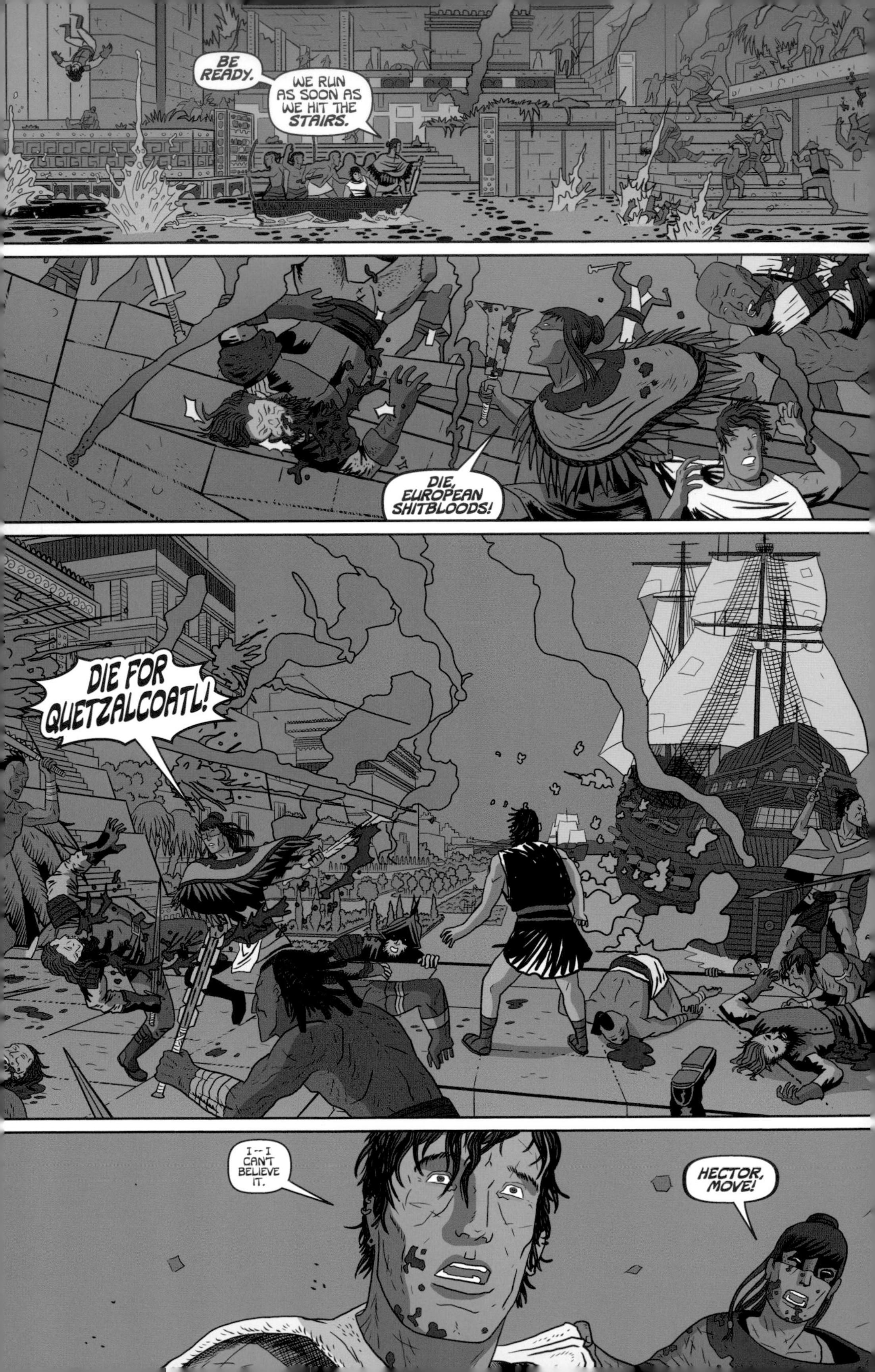
BE READY.
WE RUN AS SOON AS WE HIT THE STAIRS.
DIE, EUROPEAN SHITBLOODS!
DIE FOR QUETZALCOATL!
I -- I CAN'T BELIEVE IT.
HECTOR, MOVE!

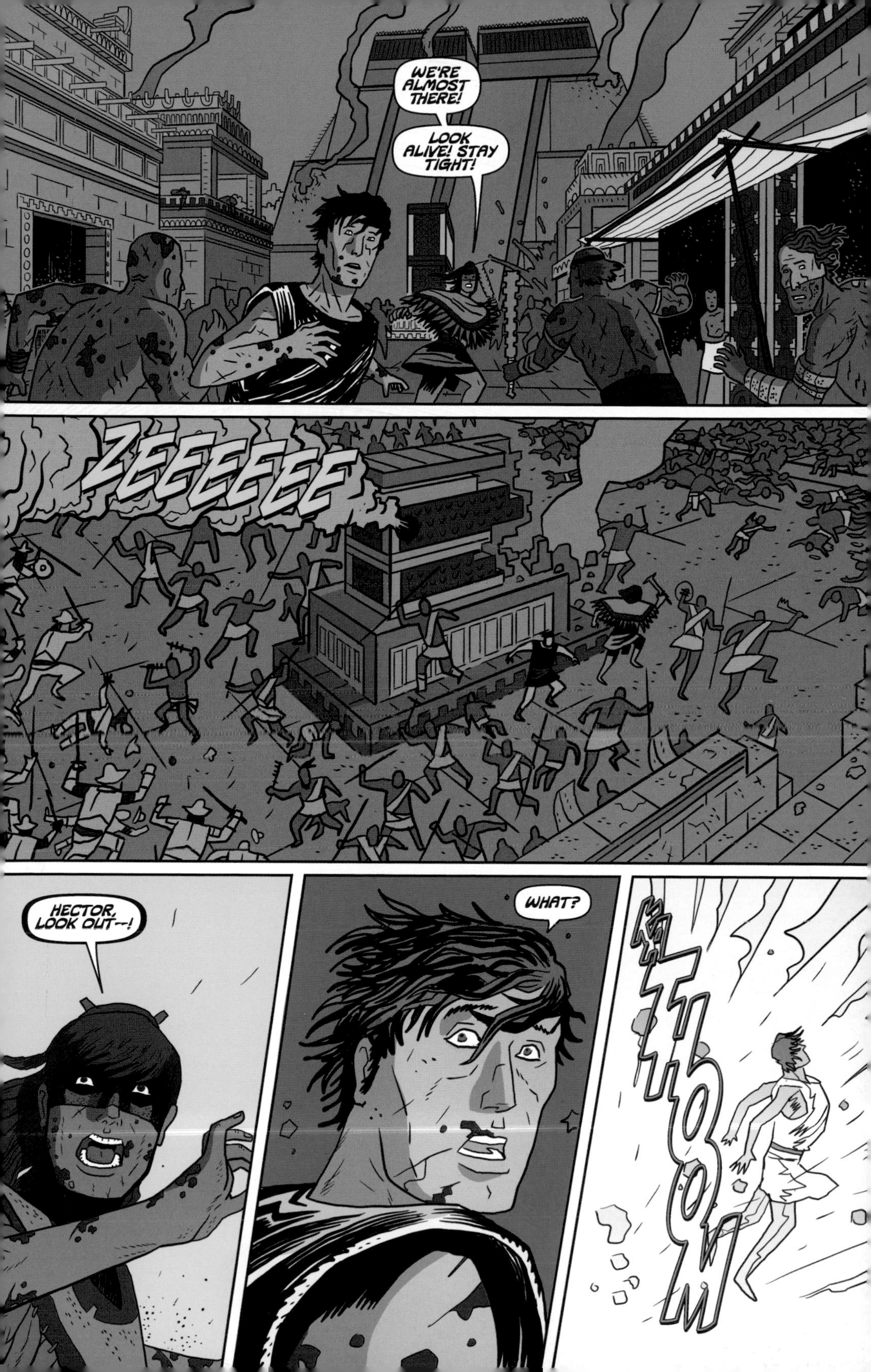
WE'RE ALMOST THERE!
LOOK ALIVE! STAY TIGHT!
ZEEEEEEE
HECTOR, LOOK OUT--!
WHAT?
THOOM

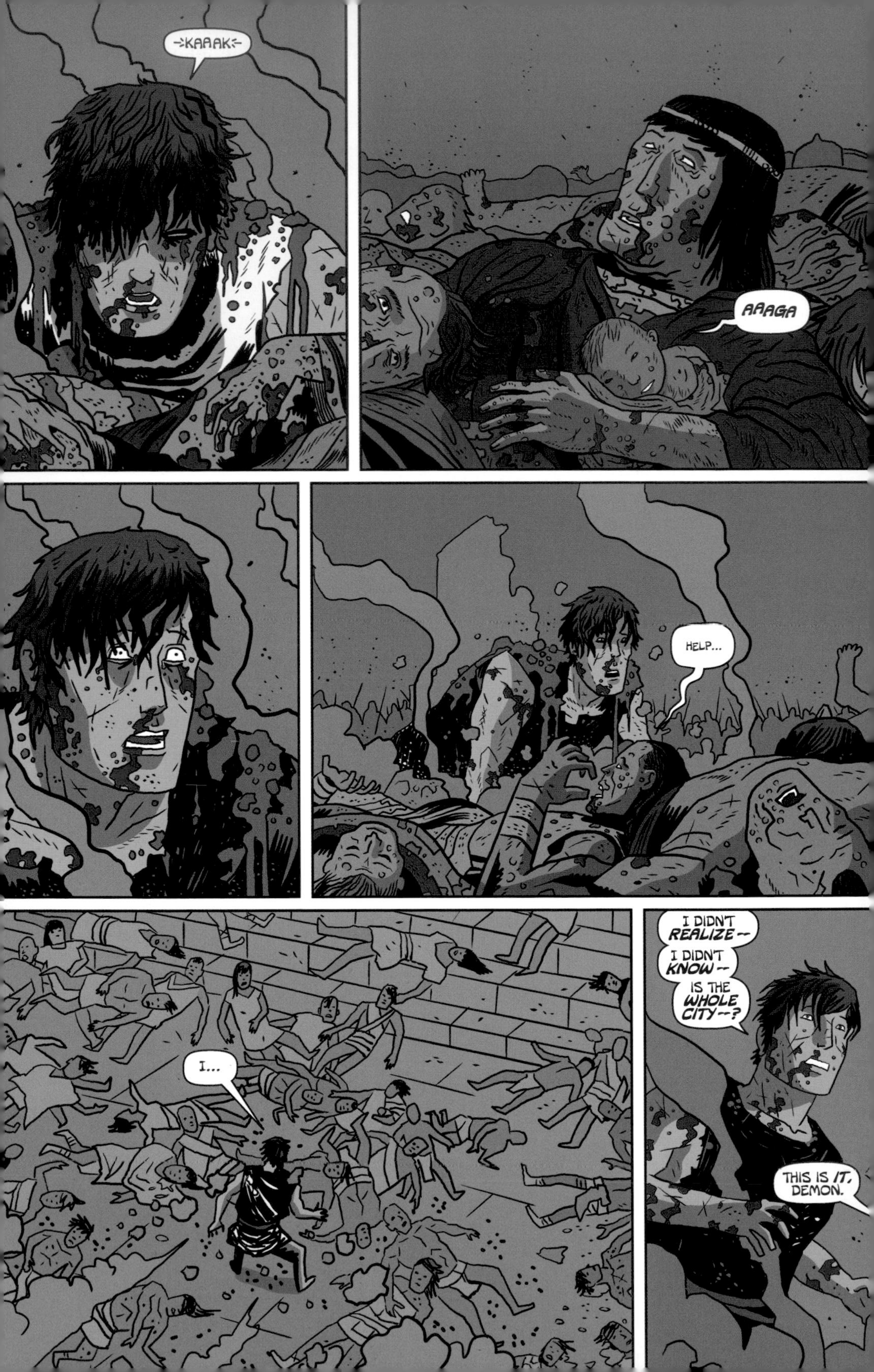
KAAAK
AAAGA
HELP...
I...
I DIDN'T REALIZE --
I DIDN'T KNOW --
IS THE WHOLE CITY --?
THIS IS IT, DEMON.

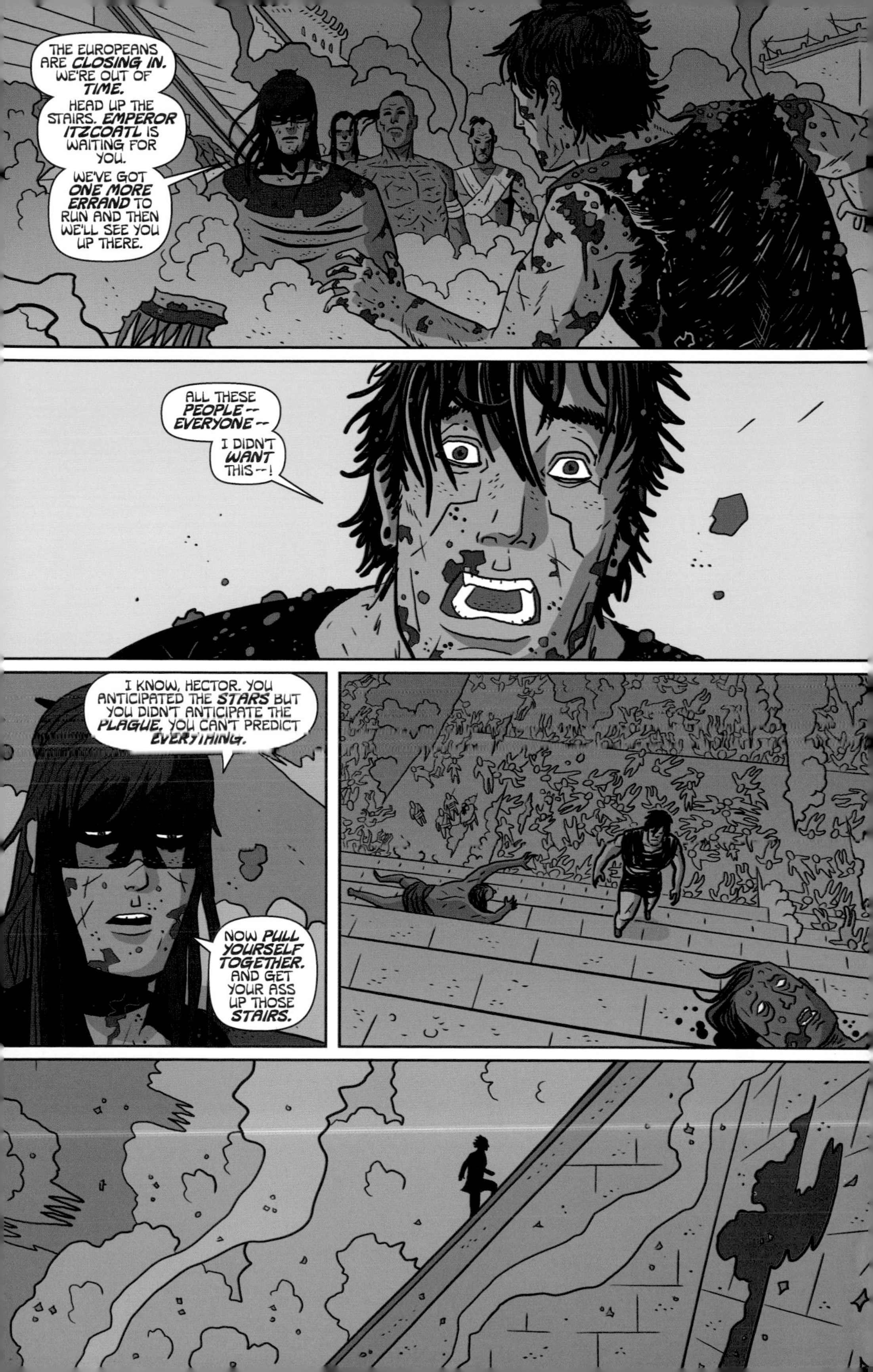

THE EUROPEANS ARE CLOSING IN. WE'RE OUT OF TIME.
HEAD UP THE STAIRS. EMPEROR ITZCOATL IS WAITING FOR YOU.
WE'VE GOT ONE MORE ERRAND TO RUN AND THEN WE'LL SEE YOU UP THERE.
ALL THESE PEOPLE-- EVERYONE--
I DIDN'T WANT THIS--!
I KNOW, HECTOR. YOU ANTICIPATED THE STARS BUT YOU DIDN'T ANTICIPATE THE PLAGUE. YOU CAN'T PREDICT EVERYTHING.
NOW PULL YOURSELF TOGETHER. AND GET YOUR ASS UP THOSE STAIRS.

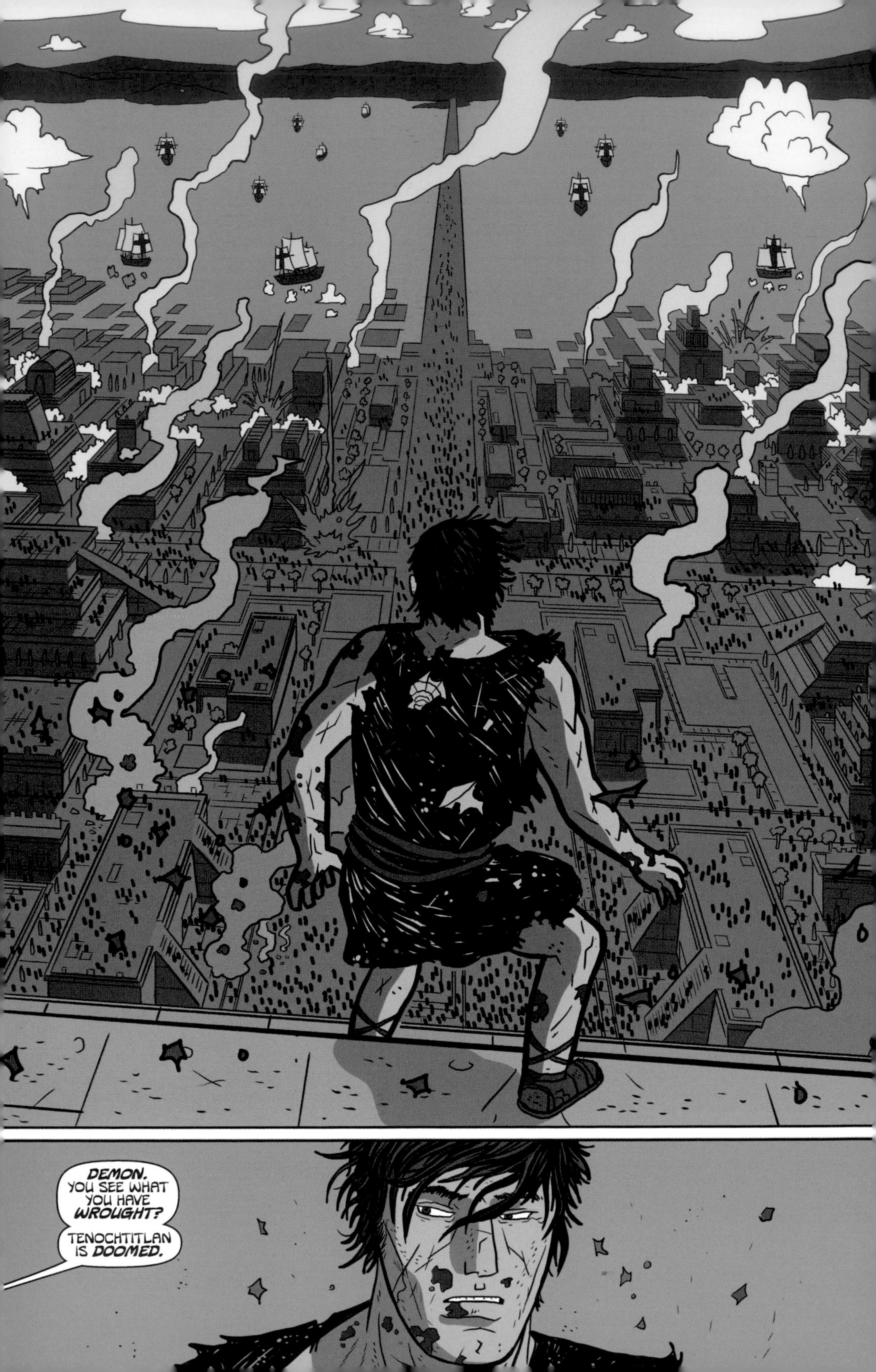
DEMON. YOU SEE WHAT YOU HAVE WROUGHT?
TENOCHTITLAN IS DOOMED.

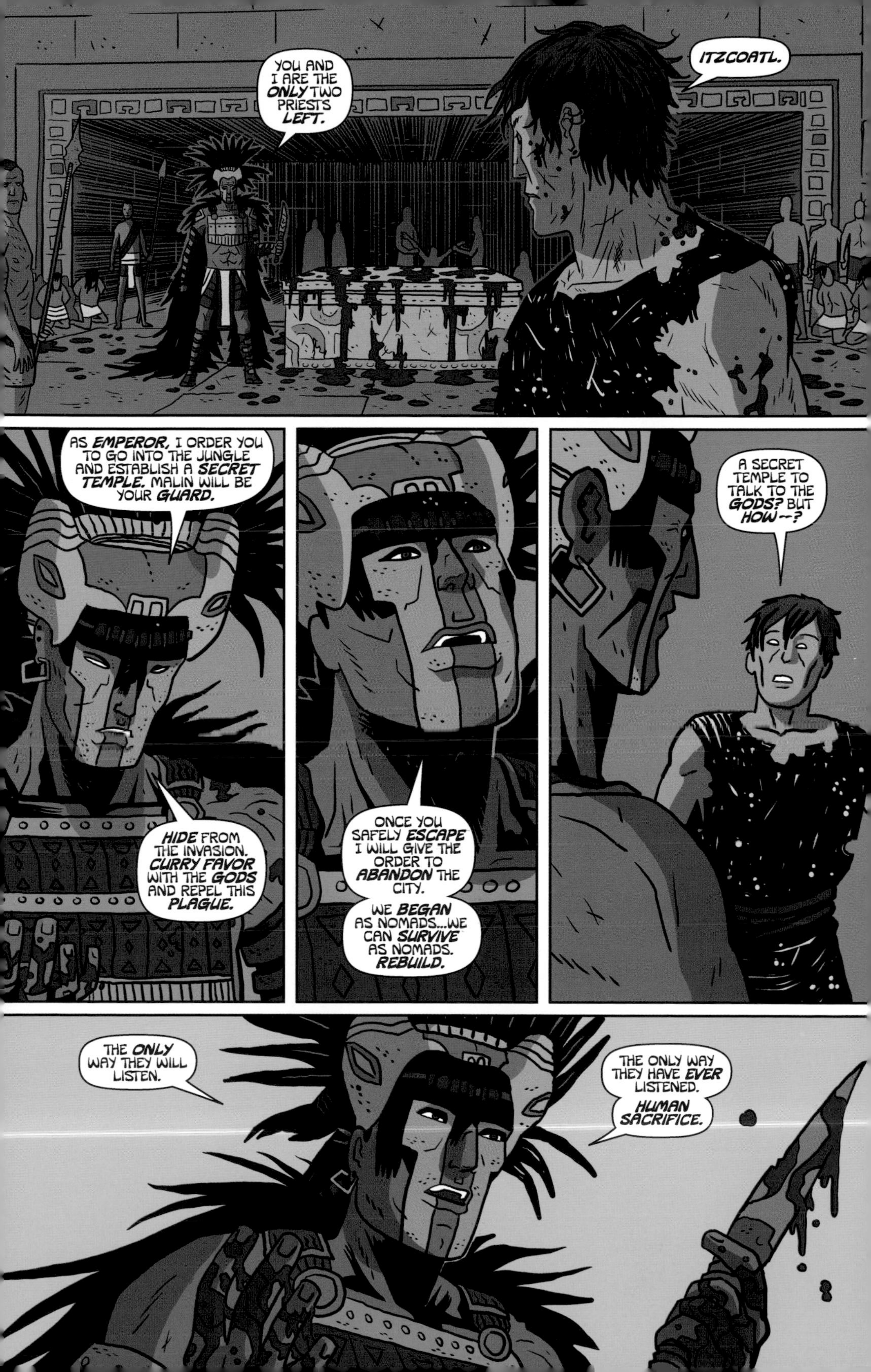
YOU AND I ARE THE ONLY TWO PRIESTS LEFT.
ITZCOATL.
AS EMPEROR, I ORDER YOU TO GO INTO THE JUNGLE AND ESTABLISH A SECRET TEMPLE. MALIN WILL BE YOUR GUARD.
HIDE FROM THE INVASION. CURRY FAVOR WITH THE GODS AND REPEL THIS PLAGUE.
ONCE YOU SAFELY ESCAPE I WILL GIVE THE ORDER TO ABANDON THE CITY.
WE BEGAN AS NOMADS... WE CAN SURVIVE AS NOMADS. REBUILD.
A SECRET TEMPLE TO TALK TO THE GODS? BUT HOW--?
THE ONLY WAY THEY WILL LISTEN.
THE ONLY WAY THEY HAVE EVER LISTENED.
HUMAN SACRIFICE.

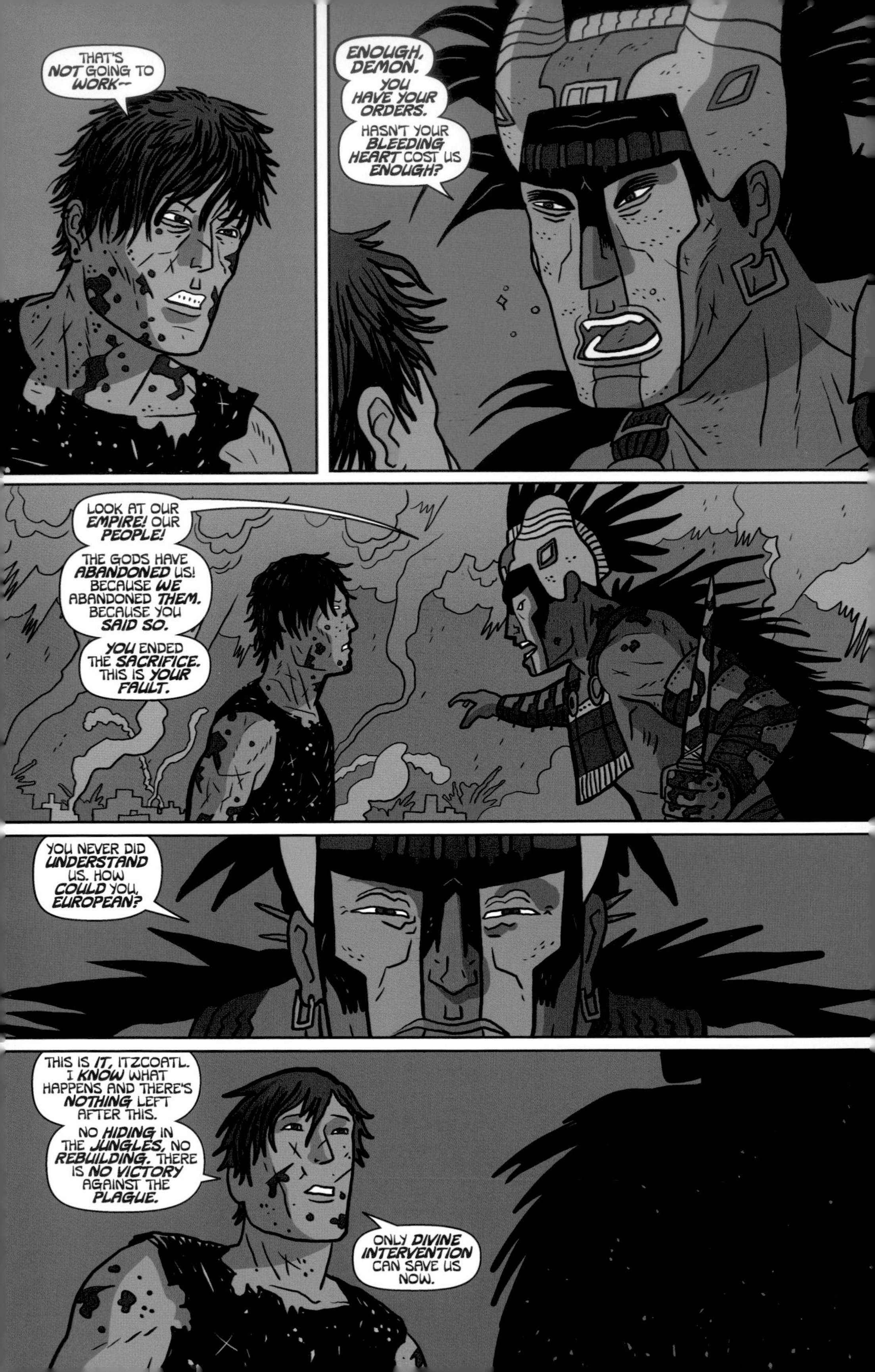
THAT'S NOT GOING TO WORK--
ENOUGH, DEMON.
YOU HAVE YOUR ORDERS.
HASN'T YOUR BLEEDING HEART COST US ENOUGH?
LOOK AT OUR EMPIRE! OUR PEOPLE!
THE GODS HAVE ABANDONED US! BECAUSE WE ABANDONED THEM. BECAUSE YOU SAID SO.
YOU ENDED THE SACRIFICE. THIS IS YOUR FAULT.
YOU NEVER DID UNDERSTAND US. HOW COULD YOU, EUROPEAN?
THIS IS IT, ITZCOATL. I KNOW WHAT HAPPENS AND THERE'S NOTHING LEFT AFTER THIS.
NO HIDING IN THE JUNGLES, NO REBUILDING. THERE IS NO VICTORY AGAINST THE PLAGUE.
ONLY DIVINE INTERVENTION CAN SAVE US NOW.

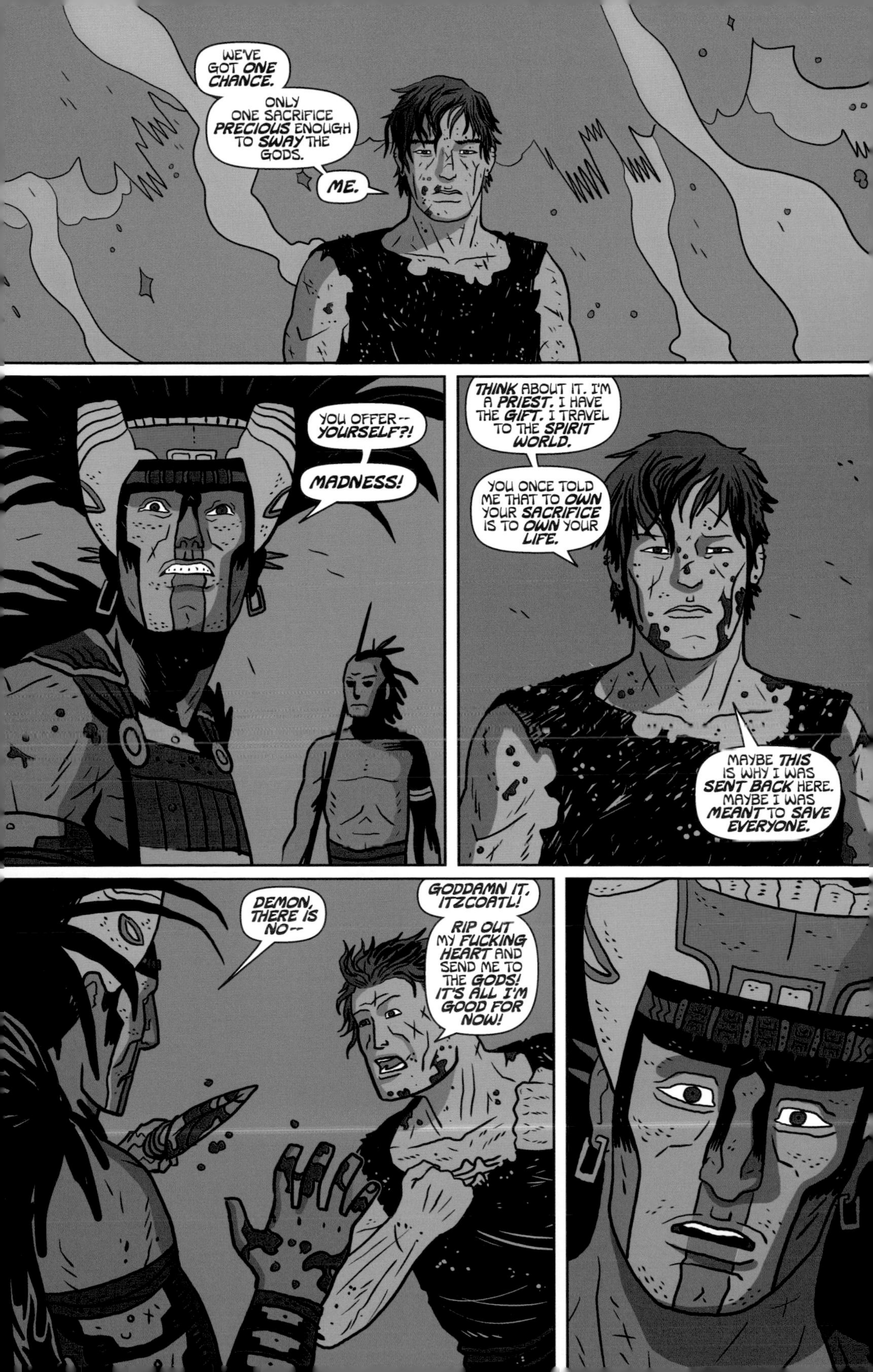
WE'VE GOT ONE CHANCE.
ONLY ONE SACRIFICE PRECIOUS ENOUGH TO SWAY THE GODS.
ME.
YOU OFFER-- YOURSELF?!
MADNESS!
THINK ABOUT IT. I'M A PRIEST. I HAVE THE GIFT. I TRAVEL TO THE SPIRIT WORLD.
YOU ONCE TOLD ME THAT TO OWN YOUR SACRIFICE IS TO OWN YOUR LIFE.
MAYBE THIS IS WHY I WAS SENT BACK HERE. MAYBE I WAS MEANT TO SAVE EVERYONE.
DEMON, THERE IS NO--
GODDAMN IT, ITZCOATL!
RIP OUT MY FUCKING HEART AND SEND ME TO THE GODS! IT'S ALL I'M GOOD FOR NOW!

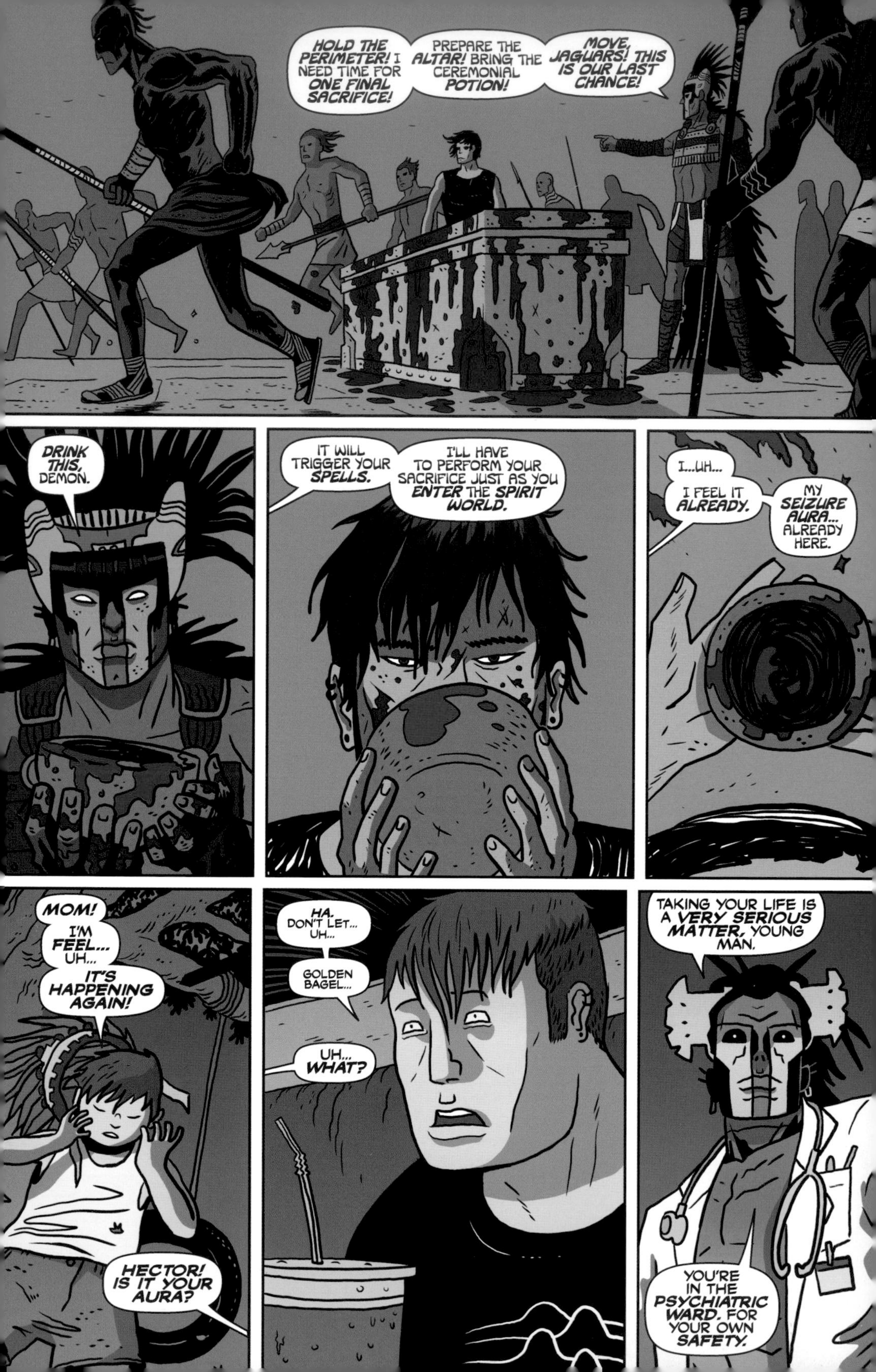
HOLD THE PERIMETER! I NEED TIME FOR ONE FINAL SACRIFICE!
PREPARE THE ALTAR! BRING THE CEREMONIAL POTION!
MOVE, JAGUARS! THIS IS OUR LAST CHANCE!
DRINK THIS, DEMON.
IT WILL TRIGGER YOUR SPELLS.
I'LL HAVE TO PERFORM YOUR SACRIFICE JUST AS YOU ENTER THE SPIRIT WORLD.
I...UH...
I FEEL IT ALREADY.
MY SEIZURE AURA... ALREADY HERE.
MOM! I'M FEEL... UH... IT'S HAPPENING AGAIN!
HECTOR! IS IT YOUR AURA?
HA. DON'T LET... UH...
GOLDEN BAGEL...
UH... WHAT?
TAKING YOUR LIFE IS A VERY SERIOUS MATTER, YOUNG MAN.
YOU'RE IN THE PSYCHIATRIC WARD, FOR YOUR OWN SAFETY.

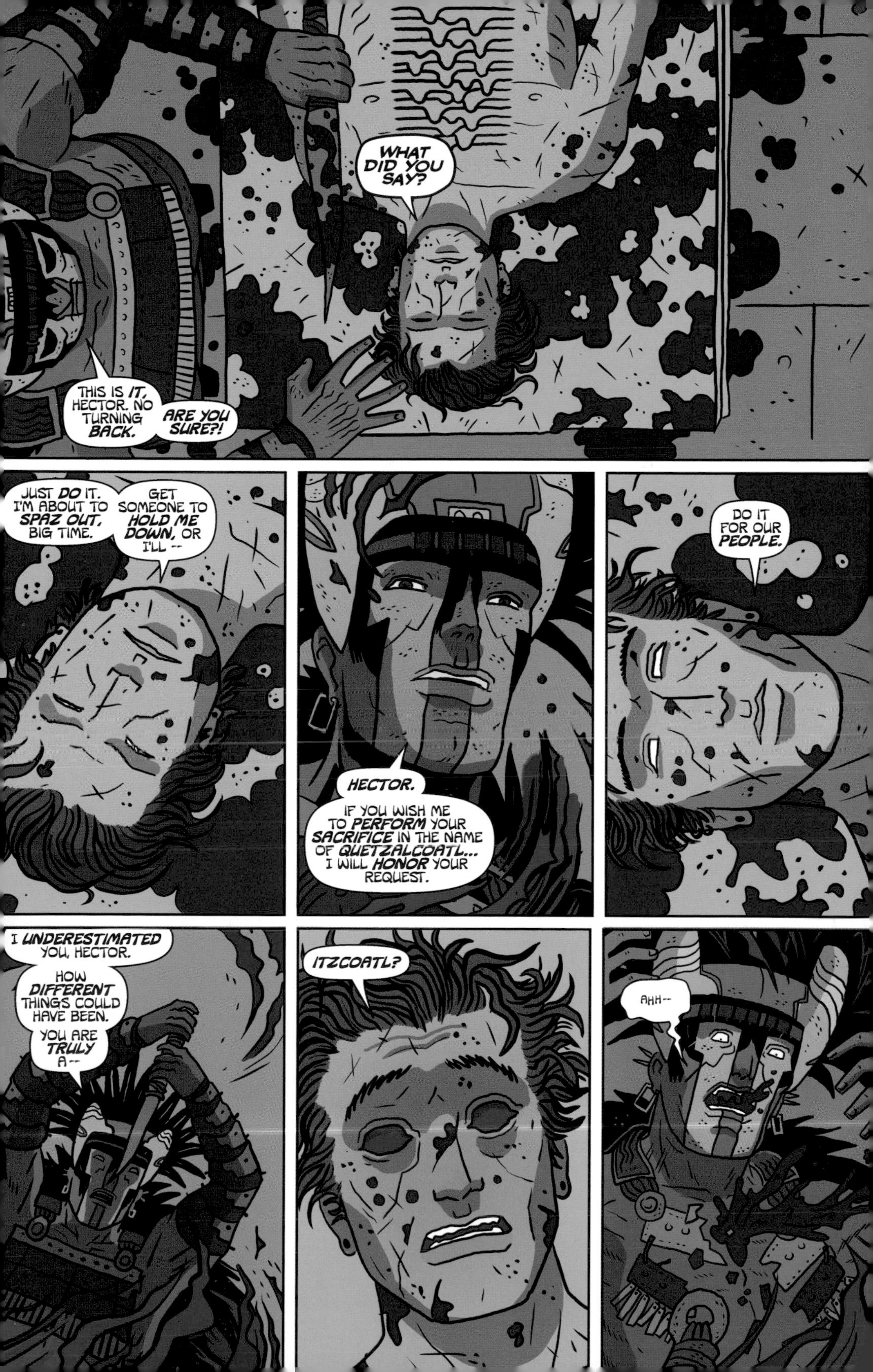
WHAT DID YOU SAY?
THIS IS IT, HECTOR. NO TURNING BACK.
ARE YOU SURE?!
JUST DO IT. I'M ABOUT TO SPAZ OUT, BIG TIME.
GET SOMEONE TO HOLD ME DOWN, OR I'LL --
HECTOR.
IF YOU WISH ME TO PERFORM YOUR SACRIFICE IN THE NAME OF QUETZALCOATL... I WILL HONOR YOUR REQUEST.
DO IT FOR OUR PEOPLE.
I UNDERESTIMATED YOU, HECTOR.
HOW DIFFERENT THINGS COULD HAVE BEEN.
YOU ARE TRULY A --
ITZCOATL?
AHH --

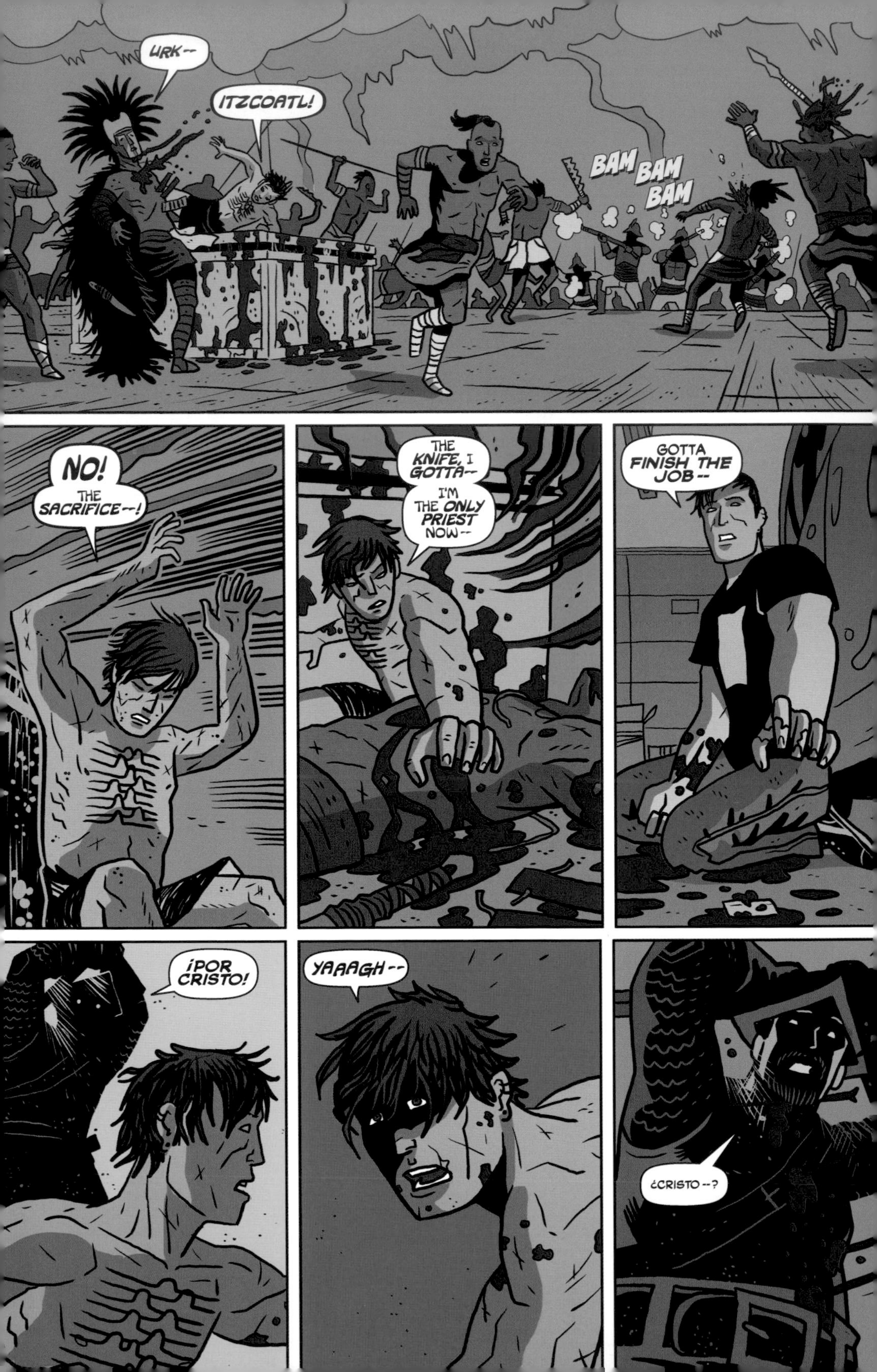
URK--
ITZCOATL!
BAM BAM BAM
NO! THE SACRIFICE--!
THE KNIFE, I GOTTA--
I'M THE ONLY PRIEST NOW--
GOTTA FINISH THE JOB--
¡POR CRISTO!
YAAAGH--
¿CRISTO--?

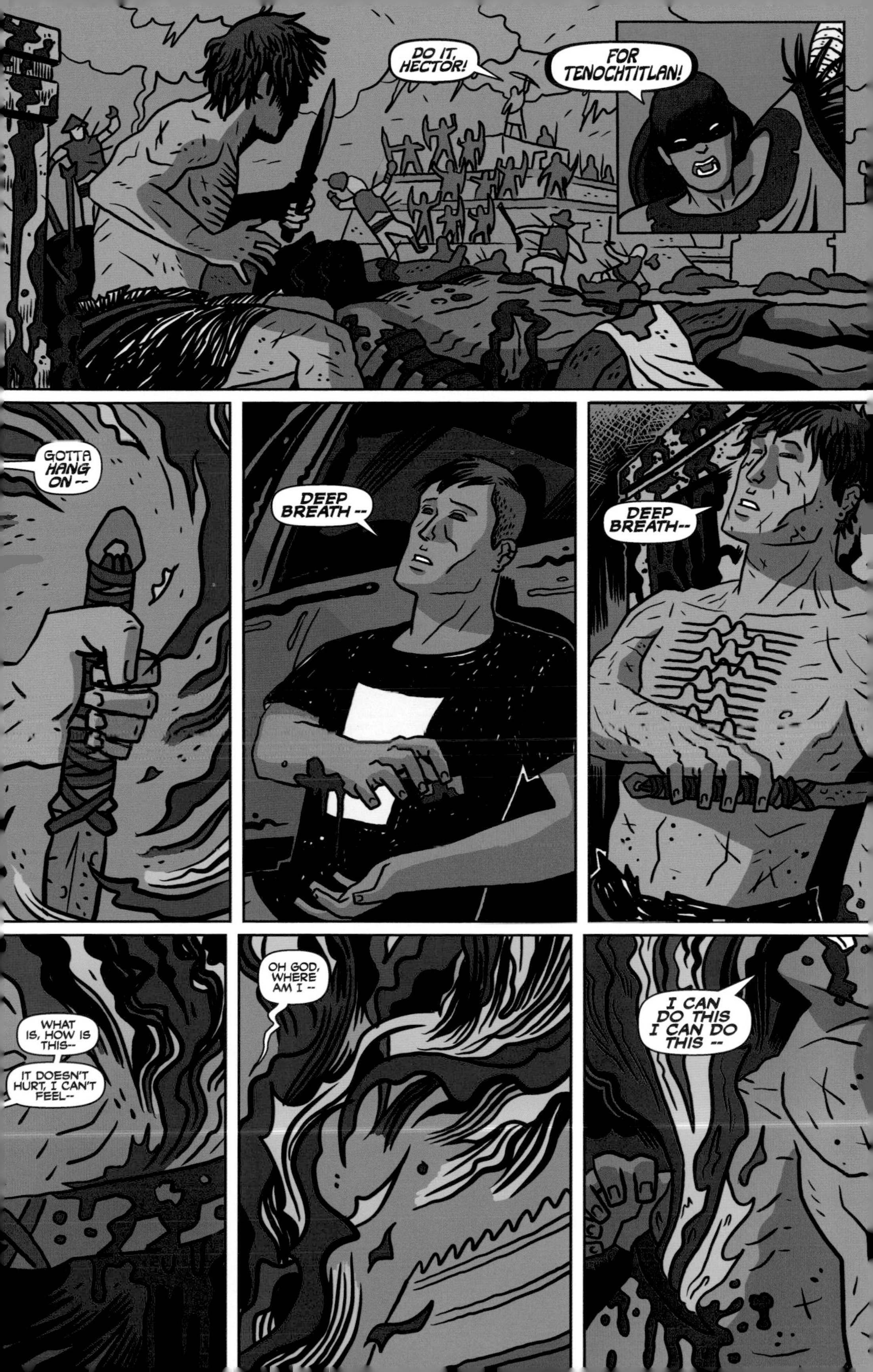

DO IT, HECTOR!
FOR TENOCHTITLAN!
GOTTA HANG ON --
DEEP BREATH --
DEEP BREATH--
WHAT IS, HOW IS THIS--
IT DOESN'T HURT, I CAN'T FEEL--
OH GOD, WHERE AM I --
I CAN DO THIS I CAN DO THIS --

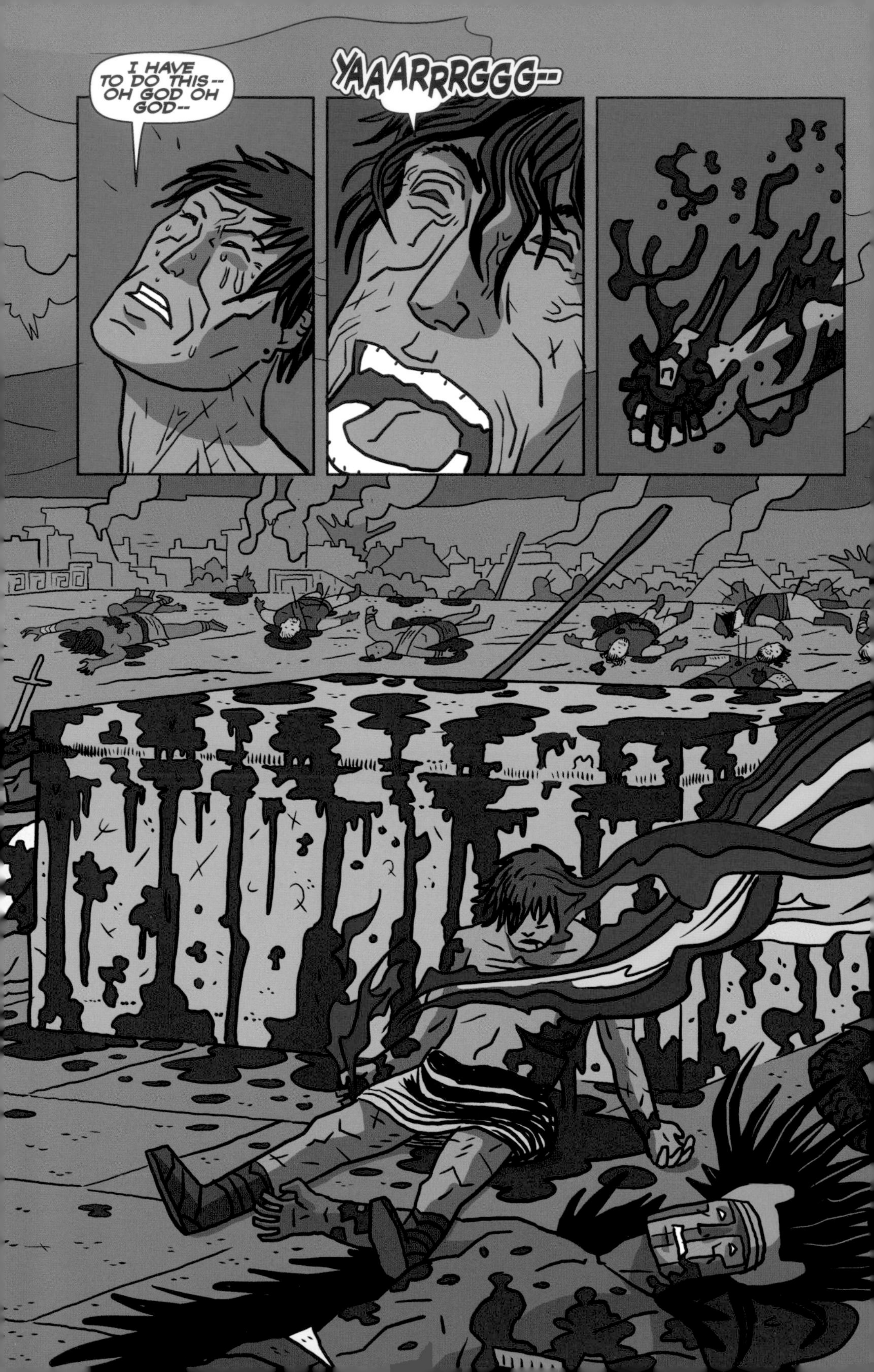
I HAVE TO DO THIS-- OH GOD OH GOD--
YAAARRRGGG--

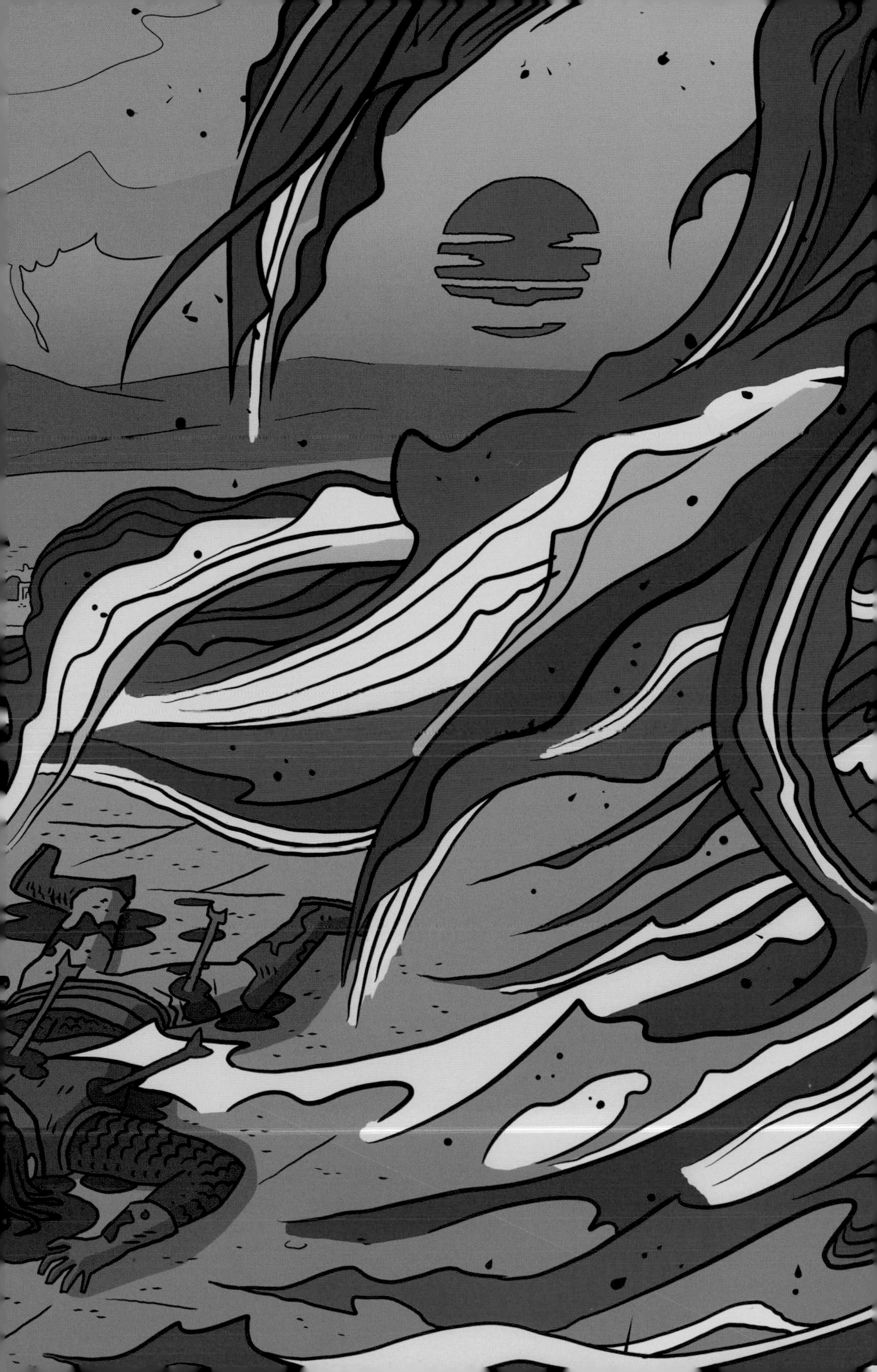

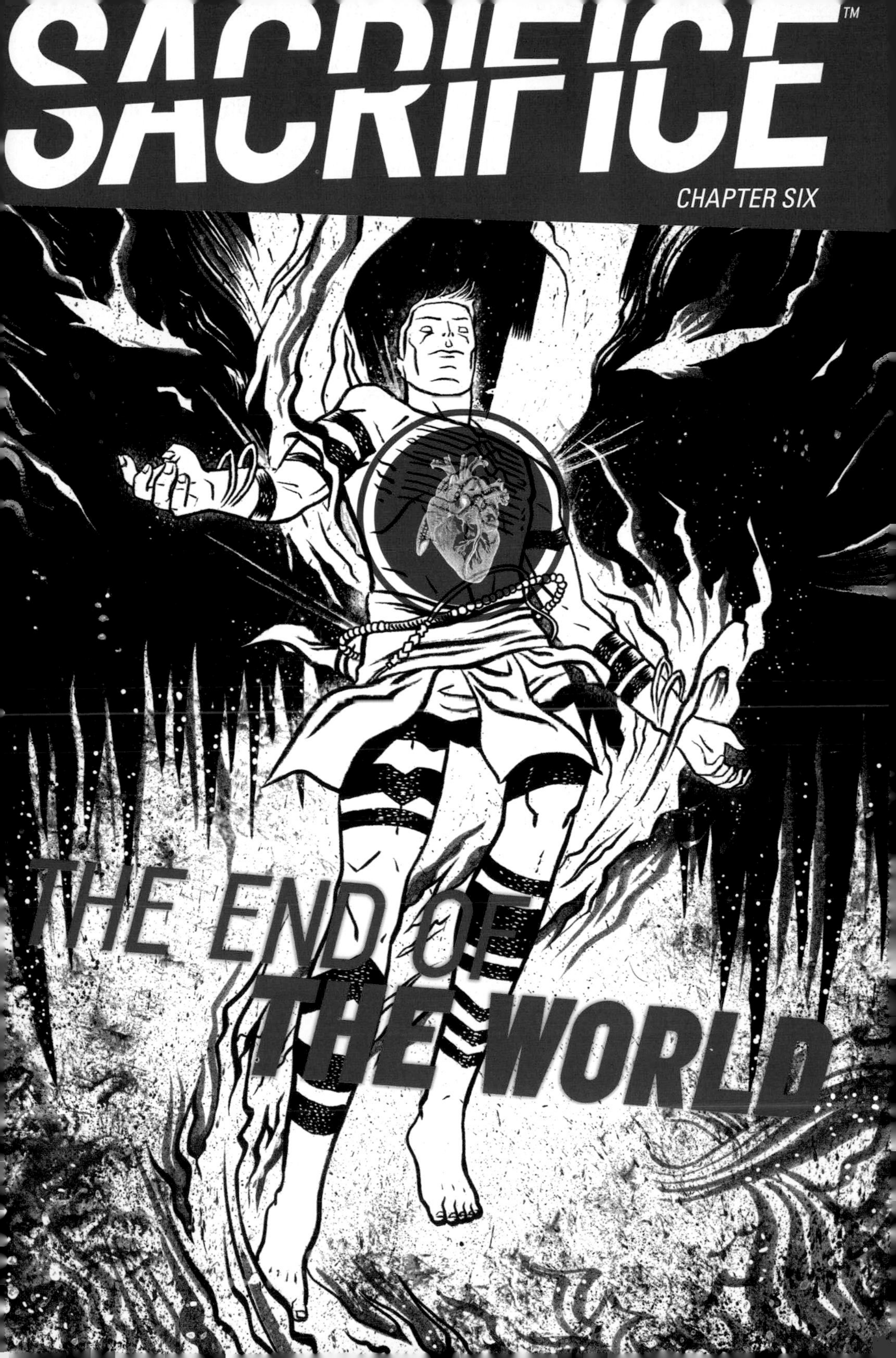
SACRIFICE™
CHAPTER SIX
THE END OF
THE WORLD

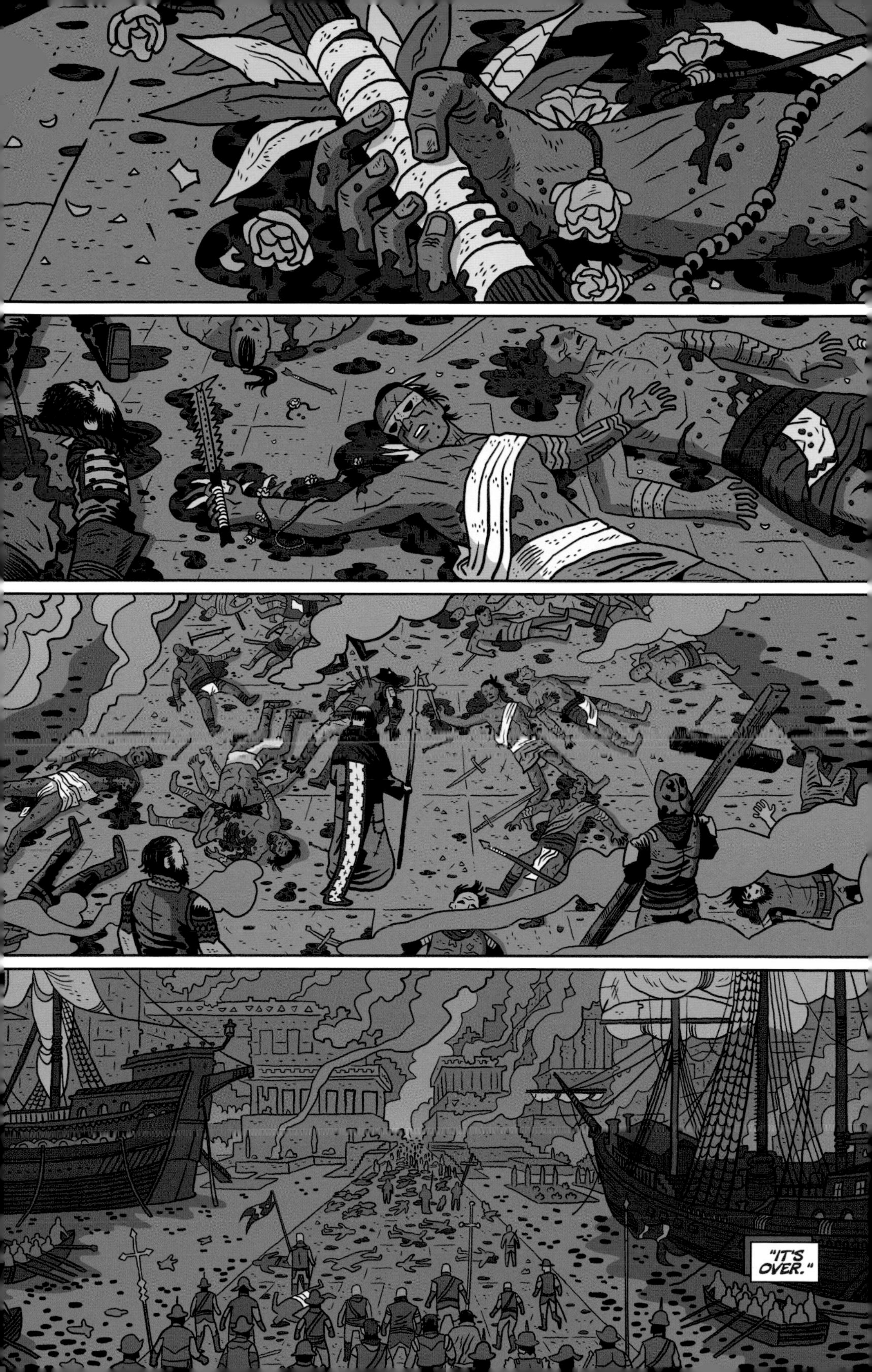
"IT'S OVER."

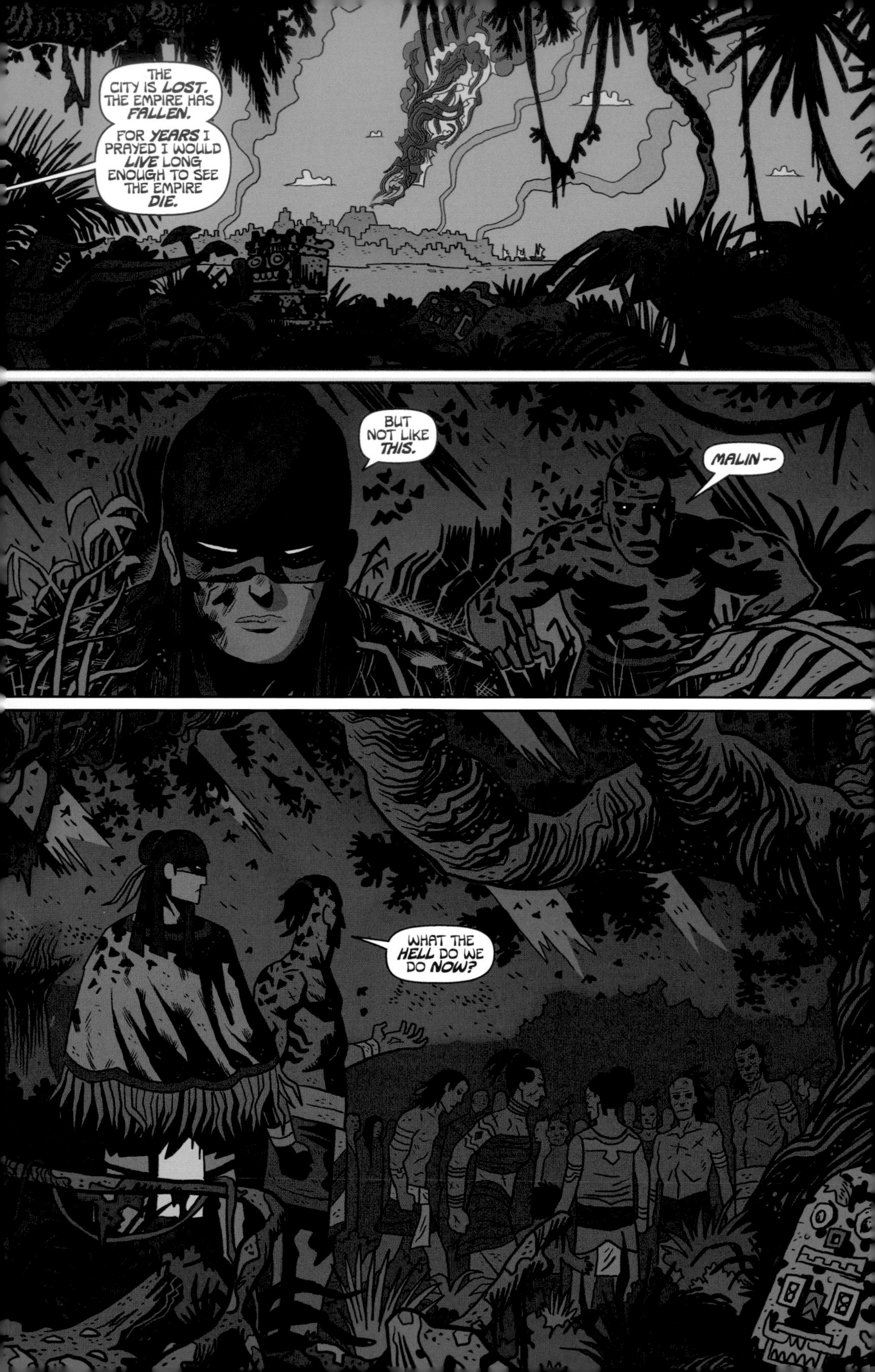
THE CITY IS LOST. THE EMPIRE HAS FALLEN.
FOR YEARS I PRAYED I WOULD LIVE LONG ENOUGH TO SEE THE EMPIRE DIE.
BUT NOT LIKE THIS.
MALIN --
WHAT THE HELL DO WE DO NOW?

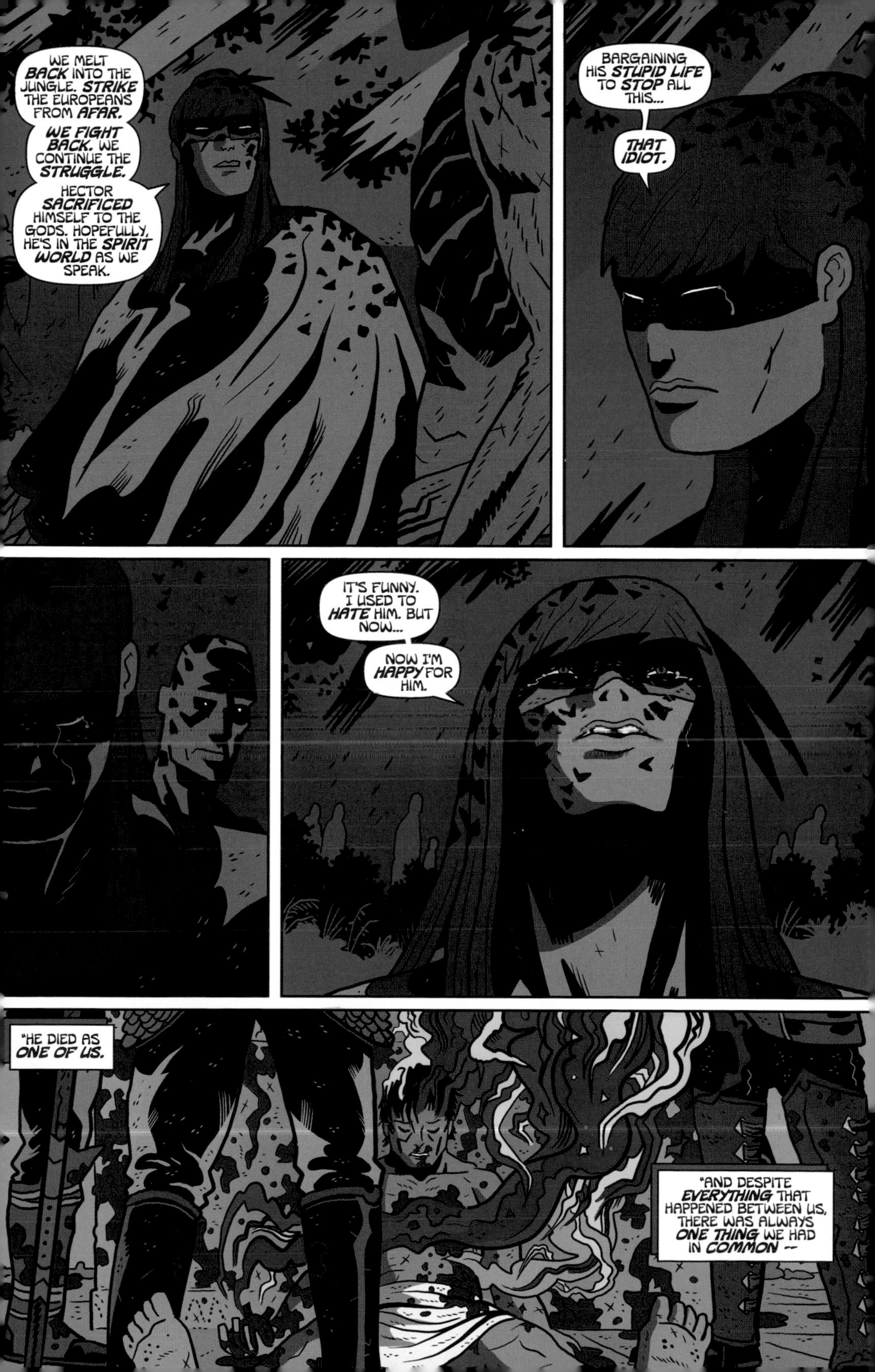
WE MELT BACK INTO THE JUNGLE. STRIKE THE EUROPEANS FROM AFAR.
WE FIGHT BACK. WE CONTINUE THE STRUGGLE.
HECTOR SACRIFICED HIMSELF TO THE GODS. HOPEFULLY, HE'S IN THE SPIRIT WORLD AS WE SPEAK.
BARGAINING HIS STUPID LIFE TO STOP ALL THIS...
THAT IDIOT.
IT'S FUNNY. I USED TO HATE HIM. BUT NOW...
NOW I'M HAPPY FOR HIM.
"HE DIED AS ONE OF US.
"AND DESPITE EVERYTHING THAT HAPPENED BETWEEN US, THERE WAS ALWAYS ONE THING WE HAD IN COMMON --

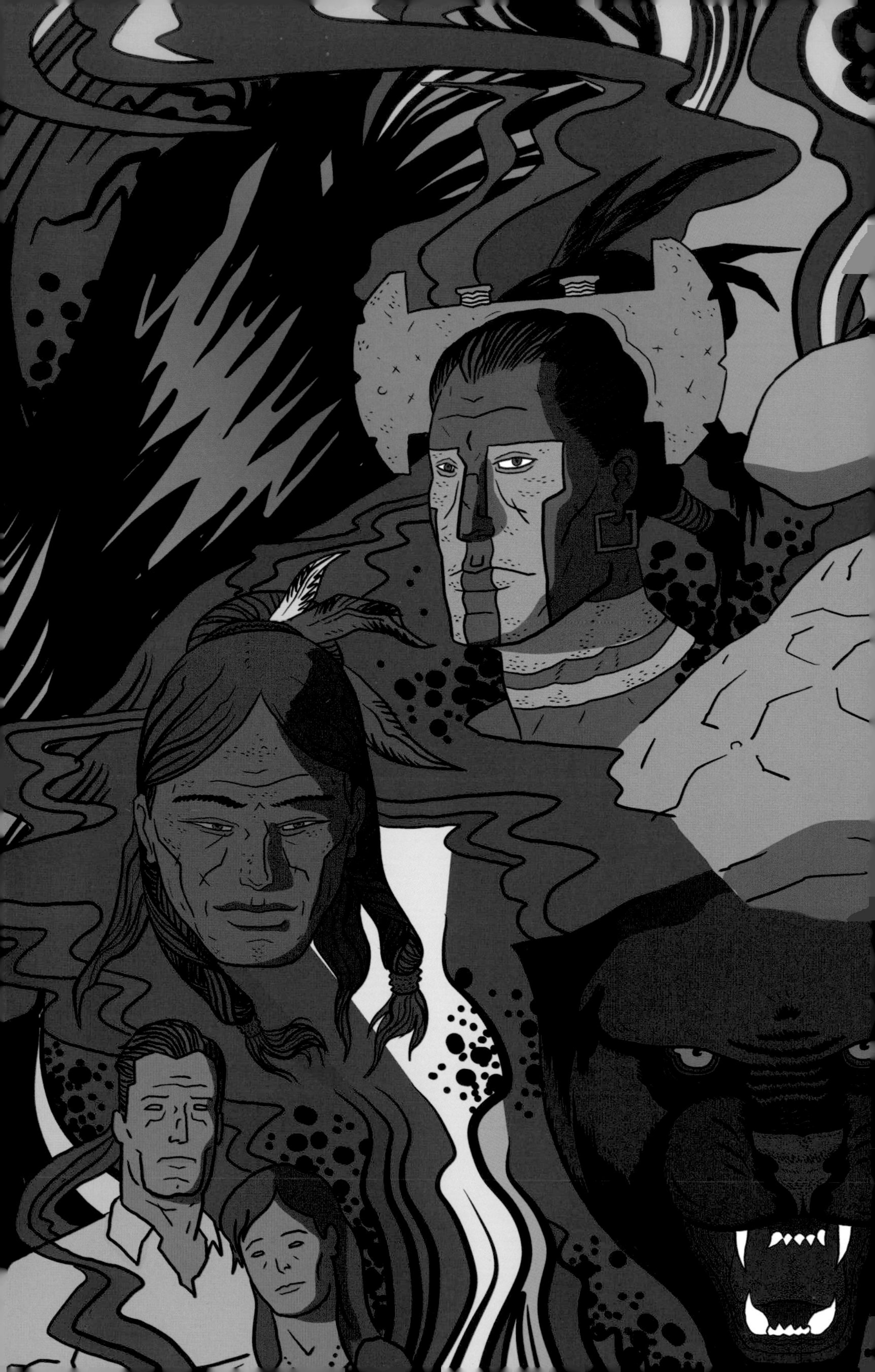

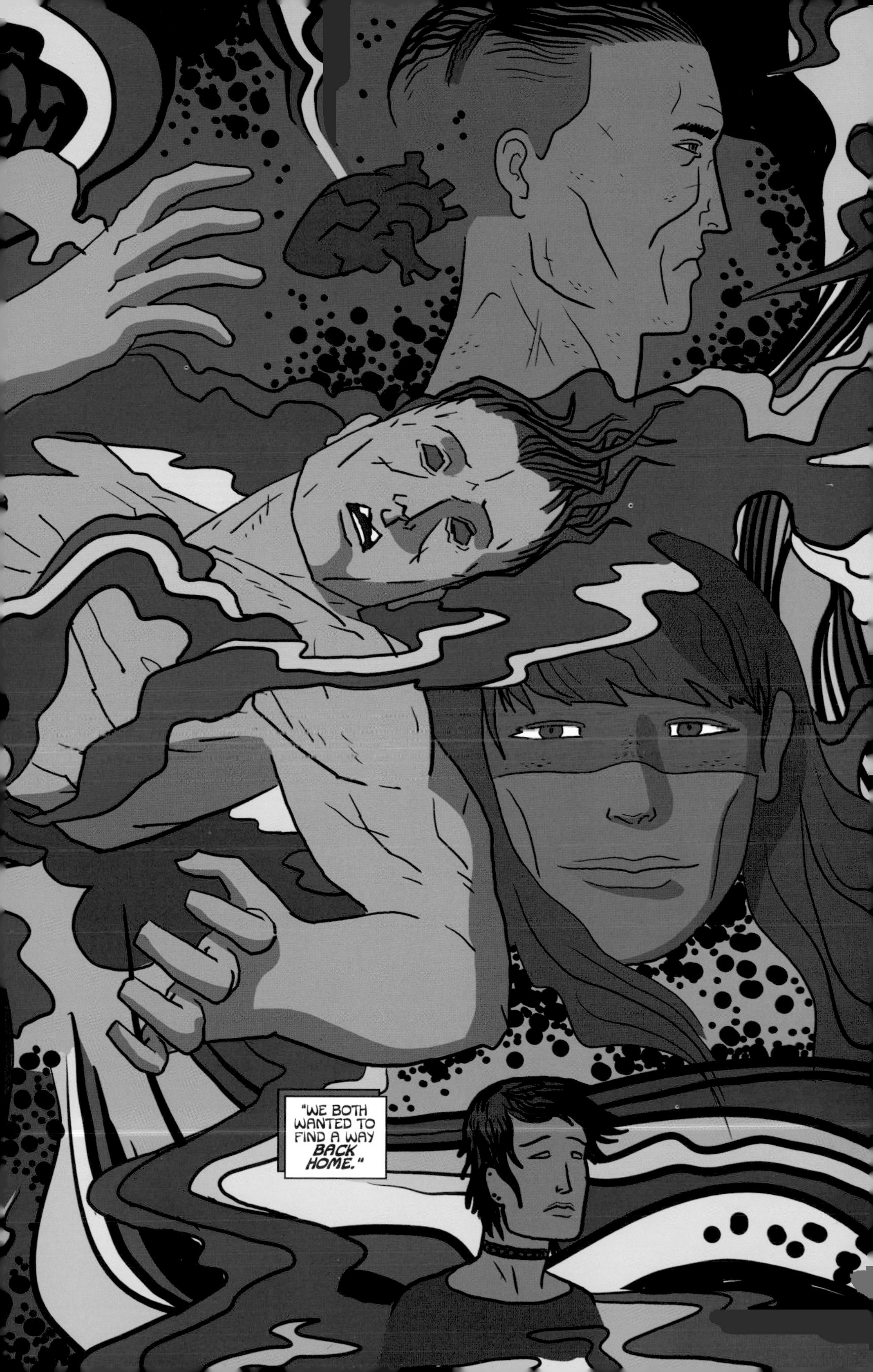
"WE BOTH WANTED TO FIND A WAY BACK HOME."

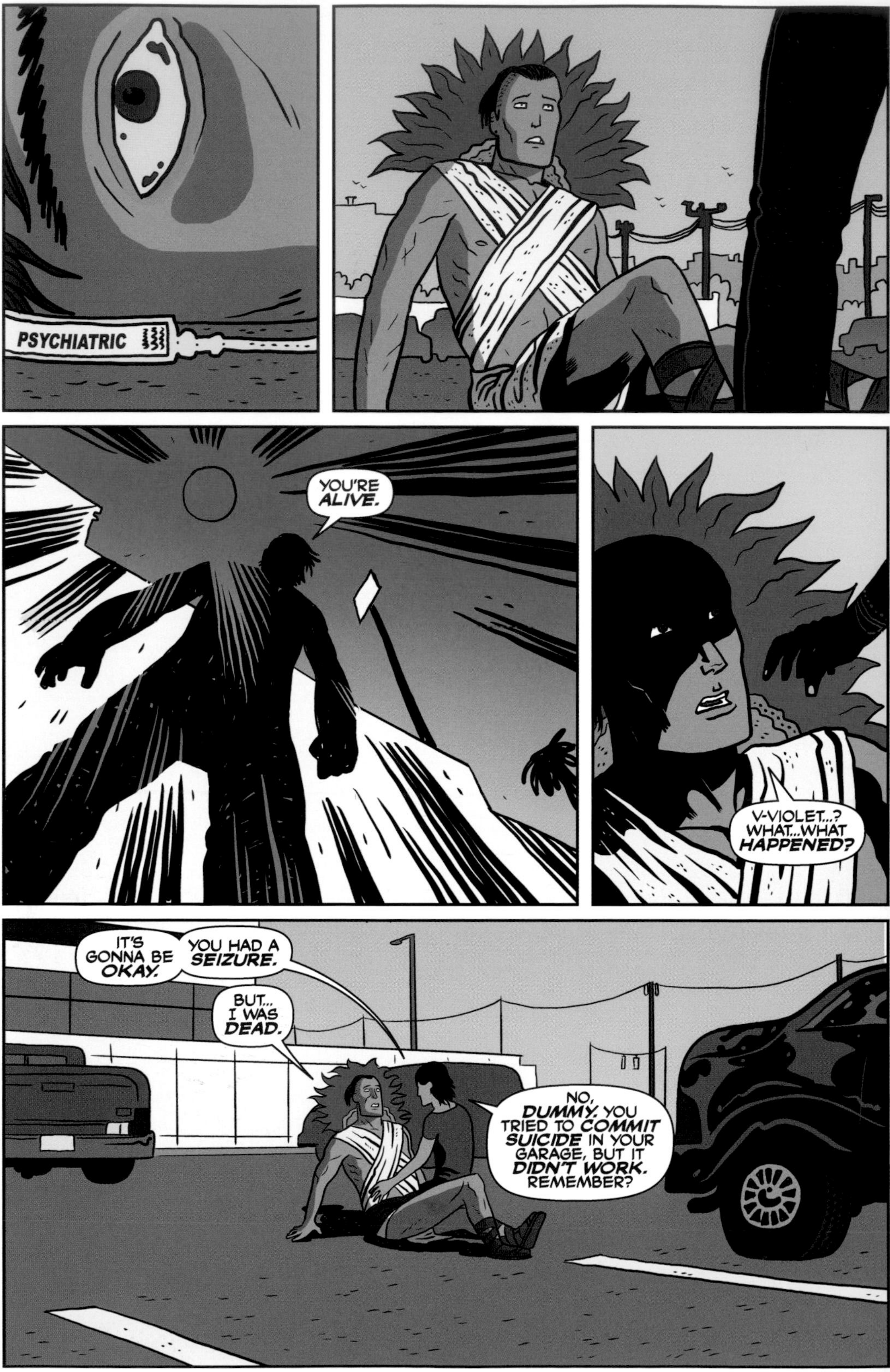
PSYCHIATRIC
YOU'RE ALIVE.
V-VIOLET...? WHAT...WHAT HAPPENED?
IT'S GONNA BE OKAY.
YOU HAD A SEIZURE.
BUT... I WAS DEAD.
NO, DUMMY. YOU TRIED TO COMMIT SUICIDE IN YOUR GARAGE, BUT IT DIDN'T WORK. REMEMBER?

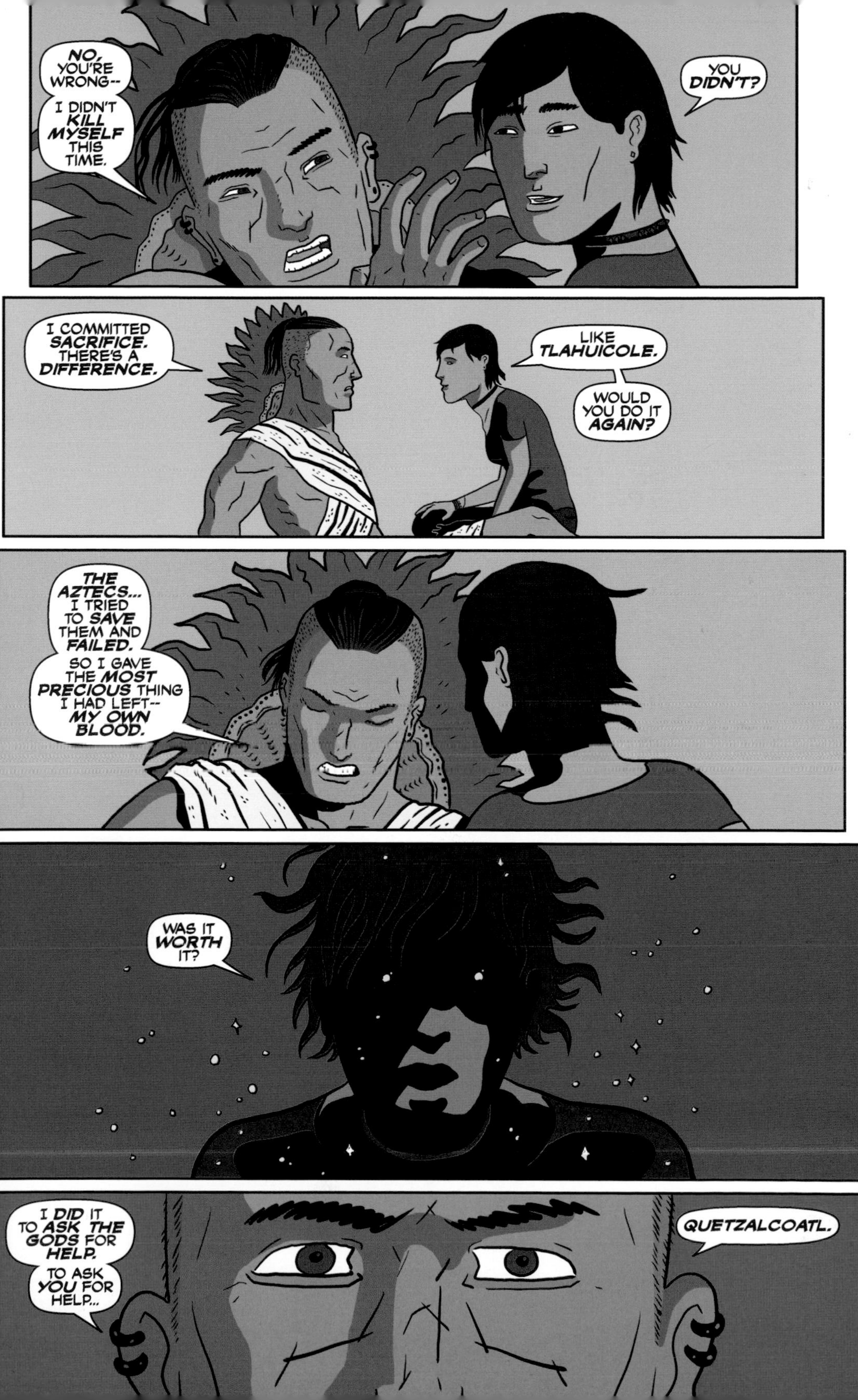
NO, YOU'RE WRONG--
I DIDN'T KILL MYSELF THIS TIME.
YOU DIDN'T?
I COMMITTED SACRIFICE. THERE'S A DIFFERENCE.
LIKE TLAHUICOLE.
WOULD YOU DO IT AGAIN?
THE AZTECS... I TRIED TO SAVE THEM AND FAILED.
SO I GAVE THE MOST PRECIOUS THING I HAD LEFT-- MY OWN BLOOD.
WAS IT WORTH IT?
I DID IT TO ASK THE GODS FOR HELP.
TO ASK YOU FOR HELP...
QUETZALCOATL.

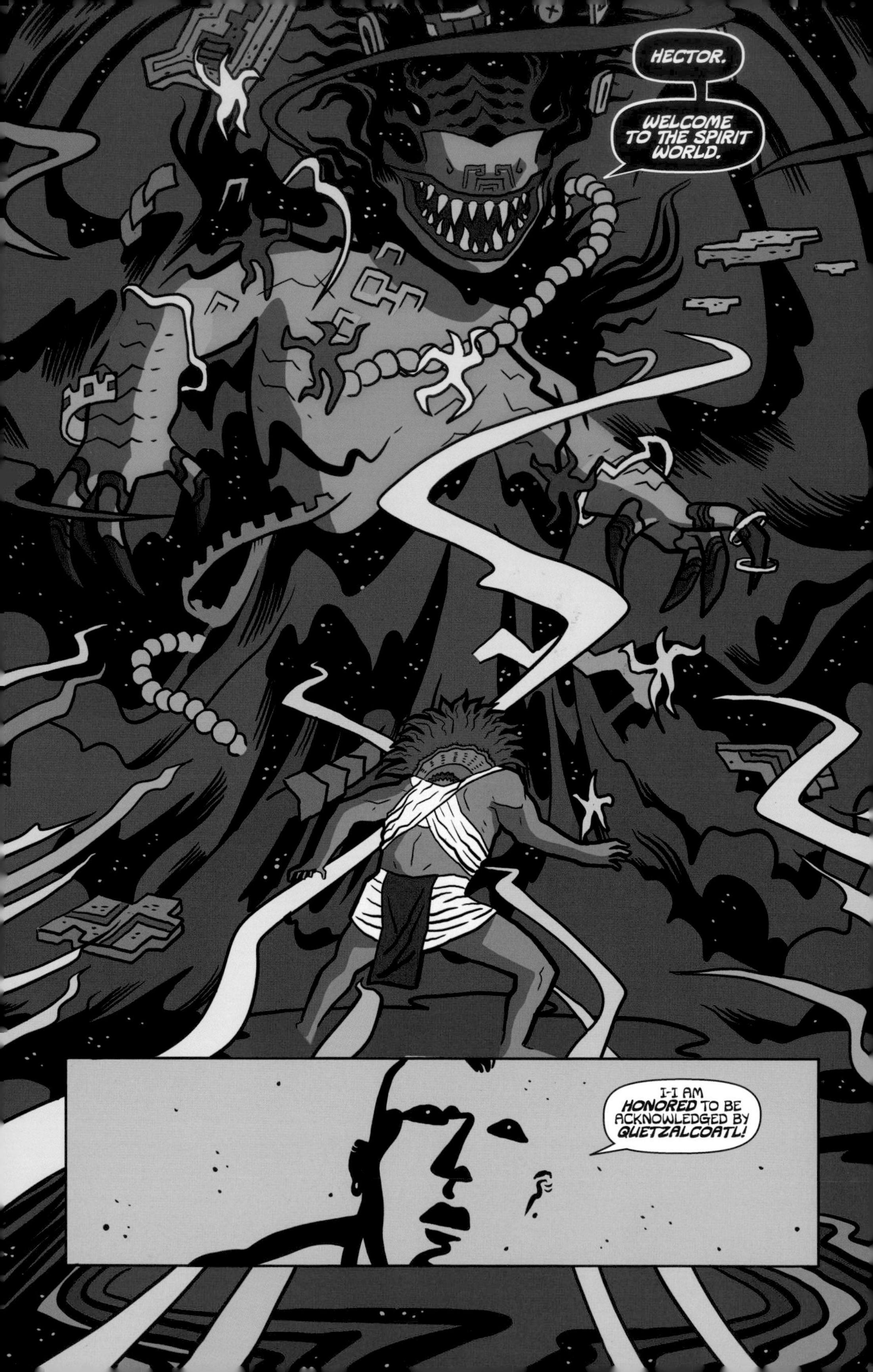
HECTOR.
WELCOME TO THE SPIRIT WORLD.
I-I AM HONORED TO BE ACKNOWLEDGED BY QUETZALCOATL!

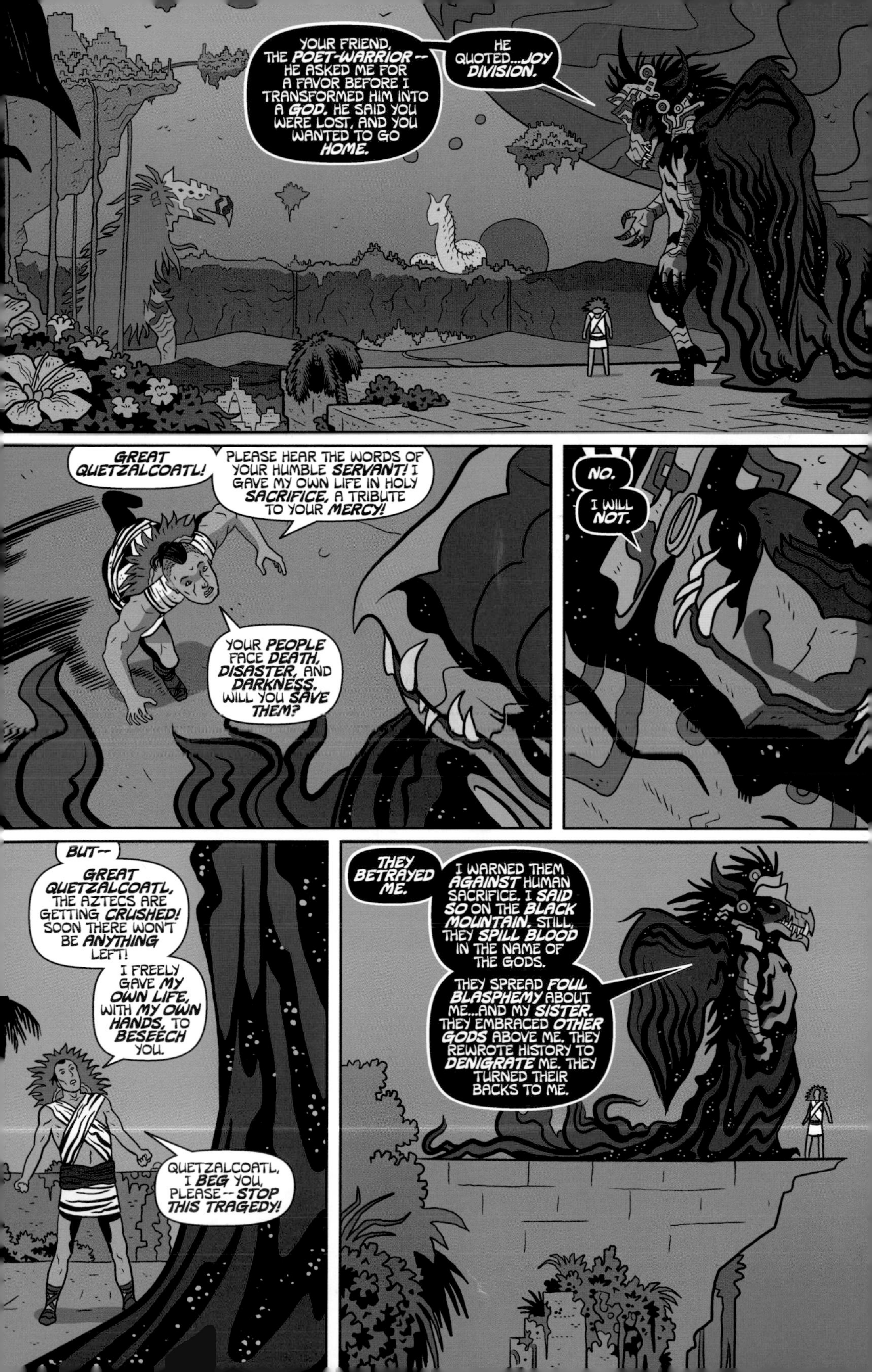
YOUR FRIEND, THE POET-WARRIOR-- HE ASKED ME FOR A FAVOR BEFORE I TRANSFORMED HIM INTO A GOD. HE SAID YOU WERE LOST, AND YOU WANTED TO GO HOME.
HE QUOTED...JOY DIVISION.
GREAT QUETZALCOATL!
PLEASE HEAR THE WORDS OF YOUR HUMBLE SERVANT! I GAVE MY OWN LIFE IN HOLY SACRIFICE, A TRIBUTE TO YOUR MERCY!
YOUR PEOPLE FACE DEATH, DISASTER, AND DARKNESS. WILL YOU SAVE THEM?
NO.
I WILL NOT.
BUT--
GREAT QUETZALCOATL, THE AZTECS ARE GETTING CRUSHED! SOON THERE WON'T BE ANYTHING LEFT!
I FREELY GAVE MY OWN LIFE, WITH MY OWN HANDS, TO BESEECH YOU.
QUETZALCOATL, I BEG YOU, PLEASE-- STOP THIS TRAGEDY!
THEY BETRAYED ME.
I WARNED THEM AGAINST HUMAN SACRIFICE. I SAID SO ON THE BLACK MOUNTAIN. STILL, THEY SPILL BLOOD IN THE NAME OF THE GODS.
THEY SPREAD FOUL BLASPHEMY ABOUT ME...AND MY SISTER. THEY EMBRACED OTHER GODS ABOVE ME. THEY REWROTE HISTORY TO DENIGRATE ME. THEY TURNED THEIR BACKS TO ME.

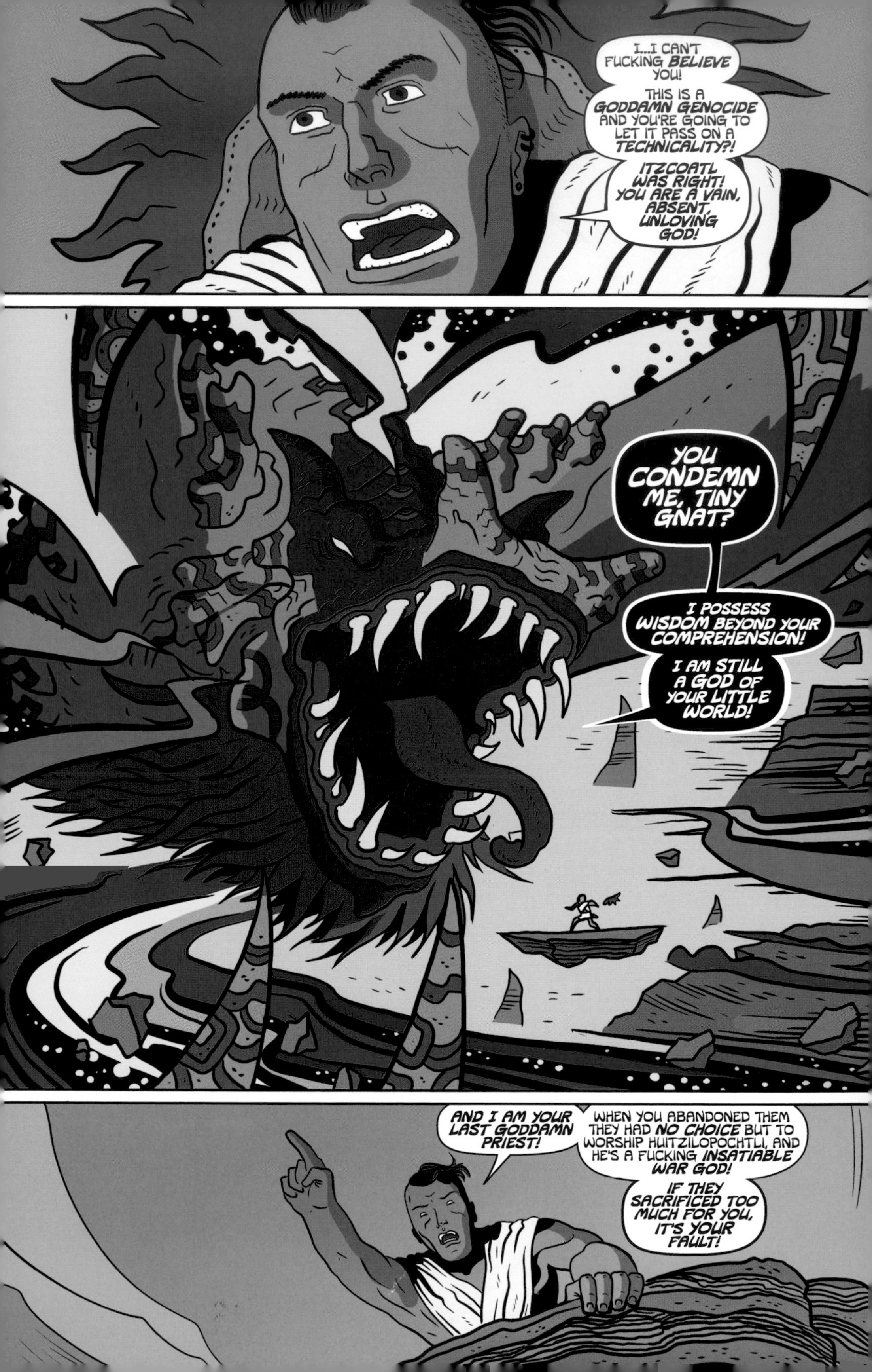
I...I CAN'T FUCKING BELIEVE YOU!
THIS IS A GODDAMN GENOCIDE AND YOU'RE GOING TO LET IT PASS ON A TECHNICALITY?!
ITZCOATL WAS RIGHT! YOU ARE A VAIN, ABSENT, UNLOVING GOD!
YOU CONDEMN ME, TINY GNAT?
I POSSESS WISDOM BEYOND YOUR COMPREHENSION!
I AM STILL A GOD OF YOUR LITTLE WORLD!
AND I AM YOUR LAST GODDAMN PRIEST!
WHEN YOU ABANDONED THEM THEY HAD NO CHOICE BUT TO WORSHIP HUITZILOPOCHTLI, AND HE'S A FUCKING INSATIABLE WAR GOD!
IF THEY SACRIFICED TOO MUCH FOR YOU, IT'S YOUR FAULT!

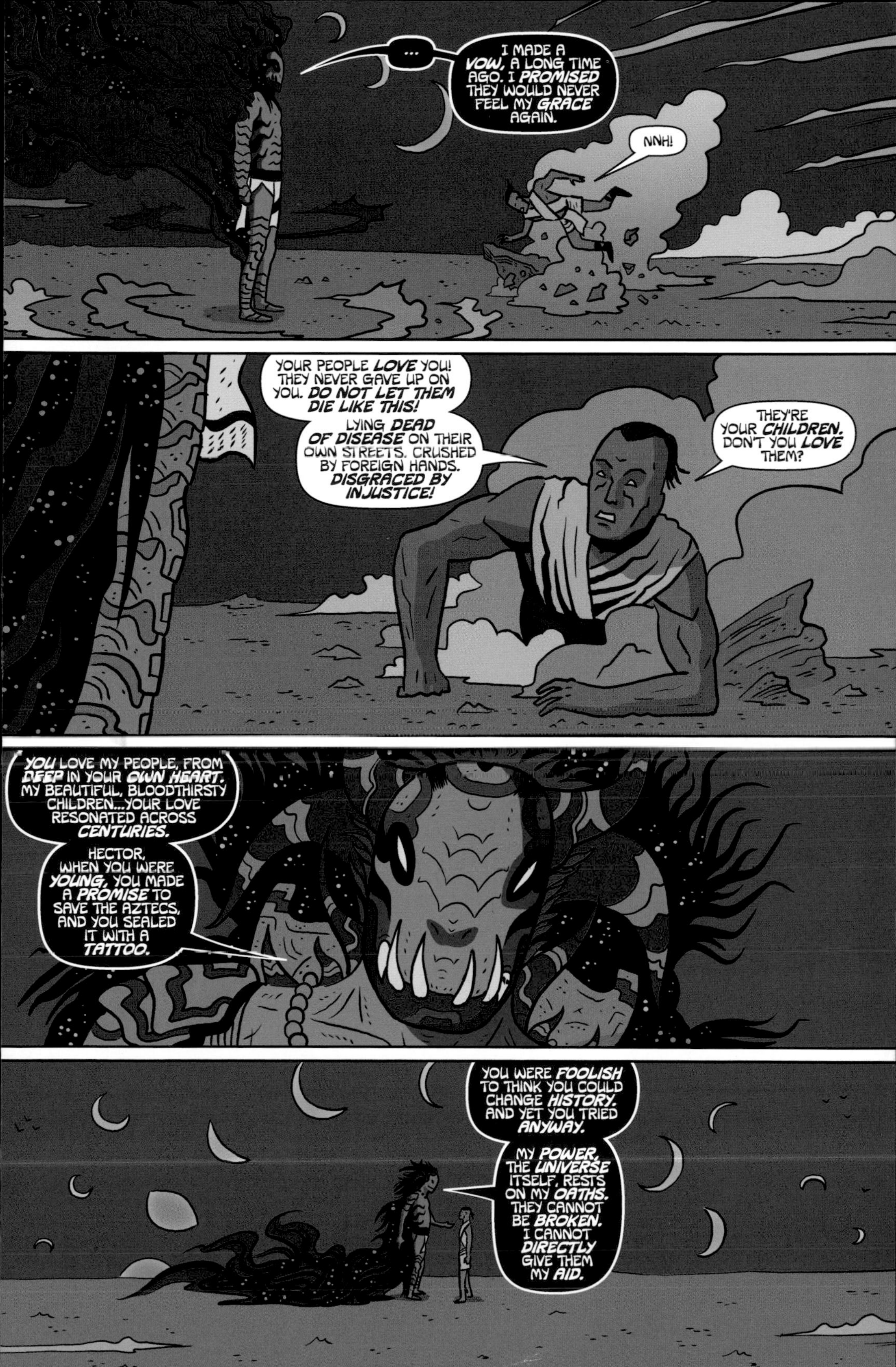
...
I MADE A VOW, A LONG TIME AGO. I PROMISED THEY WOULD NEVER FEEL MY GRACE AGAIN.
NNH!
YOUR PEOPLE LOVE YOU! THEY NEVER GAVE UP ON YOU. DO NOT LET THEM DIE LIKE THIS!
LYING DEAD OF DISEASE ON THEIR OWN STREETS. CRUSHED BY FOREIGN HANDS. DISGRACED BY INJUSTICE!
THEY'RE YOUR CHILDREN. DON'T YOU LOVE THEM?
YOU LOVE MY PEOPLE, FROM DEEP IN YOUR OWN HEART. MY BEAUTIFUL, BLOODTHIRSTY CHILDREN...YOUR LOVE RESONATED ACROSS CENTURIES.
HECTOR, WHEN YOU WERE YOUNG, YOU MADE A PROMISE TO SAVE THE AZTECS, AND YOU SEALED IT WITH A TATTOO.
YOU WERE FOOLISH TO THINK YOU COULD CHANGE HISTORY. AND YET YOU TRIED ANYWAY.
MY POWER, THE UNIVERSE ITSELF, RESTS ON MY OATHS. THEY CANNOT BE BROKEN. I CANNOT DIRECTLY GIVE THEM MY AID.

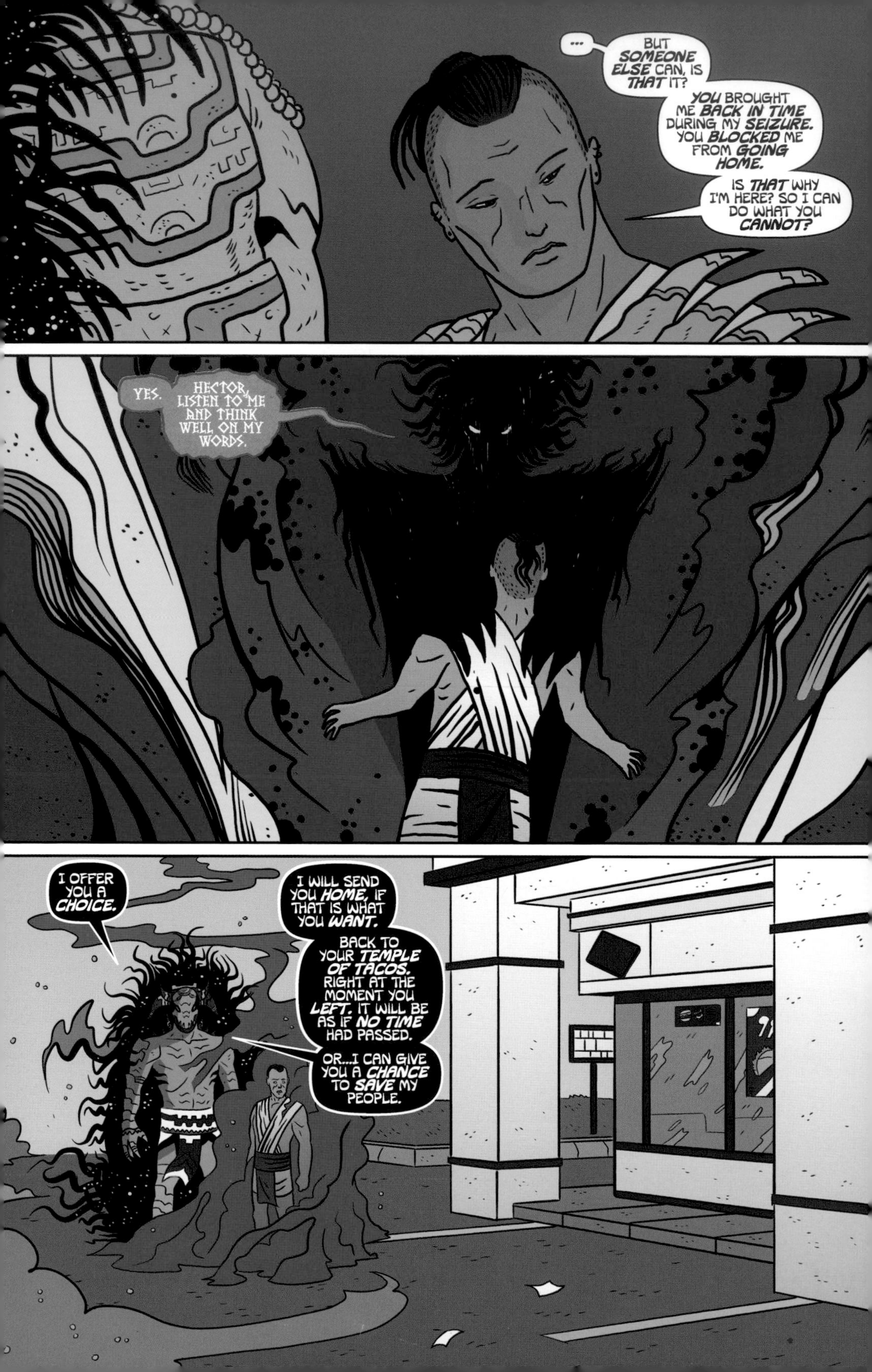
...
BUT SOMEONE ELSE CAN, IS THAT IT?
YOU BROUGHT ME BACK IN TIME DURING MY SEIZURE. YOU BLOCKED ME FROM GOING HOME.
IS THAT WHY I'M HERE? SO I CAN DO WHAT YOU CANNOT?
YES.
HECTOR, LISTEN TO ME AND THINK WELL ON MY WORDS.
I OFFER YOU A CHOICE.
I WILL SEND YOU HOME, IF THAT IS WHAT YOU WANT.
BACK TO YOUR TEMPLE OF TACOS. RIGHT AT THE MOMENT YOU LEFT. IT WILL BE AS IF NO TIME HAD PASSED.
OR...I CAN GIVE YOU A CHANCE TO SAVE MY PEOPLE.

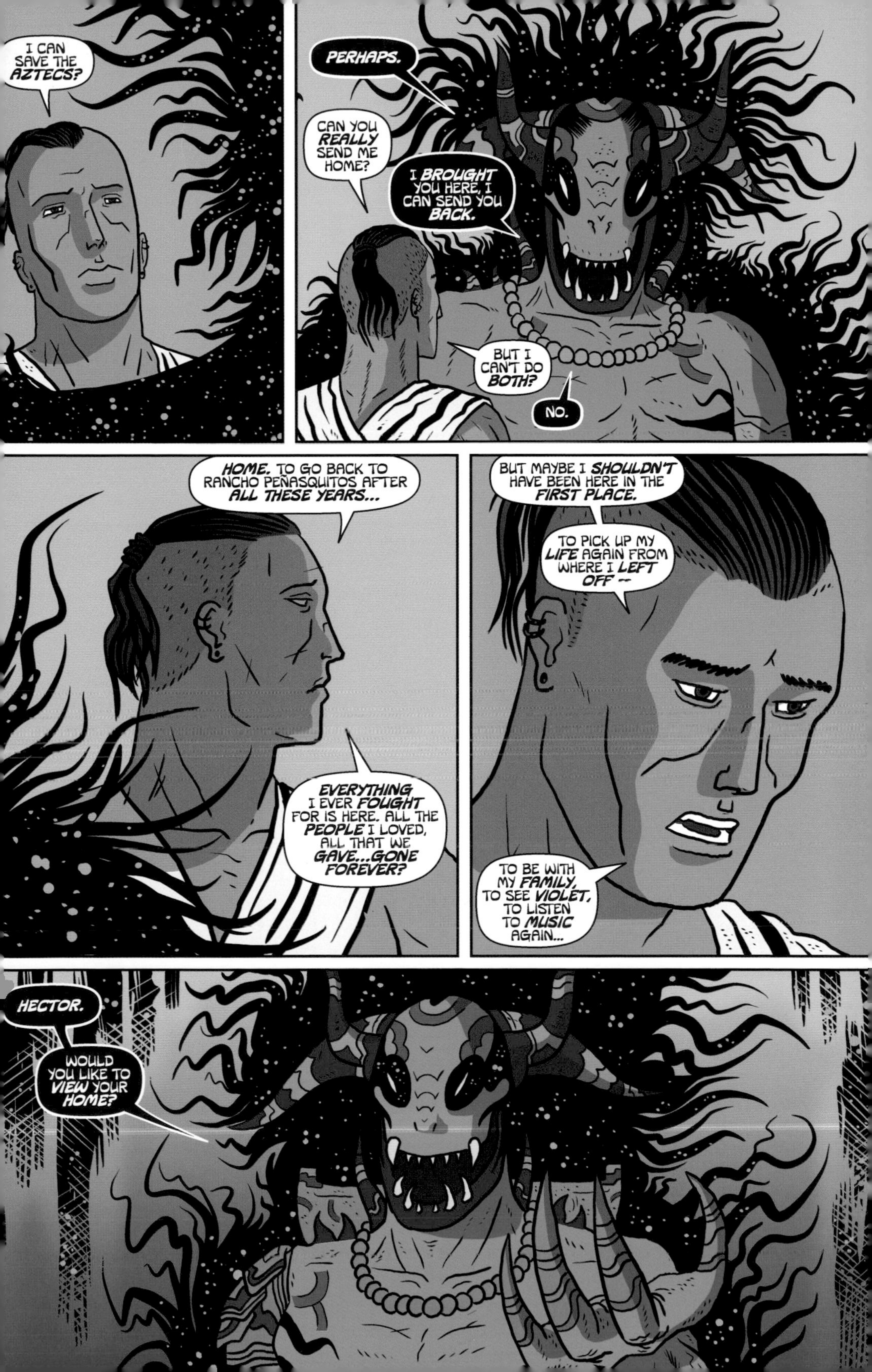
I CAN SAVE THE AZTECS?
PERHAPS.
CAN YOU REALLY SEND ME HOME?
I BROUGHT YOU HERE, I CAN SEND YOU BACK.
BUT I CAN'T DO BOTH?
NO.
HOME. TO GO BACK TO RANCHO PEÑASQUITOS AFTER ALL THESE YEARS...
EVERYTHING I EVER FOUGHT FOR IS HERE. ALL THE PEOPLE I LOVED, ALL THAT WE GAVE...GONE FOREVER?
BUT MAYBE I SHOULDN'T HAVE BEEN HERE IN THE FIRST PLACE.
TO PICK UP MY LIFE AGAIN FROM WHERE I LEFT OFF --
TO BE WITH MY FAMILY, TO SEE VIOLET, TO LISTEN TO MUSIC AGAIN...
HECTOR.
WOULD YOU LIKE TO VIEW YOUR HOME?

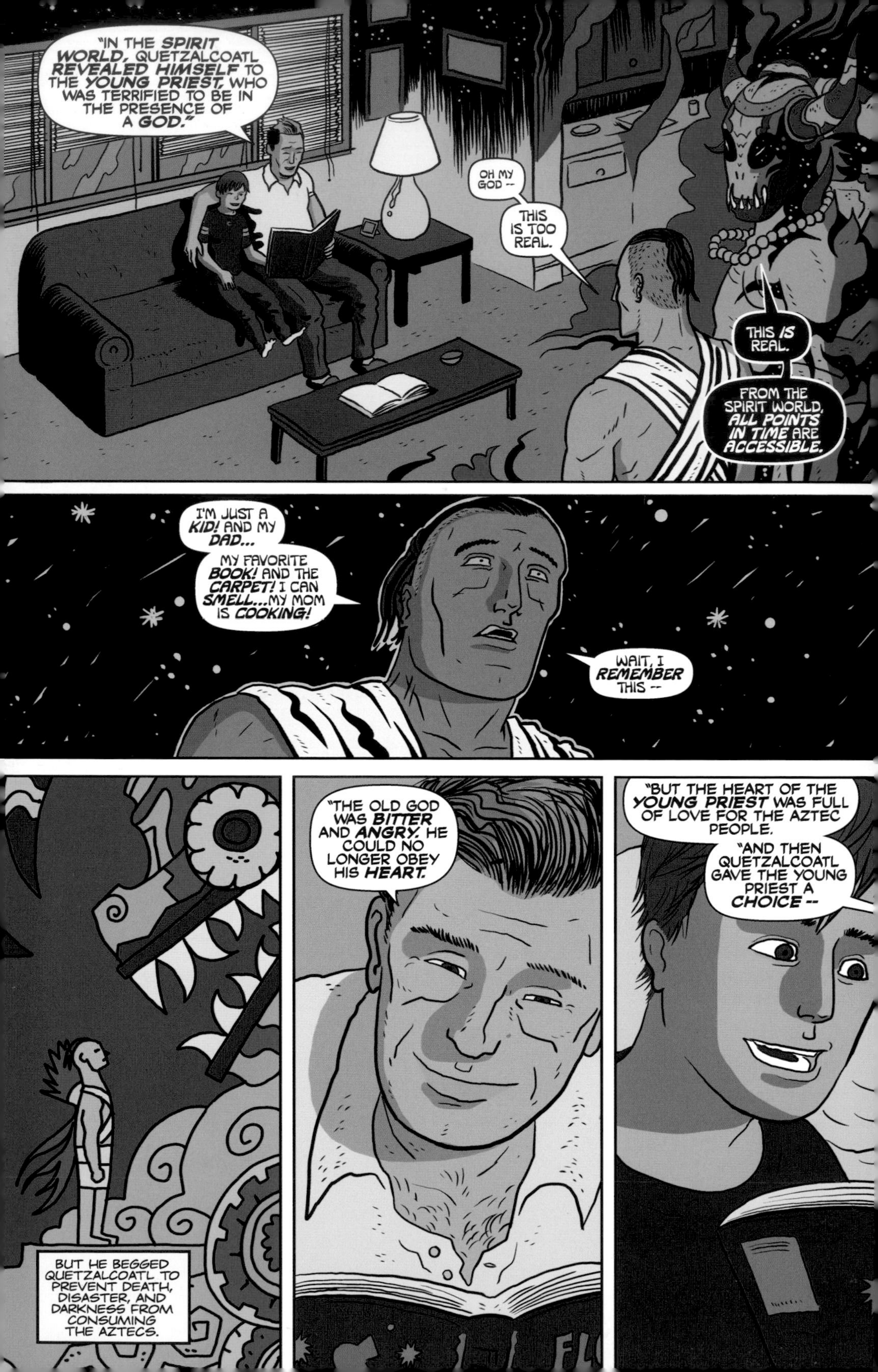
"IN THE SPIRIT WORLD, QUETZALCOATL REVEALED HIMSELF TO THE YOUNG PRIEST, WHO WAS TERRIFIED TO BE IN THE PRESENCE OF A GOD."
OH MY GOD --
THIS IS TOO REAL.
THIS IS REAL.
FROM THE SPIRIT WORLD, ALL POINTS IN TIME ARE ACCESSIBLE.
I'M JUST A KID! AND MY DAD...
MY FAVORITE BOOK! AND THE CARPET! I CAN SMELL...MY MOM IS COOKING!
WAIT, I REMEMBER THIS --
BUT HE BEGGED QUETZALCOATL TO PREVENT DEATH, DISASTER, AND DARKNESS FROM CONSUMING THE AZTECS.
"THE OLD GOD WAS BITTER AND ANGRY. HE COULD NO LONGER OBEY HIS HEART.
"BUT THE HEART OF THE YOUNG PRIEST WAS FULL OF LOVE FOR THE AZTEC PEOPLE.
"AND THEN QUETZALCOATL GAVE THE YOUNG PRIEST A CHOICE --

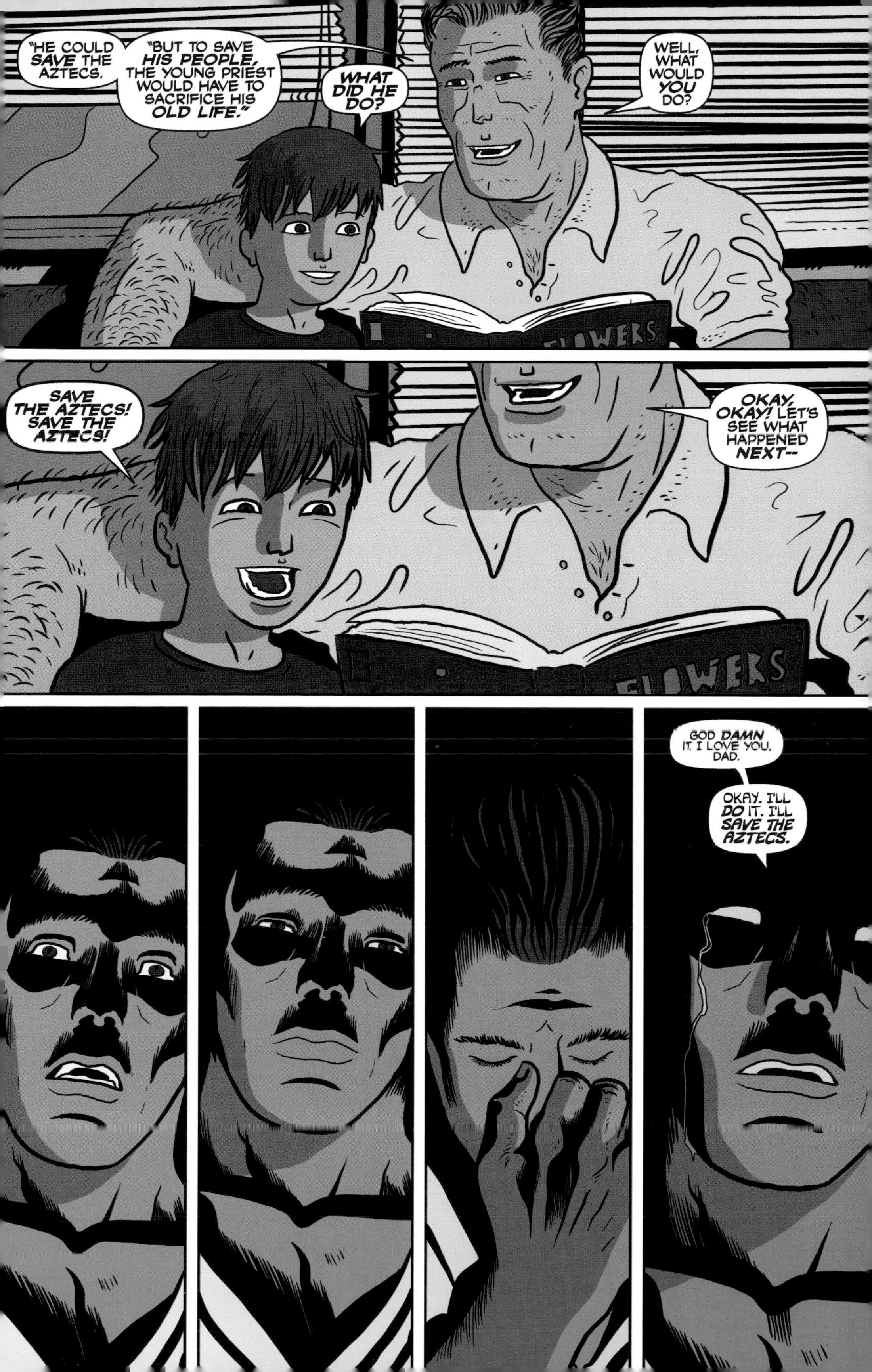
"HE COULD SAVE THE AZTECS.
"BUT TO SAVE HIS PEOPLE, THE YOUNG PRIEST WOULD HAVE TO SACRIFICE HIS OLD LIFE."
WHAT DID HE DO?
WELL, WHAT WOULD YOU DO?
FLOWERS
SAVE THE AZTECS! SAVE THE AZTECS!
OKAY, OKAY! LET'S SEE WHAT HAPPENED NEXT--
FLOWERS
GOD DAMN IT. I LOVE YOU, DAD.
OKAY. I'LL DO IT. I'LL SAVE THE AZTECS.

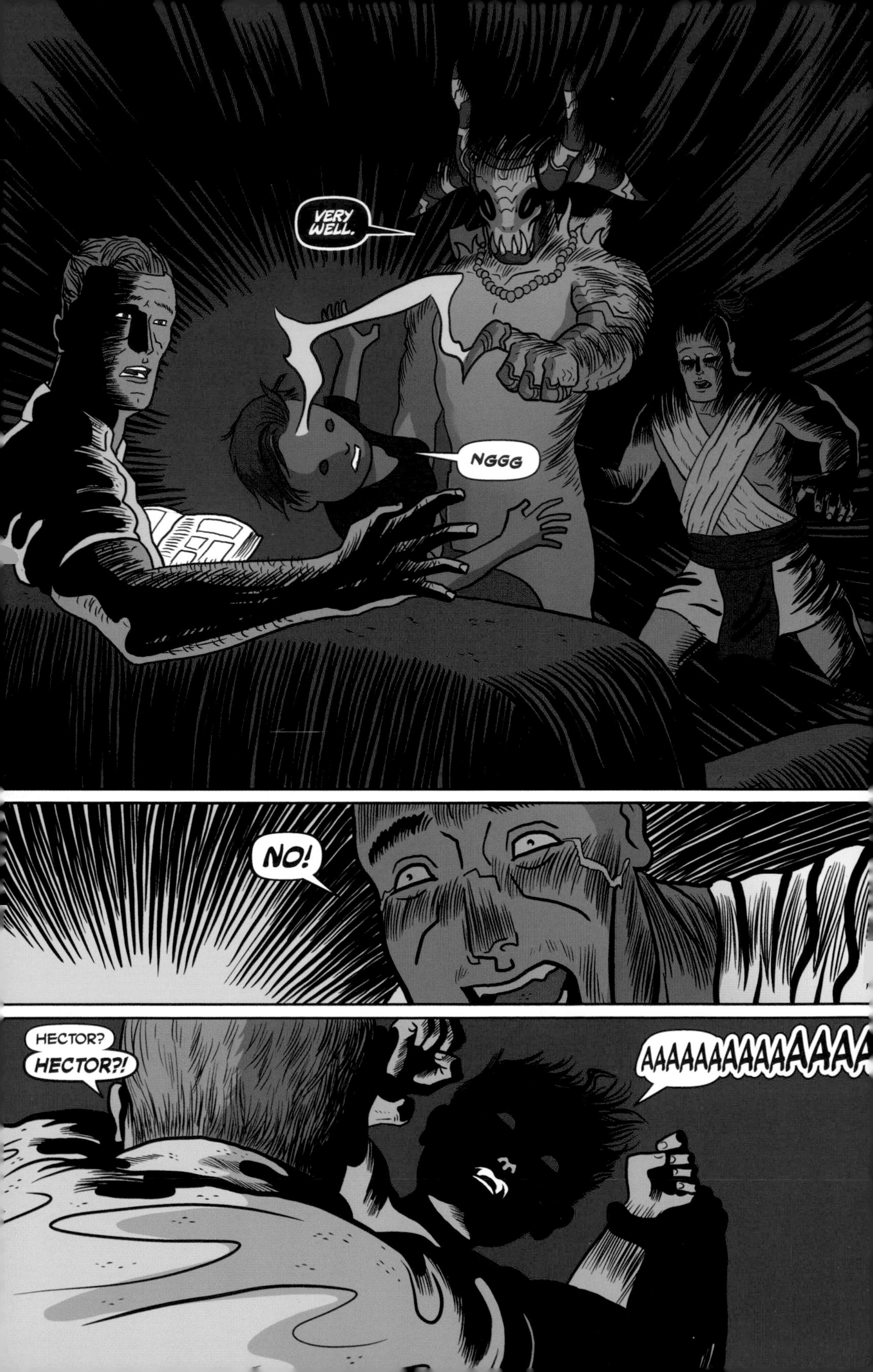
VERY WELL.
NGGG
NO!
HECTOR? HECTOR?!
AAAAAAAAAAAAAA

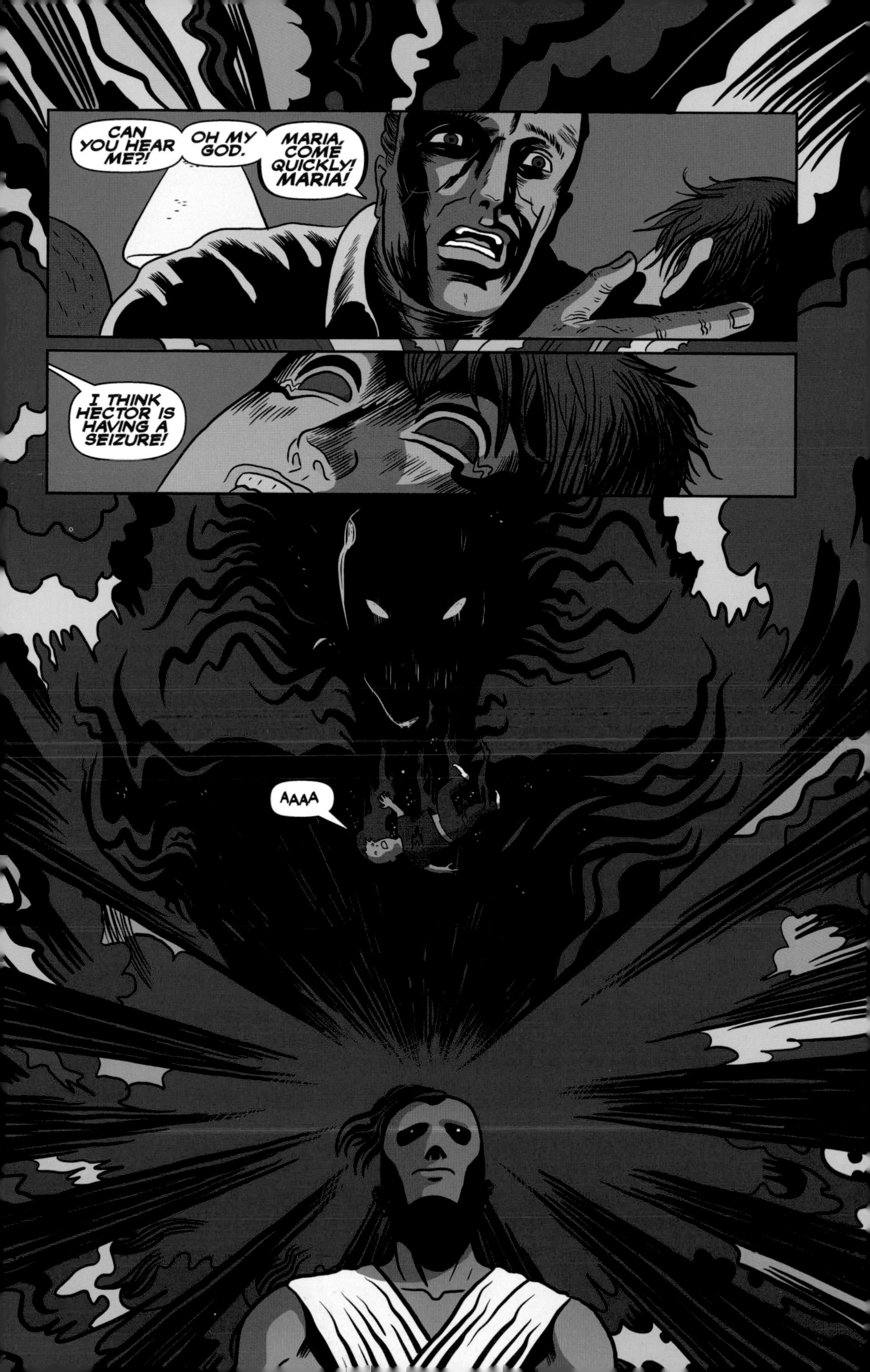
CAN YOU HEAR ME?!
OH MY GOD.
MARIA, COME QUICKLY! MARIA!
I THINK HECTOR IS HAVING A SEIZURE!
AAAA

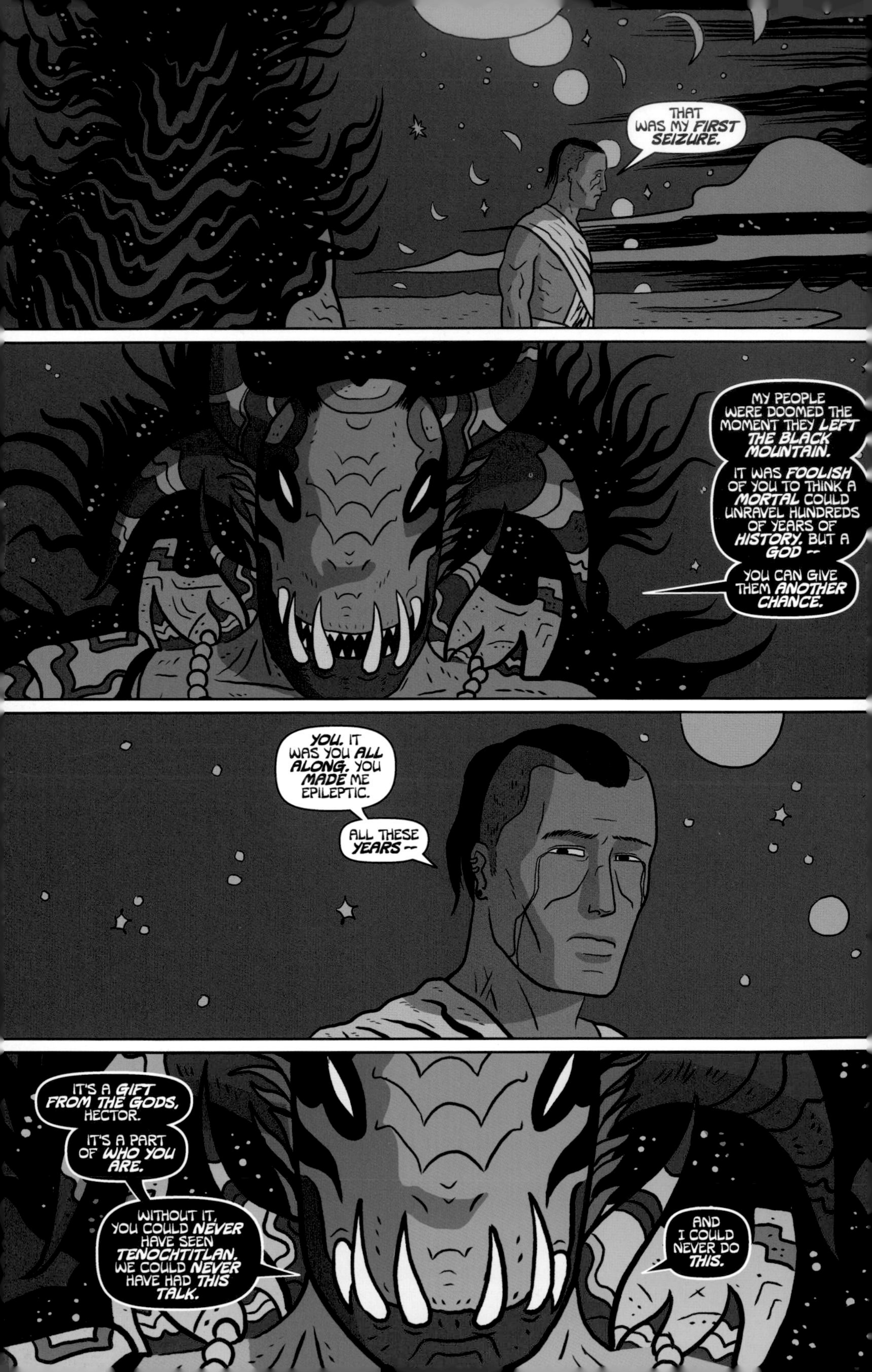
THAT WAS MY FIRST SEIZURE.
MY PEOPLE WERE DOOMED THE MOMENT THEY LEFT THE BLACK MOUNTAIN.
IT WAS FOOLISH OF YOU TO THINK A MORTAL COULD UNRAVEL HUNDREDS OF YEARS OF HISTORY. BUT A GOD --
YOU CAN GIVE THEM ANOTHER CHANCE.
YOU. IT WAS YOU ALL ALONG. YOU MADE ME EPILEPTIC.
ALL THESE YEARS --
IT'S A GIFT FROM THE GODS, HECTOR.
IT'S A PART OF WHO YOU ARE.
WITHOUT IT, YOU COULD NEVER HAVE SEEN TENOCHTITLAN. WE COULD NEVER HAVE HAD THIS TALK.
AND I COULD NEVER DO THIS.

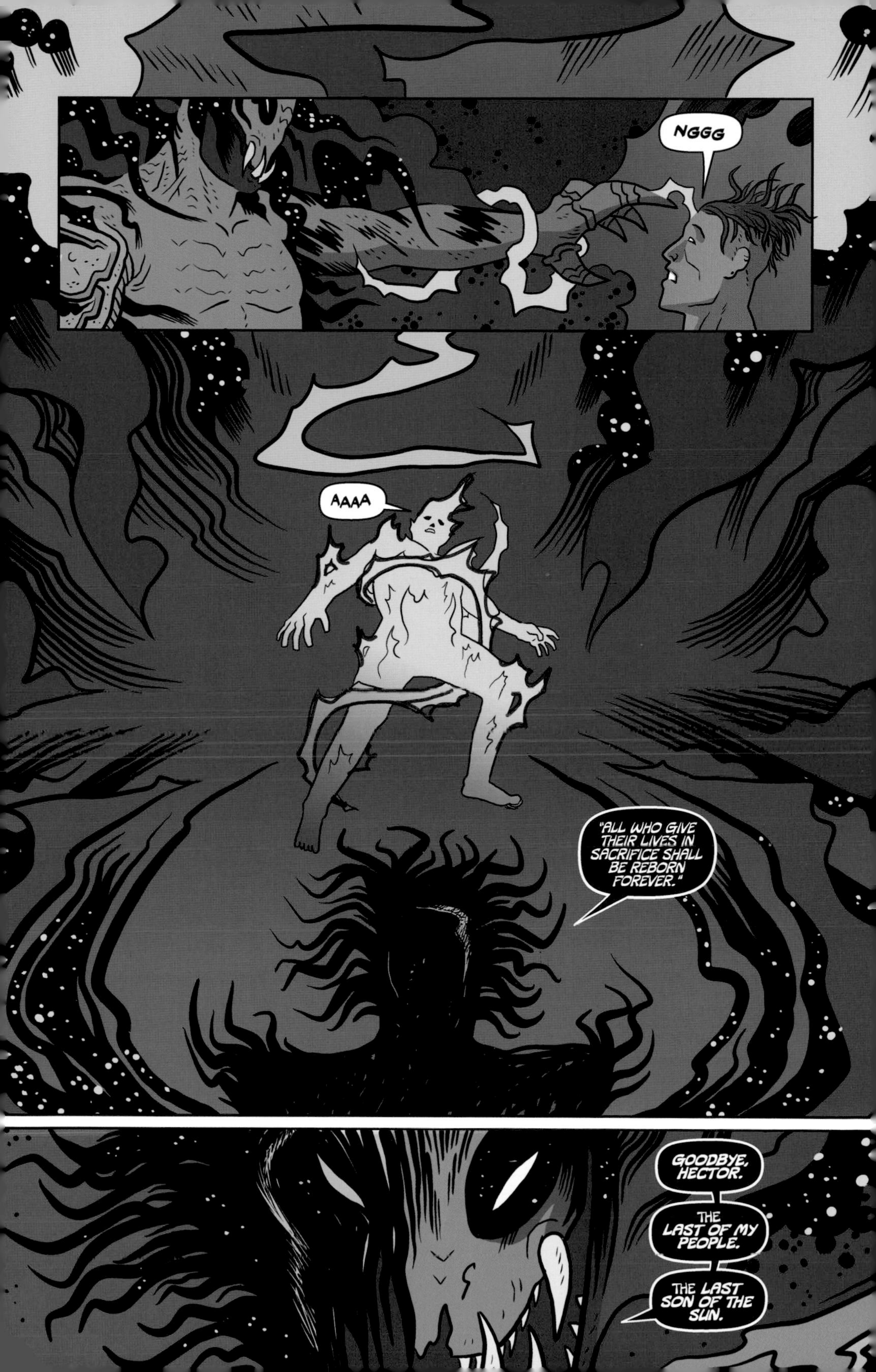
NGGG
AAAA
"ALL WHO GIVE THEIR LIVES IN SACRIFICE SHALL BE REBORN FOREVER."
GOODBYE, HECTOR.
THE LAST OF MY PEOPLE.
THE LAST SON OF THE SUN.

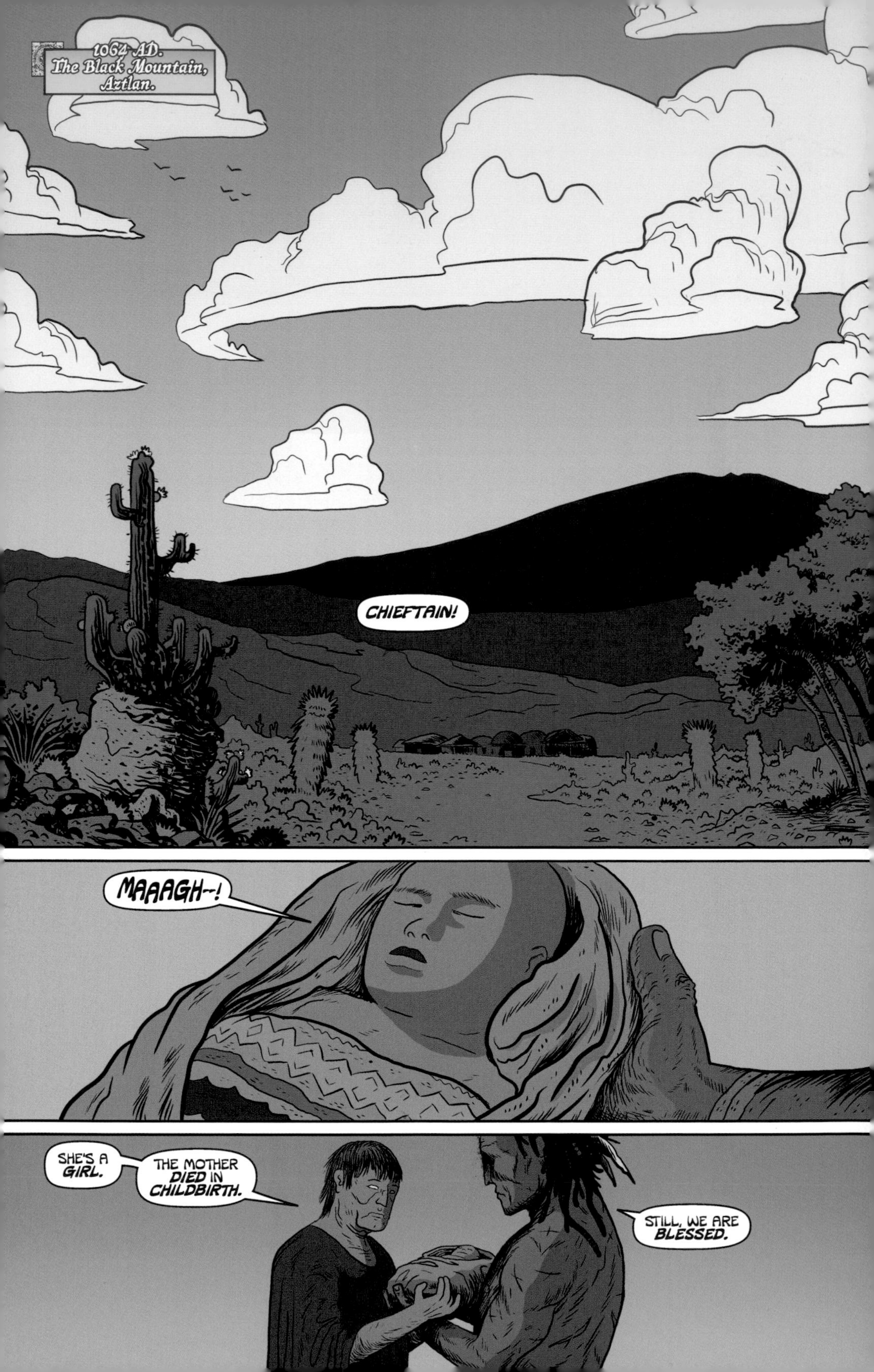
1064 AD.
The Black Mountain,
Aztlan.
CHIEFTAIN!
MAAAGH--!
SHE'S A GIRL.
THE MOTHER DIED IN CHILDBIRTH.
STILL, WE ARE BLESSED.

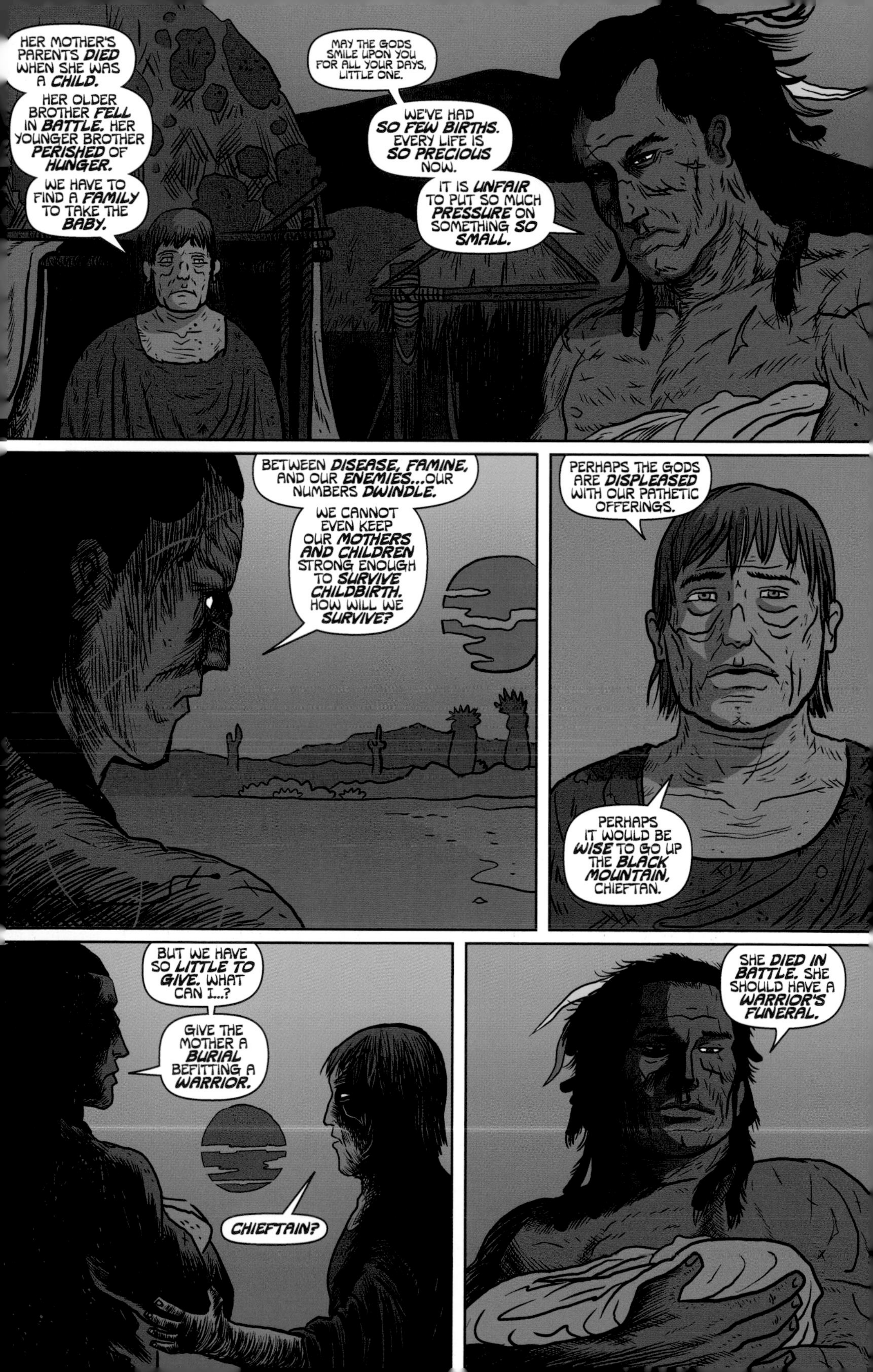
HER MOTHER'S PARENTS DIED WHEN SHE WAS A CHILD.
HER OLDER BROTHER FELL IN BATTLE. HER YOUNGER BROTHER PERISHED OF HUNGER.
WE HAVE TO FIND A FAMILY TO TAKE THE BABY.
MAY THE GODS SMILE UPON YOU FOR ALL YOUR DAYS, LITTLE ONE.
WE'VE HAD SO FEW BIRTHS. EVERY LIFE IS SO PRECIOUS NOW.
IT IS UNFAIR TO PUT SO MUCH PRESSURE ON SOMETHING SO SMALL.
BETWEEN DISEASE, FAMINE, AND OUR ENEMIES...OUR NUMBERS DWINDLE.
WE CANNOT EVEN KEEP OUR MOTHERS AND CHILDREN STRONG ENOUGH TO SURVIVE CHILDBIRTH. HOW WILL WE SURVIVE?
PERHAPS THE GODS ARE DISPLEASED WITH OUR PATHETIC OFFERINGS.
PERHAPS IT WOULD BE WISE TO GO UP THE BLACK MOUNTAIN, CHIEFTAN.
BUT WE HAVE SO LITTLE TO GIVE. WHAT CAN I...?
GIVE THE MOTHER A BURIAL BEFITTING A WARRIOR.
CHIEFTAIN?
SHE DIED IN BATTLE. SHE SHOULD HAVE A WARRIOR'S FUNERAL.

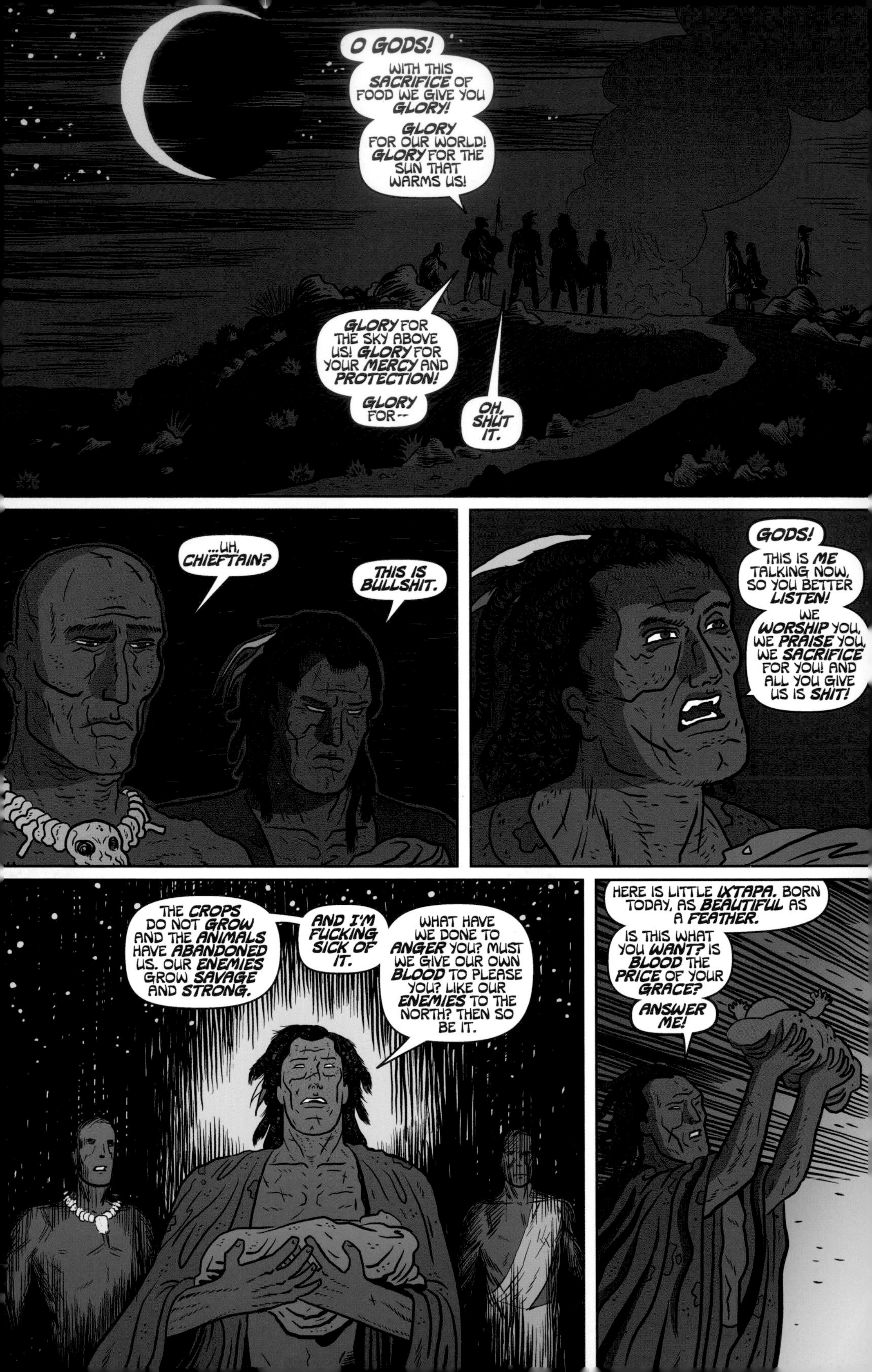
O GODS!
WITH THIS SACRIFICE OF FOOD WE GIVE YOU GLORY!
GLORY FOR OUR WORLD! GLORY FOR THE SUN THAT WARMS US!
GLORY FOR THE SKY ABOVE US! GLORY FOR YOUR MERCY AND PROTECTION!
GLORY FOR--
OH, SHUT IT.
...UH, CHIEFTAIN?
THIS IS BULLSHIT.
GODS!
THIS IS ME TALKING NOW, SO YOU BETTER LISTEN!
WE WORSHIP YOU, WE PRAISE YOU, WE SACRIFICE FOR YOU! AND ALL YOU GIVE US IS SHIT!
THE CROPS DO NOT GROW AND THE ANIMALS HAVE ABANDONED US. OUR ENEMIES GROW SAVAGE AND STRONG.
AND I'M FUCKING SICK OF IT.
WHAT HAVE WE DONE TO ANGER YOU? MUST WE GIVE OUR OWN BLOOD TO PLEASE YOU? LIKE OUR ENEMIES TO THE NORTH? THEN SO BE IT.
HERE IS LITTLE IXTAPA, BORN TODAY, AS BEAUTIFUL AS A FEATHER.
IS THIS WHAT YOU WANT? IS BLOOD THE PRICE OF YOUR GRACE?
ANSWER ME!

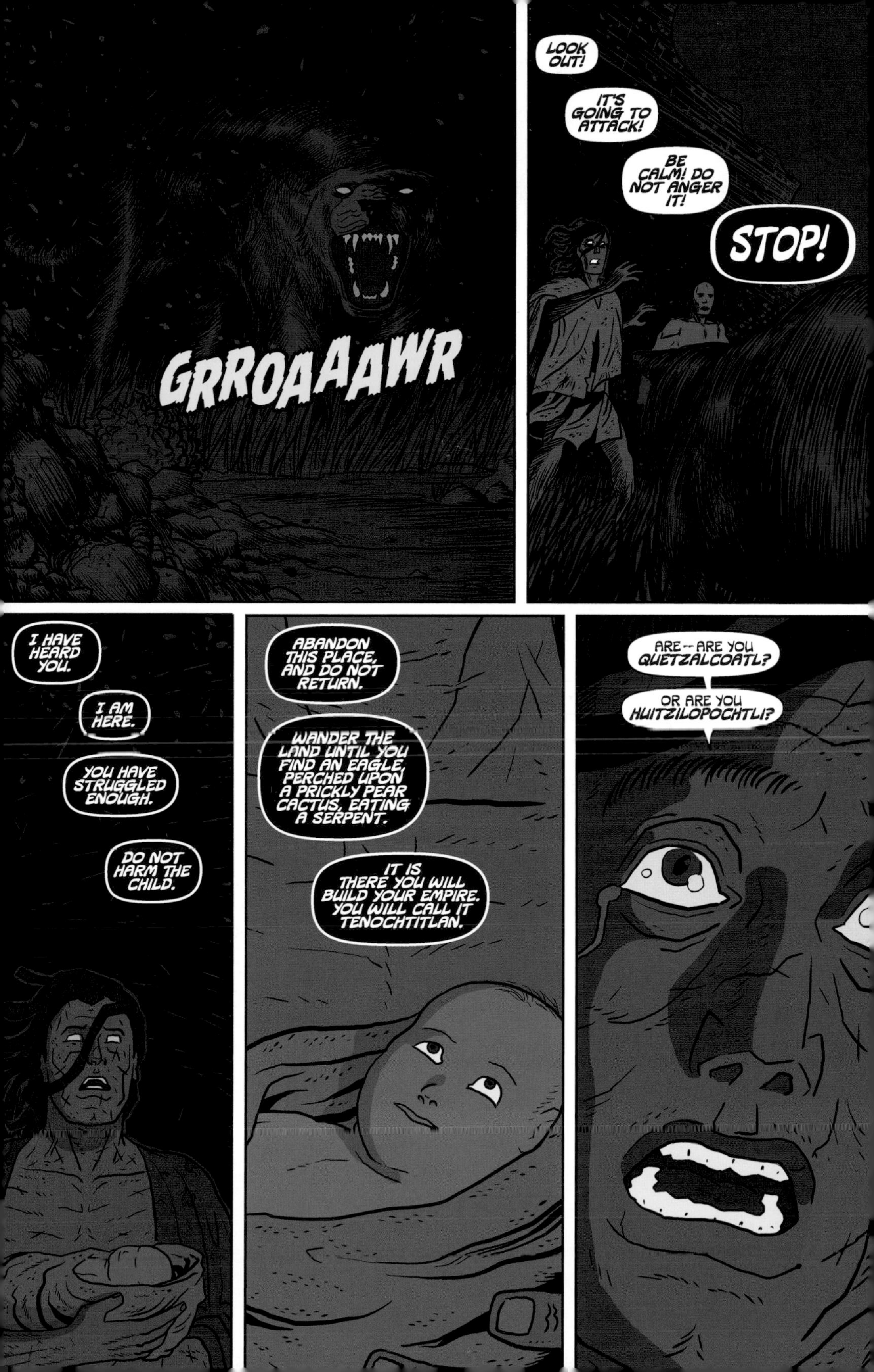
GRROAAAWR
LOOK OUT!
IT'S GOING TO ATTACK!
BE CALM! DO NOT ANGER IT!
STOP!
I HAVE HEARD YOU.
I AM HERE.
YOU HAVE STRUGGLED ENOUGH.
DO NOT HARM THE CHILD.
ABANDON THIS PLACE, AND DO NOT RETURN.
WANDER THE LAND UNTIL YOU FIND AN EAGLE, PERCHED UPON A PRICKLY PEAR CACTUS, EATING A SERPENT.
IT IS THERE YOU WILL BUILD YOUR EMPIRE. YOU WILL CALL IT TENOCHTITLAN.
ARE--ARE YOU QUETZALCOATL?
OR ARE YOU HUITZILOPOCHTLI?

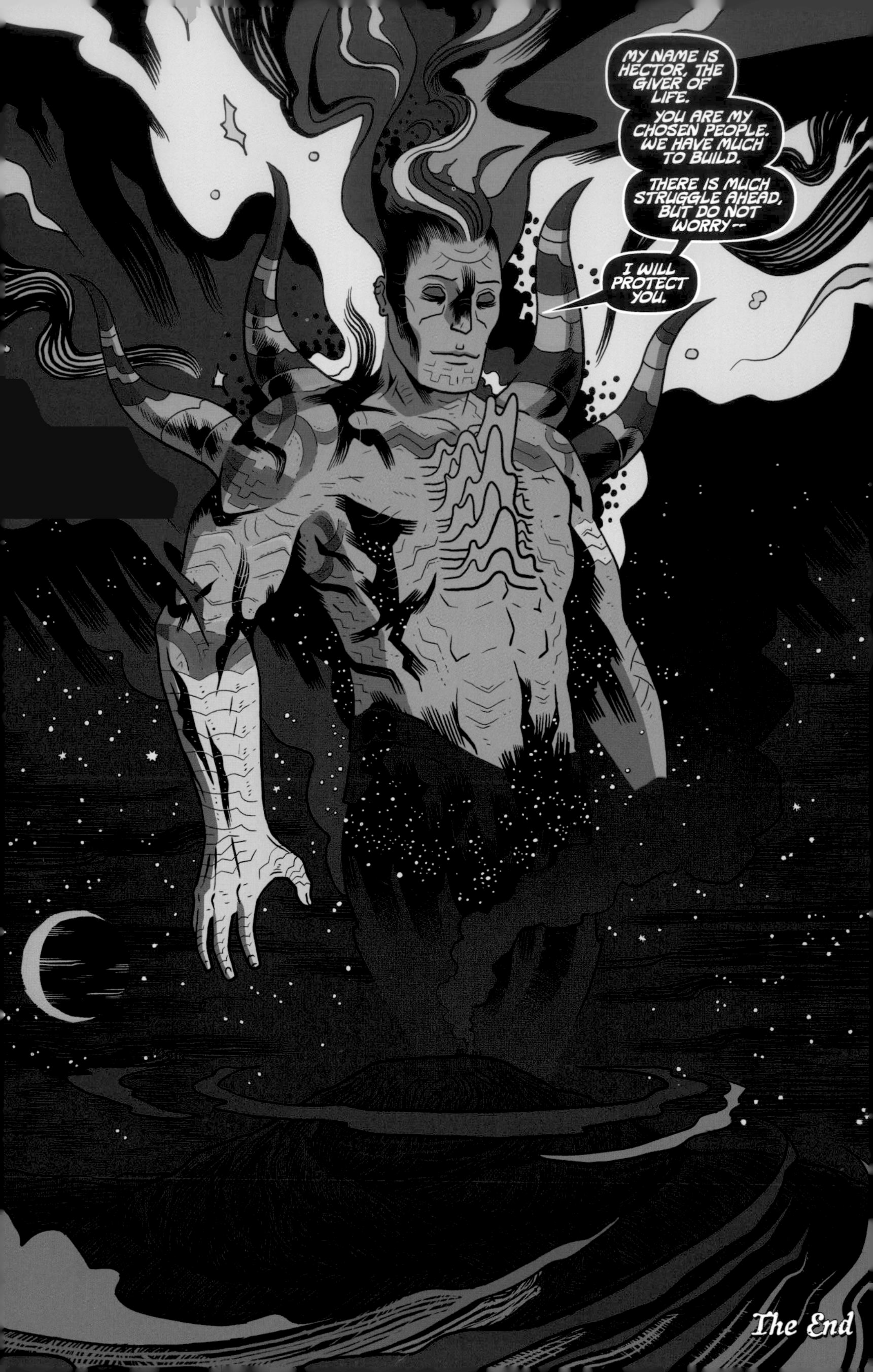
MY NAME IS HECTOR, THE GIVER OF LIFE.
YOU ARE MY CHOSEN PEOPLE. WE HAVE MUCH TO BUILD.
THERE IS MUCH STRUGGLE AHEAD, BUT DO NOT WORRY--
I WILL PROTECT YOU.
The End

SACRIFICE™

SKETCHBOOK

NOTES BY DALTON ROSE

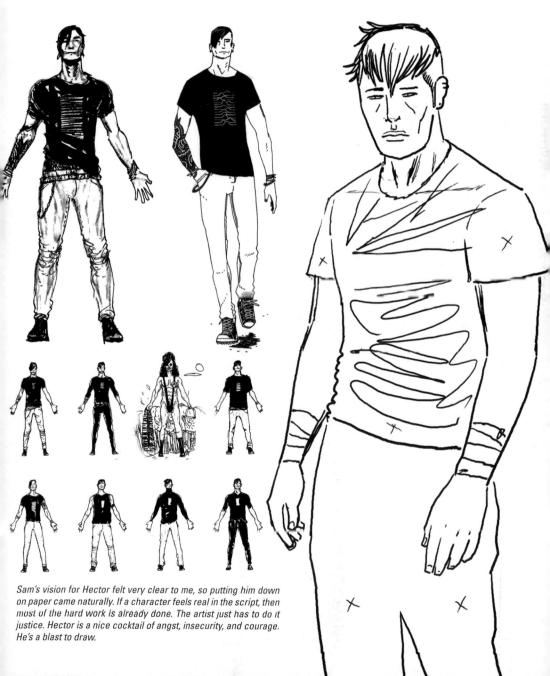

Sam's vision for Hector felt very clear to me, so putting him down on paper came naturally. If a character feels real in the script, then most of the hard work is already done. The artist just has to do it justice. Hector is a nice cocktail of angst, insecurity, and courage. He's a blast to draw.

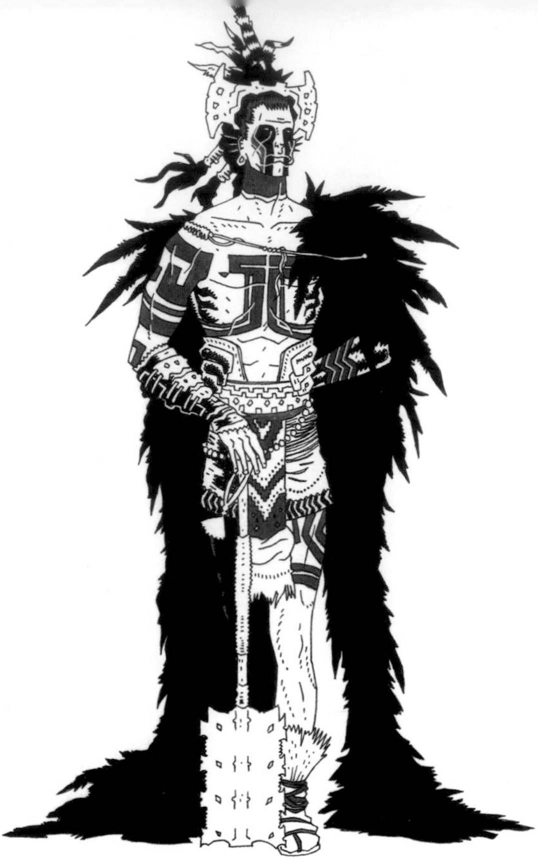

Itzcoatl is maybe the coolest character in Sacrifice. *Morally ambiguous, calculating, and enigmatic, he was an exciting challenge to depict. As he is a foil to Hector's wide-eyed vulnerability, I wanted Itzcoatl to be a study in obscurity, hidden under paint, robes, and feathers, with few clues as to the character beneath.*

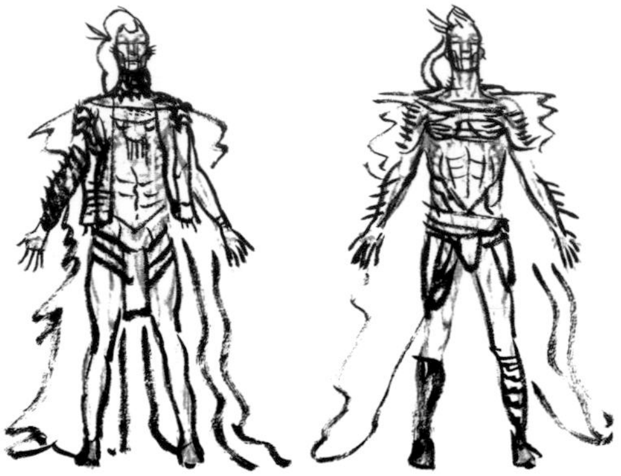

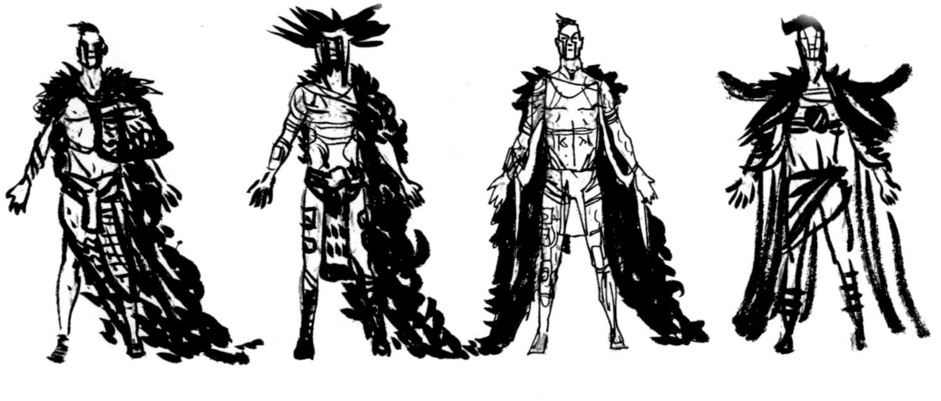

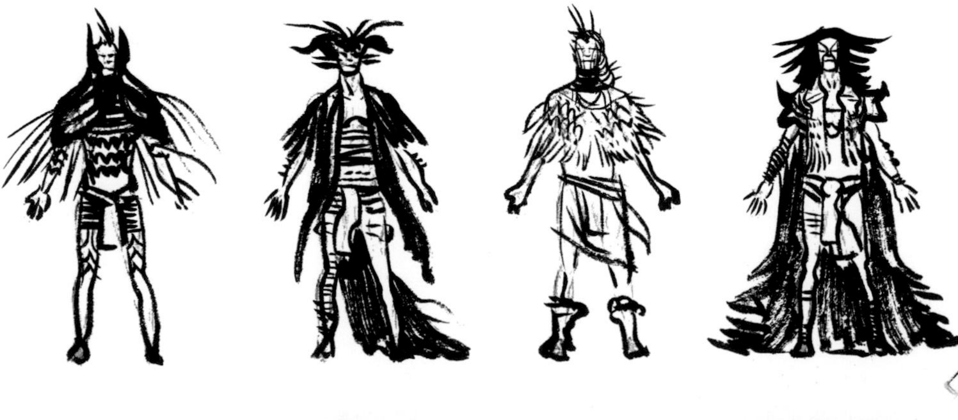

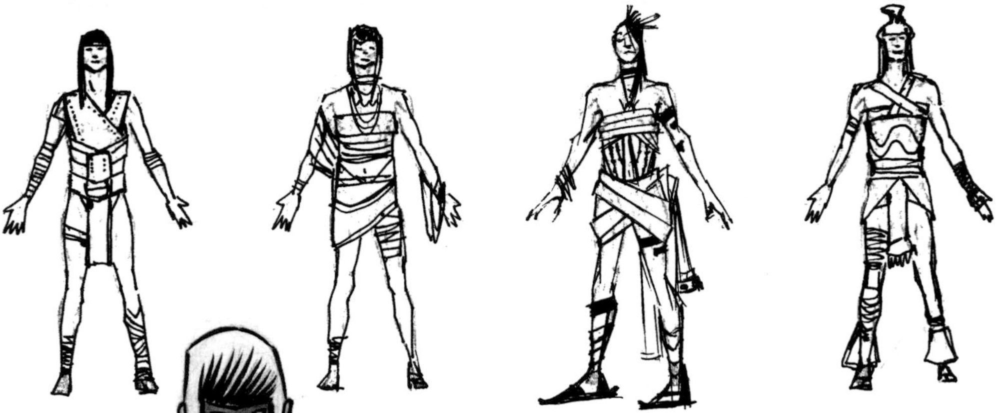

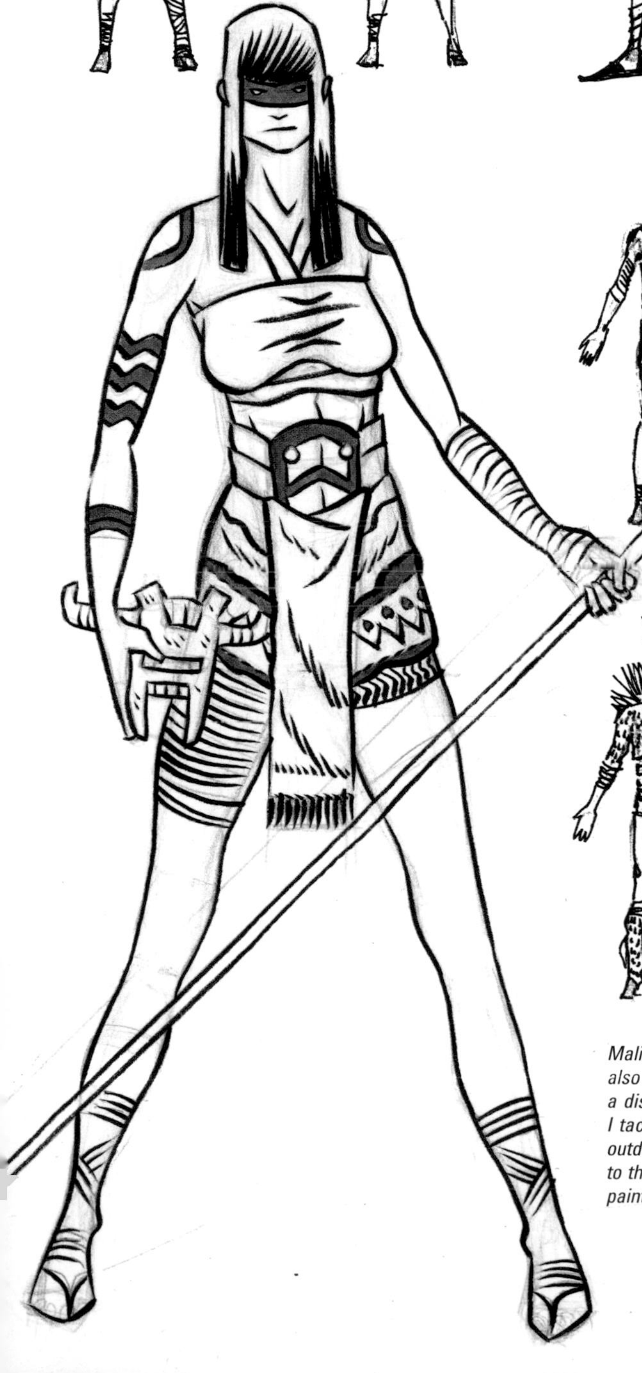

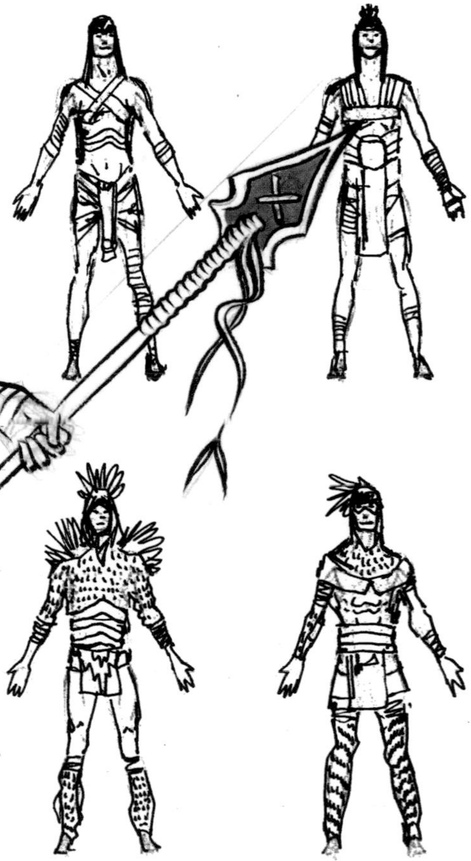

Malin is a warrior—proud, lithe, and dangerous. She also holds some serious grudges, keeps everyone at a distance, and never lowers her guard. The more I tacked on to her, the less she looked like a wild, outdoorsy, revenge-obsessed killer. It all came down to the eyes. Dark, judging, hateful eyes. A little war paint goes a long way.

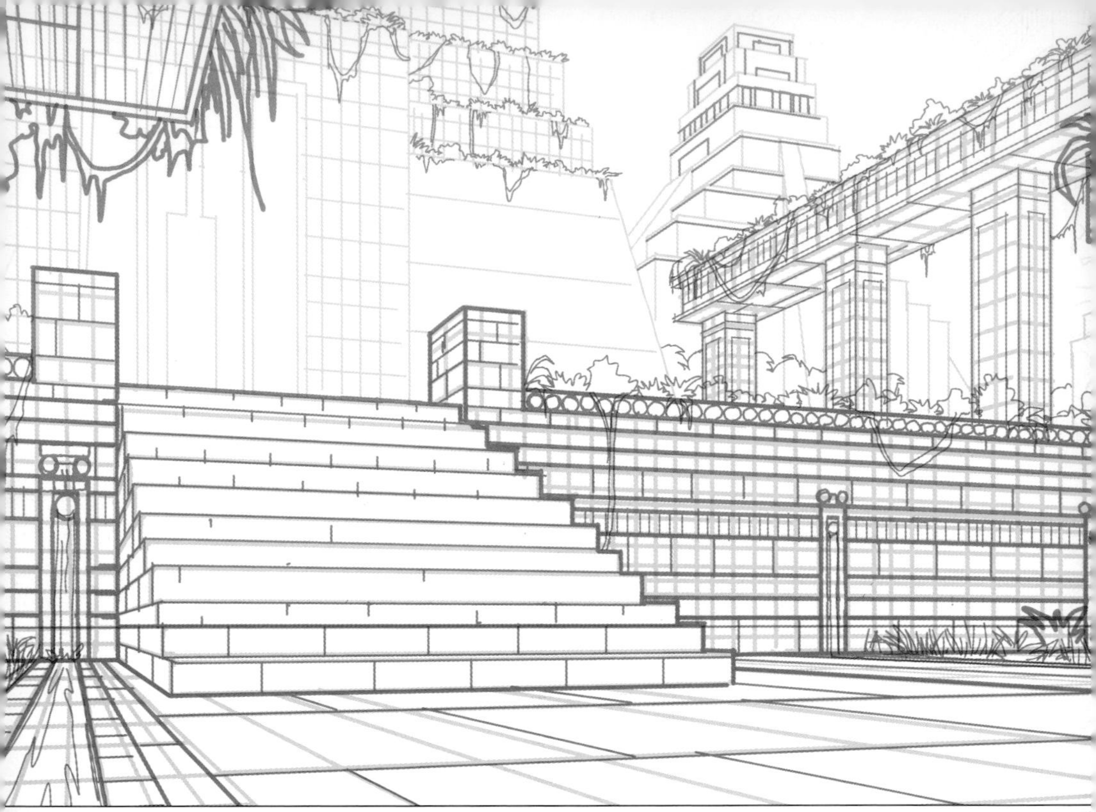

For a setting like this, I spend some time building up a solid perspective grid in Photoshop or Manga Studio. Then I add the details over the top. The characters are placed in the shot last.

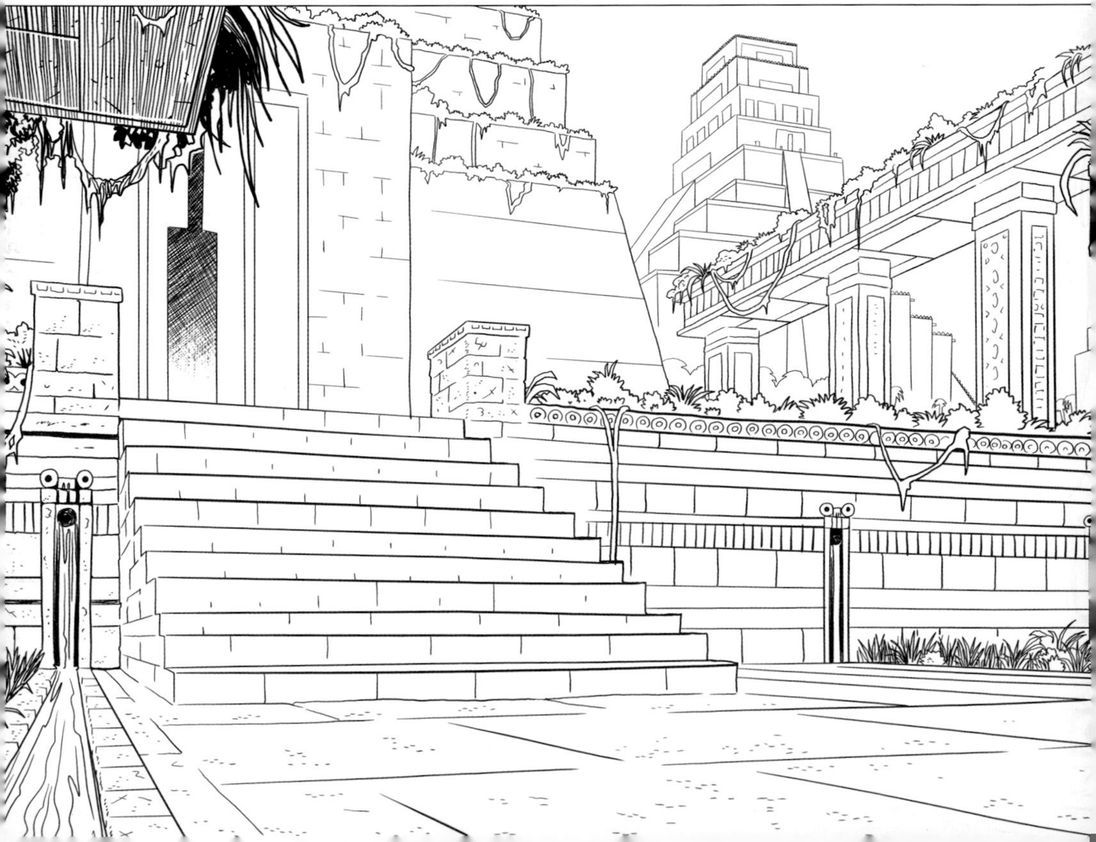

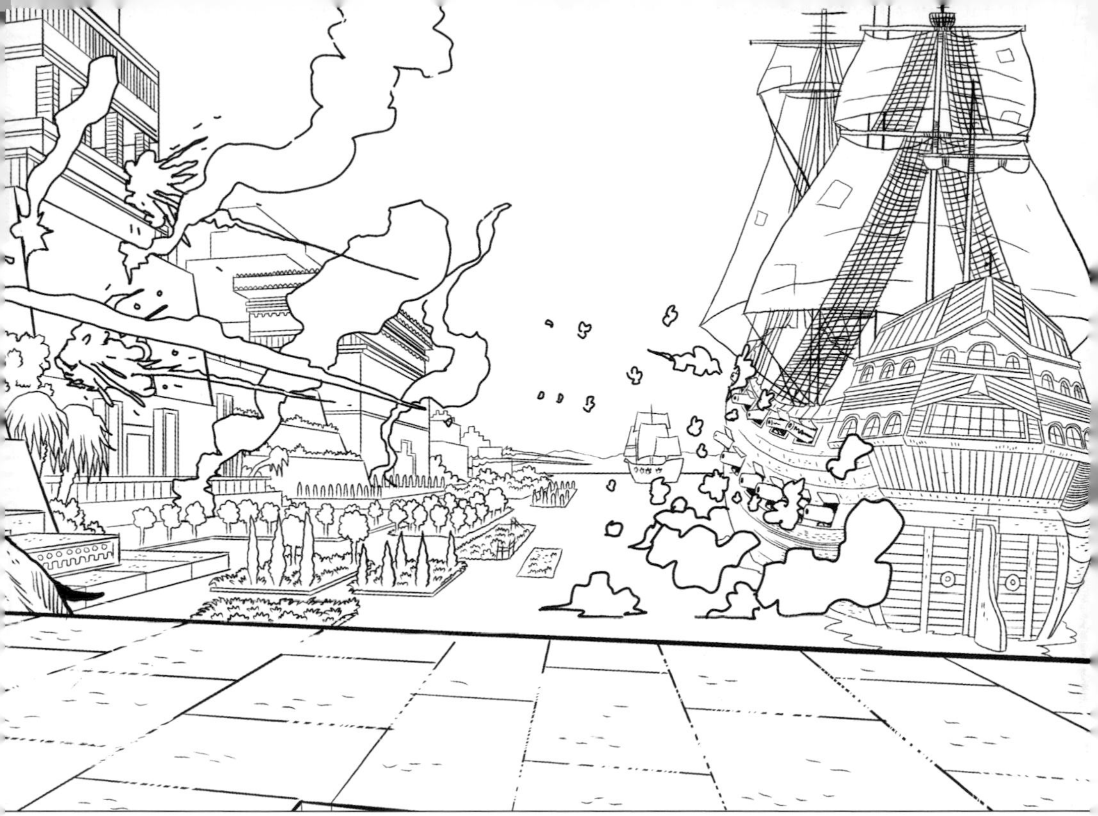

I love drawing backgrounds. Sam gave me a lot of room to pick and design the settings in Sacrifice*, and by the end they were one of my favorite parts of drawing the book.*

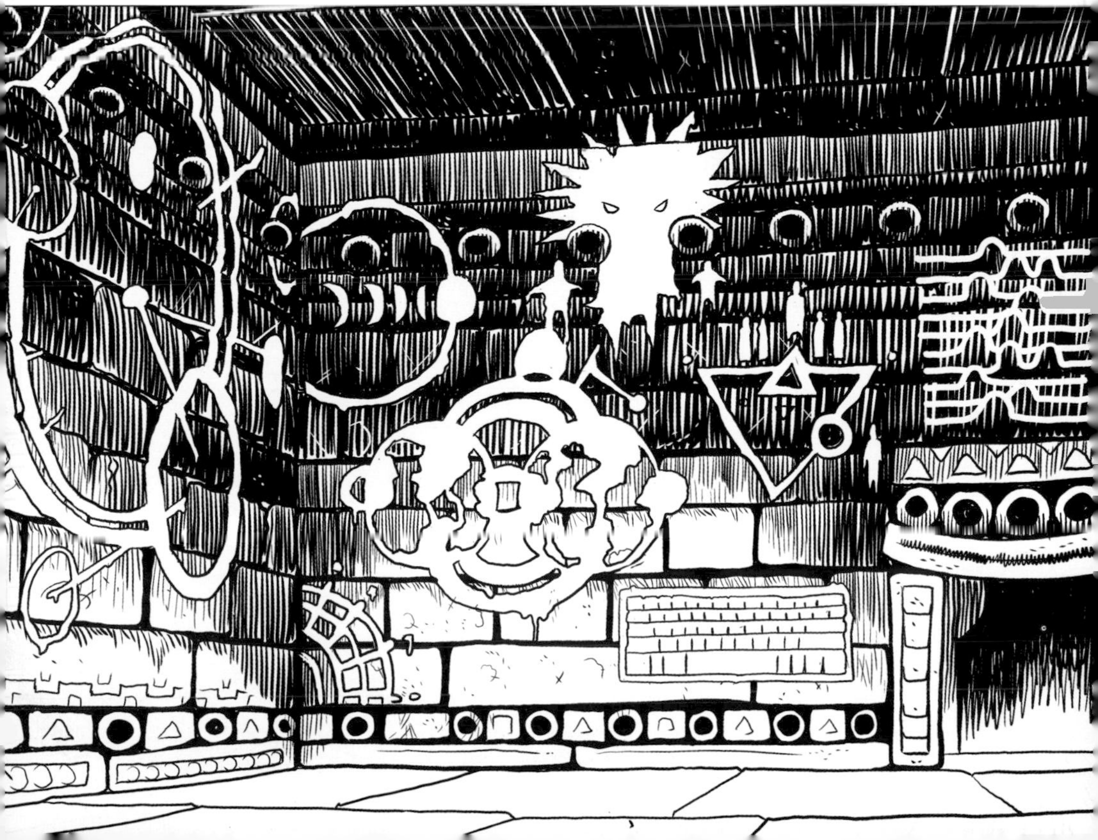

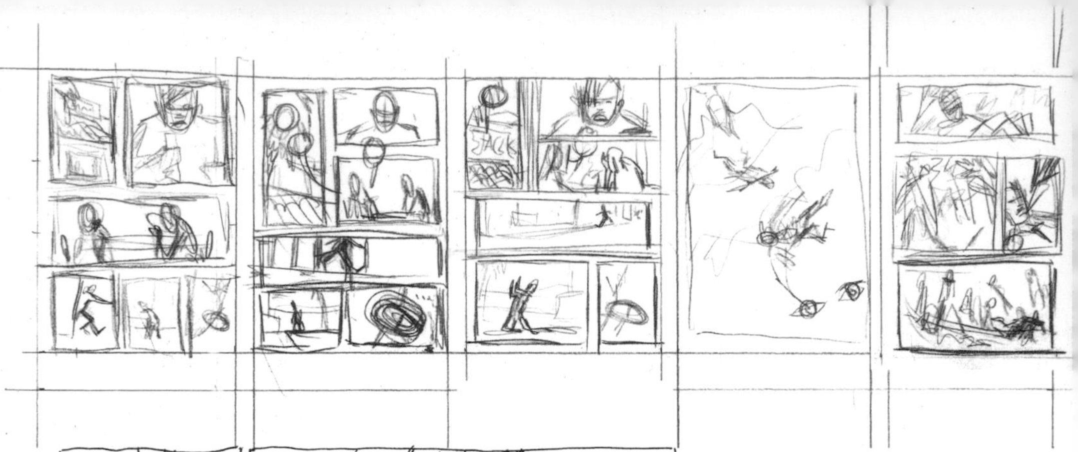

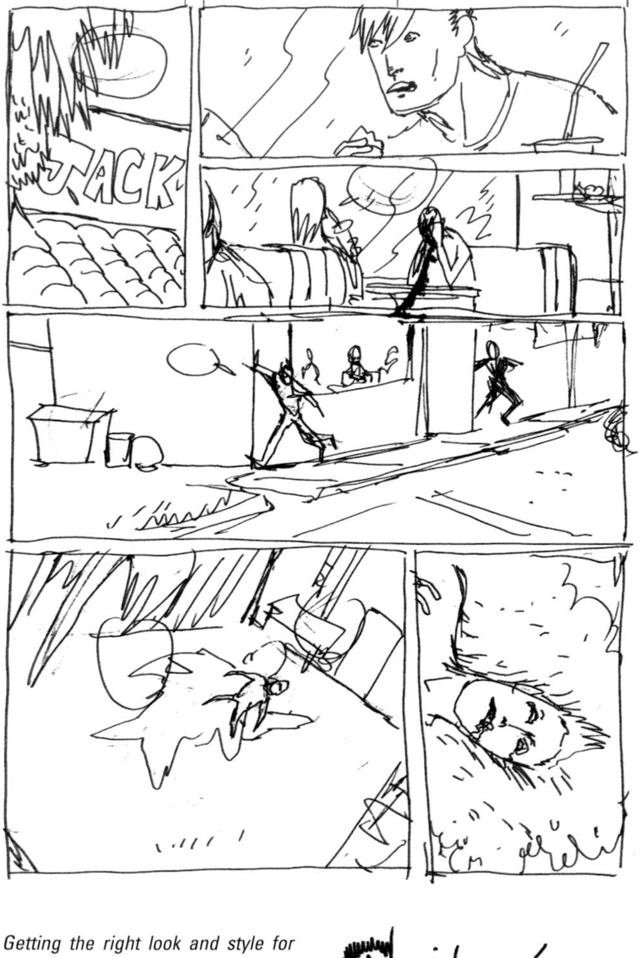
JACK

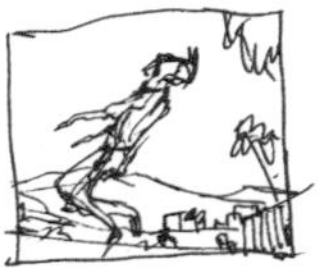

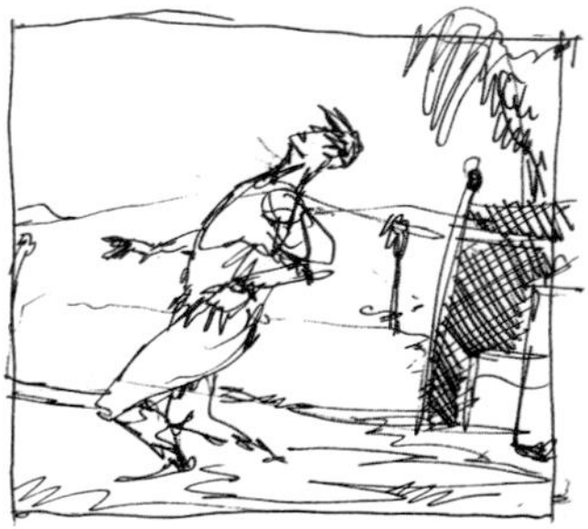

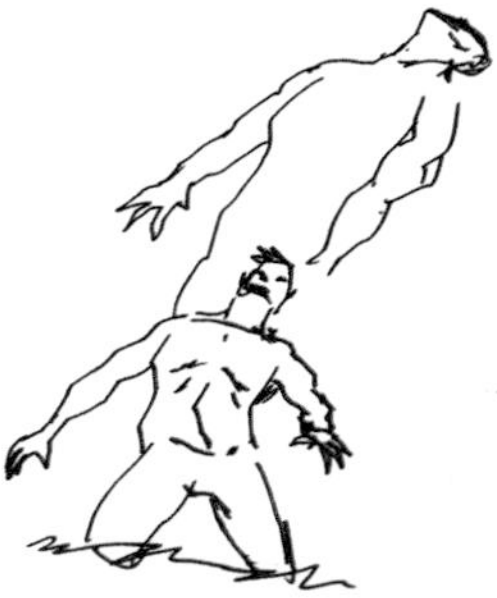

Getting the right look and style for Sacrifice *took some time, as you can see in these early drawings. On the facing page is an early version of page 1, back when the book was called* Flowers, Feathers, and Blood. *The opening scene was rewritten and redrawn before publication.*

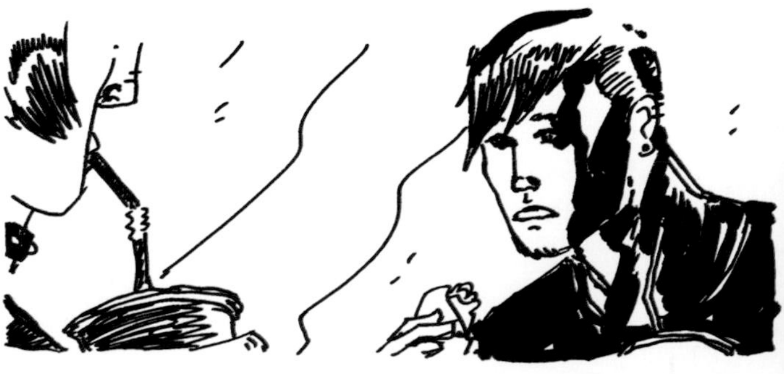

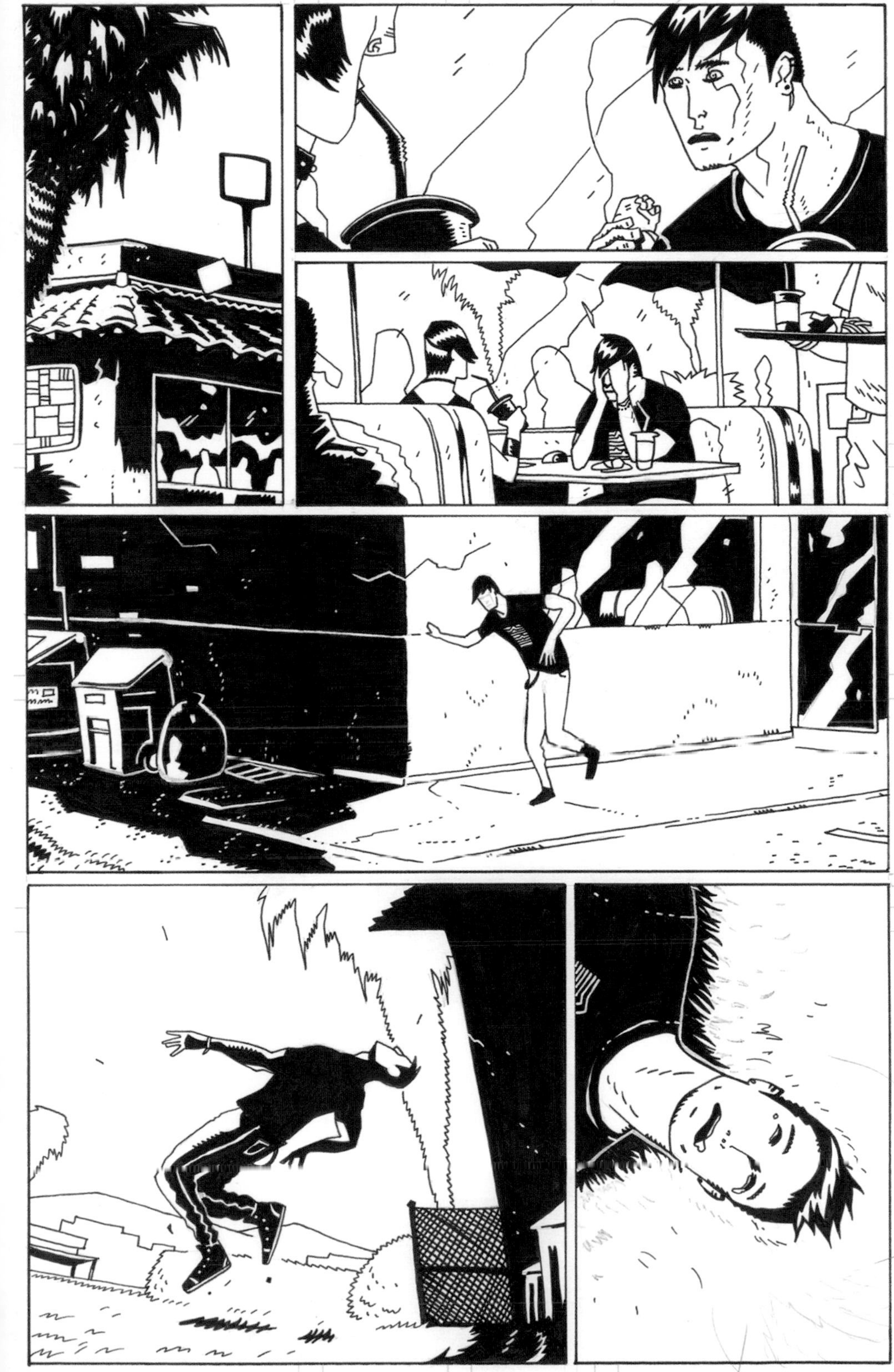

Redo

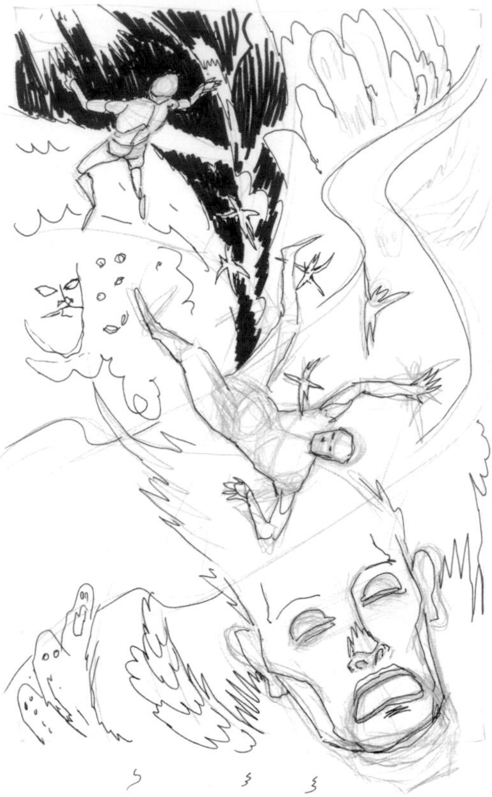

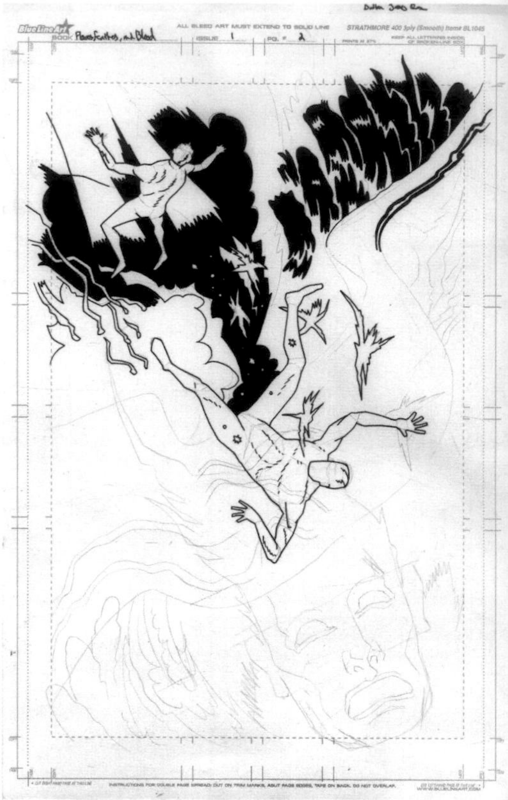
Blue Line Art
BOOK
ALL BLEED ART MUST EXTEND TO SOLID LINE
ISSUE
PG. #
STRATHMORE 400 3ply (Smooth) Item SL1045

My initial ideas about Hector's altered states were a little on the cosmic side. Sam had a very unique vision for the psychedelic travels of our hero, based on his own experiences as an epileptic. They would become more of a seething ocean of psychedelia, rather than a vast universe. I'm happy we pushed it.

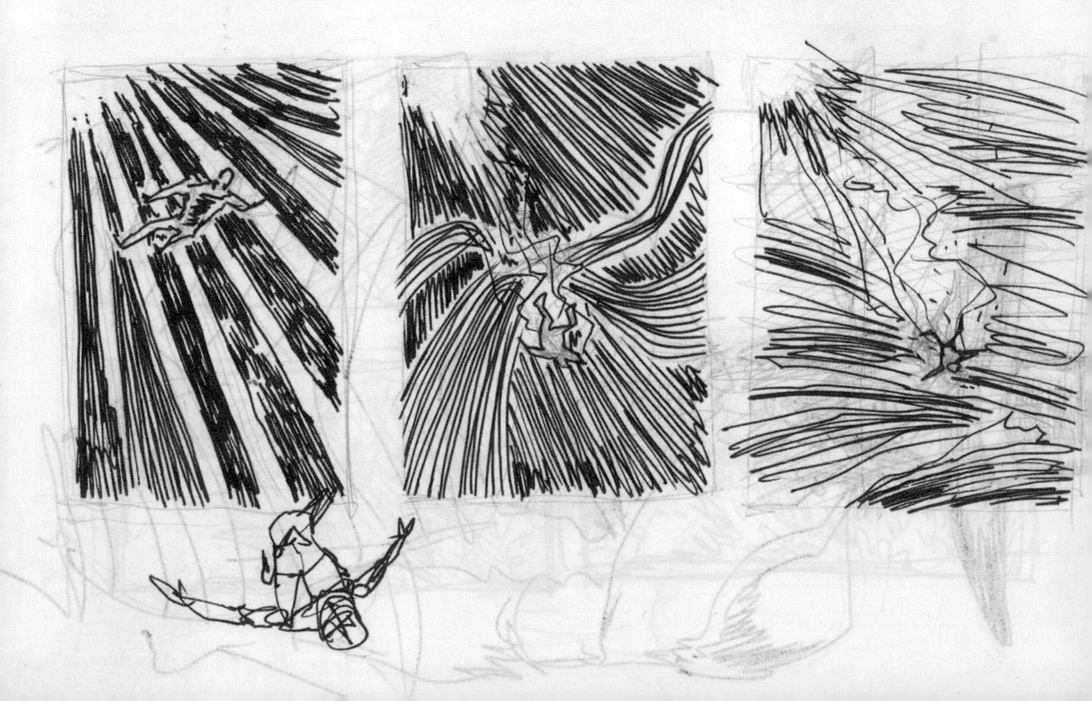

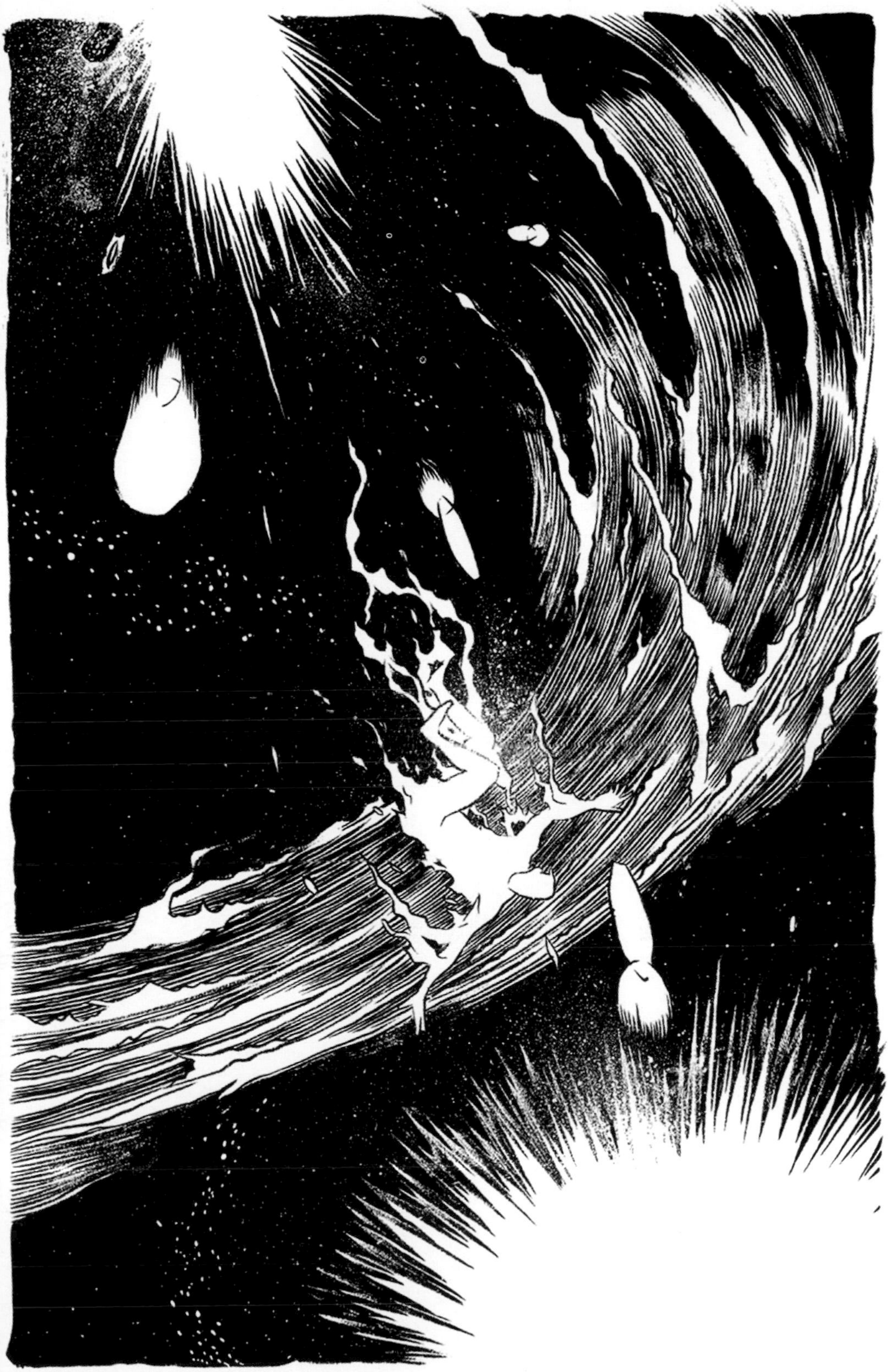

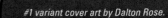

#1 variant cover art by Dalton Rose.

#2 variant cover art by Cliff Chiang.

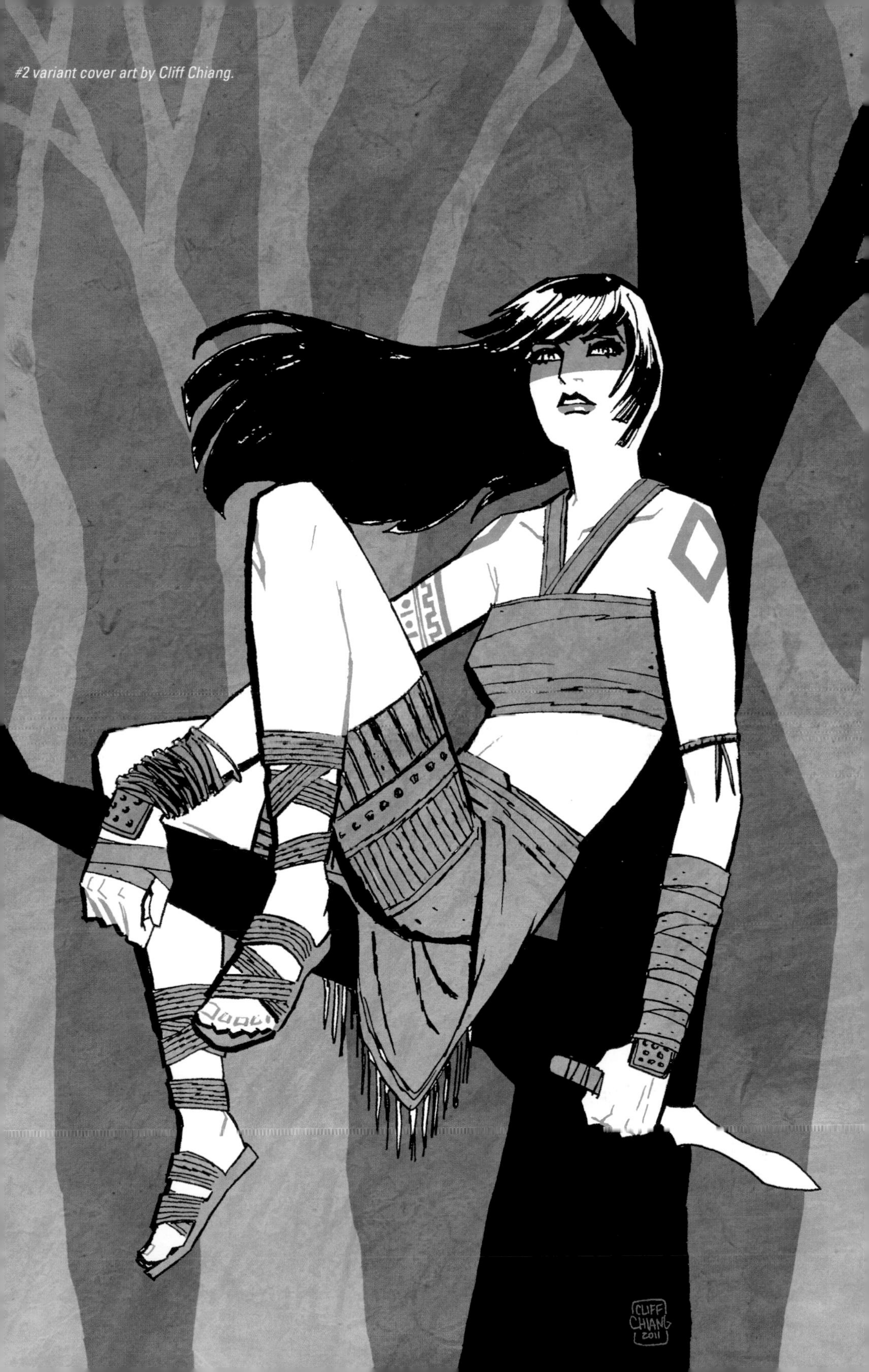
CLIFF CHIANG 2011

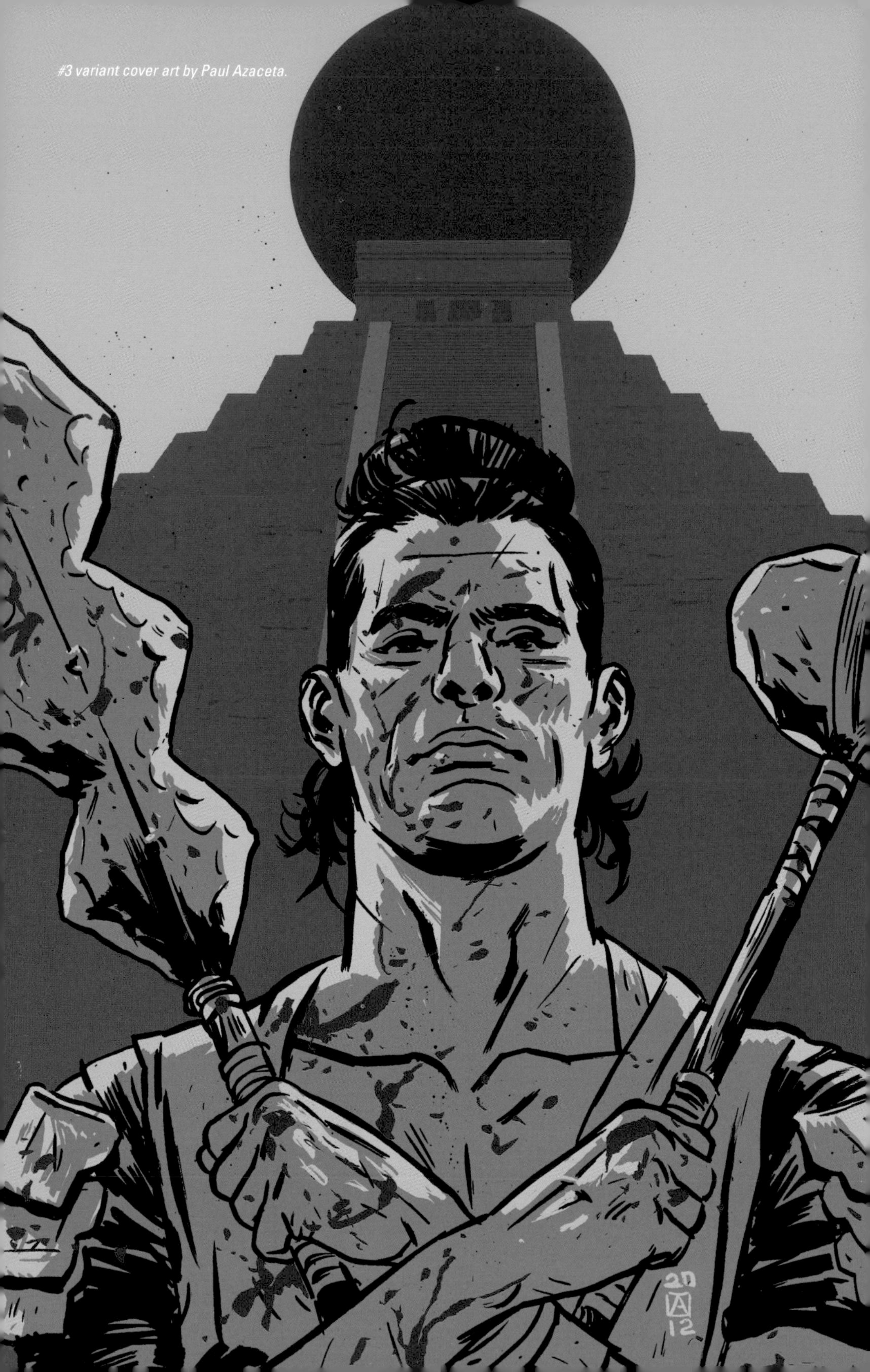

#3 variant cover art by Paul Azaceta.

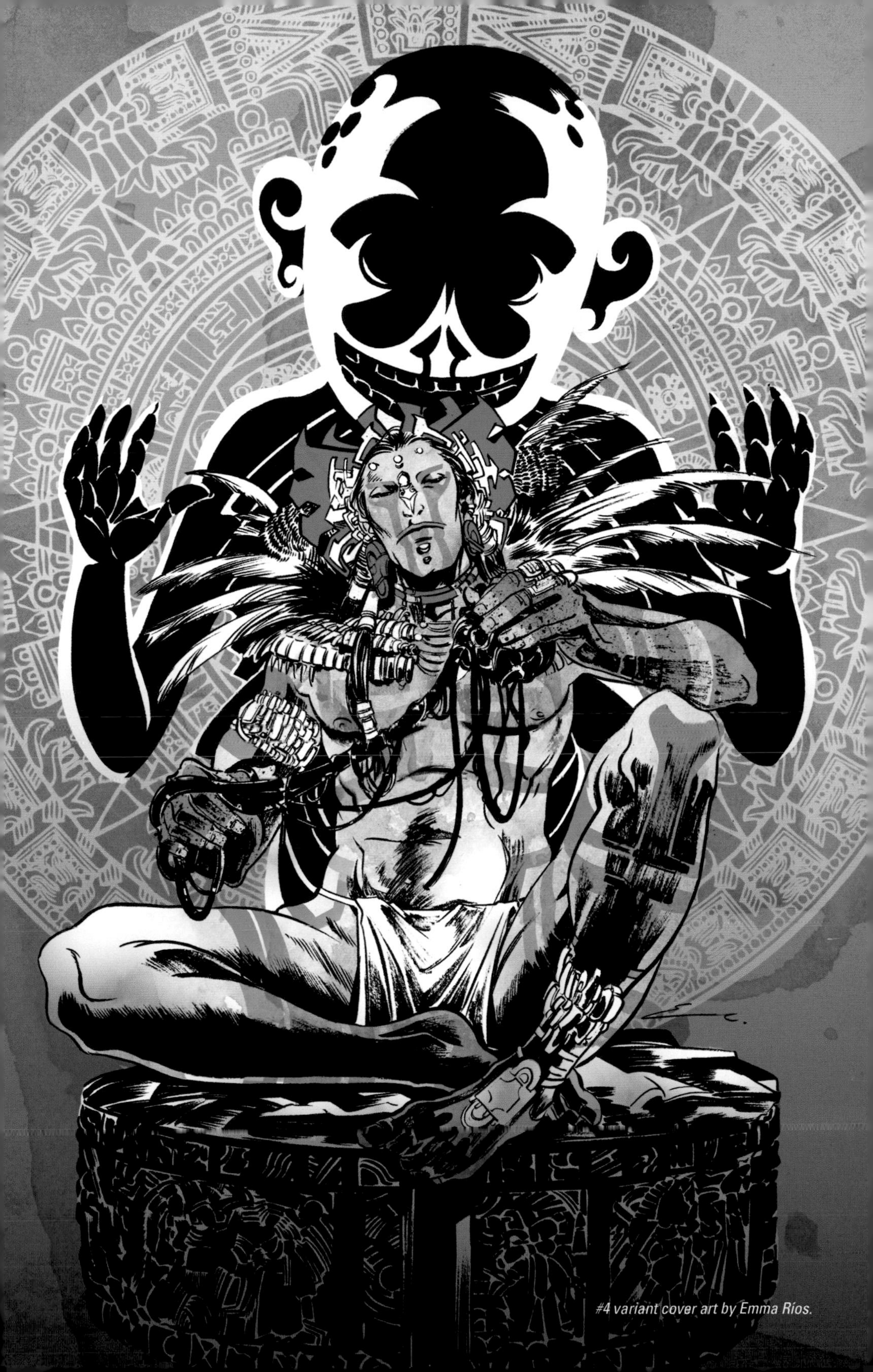

#4 variant cover art by Emma Ríos.

#5 variant cover art by Bryan Lee O'Malley.

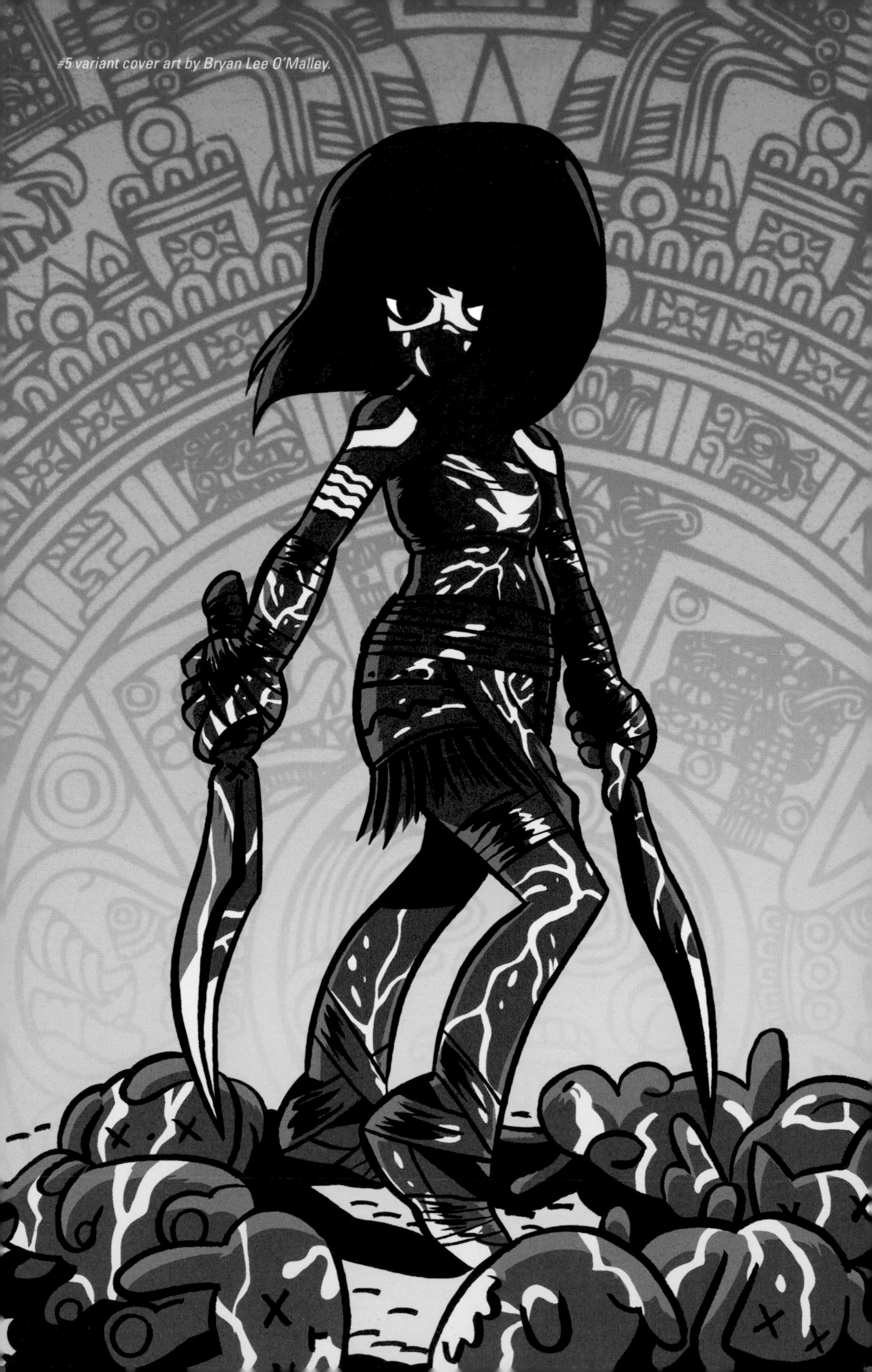

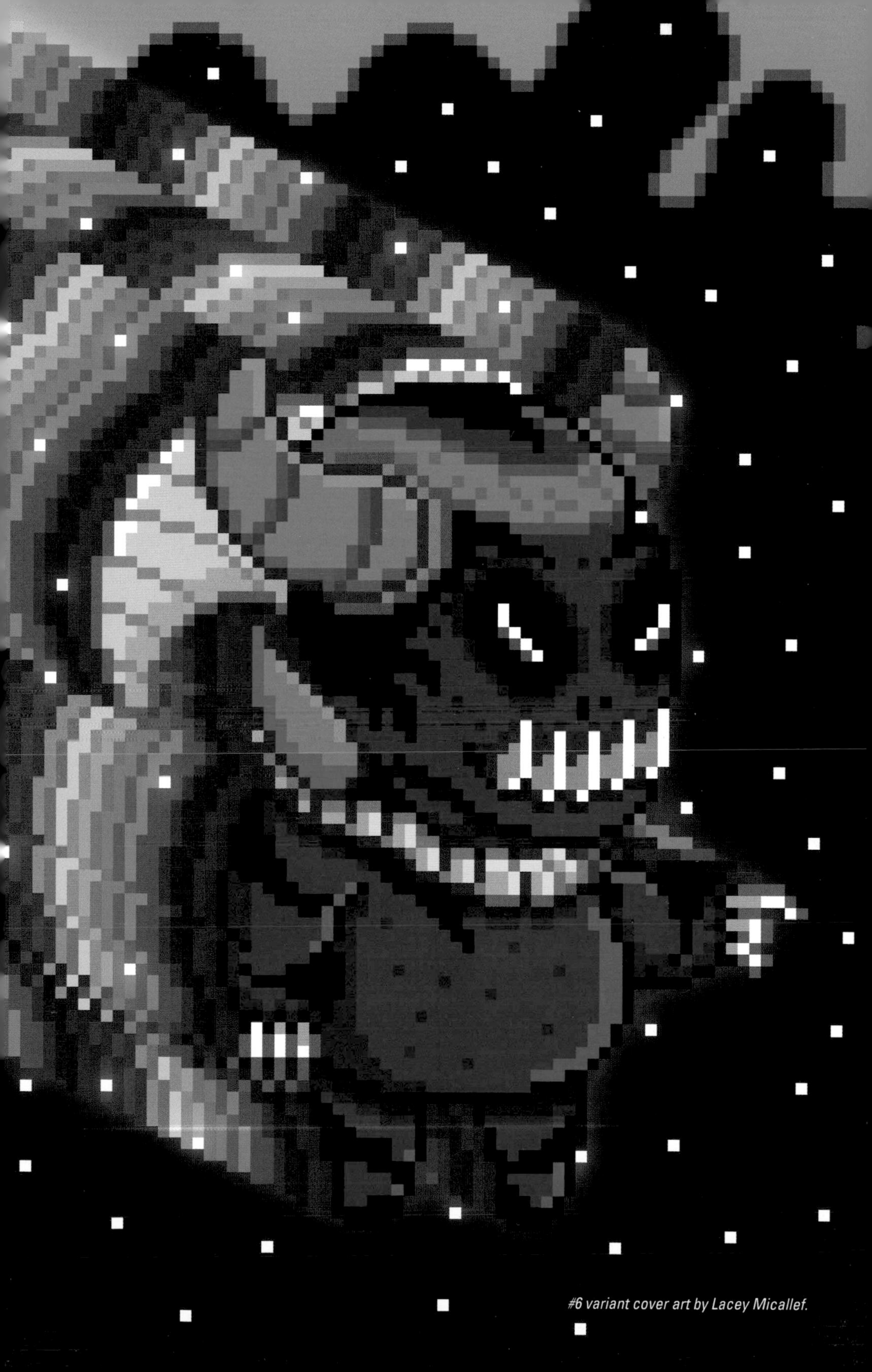

#6 variant cover art by Lacey Micallef.

SAM HUMPHRIES *is a comic book writer living in Los Angeles. His work includes* Avengers A.I., Uncanny X-Force, *and* The Ultimates *for Marvel Entertainment, as well as the indie comics* Higher Earth, Our Love Is Real, *and* Virginia. *You can find him online at SamHumphries.com.*

DALTON ROSE *grew up in the woods of Snohomish, Washington. He received an MA from the Savannah College of Art and Design in 2010. He currently lives in Portland, Oregon. Find him at DaltonJamesRose.com.*

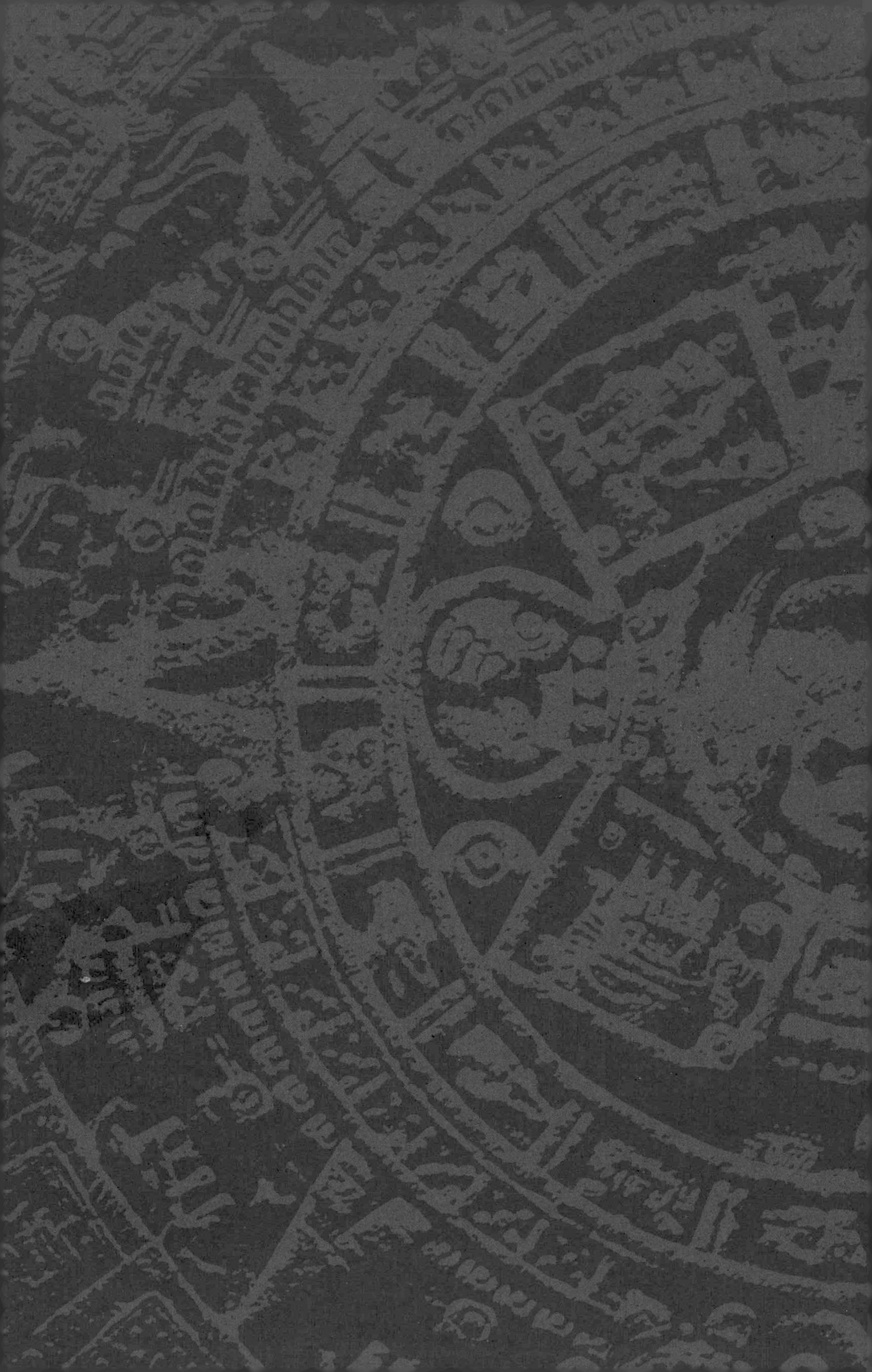